INTRODUCTION TO FRANCOPHONE AFRICAN LITERATURE
A COLLECTION OF ESSAYS

INTRODUCTION TO FRANCOPHONE AFRICAN LITERATURE
A COLLECTION OF ESSAYS

African Literature Series No 1

Edited by
Olusola Oke and Sam Ade Ojo

Spectrum Books Limited
Ibadan
◆Abuja ◆Benin City ◆Kaduna ◆Lagos ◆Owerri

Published by
Spectrum Books Limited
Spectrum House
Ring Road
P. M. B. 5612
Ibadan, Nigeria

in association with
Safari Books (Export) Limited
1st Floor
17 Bond Street
St. Helier
Jersey JE2 3NP
Channel Islands,
United Kingdom

Europe and USA Distributor
African Books Collective Ltd.
The Jam Factory
27 Park End Street
Oxford OX1 1HU, UK.

© Nigeria French Language Village

First published, 2000

All rights reserved. This journal is copyright and so no part of it may be reproduced, stored in a retrieval system, or transmitted in any form or by any means, electronic, mechanical, electrostatic, magnetic tape, photocopying, or otherwise, without the prior written permission of the copyright owner.

ISBN: 978-029-196-2

Printed by Polygraphics Venture Limited Ibadan

Contents

Preface		*vii*
Contributors		*xi*
1 Historical Threats and Resilience of Oral Literature in Francophone Africa	*Peter Okeh*	1
2 Epic Tradition in Francophone Africa	*Julie Agbasiere*	23
3 Speech Behaviour in Oral Narrative Performance: Analysis of Mfomo's French Translation of Ewondo Tales from Cameroon	*Zana Akpagu*	45
4 The Major Themes of Negritude Poetry: Protest, Revolt and Reconciliation	*Francis Angrey*	83
5 Tales from Birago Diop: Translation of a Tradition	*Imeyen Noah*	107
6 The Language of Modern African Literature	*Kester Echenim*	131
7 A Panorama of the Francophone African Novel from the 1920s to the 1990s	*Victor Aire*	153
8 The Earliest Francophone African Novels: From *Force-Bonté to Doguicimi*	*Uche Ogike*	179
9 The Radical Perspective in the Early African Novels	*Elerius John*	195
10 Modern African Literature as Illusions of African Reality: The Case of the Francophone Novel	*Olusola Oke*	215
11 Revolt and Revolution in the Francophone African Novel of the Colonial Period	*Olalere Oladitan*	239
12 The Development of National Theatres in Francophone Africa	*Raufu Adebisi*	253
13 Feminism in Francophone African Literature: From Liberalism to Militancy	*Aduke Adebayo*	275
Index		299

Preface

The study of Francophone African literature is well established in Anglophone Africa. Anglophone Africans who study and write on Francophone African Literature are usually French-speaking. They usually read and study Francophone African Literature first in the original French and quite often they also write criticism on it first in French. As the need arises, they may read the English versions of the various works of Francophone African writers; they also quite often have to write their criticism in English especially when the targeted audience is entirely English-speaking. The criticism of Francophone African literature that has been published to date comes as much from Anglophone as from Francophone Africa and, perhaps, even more from the former than from the latter. The footnotes and bibliographies at the end of the chapters attest to the abundant interest that Anglophone Africans as well as non-Africans have devoted to the study of modern African Literature in French.

The Nigeria French Language Village, Ajara-Badagry, has brought together this collection of essays first to show how the Village can meaningfully contribute to the study of French in Nigeria and secondly to highlight through a carefully co-ordinated medium the different areas of interest that have been explored over the years by different Nigerian scholars. By this, the volume is expected to contribute to the promotion of the study of Francophone African Literature in Anglophone countries the world over.

This is the first volume of the African Literature Series, a series through which the Village may be able to integrate our Anglophone colleagues into the community of specialists in Francophone African Literature in spite of their inherent handicap of being unable to read the literature in the original. The essays reflect the different critical perspectives and backgrounds from which these scholars have studied all the genres of Francophone African Literature whether Oral Literature, poetry, the novel or drama over the years.

References are made to the literary texts that have been studied both in the original and in translation, according to the choice and preference of the authors of the different essays. In some cases, quotations are side by side in French and English; in some, they are entirely in English and, in a few other cases, they are entirely in French – depending on the author's preference We are convinced that the author should be the final arbiter on his or her own style and approach.

We assume that some of the essays will appeal more to the Anglophone readers, who have mastered some French, where the former contain terms; sentences and expressions, even quotations in French and without their English translations. We also imagine that some of our Francophone readers, who might know enough English to make them understand the essays, would appreciate the use of quotations in the original in addition to the sometimes indispensable use of words and expressions from the French original in the English passages.

The use of both French and English when quoting passages is perhaps to protect the integrity of the original texts that are being criticised. The use of the original language in which the work was written, while not ignoring the difficulties that might be faced by the Anglophone reader of the essays whose knowledge of French is absolutely minimal or even totally non-existent, preserves its own originality and integrity. The use of English throughout and even when quoting passages from works originally written in French is perhaps not entirely in the interest of the works being criticised nor in that of their authors. However, the above must be seen as valid choices that were made by fully conscious authors who are within their own rights.

All the chapters are written by Nigerian lecturers of French in Nigerian universities. We were invited by the Nigerian French Language Village to contribute to a network research project on Francophone African Literature in the hope that our collective output would be more comprehensive and more rewarding than the singular production of any one of us. This is all the more important given the different areas of interest that are involved in the criticism of a whole literature as opposed to the treatment of singular authors and themes.

We fully acknowledge the risks involved in the approach that we have adopted in this collection of essays. Individual talents, imaginations and orientation can hardly be harnessed in single collections of essays without running the risk of disjointedness and disparateness. There is also the risk of unparallel levels of expression and style coupled with different degrees of depth and seriousness.

The chapters that follow would no doubt demonstrate these assumed weaknesses. We hope, however, that the fact of the chapters being edited centrally and into a single volume by a group of professors and lecturers would have reduced to acceptable levels the above inadequacies. Indeed, and in order to reduce disparateness and avoidable overlapping, the contributors to the collection of essays were brought together at the beginning in a workshop where they discussed extensively both the project and their individual contributions.

Most of the topics that are treated in the different chapters were proposed and adopted at the workshop. Some overlapping may still exist but it would hardly be the type that would make the collection of essays boring and unattractive. Each writer was advised to focus on a specific issue or on several related issues. Our individual and various efforts attest to our willingness and determination to make this endeavour a success and is also a demostration of our collective will to bequeath to and share with the larger public our intellectual distinctions, experiences, and critical sensibilities.

All the contributors are specialists in French Literature and African Literature in French. As teachers of French and Francophone African Literature in French they have all studied in the original all the literary texts which they treat in their chapters. All of them have also written extensively both in English and in French on the different areas of interest to which their topics belong.

Areas of specialisation such as oral literature (which has been translated extensively into French) and poetry (which, in its French expression, bears the indelible imprint of an African imagination and poetic heritage) are taken up by specialists who have worked in these areas for many years. These cover first five chapters (chapters 1-5). Theory of literature and general critical theory as related to modern African Literature are highlighted in chapter 6 by a critic who has various publications in the area. The novel is introduced in chapters 7-11 by several critics who are working in the area of fiction. Theatre is handled by a literary historian in chapter 12. Feminism and female writers are covered in chapter 13 by one of the foremost female critics of feminism and feminist literature in Nigeria today.

This is a collection of essays that should draw attention to all the major literary genres that have been explored by Francophone African writers including poetry, the novel and drama. It also covers the rich domain of Oral Literature in Africa with notable reference to Oral Literature in translation, an area in which the Francophones have probably made more contribution to modern African Literature than the

Anglophones. The very topical issue of feminism and female writers, which is just beginning to feature prominently in literary criticism in Nigeria, completes the rich variety of topics that are treated in this book.

Olusola Oke and Sam Ade Ojo
Lagos.
July, 1999

Contributors

Peter Okeh is a professor of French at the University of Benin, Benin City, Nigeria. He writes mainly on traditional and oral literature and has published many articles in learned journals. He holds the Masters and Ph.D. degrees of the University of Laval, Canada. He has taught French and African Literature in French in Benin for more than two decades. He does research in these areas and also in the area of Comparative Literature.

Julie Agbasiere holds the Masters and Ph.D. degrees of the University of Sherbrooke, Canada. She is a Senior Lecturer at Nnamdi Azikiwe University, Awka, Anambra State. She does research in the areas of orature, literature and feminism. She teaches French as a second language in addition to French Literature and African Literature in French. She has published several articles in learned journals.

Zana Akpagu is a Senior Lecturer of African and Caribbean Literature in French at the University of Calabar where he studied and obtained a Bachelor of Arts and a Master of Arts degree in the eighties. He holds the Ph.D. degree of the University of Benin, Benin City. He has taught for many years at the University of Uyo and the University of Benin. He has published book chapters and several articles in learned journals in the areas of criticism, oral narrative theory, feminism and Comparative Literature.

Francis Angrey lectures French and Francophone African and Caribbean literature at the University of Calabar, Nigeria. He studied at both the University of Nigeria, Nsukka and the University of Calabar, Calabar where he obtained the B.A. and M.A degrees respectively. He has published a good number of articles in learned journals on both French and Francophone African Literature. He is currently doing research work in Afro-Caribbean Literature in French for a Ph.D. at the University of Calabar, Nigeria.

Imeyen Noah is a graduate of the University of Toulouse (*Licence ès Lettres*), University of Paris-Sorbonne (*Maitrise ès Lettres*) and the University of Ottawa (Ph.D). He is a Senior Lecturer in French at the University of Calabar. His major area of research is Oral Literature.

Kester Echenim is a professor of French at the University of Benin, Benin City. He holds the *Licence ès Lettres, Maitrise ès Lettres* and the *Doctorat de 3ᵉ Cycle* from the *Université de Besançon*. He has done research and published extensively in the areas of Francophone African Literature, African Civilisation and literary criticism. He has taught these topics for more than twenty years at the University of Benin.

Victor Aire is a professor of French at the University of Jos, Nigeria, where he has taught French Literature, African Literature in French and Translation for more than twenty years. He holds the Masters and Ph.D. degrees of the University of Toronto. His research interest focuses mainly on Francophone African Literature and Caribbean Literature in French. He has taught and researched in Canadian and other Commonwealth universities. He has many publications in learned journals and is cited in national and international biographies.

Uche Ogike is an Associate Professor of French at the Alvan Ikoku College of Education, Owerri. He studied at Université de Dakar, Senegal, University of California, Berkeley and University of California, Los Angeles. He is the principal author of *Contes Nigérians* published by Hatier, Paris. He has authored numerous articles on Franco-African literature.

Elerius John is a professor of French at the University of Calabar. He studied in the University of Toulouse where he obtained the *Maitrise ès Lettres* and the *Doctorat de 3ᵉ Cycle*. He has taught French and African Literature for more than twenty-five years at the university level. His research focuses on Francophone African Literature, Comparative Literature and Cultural Studies. He has published many articles in learned journals. He is cited in international biographies.

Olusola Oke is a professor of French and Francophone African Literature at the Lagos State University. He has written many articles in learned journals on African literature in French. He holds a Masters degree in French Literature from the University of Sussex, Brighton, England and a *Doctorat de 3e Cycle* in Comparative Literature from the University of Bordeaux, France. He has taught French and African Literature in French for many years in Nigerian universities including the Obafemi Awolowo University, Ile-Ife. He does research mostly in history of criticism and theory of literature.

Olalere Oladitan has lectured French and Francophone African Literature at the Obafemi Awolowo University, Ile-Ife since 1974. He studied at the University of Ibadan where he obtained a Ph.D. in African Literature in French. He does research mainly in the area of anti-colonial and radical literature. He has published several articles in learned journals on Marxist literature and African Literature seen from the Marxist perspective.

Raufu Adebisi lectures French at the Ahmadu Bello University, Zaria, Nigeria. He holds the Ph.D. degree of the university. He has taught Francophone Literature and Culture in the university for about twenty years. He has published several articles in learned journals both locally and internationally.

Aduke Adebayo is a professor of French at the University of Ibadan, where she has taught French and African Literature in French for more than twenty years. She holds the Ph.D. of the same University in French and the M.Phil. from the Obafemi Awolowo University Ile Ife. She has edited *Critical Essays on the Novel in Francophone Africa* and written many articles in international and local journals. Her research is based mainly on Francophone African Literature and Comparative Literature.

1
HISTORICAL THREATS AND RESILIENCE OF ORAL LITERATURE IN FRANCOPHONE AFRICA

Peter Okeh

In this study, we aim at presenting a global picture of African Oral Literature with a focus on French-speaking communities. We are going to trace its history from the beginning to the present times. First, we shall see the normal events which promoted its development *ab initio*. Then we shall go on to monitor those events which subsequently constituted threats to its growth, namely slave trade, French colonialism and the inhibitions of westernised independence era. These are so because they are extraordinary in their magnitude and alien in their essence.

The dictionary definition of history oscillates between 'the record of past events' and 'the past events themselves.'[1] It is from this second perspective that we are looking at history in this work. The dictionary also defines resilience as 'the power or ability to return to its original form, position, etc. after being bent, compressed or stretched.'[2] We are talking of resilience in relation to Oral Literature in Francophone Africa and elsewhere in the continent, because, in spite of those ineluctable and extraordinary contrary forces, Oral Literature is still moving in good health, although it has tolerated and still tolerates some metamorphoses. The chief of these is made up of the French translations through which Oral Literature reaches the whole of Africa and the outside world.

Our focus on Francophone Africa is determined by the fact that we shall be concerned with Oral Literature collections in French language.

---

[1] Vide. The Random House Dictionary, p. 674
[2] *Ibid.* p.1220

These collections will be representative of the following countries: Cameroun, Tchad, Niger, Benin Republic, Togo, Ivory Coast, Senegal, Guinea, Mali, Burkina-Faso, Central African Republic, Gabon, Congo Brazaville, Democratic Republic of Congo, Rwanda and Burundi.

However, far above the French language coating, these works are essentially African, for Black Africa is one world. It cannot be otherwise, because Africans have affronted identical realities in their existence as Blacks in the continent: West Africans of the southern zone, those of the northern zone highly influenced by Islam, ethnic groups occupying the Congo Basin, inhabitants of East Africa from the Upper Nile to the river Zambezi, the indigenes of Namibia, Angola and Mozambique and the blacks of South Africa – all have a quasi-religious attachment to the mother-earth, the same worship of ancestors, the same warmth in social relations, similar perceptions of beauty and close behaviour patterns. One can even add here that the blacks across the Atlantic Ocean whose forefathers were forcibly removed from the African soil have also succeeded in keeping much of their African heritage. It is therefore impossible for a focus on Francophone Africa to exclude Anglophone Africa, Lusophone Africa, Hispanophone Africa or the Black Diaspora.

After these preliminary observations, let us now indicate precisely what we intend to do in this study. In the first section, we shall paint an authentic picture of Oral Literature with emphasis on Francophone Africa. This will include an examination of the primary nature of African Literature, an acquaintance with that literature during its golden age – when it did not experience the White Man's intrusion, alongside with its perenniality in time and space. It will also include the categorisation of Oral Literature in genres as can be seen even today.

In the second section, we shall x-ray what we consider to be the great threats, by first exposing the greatest dehumanising trade in human history – the Slave Trade. Next, we shall review the saddest story of domination, oppression and exploitation on the African soil – the Western colonisation, especially by the French. We shall then go on to highlight the problems of Oral Literature even with the official departure of the White Man and the apparent enjoyment of self-government and independence.

In the third and final section, we shall take up the issue of resilience. We shall look more closely at the continued oral nature of our literature as well as the metamorphoses it has accepted. We shall delve particularly into the psycho-ethnological factors behind the survival of African Oral Literature. Then, we shall wrap it up with the introduction of well-known collectors/translators in Francophone Africa along with the best collections in the book market. These collections are of immense benefit to experts, students and researchers in African Oral Literature in French. People often take for granted that most people - Africans and foreigners alike - understand what they say, write or hear when they are faced with the notion of African Literature. Experience has shown that this assumption is false. In our lectures in Oral Literature, we usually ask the students to answer, in not more than one page, the following question: *Que représente pour vous la littérature Africaine?* (What do you understand by African Literature?). Invariably, majority of the students end up writing about well-known African authors and their works without remembering Oral Literature. This is not just a student mistake. I know of an educated Nigerian who believes that it is unnecessary to carry out research on Oral Literature because, according to him, it is wasting time and money on the obvious. To him, they are just those old stories which everyone knows more or less.

The situation is even worse among foreign 'experts' of African literature. For example, Lilyan Kesteloot, who is known for her numerous works on African Literature, talks of the "birth of a literature" in her effort to make an inventory of Francophone literary works in Africa and America up to the 60s.[3] Robert Pageard, in his historical development of African literature, took the colonial era as his starting point.[4]

Anyone whose perception of African Literature tallies with the above examples is echoing the unfounded belief that there was not much in Africa before the coming of the White Man. He is agreeing that pre-colonial Africa was really a dark continent as she was described by European conquerors who knew neither her languages nor her civilisation. To think like that is to depreciate the primary quality of African Literature which is its oral nature.

What is literature, after all? In short, it is the reflection of facts, events and ideas in language creations belonging to a defined human group. To put the matter more clearly, let us borrow Gustave Lanson's definition:

---

[3] Lilyan Kesteloot. *Les écrivains noirs de langue française, naissance d'une littéature*, Bruxelles, 1965.
[4] Robert Pageard. *Littérature négro-Africaine*. Paris, 1969.

> Literature is, in the noblest sense of the word, a way of bringing philosophy to the reach of all. It is through it that great philosophical ideas which determine progress or at least social changes permeate our societies. It entertains souls which otherwise would have been depressed by the necessity of living and submerged by material preoccupations with concerns about big questions which dominate life and give it meaning or purpose.[5]

If we apply this definition to black Africa, we see immediately that real literature existed firmly in Africa before the colonial era and that this literature is still thriving in African villages in modern times. Really speaking, it is Oral Literature which feeds the written works in French or English which attract more attention but which, in final analysis, are only a small part of black oral and written productions.

From the evidences that abound, we need not be told that Africa had a flourishing literature, though purely oral, before the advent of the White Man, and that this literature still exists today. However, for the sake of scholarship, let us call to mind the observations made by a European expert, N.A. Chadwick:

> In civilised countries we are inclined to associate literature with writing; but such an association is accidental. (...) Millions of people throughout Asia, Polynesia, Africa (...) who practise the art of literature, have no knowledge of letters. Writing is unessential to either the composition or the preservation of literature. The two arts are wholly distinct.[6]

Having known the primary nature of African Literature, which resides in its oral existence, we are now going to see it in its pure state, starting from its golden age. The dawn of this age was when society life began in Black Africa. According to historians, the black man appeared in Black Africa about 500 B.C. Before this period, he was living in the Nile Valley where he participated, right from antiquity, in making Africa the cradle of civilisation in ancient Egypt. He also lived in the regions of the present Sahara desert which was then a grassland with trees, shrubs, rivers and lakes.[7]

---

[5] Gustave Lanson. *Histoire de la littérature francaise.* Hachette, (Avant-Propos).

[6] N.K. Chadwick. *Distribution of Oral Literature in the Old World.* Vide Ruth Finnegan. *Oral Literature in Africa.* p.25.

[7] C.f. Cheikh Anta Diop. *L Afrique noire précoloniale.* Denise Paulme. *Les civilisations Africaines* and Basil Davidson. *Old Africa Rediscovered.*

Then came a big climatic change. The Sahara regions became dry, turning into a desert. Consequently, the blacks of Africa became involved in great migrations which brought them to the wetter areas of West and South of the continent. A Senegalese historian, Cheikh Anta Diop, summed up their movements this way:

> Moving from the Nile Basin in successive bands, the inhabitants spread in all directions. Some, like the Serere and the Tuculor, went directly westwards to the Atlantic ocean.
> Others established themselves in the Congo Basin and the Tchad region. The Zulu went down as far as the Cape of Good Hope, and the Traore crossed over to the island of Madagascar.[8]

It was from that period that the history of Man in Black Africa really began. However, it was towards the end of the first millennium that we can say that *Homo Africanus* was firmly established in his new environment. From the 8th century until the White Man appeared in the 15th, we hear of his empires: Ghana, Mali, Songhai, Benin, Congo, Monomotapa, Zimbabwe, etc. These indicate that he had built up organised societies and had developed local languages. Under those favourable conditions, he did not waste time in creating his literature in his native African languages: Wolof, Fufulde, Malinke, Agni, Ashanti, Ewe, Hausa, Yoruba, Igbo, Nvema, Beti, Fang, Bantu, Zulu, Dinka, etc. He had a big advantage over his European counterpart for developing for himself a literature that would make him proud. He was at this time enjoying relative peace, social stability and prosperity. But, the European witnessed great historical upheavals like the Barbarian invasions, the struggles for the succession of Charlemagne, the Norman invasion, and the reign of insecurity which gave rise to feudalism.

In West and Central Africa which are of special interest to us in this study, three Oral Literature traditions emerged from this process; they are maintained more or less in our days. We identify them through the chief animal protagonists in various folktales and they cut through both Francophone and Anglophone countries. First, we have the Hare tradition in Senegal (Leuk-the-Hare), Guinea, Mali, Burkina-Fasso and other Sahel areas bordering the Sahara. Next, we have the Spider tradition (Kaku-

---

[8] Cheikh Anta Diop. *L' Afrique noire précoloniale.* p.177, (the translation is ours)

Ananze-the-Spider) in Ivory Coast, Ghana, Togo and the West-Coast areas reaching the Atlantic Ocean. Thirdly, we have the Tortoise tradition (Ijapa, Mbe, Kunkuru-the-Tortoise) in Benin Republic, Nigeria, Cameroun and the countries of Central Africa. Recognisable patterns are thus before us and one cannot say that it is by accident that these three animal protagonists of comparable qualities and defects dominate other animal characters in these zones.

Each of these animals (Hare, Spider, Tortoise) unites several ethnic groups in Africa into one large cultural zone with subgroups of inhabitants having homogeneous mental and socio-cultural attitudes. For these peoples, although they speak different languages today, they cherish those animals as unique cultural heroes, utilise them for framing their social ties and the education of the individual. To them, these animals are curious characters, half-men and half-animals. Physically, they maintain most of the time the appearances of their species. The storyteller even imitates their voices from time to time in his narration. But, morally, they typify human beings living in a society, men with wives who can be models to be followed or villains to be avoided. Their names vary according to the languages of the peoples who own the narratives. Their rare qualities are intelligence, cleverness, wit and resourcefulness; their defects are trickishness, cupidity, bad faith and egotism. All these are embodied in their small sizes which put them at no disadvantage vis-à-vis their bigger animal contemporaries like Goat, Tiger, Hyena, Dog, Cow, Sheep, Lion, Antelope and Elephant.

An attempt can be made to explain the Hare, Spider and Tortoise traditions through the history of North-South migrations which we discussed earlier. It is assumed that pockets of these migrants from the north of the Sahara had these animals in their folklore and already saw them as cherished ingredients in speech imagery. Each pocket had naturally a common language. In their successive movements, they would gather their young ones together, sharpen their wits with typical tales, deepen their understanding with the values these contained and make them pass this cultural heritage to their children and descendants. As time went on, the original group or groups split into smaller groups, which developed their own dialects. Again with time, the groups multiplied and increased under varying geographical and social conditions. Languages emerged later out of existing dialects. Nevertheless, the spirit of Hare, Spider or Tortoise remained with the successors of the original pockets. In this way, we have three sub-regions where people speak different languages while keeping similar oral traditions.

This hypothesis is sound for it is founded on history. Our socio-linguists tell us, for example, that Igbo, Edo, Urhobo, Efik and Yoruba belong to one family and are grouped as *KWA* languages. Let us also think of what happened in Europe. Originally, only one language, the Indo-European, was spoken in the continent. With time, it split into many languages which give us today Italian, French, Spanish, Portuguese, English, German, Dutch, Swedish, Greek, Rumanian, Slavonic and others.[9] Literatures in these languages have similar traditions which cut across national frontiers and which testify to a common European mentality. There is therefore an African mentality in African Oral Literature, which one can easily notice through comparative studies. This mentality is best conceptualised through the knowledge of the main African oral genres.

Three oral genres, namely folktales, legends and myths, form what are generally classified as oral narratives. But among these, folktales constitute what one can call the *genre par excellence*. Their occurences are more frequent than the others, their performance is within the reach of almost everybody, and they easily attract more foreigners and researchers. That was why the early Europeans were very quick to bring their existence to the notice of Africa's colonial masters. They are of three categories: animal tales, human tales and mixed tales — which combine the first two. The roles played by animals are so spectacular that when one talks of African folktales, one thinks more of animal tales more than the others. Moreover, animals appear not only in folktales but also in myths, legends and all forms of speech. And, as we explained earlier, there is always one animal dominating the stories according to the cultural zones. The situation is understandable if we remember that Africans live close to nature, that animals form part of their daily experiences and that they are led instinctively to make use of animal imagery to build their stories and enrich their languages. One of the great childhood pleasures is to listen to elders and youngsters tell these charming stories where animals, men and even spirits are involved in all kinds of adventures. It is this supernatural dimension which distinguishes radically African folktales from European fables.

Legends differ from folktales in that they are rooted in real events or events considered as such by the original producers of the literature in question. People telling or listening to folktales know that they are entirely

---

[9] C.f. W.V. Wartburg. *Evolution et structure de la langue française*. passim

fictitious. They are mainly interested in the pleasure derived from the performance and the social and moral lessons imbibed from the stories. Historical figures are the centre of legends, although animals, spirits and magic powers come in to shroud the events with the mysterious, the fantastic and the extraordinary.

The different forms of human activities from which legends are created include the founding of clans or settlements, wars between rival groups, family feuds and migration of peoples to where they now live. Unlike folktales which provide a kind of entertainment in addition to some teaching, legends are romanticised history lessons meant to give some orientation and a sense of belonging to autonomous communities. Just as it is a handicap to be ignorant of history in general, it is a sad handicap for an African to be ignorant of these legends, especially those originating from his area that still continue from mouth to mouth and from generation to generation.

Myths share with folktales and legends the animal and human ingredients. But, while the last two are concerned with the exposition and analysis of ordinary life subjects, myths are concerned with more serious stories treating sublime subjects. They have religious, metaphysical and cosmic dimensions. They touch the relationship between human beings and their creator as well as the gods of the village or the group. They explain, often in an unexpected manner, the existence of natural phenomena like the moon, the sun, the stars, the sky, death, fire, the seasons and earth features. They are fewer in number than other narratives and are often combined with folktales and legends during oral literature gatherings and in some translated collections. The black man demonstrates through his myths that he is linked up with God and the world of spirits and that he has an intimate and at times unusual relationship with the world of nature. Strictly speaking, therefore, one cannot rank him as an unbeliever, even outside Islam and Christianity. Myths can therefore be regarded as a precious genre in African Literature, which contribute enormously in shaping the African world view.

After myths, let us now come to epics. These are also 'narratives' because they tell stories that originate from legends. But they have their own characteristics which qualify them for a separate classification. Epics are stories of famous individuals in various communities who distinguished themselves by their exceptional qualities and great exploits, especially in war. They are however not pure history, for the historical details used are embellished, manipulated, magnified, and renewed by oral artists such as *griots*, *Mvet* players (Cameroun), praise singers and public entertainers. Epics are usually very long poems, not mainly prose as in the case of pure narratives. When such stories have historical significance principally or are devoid of oral literary artefact, they are called chronicles. When they are subject to the imagination of the oral artist, then they become epics. Thanks to these artists, we can still have insight into illustrious geneologies, ancient migrations, wars, victories, conquests, defeats, grand alliances, intrigues and revolutions in numerous African societies.

Epics are the historical conscience of every human group in Black Africa. They constantly remind the coming generations that anyone can achieve greatness in life and be counted among those who will ever be remembered. The epic hero is not only a strong and brave person capable of surpassing human opponents but also a very occultic figure able to command supernatural powers as he bulldozes his way against mortals and even spirit beings. Soundiata, Chaka, Silamaka Ngono and Djeky are well known African epics.

Next, we consider African oral poetry in all its ramifications. It is said that life is poetry and poetry is life. This statement is very true of many African traditional societies of old and their remnants in our times. Poetry punctuates every aspect of village life and cultural manifestations be it in prayers, rituals, ceremonies, dancing, rejoicing, leisure or work. Poetry, in essence, is an art of words – words often used in more than normal senses and in more than normal order. It is for this reason that poetic language has been said to sometimes do 'violence' to the 'resources of everyday language' in an effort to force us into 'awareness' and 'attention'.[10] But over and above this 'awareness' and 'attention', there is the more important fact that, as a result of its extraordinary nature, poetic language communicates usually by suggesting rather than by plainly 'saying something'.[11] Expressing by suggestion is the natural result of the connotative nature of poetic language which enables it to transcend the referential level of meaning and find its semantic fulfilment at the level of deliberate verbal displacement or even distortion.[12] These tit-bits will enable us to safeguard the domains of oral poetry from those of other genres.

---

[10] René Wellek and Austin Warren. *Theory of Literature*. Penguin Books, p.24.
[11] Romanus N. Egudu. *The Study of Poetry*. p.4.
[12] Michael Riffaterre. *Semiotics of Poetry*. p.1.

In practice, however, there is no clear-cut distinction between the domains of poetry and those of prose in African Oral Literature in any language, African or otherwise. They overlap in certain areas such as in the narratives where the sung parts are poetry and the narrated parts are prose. In fact, all chants or songs in all circumstances in African tradition are poetic. In spite of all these, oral poetry is distinct enough to be classified as a genre in itself.

Such a classification has been made by Egudu and Nwoga.[13] They divided the traditional verse into praise or panegeric, invocation, incantation, dance, relaxation, satirical and lamentation poems. Other classifications exist and also contribute to a better understanding of poetry in the daily lives of Africans. One can come up with a different classification provided one has a feeling for poetry and is guided by such factors as were listed by Ruth Finnegan:

> The kind of factors which it has seemed helpful to consider include: musical setting (most sung forms can be reasonably regarded as poetry); the intensity and emotion of expression, rhythm, special vocabulary; style or syntactical forms; local evaluation and degree of specialism (more marked with poetry than with prose); and finally the native classifications themselves.[14]

Two other oral genres that we would like to talk about are proverbs and riddles. Proverbs are wise sayings of invariable structures particular to a linguistic community and used without any ambiguity by the inhabitants. Riddles are short semantic combinations, sophisticated in nature and figurative most of the time, usually in form of questions or commands requiring appropriate responses. They are tests of wit whose meanings, although known in the community, are not always easy to pinpoint. Their structures are fixed like those of proverbs. In European tradition, proverbs and riddles do not qualify as genres in literature; they are simply speech tools. In African tradition, they do. Just as narratives, epics and poems are executed in communal gatherings, proverbs and riddles are also. During the meetings, people are paired to compete in the knowledge of proverbs and riddles. One witnesses then a flow of these

---

[13] Vide Romanus N. Egudu and Donatus I. Nwoga: *Poetic Heritage: Igbo Traditional Verse*. pp.25-127.

[14] Ruth Finnegan. *Oral Literature in Africa*. pp.76 & 77.

ingredients to the joy of the wise partakers, to the ridicule of those who are less knowledgeable and to the benefit of all present. In this manner, proverbs and riddles are kept alive enabling them to filter into literature, speech and discussions. The above explanations may help to understand why it is said that the Igbo understand themselves through proverbs which Chinua Achebe re-echoes when he wrote: 'proverbs are the palm oil with which words are eaten'.[15]

After this categorisation of authentic Oral Literature past and present, we shall now examine the three historical "threats" which this literature withstood for more than four centuries. They are Slave Trade, Western colonialism, especially the French and the inhibitions under independence.

* * *

The singular feature of European presence in Africa in the 15th century was the slave trade. Portuguese, French, English, Dutch, Danish – all seemed not to have been satisfied to find on the coastlands of Africa gold, ivory and spices which they needed badly. As from the 12th century, consequent on Marco Polo's travels to the East, Europe had got regular supplies of spices from Asia through Constantinople, a gate-way between East and West, South of the Black Sea. Unfortunately for the Europeans, the Ottoman Turks seized this last bastion of the Holy Roman Empire in 1453, thereby stopping this trade and cutting off Europe completely from Asia. Since geography had already established that our planet is round, Europeans looked for a solution to their spice problem by trying to get to Asia by sea. The Spaniards sailed towards the West and discovered the American continent; the Portuguese sailed towards the East through the Atlantic Ocean and discovered the West African coasts where they found the spices pushing them to Asia, including other items of trade. Sooner or later, the exploitation of the vast American continent along with the islands near it posed a problem of manpower to the Europeans. The native population was dying off rapidly because they were not strong enough for the hard manual work imposed on them by the white man. Then, the Europeans remembered the strong black people they had been trading with in Africa and decided to ship these men and women to America.

---

[15] Chinua Achebe. *Things Fall Apart*. p. 5.

They wanted to use them to produce wealth through their labour and also save the Indian population from extermination. As one historian put it, "America was discovered and Africa was sacrificed to it."

For four centuries, that is to say from the 16th century up to the 19th, slave dealers from most European countries depleted the African population without any restriction for the benefit of the New World. The number of black Africans sold in America during the notorious trade has been evaluated by various historians at between 15 and 20 million.[16] And, if we add the victims of so many raids, those who died before they reached the sea and those who perished in the slave ships, African loss in human beings ought to have been at least double that figure. Worse still, the traders looked particularly for young and vigorous individuals – children, adolescents, strong young men, beautiful young girls. These constitute the elements needed for the renewal of generations and the continuity of literature.

It was slave trade that dealt the greatest blow on African Oral Literature. Instead of peaceful evenings spent together to enjoy literature, there was general insecurity which made people seek safety at the expense of every other thing. There was a climate of war between communities who saw one another as potential enemies in search of people to sell. The empires and stable societies which were booming before went into oblivion. The loss of about 50 million human beings was like a monstrous bleeding of the population almost beyond recovery. By a kind of intervention of providence, slave trade was abolished by the same perpetrators in the course of the 19th century. The resilient Oral Literature which had managed for four centuries to keep its flickering light on, picked up once again to face new challenges.

Western colonialism which replaced the slave trade was not really an improvement on the lot of Africans except that the export of human cargoes had ceased. It all started with the arbitrary partition of Africa by the industrialised countries of Europe, who saw their action as an economic necessity. At the Berlin Conference of 1885, their delegates were able to agree on a map of their new territories, thereby avoiding diplomatic rows and war. They did not bother themselves about human realities in the

---

[16] Jacques Maquet. *Les civilisations Africaines*. p.232, Hubert Deschamps. *L'Afrique noire précoloniale*. p.64, .J.J. Schellens and J Mayer: *Le Dossier Afrique*, pp.57-58 and Ronald Segal. *The Race War*. p.32.

continent. What mattered to them were conventional elements of geography like latitudes and longitudes as well as the vital interests of their respective countries. Thus, for example, the Malinke were divided between Guinea, Ivory Coast, Mali and Senegal; the Hausa found themselves in Nigeria, Niger and Tchad; the Ewe were divided between Ghana, Togo and Benin Republic; the Yoruba were split between Nigeria and Benin Republic; the Lunda were spread through Angola, Democratic Republic of Congo and Zambia, the Baga and the Sherbro became citizens of Guinea and Sierra Leone. This action alone broke up what had remained of traditional social structures thereby removing from African communities all possibilities of natural development. This was more so in the area of culture which includes Oral Literature.

One major step taken by the French colonial government to assimilate the African and alienate him from his culture was aimed at making him look down on his mother tongue. Since literature is the art of language, any attack on the use of African languages was also inevitably an attack on the literature they vehiculate. To the average African who had gone through the French educational system, learning meant doing so in French which was presented to him as a language without rival. Moreover, going to school also meant gradually keeping away from the elders. These were the traditional experts of language and literature, and the natural instruments for the survival of Oral Literature.

This European ethnic chauvinism in language matters appears in this statement by two French administrators:

> It is indispensable that he masters the French language perfectly, for it is through it that he must have to widen his knowledge. Not to teach him a sure and supple handling of this tool of intelligence is like closing to him the horizons of thought.[17]

A Presidential decree of January 1938 is even more revealing. It reads:

> *L'enseignement doit être exclusivement en langue française. L'emploi des 'idiomes' indigènes est interdite.*
> [All teaching must be done exclusively in French. The use of native languages is forbidden].[18]

---

[17] Vide J.P. Makouta-Mboukou. *Le français en Afrique noire*. p.54. (The translation is ours)
[18] *Ibid.* p.42.

Fortunately for the cause of African Oral Literature, colonial education was not for the masses and did not go on daily for 24 hours. As a result, the majority of the black population remained illiterate and those who were made to go to school spent only a part of the day in it. In this way, a conducive atmosphere for passing Oral Literature from generation to generation was still sustained. That was how many of those who received colonial education came to be still grounded in the literature of their ancestors. They were able to strike a balance between the imported education and the non-formal education imparted by the elders. It was a survival strategy which enabled Oral Literature to witness the independence era in which we live today.

With the political departure of France, one may think that the problems of African Oral Literature in her former colonies are over. But this is not really so. They can be said to be reduced because the destiny of Africa is apparently now in the hands of Africans. But they are still real because we are living in a world of westernised values. These values have some adverse implications for pure native ones which include Oral Literature. Oral Literature inhibitions in modern times constitute what we may call the third threat after slave trade and colonial domination.

One must first realize that the tides have changed for the better with independence in the area of Oral Literature. Primary schools, secondary schools, colleges and universities include Oral Literature in their programmes. Field works are carried out extensively by scholars; collected materials in tapes and pictures are seriously examined in classes, seminars and conferences; the results are compiled in lasting recordings, transcriptions in indigenous languages and translations in foreign languages. Africans involved in these exercises see themselves as 'prodigal sons' who had abandoned their own civilisation but are now returning to their heritage in order to revive and preserve it. Successive independent governments have made and executed projects which are aimed at revitalising the study and use of African languages as well as the practice of Oral Literature.

However, the task is not an easy one. The agrarian environment of old which favoured the daily gatherings in the evenings for oral literature performances are today restricted to the villagess. Even in these villages, there is not much leisure time for people to meet often together. This is because of the poor conditions of living coupled with the daily struggle to make ends meet. People live now in cities which are less favourable to the growth of Oral Literature. This is because of their artificial nature and general insecurity at night. The drift from villages to cities is constant because of the attraction of better income and more comforts. Many of those who grew up in the cities have lost their mother tongues and are no longer in a position to appreciate Oral Literature in African languages. Other forms of amusement, especially the radio and the television, have now usurped most of the time that people could otherwise have used for Oral Literature. The excessive use of French has so much adulterated peoples' language habits that many are incapable of telling stories in their mother tongues without interjecting French vocabulary now and then. Government efforts to boost the study of native languages and literature are hampered by the fact that there are so many of them while the resources available are limited. In spite of all these odds, Oral Literature is still very much around all over black Africa. It has resolutely opposed major threats by its resilient character in the past and is likely to behave the same way in future. We are now going to look closely at that resilience.

* * *

We want to approach the issue by making an ethnological explanation of this extraordinary resilience. Tales in Africa have never been things of the past. They existed from time immemorial, they are present with our generation and they will likely continue to be. We cannot say the same thing about tales from Europe. In the Western world, fox tales belonged to the Middle ages; animal stories reigned in the 17th century and have virtually withdrawn from the 20th. In short, tales in European Literature form parts of past literature but tales in African Literature are as present and as topical as ever. The explanation of this antipodal situation can be found in their two mentalities that are entirely different.

Benjamin Worf, an American ethnolinguist, talks of Western 'objectivisation of time'. This mental and socio-cultural attitude subordinates events to time by camping them perennially in the domain of the past. It is at the origin of writing tradition, of treatment of history and literature by epochs, of the use of calendars and diaries, and of always measuring time with exactitude.[19] The same author talks of an American Indian tribe, the Hopi, who have an opposite mentality: they

---

[19] Benjamin L.Worf. *Linguistics and Anthropology* (French translation). pp.88-89.

subjectivise time by focusing more on events and happenings.[20] The Hopi attitude to time is very much like that of the African. To the African, time is a vague notion when compared to events: exact dates of births and deaths are unknown in our traditional societies; time past is rather monitored through related events. One would say for example: He was born when the Pope visited Nigeria for the first time; he left the village at the second cock-crow; the meeting will take place two markets from today; the year ends with the month of the feast of the earth goddess; locusts came last at a time now gone very far.

This vague appreciation of time explains why our ancestors did not possibly bother themselves about developing a system of writing and why they resorted to oral tradition. Writing is in effect a devise against time which inexorably passes away, while oral tradition is a devise to keep happenings with time which comes again and again. This Hopi/African mentality exists in all Africans Francophone or otherwise, who are exposed to Oral Literature. That is why they are permanently disposed to keep the literature alive in all its present forms.

From the above explanation, one can see why time was unable to carry away oral tradition in Africa. Its entities are empirically verifiable in our towns and villages since they still form part of our culture. As Pride said:

> Culture is not a static integrated whole incapable of investigation. It is made up of values that are empirical facts which may be discovered because they are ultimately subject to observable transactional processes.[21]

It is with pride that the Ivorien, Bernard Dadié, reiterates this fact when he writes:

> They (the Westerners) have their neon glow-lamps, and we have our bush lamps with the light of which we walk. They have their wireless telegraph and we, our coded drums. They have books, and we our folktales and legends in which our ancestors deposited their knowledge.[22]

---

[20] op. cit
[21] J.B. Pride. *The Social Meaning of Language*, p.11.
[22] Bernard Dadié. "Le rôle de la Légende dans la culture des Noirs d'Afrique" in *Présence Africaine*, No. XIV to XV. p.165. (The translation is ours).

Since our study is focused on Oral Literature in Francophone Africa, we are ending it with the review of translated works in French language by countries and by collectors. The efforts of the latter enable indigenous literature in these areas to be read and appreciated by non-native speakers.

Our first port of call is Senegal, and we shall undoubtedly meet its unbeatable collector and storyteller, Birago Diop. His three fantastic collections are *Les contes d'Amadou Koumba, Les nouveaux contes d'Amadou Koumba,* and *Contes et Lavanes (Folktales from Amadou Koumba, New Folktales from Amadou Koumba, Folktales and Lavans).* He is unquestionably one of the best if not the best storytellers in Francophone Africa. His stories are of the Hare tradition and they are full of humour, wit and language manipulations. One is advised to enter the world of Francophone Oral Literature through the tales of Birago Diop.

From Senegal, we go on to Cote d'Ivorie to meet another jewel of Oral Literature, Bernard Dadié. He is in fact an all-rounder for he is also a novelist, a literary critic, a playwright and a poet. He is of the Spider tradition and his two important collections are *Le pagne noir* and *Légendes Africaines (Black Wrapper* and *African Legends).*

The third country that should attract our attention is Mali, which is also of the Hare tradition. It has a traditional giant of international repute, Amadou Hampate Bâ. His major epic production, *L'Etrange Destin de Wangrin (The Strange Destiny of Wangrin)* has become a classic in African literature. He gave us two Fufulde initiation stories shrouded with mystery and full of poetry: *Koumen* and *Kaydara.* He has to his credit many tales and ethnographic publications such as *Vie et Enseignement du Tierno Bokar (Life and Teachings of Tiero Bokar), Le sage de Bandiagara (The Sage from Bandiagara), Mère de la calamité (Mother of calamity),* and *La poignée de pousiére (Handful of Dust).* He is a great defender of African oral tradition who has always insisted that all hands must be on deck to preserve our heritage. He is reported to have said in one of the interviews he had with eminent scholars: *"Chaque vieillard qui meurt et comme une bibiothèque qui brûle"* (Every elder who dies is like a library on fire).[23]

Let us now visit the Cameroun which is rated as the number one producer of literary works in Francophone Africa. We hear of such great

---

[23] Lilyan Kesteloot. *Anthologie négro-Africaine.* p.335.

names in the novel genre as Mongo Beti, Ferdinand Oyono and Francis Bebey, of Guillaume Oyono-Mbia with his plays, *Trois prétendants ... un mari* and *Jusqu'à nouvel avis* (*Three Suitors and a Husband* and *Until Further Notice*). In the same way, great names in Oral Literature abound: Eno Belinga and Towo Atangana (*Le Mvet ou L'épopée Fang*), Jacques-Mariel Nzouankeu (*Le souffle des ancêtres*), Benjamin Matip (*A la belle étoile*), Binam Bikoi (*Contes du Cameroum*), and Elelongue Epanya (*Epopée douala*). All these collections cover narratives, epics and poetry translated from various Camerounian languages into French.

We are limited by the scope of this study. Therefore, we have to limit our survey of translated Oral Literature to Francophone countries. Let us add simply that African collectors and translators of our Oral Literature are many and that most of them are successful. We are going to mention briefly the following: Fily Dabo Sissiko, translator of *Harmakhis* and *Sagesse noire* (*African Wisdom*), Julien Alapani with his *Légendes et contes du Dahomey* (*Folktales and Legends from Benin Republic*), Abdou Serpos Tidjani, translator of *Dilemme* (*Delimma*) Komla Agbetiafa and Yao Nambou with *Contes du Togo*, Djibril Tamsi Niane with *Soundjata ou l'épopée Mandingue* (*Sundiata or Mandigo Epic*), Joseph Ibrahim Seid with *Au Tchad Sous les étoiles* (*In Tchad Under the Stars*), Alkaly Kaba with *Contes de l'Afrique noire* (*Folktales from Black Africa*), Georges Agba and Gerard Remou with *Contes d'Afrique centrale*, N'sanda Wamenka with *Contes du Zaïre*, Oudiary Dantioko with *Contes et légendes Soninké*, and Ousman Socé with *Contes et légendes de l'Afrique noire*.

We are hoping that more and better French translations of African Oral Literature by Africans will continue to be produced, not only in Francophone Africa but also in Anglophone countries. Nigeria has shown worthy examples in collections like *Contes Nigérians* and *Contes traditionnels du Nigéria* by Uche Ogike, and *Olikperebu et autres contes* by Françoise Balogun (Nigerian by Marriage).

This brings us to our last remark on French translations of African Oral Literature. It is that they are not only the work of Africans but also that of Europeans, especially French-speaking scholars. French cooperation with her former colonies under the umbrella of '*La Francophonie*' is very strong in the area of culture. The members of the Francophonie cherish the slogan: '*Dialogue de cultures.*' As one would expect, African Oral Literature gets the attention it deserves in this relationship. Many scholars from France, Canada, Belgium, etc.

receive grants to enable them work on African Literature. Some of them come up with translations, which readily receive acceptance by publishers. The result is that we have a long list of books on Oral Literature whose materials were collected with the aid of African assistants who understand both French and their native languages. The Europeans are presented as the collectors while the African assistants are generally recognised. Some of these collections are: *Contes du Sahel* by Gaston Canu, *Contes de Tolé* by Luc Bouquinaux, *Contes et récits du Tchad* by Suzanne Ruelland, Jean-Pierre Caprile and others, *Contes de la Savanne* and *Contes des lagunes et de savanes* by Suzanne Lafage, *L'épopée traditionnelle* and *La poésie traditionnelle* by Laurent Duponchel, and *Da Monzon de Ségu, épopée bambara* by Lilyan Kesteloot.

This development shows that the international community also is greatly concerned with the restoration of Oral Literature in African studies. It augurs well for the future, especially as publishers are becoming better disposed towards translations from Africans as they have always been to those from Europeans.

With this, we come to the end of our panorama of the original African Oral Literature with its modern written forms in French language. We appreciated it at its golden age, when natural circumstances gave birth to it and nurtured it to full growth. We followed it through centuries of disturbances orchestrated by the Western world and its values, particularly the French colonial administration with its policies. We noted also that there are still problems even with independence from colonial rule. We observe it alive today with all its integrity but with reduced influence. It has adapted to prevailing circumstances by tolerating written forms among which are translations in European languages. Since our focus is on Francophone Africa, we introduced the translations in French language both by Africans and Europeans. It is hoped that our study will serve as a worthy compass leading to desired harbours for all those who are interested in African Oral Literature in any language, be it African or otherwise.

References

Achebe, Chinua. *Things Fall Apart*. London: Heinemann, 1958.
Agba, Georges and Gérard Renou. *Contes d'Afrique Centrale*. Paris: Fernand Nathan, 1984.
Agbatiafa, Komla and Yao Nambu. *Contes du Togo*. Paris: Clé International (N.E.A), 1980.
Balogun, Francoise. *Olikperebu et autres contes*. Lagos: Academy Press, 1978.
Bikoi, Binam. *Contes du Cameroun*. Paris: Edicef, 1977.
Bouquinau, Luc. *Contes de Tolé*. Paris: Edicef, 1976.
Canu, Gaston. *Contes du Sahel*. Paris: Edicef, 1975.
Chadwick, N.K. *Distribution of Oral Literature in the Old World*.
Dadie, Bernard. *Le pagne noir*. Paris: Présence Africaine, 1955.
────── "Le rôle de la légende dans la culture des Noirsd'Afrique" in *Présence Africaine*, No.XIV-XV. P.A. 1957.
────── *Légendes Africaines*. Paris: Seghers, 1966.
Dantioko, Oudiary Makan. *Contes et légendes soninké*. Paris: Edicef, 1978.
Davidson, Basil. *Old Africa Rediscovered*. London: Victor Gollancz Ltd, 1965.
Deschamps, Hubert. *L'Afrique noire précoloniale*. Paris: Presses Universitaires de France (Que sais-je), 1962.
Diop, Cheikh Anta. *L'Afrique noire precoloniale*. Paris: Présence Africaine, 1960.
Diop, Birago. *Contes d'Amadou Koumba*. Paris: Présence Africaine, 1961.
────── *Les Nouveaux contes d'Amadou Koumba*. Paris: Présence. Africaine, 1961.
────── *Contes et Lavanes*. Paris: Présence Africaine, 1963.
Egudu, Romanus N. *Poetic Heritage: Igbo Traditional Verse*. Enugu: Nwankwo-Ifejika, 1971.
────── *The Study of Poetry*. Ibadan: Oxford University Press, 1977.
Finnegan, Ruth. *Oral Literature in Africa*. Nairobi: Oxford University Press, 1976.
Kaba, Alkaly. *Contes de L'Afrique noire*. Snerbrooke: Naaman, 1973.
Kesteloot, Lilyan. *Les écrivains noirs de langue francaise, naissance d'une littérature*. Bruxelles: Edition de l'Institut de Sociologie, Université Libre de Bruxelles, 1965.
────── *Anthologie négro-africaine*. Paris: Marabout, 1967.

———— *La poésie traditionnelle*. Paris: Fernand Nathan, 1971.
———— *L'épopée traditionnelle*. Paris: Fernand Nathan, 1971.
———— *Da Monzo de Ségou, épopée bambara*. Paris: Fernand Nathan, 1978.
Lado, Robert. *Linguistics Across Cultures*. Ann Abor: University of Michigan Press, 1966.
Lafage, Suzanne. *Contes de la savane*. Paris. Edicef, 1975.
Lafage, Suzanne et Laurent Duponchel. *Contes des Lagunes et des savanes*. Paris: Edicef, 1975.
Lanson, Gustave. *Histoire de la littérature française*. Paris: Hachette, 1964.
Makouta-Mboukou, J.P. *Le français en Afrique noire*. Paris: Bordas, 1973.
Maquet, Jacques. *Les civilisations Africaines*. Paris: Marabout, 1966.
Riffaterre, Michael. *Semiotics of Poetry*. London: Methuen, 1980.
Niane, Tamsi Djibril. *Soundjata ou l'épopée mandingue*. Paris: Présence Africaine, 1958.
Nzouankeu, Jacques Mariel. *Le souffle des ancntres*. Yaoundé: Abbia-clé, 1965.
Ogike, Uche. *Contes traditionnels du Nigéria*. Onitsha: African Publishers, 1982.
Ogike, Uche et als. *Contes Nigérians*. Paris: Hatier, 1978.
Okeh, Peter I. "Les origines et le développement de la littérature négro-Africaine" in *Canadian Journal of African Studies*, Vol. IX, No. 3, Quebec, 1975.
Schellens, J. J. & J. Mayer. *Le Dossier Afrique*. Verviers: Marabout, 1962.
Segal, Ronald. *The Race War*. New York: Bantam Books, 1967.
Stein, Jess and Laurence Urdang, (ed.). *The Random House Dictionary of the English Language*. New York: Random House, 1971.
Pageard, Robert. *Littérature négro-Africaine*. Paris: Le Livre Africain, 1969.
Paume, Denise. *Les civilisations Africaines*. Paris: Presses Universitaires de France, 1965.
Pride, J.B. *The Social Meaning of Language*. London: Oxford University Press, 1971.
Ruelland, Suzanne & Jean-Pierre Caprile. *Contes et récits du Tchad*. Paris: Edicef, 1978.
Tidjani, Abdou Serpos. *Le Dilemme*. Paris: Silex, 1983.
Wamenka, N'Sandi. *Contes du Zaïre*. Paris:, Edicef, 1975.
Wartburg, W.V. *Evolution et structure de la langue française*. Berne: ed. A. Francke, 1962.

Wellek, René & Austin Warren. *Theory of Literature*. London: Penguin Books, 1963.
Worf, Benjamin. *Linguistique et Anthropologie* (Translated from English). Paris: ed. Gonthier, 1971.

2

EPIC TRADITION IN FRANCOPHONE AFRICA

Julie Agbasiere

Introduction

The literature of any nation usually has as its foundation the oral tradition, which comprises such genres as songs, folk-tales, fables, myths, legends and epics. Through these tales, the people in their early stages of evolution tried to explain their physical environment and existence in the universe, their beliefs, social affiliations and practices. They also tried to entertain themselves, pass on societal norms and values, and immortalise their heroes. The tales which, in particular, celebrate these heroes – extraordinary individuals in the community who distinguish themselves at trying moments in the people's history – are the epics. These tales, usually sung or recited on special occasions, have been recorded and are handed down to us in book form. Thus there are the Greek *Iliade* and *Odyssey* whose authorship is ascribed to Homer, the Anglo–Saxon *Beowulf*, the French *Chanson de Roland* and the Black African *Chaka*[1].

The epic has been defined in different terms, each definition highlighting certain characteristics of this genre. Benet describes it as "A very long narrative poem presenting adventures on a grand heroic scale, organically united through a central figure of heroic proportions" (306). This touches on form and structure. Brewer adds the historical dimension when he identifies the epic as "A poem of dramatic character dealing by means of narration with the history, real or fictitious, of some notable actions or series of actions carried out under heroic or supernatural

---

[1] These are folk epics compiled from various works of unknown authors.

guidance" (398). Seydou delimits the historicity asserting that the epic tale recreates reality rather than presents factual history (42). Kesteloot sums it up by saying that *l'épopée est la mythisation de l'histoire* (18). Irele emphasises the performance aspect. The point of interest is not on action per se and the narrating of events but *sur sa mise en scène, la charge dramatique et affective que le narrateur réussit à déployer autour du récit* (1990).

These definitions underscore the various issues that come under consideration when investigating an epic. For our study of the Francophone African epic, we shall consider the setting and socio-historical background of the tales, the form and structure, characterisation, narrative techniques and the social relevance of the epic. We shall limit our investigations to *Soundjata ou l'épopée mandingue* (1960)[2], collected and edited by D.T. Niane; *Da Monzon de Ségou, épopée bambara* (1978)[3], collected and edited by Lilyian Kesteloot; and *Silâmaka et Poullôri, récit épic peul*[4], edited by Christiane Seydou.

Setting: Socio-Historical Background

Before the European colonisation of black Africa, the people were ruled by kings and chiefs. It was the era of territorial expansionism when kings made wars on one another with the aim of defeating the adversary, annexing his land and reducing him and his successors to vassals. The more the conqueror is victorious in subsequent wars, the more his kingdom expands and the more powerful he becomes. Kingdoms flourished as long as the monarch remained invincible. Once he submitted to a more powerful conqueror, his kingdom, especially his capital, might be completely destroyed. By the force of arms, kingdoms grew into empires. Among the great empires of Africa were the ancient empires of Ghana, Mali and Songhai.

On the social scene, this was the epoch of feudalism. Chiefs and princes held their land as a fief of the overlord. The society was rigidly and highly structured and stratified. At the top echelon of the social ladder

---

[2] For the purposes of textual referencing, we shall designate this work with the letters SEM.
[3] The reference letters for this work are DMS.
[4] The reference letters for this work are SP.

were the kings and princes; next, the nobles; then, the various categories of craftsmen: goldsmiths, blacksmiths, shoemakers, wood workers, weavers; the griots, marabouts and soldiers. At the bottom rung were the slaves. Relationships were articulated in dichotomous terms - free men versus slaves, nobles versus the caste (craftsmen). Among the slaves were captives (with limited rights) versus common slaves that were mere commodity and beast of burden for their owners. It was a stable society where people accepted their situation in life and their status in the community. There was no class struggle but rather serious rivalry among the royal houses. Everybody worked for the good of the ruling family. This is the society reflected in the tales.

The action of the epics, which are under study, takes place in Western Sudan. The scenes of the action are located in the Upper Niger, cutting across large areas of present-day Guinea, Mali and Burkina Faso. Many of the towns that sprung up in those days have survived to the present day. The protagonists, Soundiata, Da Monzon, and Silâmaka and Poullôri, are historical figures. The historicity of their existence has been attested to by chroniclers, historians and geographers such as Mungo Park, El Békri, Ibn Khaldoun, Ibn Haoukal and Amadou Hampaté Ba. Camara Laye tags Soundiata's reign from 1230 to 1255 (27). C. Monteil places Da Monzon's reign from 1808 to 1827 (Kesteloot 127). Prince Silâmaka and his captive Polluôri belonged to the household of Adod Ngourôri, the last traditional chief of Macina (Seydou 40-41). They were contemporaries and rebellious vassals of Da Monzon.

The epic gives indications of the space, the actual geographical area where the action of the story takes places. The narrator in *Da Monzon de Ségou* tells us that *Da Monzon règne à Ségou* (34) and gives the extent of his kingdom in a song of praise:

De Ségou au Macina
du Manding au Sahel,
où habitent les Maures chevelus,
toi seul dispose des eaux et des hommes.
Le monde tout entier est ton fief (35)

This whole world comprises the Peul, Marka, Bambara and Maure.

In *Soundjata ou l'épopée mandinggue*, the stage is set in Soudan, *le clair pays*. Soundiata is the renowned first emperor of Mali. The vastness of his empire is best recaptured at Ka-ba during *le partage du monde*. It is the sum of all the kingdoms whose rulers receive at the hands of Soundiata the authority to govern. They include Tabon, Manding, Do, Wagadou, Mema, Sibi, Ka-ba, the land of the Koroma and of the Bobo.

Macina is a small province ruled by a patriarch, the Ardo Macina. Silámaka's confrontation with Da Monzon is an attempt to free Macina and the Peul from the yoke of the Bambara overlord in Seyou.

Form

The epic is primarily an oral genre, a performing art executed on special occasions and before a particular audience by griots. The performance of the tale is accompanied by musical instrument and the griot is the principal actor. He mimicks his characters and identifies with them. His aim is to give to his audience a rewarding performance. His renditions are never identical as he is invariably affected by his sponsors and audience. But the epic tales, now in written form, have lost to a large extent the oral trappings such as the musical background, the singing and the dramatic performance. At best, these aspects are alluded to in the written text.

By European tradition, the epic is a poem written in verse. Classical epics are written in verse form. But in Africa, the epic is written in verse and in prose, depending on the line of approach of the transcriber and editor. As an editor, he reconstructs the tale choosing from a number of traditions. The form in which he encodes the tale becomes of less significance. Thus a tale may be written both in verse and in prose. The Soundiata epic, for instance, is written in both forms. Niane's *Soundjata ou l'épopée mandigue* and Laye's *Le maître de la parole* (1978) are in prose whereas Inne's version is in verse[5]. Diabété's *Kala Jata* (1970), in prose, highlights the performance aspect by introducing an interlocutor in the tale. African scholars (Okpewho 154; Ba 83) consider the epic as a song. This negates the idea of verse as a determining element of an epic. Okpewho cautions against the strict categorisation of verse as opposed to prose saying that the line of demarcation is very thin (155). Even where the epic is in verse, the structure is loose. A griot coordinating the singing, the musical accompaniment and the theatrical aspects of his performance cannot keep to the strict rigidity of verse in the European acception of the term.

Of the three epic tales under study, *Da Monzon de Ségou, épopée*

---

[5] We could only find excerpts of this verson.

bamhara and *Silâmaka et Poullôri, récit épic peul* are in verse whereas *Soundjata ou t'épopée mandingue* is in prose. Their editors acknowledge the griot as the narrator of each tale.

Structure

The epic is a collation of the various episodes that constitute the exploits of the protagonist. This is more pronounced in the verse form than in the prose form. Each episode is a complete tale in itself while at the same time contributing to the overall story of the epic. The prosaic epic has the tendency of recounting the life and activities of the protagonist from infancy to maturity in a linear progression. The epic tale has three major parts: the prelude, the main events and the conclusion. In the prelude, the griot usually gives the main theme of the story and introduces the major characters. He then narrates the action of the tale, and at the end, he indicates that the tale is over.

The epic can also be considered as the weaving of smaller narrative units and elements to build a well-blended whole. In the oral epic, the narrative sequences of events are accompanied by musical instruments, singing and drama; each element has its rightful place in the tale. The musical tunes serve to create the right atmosphere, highlight the tempo of the action and mark the transition from one narrative sequence to another. In the written epic the elements that build the structure include the narrative sequences supported by other genres of the oral tradition – myths, legends, proverbs, songs, chants, genealogies and incantations. As Johnson rightly puts it, "the blending together of these various forms produces a generic form, the sum of which is more than its parts: the epic" (321).

The epic is built on themes and motifs. A theme is a unit of narration expressed in few lines in the same or almost the same words and reoccurring in the same or different contexts as the tale progresses. A motif expresses a broad idea that regroups a number of narrative sequences. Okpewho calls it "a frame of reference" (161). Themes and motifs form a pattern and a pivot on which rests the story.

In *Soundjata ou l' épopée mandingue*, the griot-narrator, Mamadou Kouyaté, in a prelude introduces himself and the subject matter of the tale – *l'Histoire du fils du Buffle, du fils du Lion* (10).

Thereafter, the story is told in seventeen chaptèrs focussing on Soundiata's ancestry, the arrival of his mother to Niani, his birth, childhood, exile, and battles that culminate in the defeat of Soumaoro, and the rebuilding of the imperial capital, Niani. These narrative sequences are punctuated with the recital of Soundiata's genealogy, songs composed by Balla Fasséké: *l'hymne à l' arc* and *le Niama* for the protagonist and another one for Soumaoro, as well as other songs by Sogolon and griot characters in the tale. Proverbs dot and spice the story.

The epic is developed through myths and legends. An account of the protagonist's life starts with the legendary Sogolon and the fabulous buffalo of Do. Etiological myths spring up from time to time to explain the origin of certain social groupings and relationships such as the origin of the tribe of griots, and other phenomena such as why Wagadou is a dry country. All these are deftly incorporated in the composition of the tale.

This epic is the story of the fulfilment of a prophecy. The major formulaic theme is *le destin* which is very often repeated. It is mentioned at every turning point in the narration. At times when the griot digresses, he comments on the inevitability of destiny and relates it to the case of the protagonist. He uses terms similar to *le destin* such as *la voie tracée, la voie que Dieu a tracée, la destinée*. Motifs abound and include prodigious birth and difficult childhood, occult protective powers, presages, possession rituals, totemic powers, taboos, exile, offer and acceptance of a throne.

Silâmaka et Poullôri, récit épic peul is made up of five episodes. It is narrated by the griot Tinguidji except for the third one recited by Mamadou Ham Burke de Dienne. Episodes one, three and four are different versions of the same tale. Each episode has the usual three major parts, narrative sequences, themes, motifs and proverbs. The units of narration common to all of them are tax requisition, the capture of the enormous snake, the making of the magic belt, the arrest of Ardo, battles and skirmishes, and the death of the two protagonists. Details of the information given vary to different degrees from one version to the other.

The themes can be seen within the narrative sequences. In the segments that narrate Silâmaka and Poullôri's adventure to capture the snake, the theme expresses the desire of the two young men to revolt against their over-lord:

> *Ils allaient formenter une rebellion*
> *Ils entendaient parler de rebellion*
> *Ils formenteraient une rebellion.* (83)

Subsequently they ask a fortune-teller to predict their future and the

narrator explains:

Ils voulaient se révolter (85).

Then there is the theme on *la lance*, an instrument for killing. Wanting to face the snake all alone, Silâmaka sends Poullôri to go and bring a spear:

*Je veux que tu ailles au village prendre
Une pique, prendre une lance* (89)

This order is repeated as Poullôri leaves for the village:

*il partit en quête d' une lance
en quête d' une épée
en quête d'un bâton* (91)

The theme progresses to indicate the spear as a deadly weapon. Silâmaka warns:

Ma lance est plus rapide que la guêule d'un serpent (95)

Later when they find their blacksmith making for another customer a spear similar to theirs:

Poullôri surgit, le frappa de sa lance en plein milieu de crâne au point que la lance mordit la terre (99)

The theme is repeated when their marabout repeats the same offence:

*Silâmaka fonca sur lui
le frappa avec Maléfique
au point qu ' elle mordit le tapis* (99)

Maléfique is the name of Silâmaka's spear.

The motifs in this epic include occult protective powers, presage, possession rituals, and taboos. There is the blood-letting motif. It is the urge in Silâmaka and Poullôri to kill immediately anybody who double-crosses them or is construed as an enemy. This is manifested in their killing of the craftsmen mentioned earlier, the rush to kill Bandâdo-Ardo for giving away the protective magic ring, the smiting of Silâmaka's griot, the killing of Silâmaka's impersonator, the decimation of Goundaka's men and of Amiron sa's contingents. The two heroes die, one fighting and the other resting after a good fight.

Da Monzon de Segou, épopée bambara is an epic in two volumes. The first comprises five episodes while the second volume has seven. The first traces Da's ancestry starting with Biton Koulibaly, followed by Ngolo Diarra, then Monzon, who is succeeded by Da Monzon. An episode is devoted to each of them. The remaining two episodes retrace Da's wars with Bassi de Samaniana and Diétékoro Kârta. Volume two is made up of Da's exploits against vassal chiefs and princes[6].

The structure of this epic ressembles the ones already discussed. Myths and legends occur in the episodes focusing on founding kings: Biton Koulibaly and Ngolo Diarra. The motifs which prop up the action include occult protective powers, possession rituals, taboos, divination, treachery, exile, offer and acceptance of a throne. There is also the provocation-response motif. It manifests when there is an insult in words or in deeds, a physical or verbal aggression, the laying of claims on a throne by rival kings. Almost immediately, the aggrieved takes up arms. Da's exploits hinge on this motif. He is either responding to insults from his vassals such as Bassi de Samaniana or provoking others with the intention of fighting and killing them as in the case of Bakoroba and Niagnia Kami.

One of the grand themes in *Da Monzon et Bassi de Samaniana* is hinged on the procurement of personal objects from the invincible Bassi. The marabouts order the procurement of certain objects in order to work on them and destroy Bassi's invincibility. They demand:

la sandale de son pied
la coiffure de sa tête
la première bouchée de mil de sa journée

Da repeats the order to his courtiers, to his griots, to his wives and slaves in a bid to find people who can go and get the items from Bassi. The slave women rehearse the order; Bassi itemises them in counting his losses. This injunction is repeated six times and each repetition advances the action. Injunctions usually constitute a theme in an epic tale.

Characterisation: The Protagonists

The epic underscores the inexorable intervention of supernatural forces – fate, or the gods in human affairs. The ambition of kings and princes is the conquest of adversaries which ensures the aggrandisement and safeguard of their territories. To realise this ambition they seek divine

---

[6.] Unfortunately, we could not lay our hands on this second volume. All our observations are based on our reading of volume 1.

help. A prince is powerful and invincible inasmuch as the gods are favourable to and approve of his exploits. The gods accord him supernatural powers but decree an interdiction, a taboo. This becomes a sort of covenant between the gods and man. As long as the interdiction is observed, the prince remains unbeatable. But once he transgresses, the gods divest him of his powers and he becomes vulnerable. Unlike in the Greek mythology, the gods do not intervene in the affairs of princes to settle their own scores. They allow the princes to live out their destiny which is a strict compliance with the will of the gods.

The characters that people the tales are drawn from various walks of life as has already been indicated. The ones on whom the tales hinge are kings and princes. The rest contribute to further the cause of the protagonists. They comprise the marabouts, griots and women. The epics under study derive their title from the protagonists whose exploits they extol. The protagonists exhibit the characteristics of an epic hero.

Silâmaka and Poullôri

These are two inseparable companions from the royal household of Ardo, the patriarch of Mâssina[7]. Silâmaka is the prince and Poullôri is his captive. Right from infancy Silâmaka is marked by a portent, a mark of an epic hero. As an infant and before tax collectors from Ségou, he does not cry or bat an eyelid as a big fly perches on his forehead, sucks blood to saturation and then falls off. This incident portends trouble for Ségou; the tax collectors are struck by it and warn the king. As young boys, Silâmaka and Poullôri resent the idea of their father paying tribute to another boy's father. Their disaffection grows into a revolt and soon after they prepare to organise a rebellion.

The first task of the two young men, as epic heroes, is to fortify themselves with supernatural powers. A diviner prescribes to them to catch and kill an enormous snake that lives in an anthill at the outskirts of the village. This snake is a spirit. The struggle with and the capture of the spirit snake is a feat that both men must accomplish to attain a physical and mystical maturity. The snake when caught is used in making magic belts for the two, and this confers on them the power of invisibility in battle. Thus fortified, the duo are poised to carry their rebellion to its

---

[7] This is another version of Macina. The two spellings occur in the epic under study.

logical conclusion. They provoke Amirou Sâ by withholding Mâssina's tribute to Sâ. The latter sends a contingent of soldiers with his son Moulbali Dâouara at the head to arrest the Ardo, and fighting starts.

Silâmaka and Poullôri are intrepid and fearless in battle. The two of them alone scatter and decimate Amirou Sâ's soldiers. They kill the soldiers that come for the expedition and hang the head of the king's son on a pole in front of their father's house. Reinforcements keep pouring in and the two continue slashing throats:

> *Le lendemain ils en envoyèrent encore cent;*
> *qu'ils exterminèrent*
> *Le surlendemain, ils en envoyèrent encore cent,*
> *qu'ils exterminèrent*
> *Le jour suivant, ils en envoyèrent encore cent;*
> *qu'ils exterminèrent*
> *Tout ce qu'ils envoyaient, il l' extermnanit* (107)

And this lasts for five months.

Silâmaka is remarkable not only on the battlefield but also in his private life. He upholds the tenets of his people's culture: he eats in seclusion and only with Poullôri, he does not go in to his wife during the day and above all he observes frugality in his mode of eating. All these bring out the nobility in him. It is also the mark of nobility that he should want to face danger alone. In trying moments such as the capture of the spirit snake and the imminence of his death, he sends away Poullôri on an errand. The latter understands, acquiesces and leaves him to face his destiny the way he wants it.

Silâmaka and Poullôri resent insults and mockery and when their pride is hurt, they take up arms. A hurt pride is enough justification for a hero to go to war. Their brush with Amirou Goundaka stems from the fact that they felt insulted when Amirou's slave insinuated that both young men are not the type that can bring about disaster. Their self esteem is at stake and they move into action. They kill five and maim two of the king's seven cattle keepers, seize the herds of cattle and dare the king to meet them at the king's grazing ground. The king arrives with his soldiers and these are slaughtered. Silâmaka releases the cattle only when Amirou Sâ's wife, Silâmaka's former sweet-heart, sends a message to Silâmaka that the herds of cattle are hers.

Silâmaka is the embodiment of the resistance of Peul vassal princes against the domination of a Bambara overlord. The king had to plot a marriage alliance with one of the princes, Ham-Bodêdio, to be able to deal decisively with Silâmaka. However, discountenanced by Silâmaka's successful and sustained resistance, the king seeks other means to neutralize his powers. This opportunity knocks at his door with the defection of Silâmaka's griot.

Silâmaka's fiery temper, an asset in war, proves his undoing in his private life. Unable to restrain himself in the face of provocation, he slaps his late father's griot. Disillusioned and angry, the griot joins forces with Amirou Sâ, denounces the young impetuous prince and discloses the source of his invincibility. Silâmaka becomes the architect of his own downfall and triggers off a chain of events that culminates in his death. He meets death not on the battlefield but in the privacy of his home, unarmed and at rest. He is confounded:

ni cavalier ne m'ont tué
et voilà qu'un enfant nu est venu et m'a tué!
Je meurs ignominieusement, moi Silâmaka Ardo Mâssina (127)

The golden ring, Silâmaka's source of life protection par excellence, becomes an active ingredient in the ritual that renders the young man vulnerable. Despite what Silâmaka thinks of his death, he is a great hero both to the Bambara as well as to the Peul. He is as much sung by griots in Macina as in Ségou.

Da Monzon

Da Monzon is the grandson of Ngolo Diarra, the founding monarch of the Diarra dynasty. He inherits from his forefathers a vast kingdom, which has a relative internal peace. He comes to power as a wealthy absolute monarch, the lord and master of the known world and its riches. He is the *Djitigui et Matigui ... celui qui est riche en eau et en hommes* (35). What is emphasised in this epic is not so much his personal prowess, for his *tondyons* (warriors) are there to fight his wars, as the values that he symbolises.

The monarch is the symbol of authority. He is the one who decrees what is to be done, and his word is law. The vassals are presumed to hold their land from his hands, and pay him a yearly tribute in gold.

Da Monzon is slow to anger and shows some measure of restraint. When an insult is communicated to him, he tries to ascertain the veracity of the allegation. Once he is satisfied that there is an insult, he takes up arms and there is no going back until victory is achieved. He remains resolute and tenacious. Insults to the king come from Peul princes who mock his ethnic culture and despise his non-noble ancestry. They tell him to his face that he is socially inferior to them. Bassi de Samaniana sends him the head, skin and feet of a bull. The Bambara are reputed to prefer bony to fleshy part of meat. As for Diétékorro Kârta, he refuses to give his daughter's hand in marriage to Da Monzon because of the latter's inferior social status. He makes this abundantly clear to the king through the king's messenger:

Retourne à Ségou,
dis à Da qú il est un Monzon
et que Monzon est fils d' un captiff de case
Monzon est le fils du captif Ngolo
qu' on a fait venir de Niola
comme complément au prix du miel
de mon grand-père Biton Koulibaly à Ségou Koro;
si un homme oublie ses racines,
sa fin lui chauffera le ventre (98-99)

Because he has absolute power over those under his dominion, Da Monzon takes liberties and goes to excesses. He becomes tyrannical and sadistic. He goes to the extent of capturing two of his vassal chiefs, Bakoroba and Niagnia Kami, and sacrificing them to his oracle in commemoration of his marriage with Diétékoro's daughter. He also slaughters Diétékoro Kârta as sacrifice to his oracle.

Da Monzon is ruthless and uses fair and foul means to achieve his ambition. When he fails to obtain the results expected by force of arms, he resorts to witchcraft, ruse, and complicity of certain individuals with gold. Women are generally his agents. Before the excesses of kings and princes, the people are helpless and resign themselves to fate. As the people of Niagnia whose chief, Kami, is captured by Da Monzon say,

Ici ou à Ségou nous ne serons que des captifs (123).

Their chief having been defeated, the subjects become captives.

Soundiata

Soundiata is the quintessence of the epic hero in Francophone African Literature. His life is marked by portents and feats of heroic proportion. The height of his greatness and achievements are prophesied ever before he was born. He is:

*celui qui rendra le nom de Manding inmortel à jamais,
l' enfant sera le septième astre, le Septième Conquer-ant de la
terre, il sera plus puissant que Djolou Kara Naïni.* (20).

The arrival of his mother, Sogolon Condé, to Niani is also prophesied. She is extraordinary, being the "double" of the legendary buffalo of Do. His birth is extraordinary, too, in that it is heralded by a portent: a rainstorm occurs in the peak of the dry season!

Soundiata starts early in life to overcome formidable obstacles. For ten years he is paralysed in both legs and this becomes a source of anxiety and insults to Sogolon. The king even despairs and doubts the possible fulfilment of the prediction concerning the handicapped boy. But when the hour strikes, he walks. The iron bar he holds to straighten himself up bends, taking the shape of a bow. Diata walks and takes giant steps. He stuns spectators by uprooting a baobab tree and planting it in front of his mother's hut. Just as his paralysis was a big disadvantage, his walking and uprooting of a baobab tree lift him above boys of his age group. This is a heroic feat which receives immediate acknowledgement. Mothers send their boys to become playmates of the super-hero. As the King observes: "Soundiata's childhood is typical of that of many epic heroes, who must overcome extraordinary obstacles to gain a super human power" (89).

As a result of domestic squabbles, the protagonist goes into a forced exile. Rather than being a misfortune, the exile turns out to be a preparatory period for the brilliant and spectacular rise to power of the budding monarch. It provides opportunities for the young man's education in endurance, perseverance, hunting, leadership and warfare. In Mema, he so much distinguishes himself by his courage, bravery in battle, and leadership qualities that the king of Mema makes him the deputy king. He is feared and loved by all and sundry because he is powerful. This exile becomes a sort of initiation rite at the end of which Soundiata attains the maturity needed to accomplish his destiny. It offers him the opportunity of travelling to the various parts of the Soudan and of making friends and contacts. From these contacts, he is able to raise an initial army with which he confronts Soumaoro, king of Sosso, the scourge of the Soudan in those days.

Soumaoro incurs the wrath of Soundiata by ravaging Niani and keeping Diata's griot. The time is now ripe for Soundiata to claim his kingdom and punish Soumaoro for all the atrocities he has been committing in the

Soudan. After the initial skirmishes, Soundiata's fame spreads like wild fire and aggrieved chiefs start flocking to him. His fighting prowess becomes legendary. At Tabon he lets go his fury:

> *En un instant le fils de Sogolon ,tait au milieu des Sossos tel un lion dans une bergerie; les Sossos meurtris sous les sabots de son fougueux coursier hurlaient. Quand il se tournait ... droite les forgerons de Soumaoro tombaient par dizaines, quand il se tournait ... gauche son sabre faisait tomber les têtes comme lorsqu' on secoue un arbre aux fruits mûrs* (93).

In the true epic tradition, Soundiata does not unobtrusively accede to the throne. He fights to reclaim what is his by right. He has been predestined to rule the Manding and West Soudan. Twice the throne is offered to him and twice he accepts. First is at Mema during his exile. Emissaries depart from Niani and request him to come home and redeem the throne of his fathers. He accepts and this implies going to war with Soumaoro who bars the route to Niani. The second time is after the defeat of Soumaoro at the battle of Krina. All the princes that fought under his command pledge allegiance to him thereby making him king of kings. He accepts and becomes the supreme king and emperor of the huge empire of Mali.

Soundiata is an avenger with a keen sense of justice. That is why all the wronged princes of *le clair pays* rush to him for redress, including Fakoli Koroma, Soumaoro's nephew whose wife is abducted by his uncle. His griot, Balla Fassék, composes to his honour the song "Niama" showing Soundiata as the rampart to which people rush for protection and redress.

Of all the monarchs under study, Soundiata is the only one who has a deep-rooted concern for his people's progress and welfare. As an emperor he makes sure that peace, stability, happiness and abundance prevail. He ensures that peace and justice reign in the various vassal kingdoms by summoning their rulers to a yearly meeting to give an account of their stewardship.

Like other epic heroes, Soundiata derives a lot of power and benefits from supernatural forces. But on one incident, the protagonist does not seek the help of the supernatural forces; he rather inherits the forces and therefore becomes one with them. This is emphasised in his transfiguration at Kita. Having enlisted the services of the mountain gods in his assault on Kita, he goes back to their pond-abode to thank them after the capture of Kita. He drinks from the pond and washes his face and thereafter he becomes transformed: *Ses yeux avaient un éclat insoutenable; il rayonnait tel un astre, le Moghoya - Dji l'avait transfiguré!* (129): Soundiata is not only superhuman, he is supernatural. That is why there are no taboos that can render him vulnerable. He is *l'homme aux noms multiples contre qui les sortilèges n' ont rien pu.* (11).

The "Adjuvants"

We now discuss the people who render substantive help to the protagonist. These are the warriors *(les tondyons)* who fight the king's wars. But as Da Monzon acknowledges:

Le roi est toujours assisisté de certaines personnes, ses griots, ses marabouts et enfin les femmes (117-118).

Each one has a specific service to render.

The Griot

The general image of the griot is that of a musician who accompanies his songs and recitals with musical instrument. The griot is widely acclaimed as the repository of the history of kings and princes (Echenim 91). In the epic tales, his roles and functions go further than this.

A griot is part and parcel of the heritage of princes. He is the companion and educator of the young prince, the witness and recorder of his exploits from boyhood to manhood. When the prince becomes a king, the griot renders him more services. He is the chief adviser to the king, and his confidant. As his spokesman, the griot transmits the king's address spoken in a low voice. When the king does not speak at all, it is for him to deduce what the king wants to be said and say it. A nod from the king indicates that the griot has spoken well. During wars, it is the griot, who spurs the prince to valorous deeds. A reminder from the griot of the feats performed by the prince's ancestors catapults the belligerent to the limits of his capabilities. During festivities, the griot is the grand master of ceremony who through his organisational skills and oratory adds grandeur and colour to the occasion.

At other times, the griot is involved in intrigues and diplomacy. He is subtle, trickish and cunning. Where brute force fails, the griot invariably succeeds using his sweet tongue, diplomacy and persuasive powers. He can even twist the king's arm. A griot goes on diplomatic missions and functions as his prince's ambassador to an overlord king.

The griot is the alter ego of the king. In this regard he is accorded great respect and given lots of presents. He is very well taken care of. As Silâmaka learns to his detriment, any incivility meted out to the griot attracts disastrous consequences. The griot is the one character who is quite versatile in the epic tale.

The Marabout

The marabout is indispensable to the king. The latter consults him in whatever he does. The marabout predicts the future, interprets signs and omens, and advises the king accordingly. He prescribes the sacrifices to be made to obtain the favour of the gods, and these are religiously adhered to. He prescribes other sacrifices and rituals to render powerful princes vulnerable. He offers prayers and makes charms to protect those who go on dangerous missions. His powerful influence over the king is accentuated in the following lines:

> *Avant de décider guerre, voyage*
> *ou entreprise diplomatique,*
> *l'on consultait les marabouts:*
> *Sirabl, mori,*
> *Mori Zoumana*
> *Mori Souleymane*
> *Mori Diankin,*
> *Sur leur parole, c', tait la guerre ou la paix.*
> *Si les marabouts disaient : "Montez !"*
> *Da Monzon levait sa "main de guerre"*(DMS 38)

Women

Women are instruments of war at the disposal of the king. In the cases where *les todyons* and griots fail, the king has recourse to women. This is an important and surer war tactic of Da Monzon. They go on delicate and risky missions to obtain vital information or personal effects of the adversary, necessary ingredients in preparing possession rituals. The king offers gifts and gold to the women. But once the mission is successfully executed, the women are forgotten or killed off. In carrying out their precarious assignments, class distinction is abolished and slave women co-habit with princes.

Narrative Techniques

Griots are products of the traditional society and they exemplify the traditional art of good speaking. As narrators of stories they exploit all the traditional techniques to render their stories pleasurable.

In epic tales, the griot makes frequent use of repetition. Ideas are repeated in the same or almost the same words. They come at various intervals in the narration. Praise names and titles of monarchs are often repeated especially in addressing the king. In the Diarra dynasty Ngolo to Da Monzon are addressed as *Djitigui et Matigui* (DMS 35) and this means owner of men and the waters: that is, source of production. At times, the narrator prefixes to a prince's name the name of his mother. Thus Da Monzon is at times called Makoro Monzon. Diata is called Sogolon Diata which, when shortened becomes Soundiata.

As has already been indicated, themes and motifs are repeated throughout the tale. They have a cohesive effect on the story being narrated.

Repetition underscores the intensity of the action and the feelings of the characters. Thus the time it takes the marabout to write on the snake brought by Silâmaka and Poullôri is highlighted in the repetition of an on – going action:

> *Il écrit et, au fur et ... mesure, eux y enroulent une bande de coton*
> *Il écrit et, au fur et ... mesure, eux y enroulent une bande de coton*
> *Il écrit et, au fur et ... mesure, eux y enroulent une bande de coton*
> *Il écrit et, au fur et ... mesure, eux y enroulent une bande de coton*
> *Ainsi, jusqu' ... la fin* (S P 119)

Through repetition, an explanation to an order is supplied and the action of the story progresses. When the order "Samaniana" is given to Da Monzon's army, the griot gives the significance of the one-word order:

> *C' est dire qu' il faut aller ... Samaniana,*
> *C' est dire qu' il faut conquérir Samaniana,*
> *C' est dire d' aller piller Samaniana,*
> *C est dire d' aller en guerre ... Samaniana.* (DMA 59)

In the case of the inseparable companions, Silâmaka and Poullôri, repetition underscores the similarity in their behaviour, in their private and public engagements and in the treatment given to both of them in the family. The griot comments:

> *On aurait beau faire, on ne saurait les distinguez:*
> *y passâ-t-on cent ans,*
> *le captif,*
> *on ne saurait lequel est le maître,*
> *on ne saurait lequel d' entre eux est l'esclave.*(S P 79)

The similarity is evident in their fighting prowess against the detachment of soldiers sent from Ségou:

> *L' un en prit vingt-cinq, l' autre en prit vingt-cinq*
> *L' un vint ... bout des siens, l'utre vint ... bout des siens.*(S P 105)

Soundiata ou l'épopée mandinque being a story of a prophecy come true, the idea that is very frequently repeated is expressed in *le destin, le présage, la destinée*. By bringing up these words, the griot keeps constantly in view the main theme of the story.

The griot has a preference for figures of speech such as metaphors and proverbs. The proverbs are sourced from the fauna and flora of the savannah and from the day to day life of the people. Thus are found proverbs such as:

> *Quand bien même il n' existerait plus de vaches des Peuls*
> *n' iraient pas garder des hyènes!* (S P 159) *un esclave, si*
> *beau soit - il, a toujours les pieds larges* (DMS 153)

Many of the proverbs in *Soundjata ou l'épopée mandingue* are drawn from the flora. Despite his relatively small army, Soundiata shows his confidence in overcoming Soumaoro saying:

> *Si petite que soit une forêt. . . on y trouvera toujours*
> *de fibres pour lier un homme* (SEM 91)

To describe the imminent fall of Soumaoro due to his excesses and arrogance the griot says:

> *L' arbre que la tempête va renverser ne voit pas*
> *l' orage qui se prépare à l' horizon* (SEM 80)

The griot chooses apt metaphors to show the social standing of his heroes. For Soundiata, he chooses the Fromager, a giant tree and king of the savannah forest. He uses it to compare Soundiata's social ascendancy, his stature, his strength and powers. When the king (Soundiata's father) is worried over whether the prophecy on Soundiata will ever come true his griot, Gnankouman Doua, reassures him saying:

> *Le fromager sort d'un grain minuscule ...... Quand le grain germe, la croissance n'est pas toujours facile; les grands arbres poussent lentement;mais ils enfoncent profondément leurs racines dans le sol* (SEM 38-39).

In addition, he demonstrates the use of sustained metaphors and elaborated proverbs in debates and litigations. This is well illustrated when Soumaoro and Soundiata lay claims to the throne of Mandigue and declare war:

> *-Je suis le champignon vénéneux qui fait vomir l'entrépide.*
> *-Moi je suis un coq affamé, le poison ne me fait rien.*
> *-Sois sage, petit garçon, tu te brûleras le pied car je suis le cendre ardent.*
> *-Moi, je suis la pluie qui éteint la ceandre, je suis le torrent impétueux qui t'emportera.*
> *-Je suis le fromager puissant qui regarde de bien haut, la cime des autres arbres.*
> *-Moi, je suis la liane étouffante qui monte jusqu' à la cime du géant des forêts* (SEM 112).

The griot makes a number of digressions when narrating a story. It serves as an opportunity for him to give relevant information to clarify or give more details on an issue in a narrative segment. He uses it to comment on the people's mores or make fun of people. The narrator of *Da Monzon et Diétékoro* stops his recitation from time to time to comment on wealth, poverty and women. Beautiful, ugly and avaricious women come under his humorous tongue. Describing an ugly woman he says:

> *Si Dieu n'aime pas une femme,*
> *il la fait vilaine avec un gros ventre,*
> *fesses dessechées et jambes tordues*
> *galeuse, sans oublier la bouche qui pue* (DMS 106).

Another technique is the use of dialogue. The griot-narrator makes the characters engage in conversation. To open a conversation, the narrator uses the sentence, *Il dit*, to mark off each person's statement. The exchanges are usually short and that makes the narrative lively and dramatic. The following is a conversation between Silâmaka and a spy mâbo:

> *Il dit: "Qu'est-ce qui t'amène, grand mâbo?"*
> *Il reprit: "Je te donne cinq chevaux" Il dit: "Je n'en veux point."*
> *Il dit: "Je te donne cinq serves. Il dit: Je n'en veux point."*
> *Il dit: "Que veux-tu?" Il dit: "Je ne veux rien..."* (SP 119)

And the mâbo tells the prince that he only wants to be his griot and live in his house. In other situations, he makes characters call on one another as a prelude to a conversation. For instance, the women who go on a mission to Samaniana call on one another:

> *Ô soeur aînée ... Oui petite soeur* (DMS 50)

The griot expresses strong emotions – disgust, wonder and disappointment – by the use of local interjections such as *Njak!* (SP (149), *Karja!* (SP.107). He makes a literal translation of local idioms such as *Bassi me chauffe le ventre* (DMS 41). Da Monzon sends soldiers to Bassi in order to *ramener sa tête de Samaniana* (DMS 40). There are also responses to greetings by the king, *Marhaba* (DMS 83). When a request or a suggestion is made, characters, especially Da Monzon, answer *C'est bien, C'est simple, Ce n'est rien, cela est peu de chose.* Thereafter he moves into action. All these bring out the oral nature of the epic.

The griot takes cognisance of his audience by referring to their culture and shared experiences. He refreshes their memory by giving them in a sort of summary the origin of customs and practices. Ngolo Diarra outmanoeuvres and eliminates a number of rival *tondyons* and the griot observes:

> *C'est à partir de ce moment qu'on commença à sacrifier des hommes à Moakongoba.* (SEM 82)

He authenticates his story by giving geographical landmarks that continue to bear witness to the great events narrated in the story. On one occasion he says to his audiences:

> *Si tu vas à Ka-ba, va voir la clairière de Kouroukan Fougan, tu y verras planté un linké qui perp,tue le souvenir de la grande assmblée qui vit le partage du monde* (SEM 142).

Social Relevance

The epic has as its main objective, the edification of the present day generation by presenting to them models of behaviour attributed to their forefathers. It teaches the youth such virtues as heroism, fidelity, honour, uprightness and human dignity. It creates in them *ce besoin d'identification à des figures prestigieuses d'une époque re,volue* (Chevrier 155). While writing on Chaka as a mystical figure, Modum notes that African writers present this figure from the African past to question the contemporary political situation (85, 92). In the same vein, the Soundiata epic, in particular, targets those in governance from whom are expected justice, compassion, fairness, patriotism, tolerance, altruism – values necessary for nation-building. Johnson (like King who cites D. T. Niane - 89) asserts that "this epic plays a definite role in building a sense of national identity in spite of the fact that political boundaries drawn by French and British colonial powers persist in dividing these people" (319). Epic heroes are worthy of emulation.

Conclusion

The epic is the most complex and most elaborate of the genres of the oral tradition. On the social scene, it accentuates the customs, beliefs and socio-economic values dear to the people. On the political scene, it offers a model for good and just governance. On the literary scene, it encapsulates the other genres of the oral tradition. It is the oral traditional prototype of the modern African novel. It affirms the African root of the novel and disproves the erroneous assertion that the African novel is a foreign and borrowed form. We agree with Chinweizu *et al* that the African epic narratives "have made thematic, technical and formal contributions to the African novel" (27). It is the bridge between the ancient and the modern.

References

Bâ, Amadou Hampaté. "Silâmaka, Ardo du Macina". *Poésie du monde noir.* Ed. Maguy Cuingnet. Paris : Hatier, 1973, 82-86.

Benet, William Rose. *The Readers Encyclopedia.* London : A & C Black, 1987.

Brewer, E. Cobham. *The Brewer Dictionary of Phrase and Fable.* Hertfordshire: Omega Books, 1966.

Chevrier, Jacques. *Littérature Africaine : Histoire et grands thèmes.* Paris: Hatier, 1990.

Chinweizu et al. *Toward the Decolonization of African Literature.* vol, 1. Enugu: Fourth Dimension, 1980.

Diabaté, Massa Makan. *Kala Jata.* Bamako: Editions Populaire, 1970.

Echmin, Kester. "Aspects de l'écriture dans le roman Africain." *Présence Africaine,* 139.3 (1986): 88-114.

Irele, Abiola. " L'épopée dans la littérature africaine traditionnelle". *Présence Africaine.* 139.3 (1986): 185-191.

Johnson, John William. "Yes, Virginia, there is an epic in Africa." *Research in African Literature.* 11.3 (1980) : 308-326.

Kesteloot, Lilyan (ed). *Da Monzon de Ségou : épopée banbara.* Tome I. Paris: Fernand Nathan, 1978.

King, Adele. *The Writings of Camara Laye.* London, Ibadan : Heinemann.

Laye, Camara. *Le Maître de la Parole.* Paris: Plon, 1978.

Modum, Egbuna. "Le Mythe Dans la littérature Négro-Africaine : Le cas de Chaka. " *Nsukka Studies in African Literature* (NSAL). 2.1 (1979): 77-94.

Niane, D.T. *Soundjata ou l' épopée mandingue.* Paris: Présence Africaine, 1960.

Okpewho, Isidore. *The Epic in Africa: Towards a Poetics of the Oral Performance.* New York: Columbia University Press, 1979.

Seydou, Christiane. *Silâmaka et Poullôri, récit épique peul.* Paris: Armand Colin.

3

SPEECH BEHAVIOUR IN ORAL NARRATIVE-PERFORMANCE: ANALYSIS OF MFOMO'S FRENCH TRANSLATION OF EWONDO TALES FROM CAMEROON

Zana Akpagu

Introduction

Oral literary scholarship in Nigeria and indeed in the Anglophone world gives only token acknowledgement to the rich traditional folklore existing in Francophone Africa. Equally ignored are the invaluable contributions of its researchers, collectors and translators, due mainly to the linguistic barrier. There is, therefore, the cogent need to open up folklore in French translations to non-French speakers. This in fact is the focal interest of this chapter.

We have chosen to discuss speech behaviour in oral narrative performance for obvious reasons. Much of what has been published by folklore scholars even in Anglophone Africa has concentrated on the content of the oral text itself with little attention paid to the role of speech, or *Nkobo* in Ewondo, in the rendition of the oral text. In as much as we acknowledge the incisive studies carried out by scholars like Dell/Hymes[1], Richard Bauman[2] and Denis Tedlock[3] in this aspect, speech as a means of verbal communication in oral narrative performance deserves greater attention beyond mere preview.

---

[1] Dell Hymes, "The Ethnography of Speaking" in *Anthropology of Human Behaviour*, 1962.
[2] Richard Bauman, *Verbal Art as Performance*, 1977.
[3] Dennis Tedlock, "Dialogue", *Alchering Ethnopoetics*, vol.2, 1976.

Scholars like Idris Makward[4], Gordon Innes[5] and Chukwuma Azuonye[6] have made cursory mention of the types of speech modes in storytelling in their respective studies, but emphasis is on the dramatic and performance-related aspects to the exclusion of the speech substratum of the storytelling process.

The oral text remains lifeless except when verbally actualised through the speech act. Ruth Finnegan spoke in the same vein when she said: "In the case of oral literature, the bare words cannot be left to speak for themselves"[7]. It is that need to investigate speech as the aspect that gives life to and helps in the proper understanding of the meaning of the oral text that has informed this study.

Our aim is primarily to analyse speech behaviour in the composition and delivery of Ewondo tales in Mfomo's *Au pays des initiés*[8] as seen in the light of various theories and principles enunciated by experts in the area; to examine the whole spectrum of this collection in terms of 'how' the tales are told; to study the various devices employed by the bards in their oral enactment of the tales and to probe the aesthetic basis for the effectiveness of the devices used.

Cameroon is selected for this study for several reasons. Its central position makes it appear fairly representative of Francophone Africa. Perhaps, more importantly, Cameroon has produced great folklorists in the persons of Eno Belinga, M.F. Minyono Nkodo, J.M. Awouma, J. I. Naah, E. E Yondo and Meva'a M'eboutou among others.[9] There is the need to bring to view the equally rich indigenous tradition which has

---

[4.] Idris Makward, "Two Griots of Contemporary Senegambia" in *Oral Performance in Africa*, 1990, pp.28-29.

[5.] Dordon Innes, "Formulae in Mandika Epic: The Problem of Translation", in *The Oral Performance in Africa*, 1990, p.102.

[6.] Chukwuma Azuonye, "Kalu Igrigiri: an Ohafia Igbo Singer of Tales", in the *Oral Performance in Africa*.

[7.] Ruth Finnegan, *Oral Literature in Africa*.

[8.] Gabriel Evouna Mfomo, *Au pays des initiés: contes Ewondo du Cameroun* (Soireé au Village, tomeII), 1982. Futher references are to this edition henceforth referred to simply as *Initiés* and acknowledged immediately after quotation. It shall bear the page number and be put in brackets.

[9.] For example, see Eno Belinga, S.M., *Les Chantesfables du Cameroun* (1970). *Decouverte des Chantesfables beti, bulu, fang du Cameroun* (1970), *Lépopée Camerounaise* (1978) and *Poésies orales* (1978) co-authored by M.F. Minyono Nkodo; J.M. Awouma and J.I. Naah, *Contes et Fables du Cameroun* (1976), E.E. Yondo, *La littérature orale Douala* (1966); Meva'a M'eboutou, *Les Aventures de Koulou In Tortue*.

inspired vigorous creative genius among many Cameroonian oralists.

It is our belief that knowledge of the oral legacy of this Francophone Central African country would lead not only to a better understanding of Ewondo folklore and world view but also to a better appreciation of the literary style of Francophone African bards as exemplified by Ewondo storytellers or 'Nkat Minkanà' of Cameroon. In fact, while reading through these Ewondo Cameroon stories, one cannot help but agree with what Charles Binam Bikoi said: "one recognises the undoubted 'African culture' in them and not the Cameroonian culture alone".[10] Therefore, acceptable generalisations can be made from analysing them, for speech performance in other Francophone oral cultures.

Gabriel Evouna Mfomo is one of Cameroon's best known folklore scholars. He is an immensely qualified expert folklorist who has done much to promote oral narrative scholarship and whose contributions were crowned with the award of the very prestigious *Prix de L'Académie Française* for his very successful first French translation of Cameroon tales, *Soirée au Village*. Tales in his second collection, *Au pays des initiés*, which we are analysing, are performed by various highly articulate connoisseurs whose enactment styles and speech behaviour seem to be truly representative of the oral tradition.

To achieve our set objective, an integrated analytical approach will be adopted, by including relevant perspectives from verbal arts, communications, linguistics and literature. This approach will create a meeting ground for those separate disciplines involved in speech performance of oral narratives. Although examples are drawn from Ewondo of Cameroon, findings will have wider implications for other Francophone African cultures.

Speech Behaviour in Oral Narrative Performance

The primacy of speech or *Nkobo* in oral narrative performance cannot be overemphasised. Written text of tales is dormant, waiting to be actualised through the speech process. The story rests on the pages of paper until given life by speech or what Jacques Chevrier refers to as *l'art de la parole*.[11] The interest of the story is vastly enhanced and it is

---

[10] Charles Binam Bikoi; "The Literary Dimensions of Camerounian Cultural Identity" in *Cameroon Cultural Identity*, 1982, p.92.
[11] Jaques Chevrier, *Littérature négre*, 1995 Edition, p.195.

given its proper character by the manner in which it is told. This is the view Jean Cauvin reiterates when he says: *le conte n'est pas un simple texte statique (...) la manière dont il est produit est importante.*[12]

Speech is a creative activity, realised in storytelling. It is through speech that the story is made manifest and through it a story is communicated. Therefore, in the context of our discussion, speech can be taken to mean the dynamic process by which the tales or *Minkanà* in Ewondo are actualised. Speech behaviour of a narrator or *Nkat Minkana* is the act of giving verbal expression to the stored-up knowledge of stories, literary motifs and formulae inside the bard's head, a point recently made by Lilyan Kesteloot.[13] It places the narrator-performer in a creative capacity. With speech, the content of a story transforms into a lively artistic experience. Speech and acting interact to render the text socially established, well transmitted and received.

Through speech, the artistic talents of the *Nkat Minkanà* are put into audible and visible form with gesticulations and songs to entertain. The manner and style of enactment constitute the appeal of the oral rendering of a tale. And this comes about only through speech.

In oral performance, the speech act is considered as a communication system in which a social discourse takes place principally between a narrator-performer and an audience. The bard has to employ appropriate verbal techniques to enhance the magic of rendition and the entertainment value of the tale. Through the speech act a bard executes a tale or tale-song before an audience, using the appropriate speech modes of narration.

Among the Ewondo of Cameroun, to be considered as *Nkat Minkanà* one must possess the attributes of a raconteur: a rich repertoire of tales, a good and charming voice, an oratorial capability/facility with language, ability to gesticulate and improvise, possession of wit and humour. What this implies then is that not every and anyone qualifies as a bard. This is rightly observed by Alain Ricard:

> *Tout African qui parle ne produit pas de la littérature orale! La parole s'inscrit dans des cadres sociaux, des cadres linguistiques, et s'organise autour de schémas prosodiques et ou génériques pour être vraiment une forme d'art oral"*[14]

---

[12] Jean Cauvin. *Comprendre les contes*, 1992, p.6.
[13] Lilyan Kesteloot, *Momento de la littérature Africaine et Antillaise* 1995, p.5.
[14] Alain Ricard, *Litteratures d'Afrique Noire*, 1995, p.33.

Thus, to qualify as an oral artist, one has to be talented, gifted, unique, competent and must stand out from the crowd. An oral artist's voice should possess the following qualities: beauty, flexibility, audibility and clarity. In oral performance, much attention is paid to the narrator's voice because, an inaudible voice is as bad as an illegible script. Lucidity is crucial during delivery of the tale. The bard has to avoid decorative phraseology and tell his story in a straightforward manner and articulate the facts clearly. This point is stressed also by Chinweizu thus:

> Orature, being auditory, places high value on lucidity, normal syntax and precise and apt imagery. Language or image that is not vivid, precise, or compels the listener to puzzle it out, interrupts his attention and makes him lose parts of the telling.[15]

Modes of Verbal Communication in Ewondo Tales

To give verbal expression to their tales in *Au pays des initiés*, the bards use three modes of vocalisation or voices: the speech mode, the recitation mode and the song mode. The narrators gravitate between the narrative, the reciting and the singing modes of vocalisation. This is so because the *Minkana* are besprinkled with a generous dose of proverbs, magic incantations and esoteric formulae interspersed with tale-songs. The narratives and incantations are solo recitatives while the songs require the active participation of the audience. Thus, one can conclude that the praxis of Ewondo oral narrative allows for dynamic and creative variations in modes. This enhances the aesthetic value and emotional effect of the stories. With this mode-mixing, the tale sessions look like an oratio-drama.

Most of the tales in Mfomo's collection are borne on the speech mode (referred to as *le mode de la parole* by Alain Ricard[16]) which is the appropriate mode for storytelling. It is more like ordinary speech used to narrate memorised stories or to recount a personal experience. This mode carries the momentum of the tale. Mfomo's bards are omnipresent narrators using the free-form narrative style to re-enact the experiences of the characters in the tales. The stories are told in the third person pronoun.

---

[15] Chinweizu et al, *Towards the Decolonization of African Literature*, 1980, p.247.
[16] Alain Ricard, 1995, *Op. Cit.*, p.44.

Although a great bulk of Ewondo tales in Mfomo's collection are cast in the speech mode, one finds incantations, proverbs, praise chants (which Alain Ricard calls *mode élogieux*[17]) and other fixed-phrase passages in the recitation mode. These are usually used to express philosophical thoughts and often couched in formulae in fixed diction of high emotive value. Memorisation is essential for a good delivery in this mode because it is the praise-singing mode where genealogies have to be remembered and names of persons and places recalled. This is exemplified in the short praise of Tortoise below. Tortoise outwits the chief of ancestral spirits, Zameyo-Mebenga and wins the latter's daughter's hand in marriage. In this panegyric, Tortoise is nicknamed :

koulou, fils d' Etougou, de la tribu des pieds - ongulés, beau - fils de Zameyo - mebenga L'animal - aux - cent - solutions (Initiés, p.77).

Tortoise's genealogy is traced in this short praise passage. Tortoise is himself a reputed genealogist, praise singer and oral historian of sorts:

Maître expert des généalogies ancestrales, il appela ses congénères, chacun par son sobriquet, non sans avoir évoqué, pour les flatter, la noblesse de leur ascendance et la vaillance de leurs descendants (*Initiés*, pp.79 - 80).

Divinatory incantations and esoteric formulae are expressed in the recitation mode. This can be gleaned in this story about the hummingbird, entitled *Mbiam - Ntsotsoli - le -Colibri, un expert devin*. In the story, the elephant, *Nyogo-le-daman*, and the small river bleak, *Mvaa - l'ablette*, have been condemned to death by the oracle. Both come to the expert diviner and witch-doctor, the hummingbird to enquire, through divination, the cause of their impending death.[18] The scene is captured by the bard thus:

Le Colibri alla prendre son sachet de pions et le secoua à plusieurs reprises en récitant une formule divinatoire:
- Tcharrrrrrrr! ma natte s'étend de derrière ma case jusqu' au - delà de ma cour. Tu me trouves en train de depécer la tête d'une tourterelle, ce n'est pas la tête d' une

---

[17] *Ibid.*, p.44.
[18] For a typical divination session in Africa, see Senteza W. Kajubi *et al*, *African Encyclopaedia*, 1974, p.168.

tourterelle, c'est la tête d'un pigeon gris, plutôt la tête d'un cancrelat, non la tête d'un cancrelat, plus exactement celle du margouillat, mieux, la tête d'un makalafifiè !
(*Initiés*, p.34)

Esoteric formulae are often groups of words that are not discernible and do not make meaning to the non-initiate. They are usually characterised by high poetic afflatus as can be seen from the above example. The same can be said of this incantation by an ancestral spirit who tries without success to initiate his son in the art of necromancy:

Il arracha une touffe d' herbes, la brandit en l'air en pronoçant une formule incantatoire:
- Ici, les fantomes, là les magiciens, là - bas, les termitières: ô fantomes, repondez - moi !"
- Hé - é - é - é! hurlèrent en choeur les mystérieux personnages (*Inities*, p.92).

The third mode of vocalisation is the song mode (what Alain Ricard calls *le mode chanté* [19]). As the name implies, it is used in singing the tale-songs that occur occasionally in the stories. In Ewondo narrative tradition, stories can be told to the accompaniment of music which occurs in form of tale-songs, embedded in the tale and forming part of the narrative process or as interludial devices, in between the tales. As Isidore Okpewho rightly posits:

> Music plays an inestimable role in the oral narrative performance; and some bards sometimes have a tendency to indulge the musical feeling which the song interludes within the tale tend to enhance.[20]

The narrator may sing the songs himself or this can be done by an accompanying singer. The songs are usually cast in the leader-chorus structure. The lead-singer or cantor (or cantress) is the antiphonic leader while the audience intone the chorus or refrains. With a charming and beautiful voice, aesthetic harmony is achieved.

Musical instruments like the 'mvet' or 'kora' (a cithare), the flute,

---

[19] Alasin Ricard, 1992. *Op.Cit.*, p.44.
[20] Isidore Okpewho, "Towards a Faithful Record: On Transcribing and Translating the Oral Narrative performance" in *The Oral performance in Africa*, 1990, p.125.

the wooden or metal gong, the drum or a resonating pot, rattles or a bell are used. At times, just an empty bottle or some other ideophonic instrument can provide background rhythmic accompaniment to which the song coheres. If the narrator is playing an instrument, it should be a hand-played instrument to allow the mouth extensive freedom. The narrator-performer can accompany the songs with dance steps in appropriate choreography.

An example of a tale-song can be found in *Comment Orongo-Man-Bela devint fataliste* which recounts the unfortunate experiences of the hamster, alias Koë-Sii, the earth monkey. As many times as he got married, he became widower in equal number of times. His siblings either died at birth or before puberty. So, he lived one long endless life of mourning. Despite the sacrifice, the purification ceremonies and the expiation rites he performed, oracles only foretold of worse times ahead. At wit's end, he intones this elegiac song of lamentation which he bequeaths to posterity as testimony of his fatalism:

> *Vòlat! Vòlat! Ovongo - Man - Bela! Vòlat!" Cri*
> *du rongeur vaincu par un destin inexorable:*
> *- Ah! pauvre de moi!*
> *Que je sorte pour aller boire au ruisseau:*
> *Me voici pris au piège !*
> *Que je me cache dans mes galéries:*
> *Me voici asphyxié par la fumée.*
> *Que je veuille aller me ravitailler aux champs:*
> *Me voici écrasé par un piège - assommoir !*
> *Quel crime ai - je donc commis*
> *pour qu' on me traite de la sorte?*
> *Certes, bien triste que mon sort!*
> *Mais, ô jeunes gens et jeunes filles*
> *Qui mangerez de ma chair:*
> *Gare à vous!*
> *A mon tour je vous coincerai le gosier*
> *Avec un fruit*
> *Que vous pourrez ni avaler ni rejeter!*
> *Car enfin, pourquoi me persécute - t - on?*
> *Est - ce parce que ma queue est ornée d' anneaux?*
> *O mystère! Vòlat! Vòlat! Ovongo - Man Bela!*
> *Vòlat !* (*Initiés*, p.32).

This tale-song is part and parcel of the story being sung instead of narrated and tells of his numerous efforts in vain to escape the wicked hands of destiny. This song variation helps to combat boredom among members of the audience who become involved. Voice parts are allotted to the audience who join the bard in acting out the lines. This helps to maintain the interest of the audience, and creates a renewed interest and greater zeal after the song. This is achieved through the psychology of change and variation. Thus, the incidence of songs heightens entertainment value and sustains performance. Thus, the skillful bard should not only be a reciter of tales, but also a good composer and singer, a complete and versatile entertainer.

Among other virtues of the Nkat *Minkanà*, his voice should be sufficiently flexible to be able to simulate the varied mood of the tales and to represent the various emotional states of the various characters. For example, he should be able to simulate a lament in such a manner as to excite pity, to dramatise grief in an elegiac story and to express an impassioned appeal and desperation in the apostrophic tale. He should also be able to express joy and happiness in the rhapsodic form. Since tales incorporate the three modes most often than not, the proficient bard should have a flexible voice, rich enough to intone easily the various modes of the tale – lyric, invocation and oratorical narrative – in their proper modulations.

Performance Strategies: Narrative Devices in Ewondo Oral Tradition

It is necessary, at this juncture, to examine some of the ways the performer - narrator dispatches himself verbally in order to maintain the audience's interest, the elements he employs in the art of telling the story.

Use of Verbal Formulae

Ewondo oral performance is marked by use of verbal formulae. For the purpose of our discussion, formulae are simply taken to mean abstract - pattern sentences strung together and uttered in the recitation or singing mode. During narration, formulae ensures stability and facilitates control of audience by the bard. Formulae also conserve as recognition cues for audience as well as mnemonics for the bard. Formulae occur as opening and closing statements in tales, as proverbs or as incantations.

(i) Introductory and Closing Formulae

A notable feature of performance of Ewondo prose narratives is the use of formulae as a form of introduction to the story proper. The use of the term formulae in this context is as defined by Gorden Innes:

> A fixed form of words which are used in particular circumstances, in the sense in which we speak of greeting formulae such as 'How do you do?' in ordinary conversation and of opening and closing formulae in tales[21]

Introductory formulae are preliminary remarks used as prelude, or as formal courtesies by the Ewondo storytellers to the audience. The usual opening formula is: *Ndon Hina* ! translated into French as *Voici l' Histoire* which prefaces tales. At this utterance, all conversations cease and the bard starts his story under prevailing calm. It can be repeated to obtain fuller attention of the audience. It sets the scene and prepares the audience for the forthcoming narrative.

The purpose of preliminary formulae is to provide transition from the everyday world in which the audience is situated into the fantasy world of tales into which they are to be plunged. It announces a shift from the factual world of the audience to the fictional experience about to be evoked by the narrator. The following observation by Jacques Chevrier underscores these points:

> *La formule liminaire a donc deux fonctions: d'une part elle permet d' attirer et de fixer l' attention du public avant même le début du récit, d'autre part, radicalement différent ou le surnaturel est la règle et ou l'ordre habituel des choses est renversé.*[22]

In Ewondo oral narratives, this setting for the events of the stories is usually the extraterrestial world of the spirits, *l'autre - tombe, le pays d'en haut, mystérieux pays* (*Initiés*, p. 134). It is a never-never world, inhabited by ghosts and souls of dead ancestors. The Ewondo of Cameroon are located in the equatorial rain forests with their peculiar

---

[21] Gordon Innes, 1990, *OpCit.* p.103.
[22] Jacques Chevrier, 1995, Op. Cit, p.192.

flora and fauna. The forest naturally constitutes another favourite psychic or imaginary milieu in which tales are set. The following formulae serve as formal conclusion or closing courtesies to the stories:

>Bard: *Gasi Na La' a*
>Audience: *Na la' a!*

It is translated into French thus:

>Bard: *N' est - ce pas ainsi?*
>Audience: *Parfaitement!*

The English translation is

>Bard: Isn't it so?
>Audience : Perfectly so!

At the end of the tale, the Ewondo bards give the audience the chance to be the arbiter and judge of the merits of their performances. The bards seek to verify if they have respected the facts of the tradition. By making a sentence of judgement: "Perfectly so!" in response to the bard, the audience is showing that they are in agreement with the details of the story.

From this post-mortem or appraisal formulae in Ewondo oral tradition, it can be seen that a relationship of mutual reciprocity exists between the bards and the audience. With this formal conclusion, verbal commendations in the form of praise-names or eulogistic courtesies may be made. Another tale can then be introduced, otherwise the storytelling session is ended.

(ii) *Greeting Formulae, Praise Epithets and Esoteric Incantations*

In Ewondo oral tradition, ordinary everyday exchange of greetings occur as formulae and are uttered in the recitative mode. These are fixed-phrase passages used as formal courtesies or friendly invitation made by a speaker to his listeners. It is an oratorical formula whose aim is to arrest audience's attention, raise expectations and curiosity and create the appropriate atmosphere and emotional state in the listeners for a speech about to be delivered.

Tortoise, the hero of Ewondo forest animal tales and reputed for his enormous oratorical skills, makes profuse use of greeting formula each time he is addressing a plenary session of animals which he enjoys summoning. He is reputed for his high intelligence and feared for his mystic powers as witch-doctor and necromancer. The invisible world of ancestral spirits is inaccessible to mere mortals except for a few initiates. The journey to the spirit world is hazardous. Not all who go there to 'consult' return alive. The awe and secrecy associated with this world, due to the image of ancestral spirits as the final arbiters of justice is seen in the tale *La tortue cite le léopard au tribunal des ancêtres*. Tortoise is the only one that literally strolls in and out of it as if it were just a neighbouring village from where he brings back the deep secrets of the spirits. In *Comment Bëmë manqua de cornes alors que son oncle en fabriquait*, he returns from one of such miraculous journeys, with a sack full of horns and magical powers for distribution to other animals to enable them defend themselves against their all-time enemy and aggressor, man! When the hero mounts the podium to speak, he salutes his homologues with this formulaic greeting:

> *- fils de mon père, filles de ma mère, de l'amont*
> *à l'aval, de la haute et de la basse forêt: honneur*
> *à tous!*
> *- Hé - é - é - é - é!*
> *- Honneur à tous!*
> *- Hé - é - é - é - é!* (*Initiés*, P. 27)

In similar circumstances, in the story *La tortue cite le léopard au tribunal des ancêtres*, he uses the same formulaic greetings. Also in *Fétiche de mon père, vas - y !*, the village patriarch uses the same formulaic greeting. Greetings in form of formulae become a speech device for the oratorical speaker to create in his listeners the appropriate affective climate. Both Tortoise and the community leader want to persuade others. And the main intention of oratory is persuasion according to Eno Belinga:

> *L' inspiration oratoire exprime une idée avec passion, pour*
> *convaincre, persuader, modifier la volonté de l' auditeur.*
> *C'est de cette facon que l'on arrive à décider tout un*
> *clan, toute une tribu, à une campagne idéologique, a*
> *poursuivre un combat ou à entreprendre une guerre*[23]

The Tortoise is the object of praise and admiration especially after performing his magical or supernatural feats. Praise epithet and eulogistic

---

[23] S.M. Eno Belinga, *Comprendre la littérature orale Africaine*, 1978, p.123.

names are given to him as mark of honour. One of such occasions in which such is given to him is during his epic capture of the sorcerous river snail that frightened the whole village:

> *Les animaux n'en croyaient pas leurs yeux. Ils accourent à la rencontre du héros avec des cris d'acclamation. Quelle joie dans le village. On decerna au conquérant des titres élogieux (. . .) race des quadrupèdes (...) l'animal - aux - cent -solutions. (Initiés, p.72).*

Among other endowments, Tortoise is the magician and trickster of the animal kingdom. His shell or mobile house and his slow movement excite great curiosity and awe. In *La tortue porte l'éléphant* he dresses up like a magician ready to perform in front of his grotto. He recites magical formulae during demonstrations as we hear from Ambroise Bala, the bard:

> *Que vous dire! Le féticheur s' assit à côté de l'éléphant, debout au milieu de la cour. Il procéda à des incantation magiques, répétant toujours les mêmes mots:*
> *- koul' antoa, koul' antoa, koul' antoa. (Initiés, p . 59)*

Incantation here is for magic inspiration for the performer and to develop an appropriate emotive state of mind and create the right psychological atmosphere among the audience. Elsewhere, we find this esoteric sentence: *Toum voum! Tu ne te moques que de toi - même* uttered intermittently at regular intervals at the providential palace by the mystic voice of the forest spirit. This enigmatic formulaic utterance creates an effective climate in the fairy house.

(iii) Use of Supportive Proverbs

The Ewondo are prone to using proverbs and this trait amply manifests in their oral narratives. Charles Bird defines a proverb as a fixed-word formulae, an abstract-pattern sentence, a phrase or clause that is formulaic, compact and metaphorical. [24] According to Jean Cauvin, proverbs occur as formulaic utterances, as figurative statements or as expressive formulae used in an oral medium. [25] They have no separate existence,

---

[24] Charles Bird, "Heroic songs of the Mande Hunters" in *African Folklore*, 1972, p.283.
[25] See Jean Cauvin, 1992, *Op. Cit.*, pp.19-29.

they are part of speech performance in tales and other oral genres. Proverbs are associated with wisdom and verbal sophistication on the part of the user. They are terse, memorable and popular. Going by G. Milner's definition:

> *Un proverbe est laconique, lapidaire, facile à retenir. Il sent le terroir, fait comprendre immédiatement une situation, valorise le discours. Son message abstrait et universel est fondé sur l'expérience et l' observation*[26]

Among the Ewondo, proverbs constitute a core aspect of a living speech tradition. They are supposed to be wise sayings bequeathed to them by their forebears, a fact acknowledged before every proverb with phrases like *nos ancêstres ont dit que, voilà pourquoi nos ancêtres nous ont transmis ce proverbe..., et nous tenons de nos ancêtres ce proverbe...*, etc. These words that preface proverbs are to authenticate them. The Ewondo show respect for tradition, therefore, they accept proverbs without questioning, as time-tested and proven truths. Thus a proverb consists of a short speech utterance that is considered as true, valid and popular.

In speech performance, proverbs play ornamental and seasoning roles. They add flavour to *Nkobo*, they are the palm oil with which words are eaten (to borrow Chinua Achebe's words). They create a certain atmosphere of grandeur with expressive force. Generally, people do not bother about origins or coiners of proverbs. Among the Ewondo, daily experiences of individuals give rise to their coinage. Accepted ones find their way into the pool of existing proverbs. They are not ascribed to authors, they are considered as part of the community's living speech tradition. This applies to all oral literary items. Therefore there is sense in what Eno Belinga is saying in this regard:

> *Les oeuvres littéraires orales de l' Afrique Noire ont été créées par des auteurs qui restent généralement inconnus, quoique l' on puisse parfois les identifier de façon directe ou indirecte. L'oeuvre littéraire, née dans ces conditions, devient, par la suite, le patrimoine esthétique et spirituel de sa communauté d' origine*[27]

---

[26] G. Miller, "*De l'armature des locutions proverbiales. Essai de taxonomie sémantique*", in L'homme, vol. 3 No 1, 1969, p.51.
[27] S.M. Eno Belinga, 1978, *Op. Cit.*, p.103.

The core element of Ewondo proverbs is pedagogy. They communicate lessons on human existence and relationships with others. For example, the following proverbs stress the necessity of merging honesty with wit and cunning in order to survive in this world:

Vivre, c'est user de ruses (Initiés, pp.37, 67)
(To survive is to employ wit)[28]

Qui dit vivre, dit user de ruses (Initiés, p.30)
(He who says to you, live! says use wit).

These proverbs are predicated on a machiavellian notion of survival as a philosophy of life. Canny survival is important to the Ewondo and the proverbs show that cunning and wit are of advantage to man. In the jungle where the law is survival of the fittest, Tortoise with its physical handicap resorts to scheming for survival.

Proverbial items transmit instruction and correction on how to and how not to live. For instance, children are taught to be obedient to their parents. This advice is expressed in this proverb which states that:

La désobéissance au père apporte malheur
(*Initiés*, p.105)

(Disobedience to the father brings ill-luck)

Those who obey parents prosper while those who do not are deprived of parental blessings.

Another didactic proverb stresses the need to be kind to others because the person you help may turn out to be of help to you in the future:

On ne casse pas les pattes à la perdrix sa voisine (Initiés, p. 47).

(One does not break the legs of the patridge, your neighbour)

The lessons of the "Good Samaritan" are being preached here. In the illustrating story, Oling' Nga Ngoa, the hunter showed kindness to a patridge (Man-Bekon the spirit had transformed himself into the patridge). The patridge later saved this hunter's life in its capacity as head of the spirits' tribunal. The lesson is that one good turn deserves another. Similar

---

[28] All English translations are done by us.

advice is communicated through this proverb:

> *La générosité enrichit le donateur lui - même, tout comme l'avarice prive l'avare (Initiés, p. 97)*
>
> (Generosity enriches the giver himself, just like greed deprives the greedy)

In the story *L' Orpheline et la vieille femme*, the orphan's kindness and humility are rewarded by the old woman fairy with riches while her unkind and arrogant half-sister is repaid with evil.

The theme of ingratitude is given adequate verbal exposition in Ewondo proverbs. Proverbs such as the one below are coined to show the evils of ingratitude:

> *Tu ne te moques de personne d' autre; tu ne te moques que de toi-même! (Initiés, p. 118)*
>
> (You mock no one else, you mock but yourself)

The advice here is that if you bite the finger that feeds you, you make a mockery of no one else, but yourself as illustrated by the events in the tale.

Another proverb is derived from the evil of over-confidence:

> *L'assurance du sucès peut conduire à l'échec (Inities, p. 29)*
>
> (Assurance of success can lead to failure)

There are laid-down behavioural patterns in Ewondo society. Deviations from these patterns are criticized. For example, double-dealing and telling of lies which men indulge in are considered anti-social. Ewondo elders caution against such attitudes in this proverb:

> *Si tu fabriques ton piège en jouant la comédie, si tu l'enclenches par mode d'amusement, tu attraperas ta vérité! (Initiés, pp. 57 - 58)*
>
> (If you set your trap on falsehood, if you set it in fun, you will catch your truth)

The dove reaps what he sows in the story of *Zoumfèbë-la Tourterelle*. His conduct is based on lies, so he loses his wives when the truth is finally discovered.

Again, man must not be talkative or indiscreet. An Ewondo proverb attests:

> *La bouche de Nlo - Modo tua Nlo - Modo lui - même (Initiés, p. 112)*

(The mouth of Nlo - Modo killed Nlo - Mode himself).

Another attitude abhorred by the Ewondo is disobedience. The dire consequences of disobedience are communicated through this proverb:

La désobéissance coûta la vie à l' homme tronqué (Initiés, p. 102).
(Disobedience cost the truncated man his life)

The proverb in Ewondo is a pseudo-form of schooling. They pass on social messages on life. For instance, generosity is preached but to succeed in life, man must not be too indulgent as suggested in this proverb:

L' homme indulgent ne prospère jamais (Initiés, p. 121)

(The indulgent man never prospers).

To achieve success and prosperity, man must be daring, ruthless and bold. This other proverb drawn from *Les accords sont inviolables au pays des fantomes* impresses on man to fulfil his promises and avoid unpleasant consequences of violating an accord:

Ce qui, une fois, est entré au creux de l' oreille, n'en ressort plus jamais (Initiés, 135)

(That which, once enters the ear, never comes out again)

Once made or undertaken, one's word of honour becomes sacrosanct and inviolable.

Another Ewondo proverb stresses the need to make hay while the sun shines:

On visite les pièges dans la mesure où ils attrapent le gibier (Initiés, p.99)

(One visits the traps as often as they catch game)

The idea here is that opportunities are difficult to come by and so should be seized whenever they present themselves.

The ultimate superiority of wisdom and wit over brute force is presented in the heightened and compressed form of proverbs, which demonstrate the validity of this fact of life. This is what the proverb below is saying:

La sagesse est l'aînée et la force, cadette (Initiés, p. 67)

(Wisdom is the elder sister and force, the younger)

In the story, *Concours de vitesse entre la tortue et le léopard*, the weak but artful Tortoise uses his wisdom to defeat the awfully powerful leopard in a racing competition.

Endurance and hope are major themes in Ewondo oral narratives. Advice on these cherished ideals of life are transmitted in the condensed form of proverbs:

> *L' éléphant ne se lasse guère de porter ses ivoires* (*Initiés*, p. 28)
>
> (The elephant hardly gets tired of carrying its tusks)
>
> *On n' abandonne pas un poussin qui crie encore* (*Initiés*, p. 30)
>
> (One does not abandon a chick that still cries)

The odyssey of Ovongo-Man-Bela the hamster is intriguing and his reaction is worth emulating. His is the saga of persecution upon persecution, one mishap after another. Although he becomes fatalistic, his reaction is philosophical: once there is life, there is hope!

The future is unpredictable no one knows what the future holds for man. This fact of life must have given rise to this cautionary proverbial statement:

> *L'avenir est aveugle; nul n'est maître de l'avenir* (*Initiés*, p . 68)
>
> (The future is blind; no one is the master of the future)

The Ewondo believe in the existence of God, *Zamba - Dieu, Dieu - créateur - des - hommes*, as the ultimate force who directs an individual's destiny. This is attested to by this ancestral wise saying:

> *Toute chose arrive par prédestination* (*Initiés*, p.133)
>
> (All things come through predestination)

However, man must take precaution to arm himself with charms as the individual's immediate force, directing, manipulating and channelling man's affairs. This concept is given as advice by ancestors thus:

> *On ne descend pas une colline glissante sans tenir en main un baton* (*Initiés*, p. 106)
>
> (One does not descend a slippery hill without holding in his hand a walking stick)

The Ewondo believe that charms are potent and useful. They are used when human effort fails. Thus, there exist charms for hunting, for fertility, for good luck, for riches and prosperity , tor love and admiration, for wrestling, etc. The reason is expressed in this proverb:

> *Qui dit fétiche, dit sagesse de l' homme. Qui dit fétiche, dit art de vivre* (*Initiés*, p.139)

(He who says fetish, implies wisdom of man. He who says fetish, implies the art of survival)

Idols and charms protect and help to keep man's life on a leash.

In Ewondo belief system, God is omniscient. So, even if a wrongdoer escapes notice, God effects justice through nemesis by punishing the wrongdoer as demonstrated by the story *Le kaiser et les deux domestiques*. This principle is expressed in this proverb that says that nothing is hidden under the sun:

Cadavre d'un homme ne peut rester caché (*Initiés*, p. 114)

(The crops of man cannot remain hidden).

The murdered man in question had warned his assailant that *le soleil qui nous voit publiera ma mort* (the sun that was their only witness would publicise his murder).

To conclude, one must stress the fact that in Ewondo society, proverbs are more than mere flavouring items in speech. They are statements of advice in formulaic form and are transmitted through tales and other oral genres.

The Oral Style

One of the characteristics of oral delivery of Ewondo *Minkana* is the adoption by the *Nkat Minkanà* of the oral method. According to this style, tales are recounted in everyday diction, but with the narrative discourse encapsulated in an aesthetic form. It is an informal style of delivery, detailed and complete. There is a quick facile transition of roles by the storyteller. At one time, he is the narrator, recounting events and at another time, a character within the same story. With the oral style, narrators adopt the direct speech as characters. Direct speech brings the quaint reported speech at one time and at other times, they adopt the narrative alive, this gives it greater immediacy and impact.

Dialogue and monologue are oral delivery devices. Ewondo tales offer numerous examples of good dialogue and monologue. Skilled bards can exploit to a great advantage the dramatic potentials of dialogue in the stories, they can vividly recreate the episodes by means of dialogue. At times too, the characters in the tales engage in monologue like Bëmë, the Wildboar in his stupid contemplations. Each time he sees others do extraordinary things, he engages in monologue and accuse them of having stolen the charm bequeathed to him by his late father:

> ... *sous le regard de plus en plus curieux de Bëmë qui se dit en lui - même: "Encore un qi m'a volé le fétiche que j' ai hérité de mon père!* (*Initiés*, pp 22, 24)

A peculiar feature of Gabriel Mfomo's collection is that most of his bards are modern raconteurs, with the power of speech, who incorporate in their narratives elements of contemporary socio-political history, terminology and concepts drawn from modernity. They are at ease with urban setting. For example, Paul Messi Manga narrated *Les proverbes de Ngasoumou* in Hambourg while Paul Ndougsa Balla performed *Zoumfëbë - la - tourterelle* in Lyon. Jean Pierre Enyegue - Amvouna performed *On ne casse ...* in Paris.

The above observation explains why one finds words and ideas that clearly belong to technologically advanced Europe in the tales. Some of these modern concepts include: *l' aéronaute* (p. 109), *oiseaux - moteurs* (p. 106), *météore* (p. 71), *pétrole* (p. 132), *police* (p. 114), *investigations policières* (p.113), *soldats* (p. 132), *écriture* (p. 156), *secrétaire* (p. 156), *enqueteur* (p. 157), *amphithéâtre* (p.59). A word like kaiser (pp. 106, 160) is an evidence of German influence in Cameroon.

Witticism and humour are added to the tales to pad out the narratives. These elements are introduced to be enjoyed on their own as items in a mixed programme of verbal artistry.

Schematic and Thematic Structure of Ewondo Tales

Ewondo tales are basically prose narratives, written in run-on lines. Although in prose form, they are besprinkled with proverbs and interspersed with songs. In them, there exists a whole range of social issues from public morality to private relationships.

Life is depicted in the tales as a mixture of the contradictory principles of cruelty, trickery and obedience. Some of the stories appear as deep contemplation on man's destiny and the incomprehensibility of God as can be seen in the *beti* version of the biblical book of Job, recreated in the story of *Abobo - l' araignée interroge Dieu* (*Initiés*, pp 156 - 159). The tales take the listener through a spiritual and philosophical journey during which the listener is invited to dialogue and meditate with the *Nkat Minkanà*. They attempt to provide answers to epistemological problems.

On the whole, Mfomo's collected tales are entrenched in the moralistic principle of good and evil and their ensuing conflict. This bipartition or polarisation is typical of African tales. At the end, conflict is resolved with evil being punished while good triumphs. The tales communicate some general truth, a moral or lessons, which are implicit in the story or explicitly stated in the middle. In some other stories, the lessons appear at the end as tag morals in final statements or in form of proverbs. An example can be found in *La vertu d'obéissance* which ends thus:

> *Ainsi, le benjamin de la famille - par son obéissance-devint l' homme le plus riche du pays (...) car, dit le proverbe : "La desobéissance au père apporte malheur! (Initiés,* p .105).

Some tales end with conundrums or questions, leaving the audience to work out the solution to the unresolved issue from the content of the story. For example, *Les trois jeunes gens et la fille du kaiser* ends with a puzzle:

> *A votre avis, qui des trois féticheurs mérite d' épouser la jeune fille miraculée? (Initiés,* pp. 109 - 110)

The aetiological element is preponderant in Ewondo tales: some of the tales purport to formulate explanations for the existence of the natural and supernatural order. For example *Les sept fils de Zamba - Dieu* explains why God separated man from other animals and gave him power over them . The tale *Dieu - créateur - des - Hommes* is also aetiological and explains that God left man here on earth because of the latter's disobedience. It explains also the origin of the use of charms and the practice of burying corpses. In some tales, the aetiological element is stated and incorporated in titular form such as in *Comment la mort fit son entrée chez les hommes* which reveals the origin of death. Also *L'origine de la maladie Akiae* tells how hydromniosis came to infest humans. *L'histoire des deux frères* draws attention to why the viper's meat is taboo to Beti youths and women (*Initiés*, p. 100).[29]

Structurally, Ewondo tales are made up of a combination of incidents determined by actors and actions linked together in an ordered sequence to make up a story. The characters in tales vary from tale to tale. The archetypes in tales vary from tale to tale. There are archetypes like the trickster, the villain, the dupe and the intervener in animal tales. In Ewondo

---

[29] This taboo is a source of conflict in *Trois pretendants... un mari* by Guillaune Oyono-Mbia.

animals tales,[30] the trickster is Tortoise, and at times the turtle, or the dove. In human and supernatural tales, there are archetypal character too represented by the villain or superior, the underdog or dupe, the helper or intervener, the hinderer and the companion.

(i) Unistructure and tale Embedding

Ewondo tales exhibit some form of homogeneity in their structure. The storyline, the plot and sequence of the actions follow a parallel or similar narrative pattern. Most of the tales adopt the simple unistructure. A few others however are multi-structured, having more than one plot unit. This phenomenon is called tale embedding or tale merging. An example is seen in *Un jeune enfant sauve l'humanité* where, in disobedience to the law and for want of adventure, a young man wanders into the forest. He is confronted by Emomodo, the forest monster and is swallowed up. The tale is supposed therefore to draw to a close with the resolution. But it continues with fresh episodes and the introduction of a new range of characters: the messianic child, the other villagers hitherto swallowed by the monster, including the arrogant rebel Ngoulétama.

New conflict is introduced between the saviour-child and the ogre, Ngoulétama, who refuses in his arrogance to recognise the power and leadership of the saviour-child. He is left behind in the stomach of the monster while others are freed. Somehow, the young adventurer in the first part is never heard of again and the second part of the story bears very little relation to the first part. This is a clear example of tale merging. The second part of the story can constitute a complete story in itself, though it will be short.

The story of *Fétiche de mon père, vas-y*! shows the same merging form by bringing together two unrelated episodes. The first part of the story deals with the traditional blessing-cum-coronation of the heir apparent by the eldest statesman. The second part is a story within a story. To buttress his advice, the old man narrates the story of a lazy dependent crown prince who, instead of stamping his own footprints on the sands of time, depends on his late father's reputation and achievements. Both episodes could consist of separate stories, i.e. "The Coronation of the Prince" and "The Lazy Hunter." This points to an instance of tale

---

[30] For another type of classification of tales, see Jean Cauvin, 1992 *Op. Cit*; p.13.

embedding.

(ii) Structure of Ewondo animal tales

The traditional narrative schemata of Ewondo tales is generally herocentric, i.e. all actions, situations and even locations are organised in such a way as to reveal the hero. This schematic structure usually pitches two characters – the hero and the anti-hero – against each other. The hero is usually the dupe, presented as a peace-loving victim. The anti-hero is the villain – the aggressor or victimiser who confronts the dupe. At the end, the villain is punished. There is a third minor character, the intervener who takes sides with either of the two opponents. He tilts the power balance and helps in the resolution of the story.

The narrative pattern is fairly consistent. The story starts by presenting the characters, their traits and relationship, as a launching pad for action. The body of the story tells of their confrontation which opposes a weak character with a strong one. One suffers persecution and this sparks off a series of actions aimed at resolving the situation. There is suspense. The story ends with resolution or rectification of the situation.

By way of illustration, *La tortue cite le léopard au tribunal des ancêtres* manifests the analytic structure above. Schematically, this story can be broken down as follows:

Introduction
Two neighbours: - Tortoise plants maize and obtains good harvest.
Tortoise and Leopard   - Because of draught, Leopard has bad harvest.
are in conflict   - Leopard envies and covets Tortoise's farms.

Act 1
Confrontation:
Tortoise versus Leopard - The powerful and aggressive Leopard chases away Tortoise from his farms and home. Claims that the land is part of his heritage.

Tortoise loses: Defeat   - The weak and helpless Tortoise leaves to settle
Leopard wins: Success   elsewhere.
                         - Three times, Leopard repeats same persecution by confiscating Tortoises land and farms.

Act II
Confrontation:

Tortoise versus Leopard - Tortoise resorts to tradition to seek redress and justice.

Tortoise loses: Defeat - Summons other animals and presents case before their tribunal.

Leopard wins: Success - For fear of reprisals, animal assembly returns verdict of 'Guilty' on Tortoise. Tortoise suffers injustice.

Act III
Confrontation:

Tortoise versus Leopard - Tortoise takes case to Court of Appeal of ancestral spirits. (Seeks vengeance, reverses tale back to another beginning in form of tale embedding).

Tortoise wins: Success - Tortoise uses trickery. Both are buried so as to present themselves before spirits court.

Leopard loses: Defeat - With the help of the hamster (intervener) Tortoise digs tunnel from his grave to his house.
- Purported judgement passed by ancestors. Leopard suffocates and dies. Tortoise emerges triumphantly alive to report verdict.

Denouement

Resolution of Conflict: - Restitution: Tortoise regains his land and farms

Return to normalcy - Tortoise is given a hero's welcome and grows in esteem before other animals.

Ultimate goal: Tortoise attains justice.

This story can be summarised and diagrammed thus:

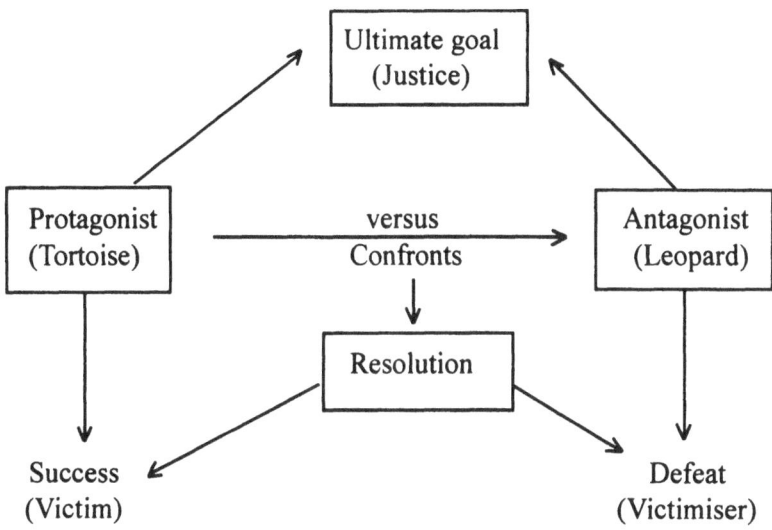

(iii) Structure of Tales with Human and Supernatural Characters

Tales with human and supernatural characters are usually longer and more developed. We find characters being contrasted and opposed to one another. The schemata reveals a pattern of relationships between victimiser/victimised, exploiter/exploited, superior/underdog, helper/hinderer, hero/villain. Often, metamorphosis occurs with an underdog emerging as the hero at the end of the tale.

In terms of characterisation, the 'superior' is he who wields authority and uses it to intimidate and bully. This triggers the action. The 'underdog' is victim, suffering from bullying, anxiety and apprehension and seeks alleviation. When metamorphosis occurs, we see a reversal of roles from underdog to hero. There is often a 'helper' a *deus ex machina* who is usually a supernatural being who intervenes to effect the betterment of the underdog. They are benevolent spirits that come in animal or human forms as an old woman, a bird, etc. She helps the victimised and punishes the victimiser. At times, there is also the hinderer who in contrast to the helper impedes the progress of the underdog.

L' Orpheline et la vieille femme has a structural pattern that very closely parallels the one established above. It is the story of the stepmother character archetype, stereotypically portrayed as villain, bullying her stepdaughter. The schema below illustrates this:

Introduction
Stepmother visits
villainy and cruelty
on stepdaughter.

- The stepdaughter is made to perform impossible chores, especially fetching water during meal times from the forest, day and night.

Act I
Rescue: Help in aid.
Stepdaughter's Metamorphosis

- Meets supernatural spirit in the form of an old dirty woman.
- Stepdaughter undergoes a test of courtesy and kindness.
- Impressed, the old woman blesses her power to become rich and happy.

Act II
Confrontation:
Stepmother versus Stepdaughter
Stepdaughter wins : Success
Stepmother loses : Failure

- The stepdaughter returns a changed person.
- When beaten up, she opens her mouth to cry, gold, ivory and other precious objects come out.

Act III
Hinderer introduced:

- Stepmother sends her own daughter to the same stream so as to get same blessings

Daughter loses: Failure

- Daughter undergoes test of courtesy and kindness. She fails.

Daughter cursed.

Spirit enraged, fairly curses daughter for her haughtiness and unkindness.
- Daughter returns. Vomits vipers, snails, crabs, etc.

Denouement
Resolution: Justice.
Stepdaughter attains happiness
Stepmother frustrated

- The stepdaughter achieves peace and becomes prosperous.
Stepmother punished for her villainy, runs off and abandons home.
Her daughter is banished from the village.

The summary of the basic structure of this story will look like this diagram:

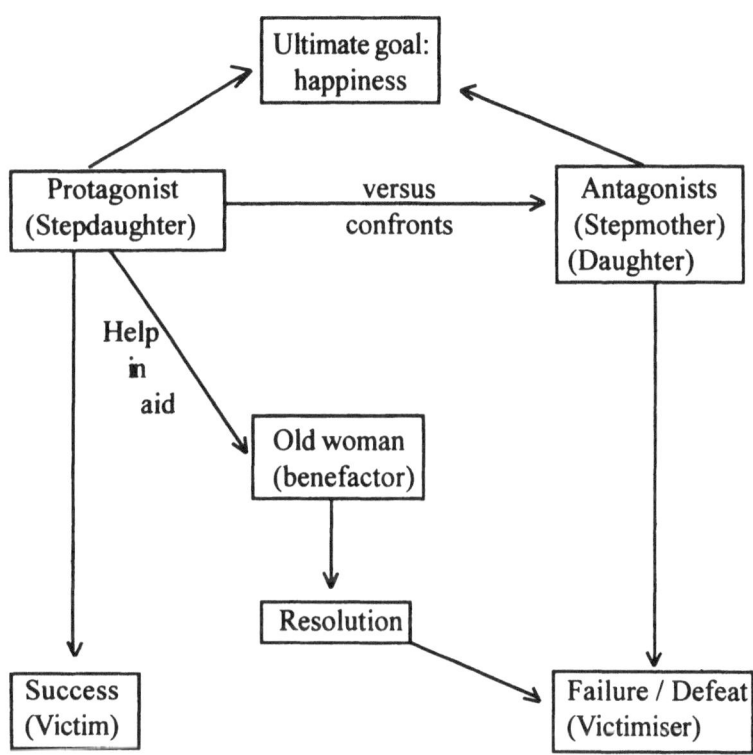

With these polarities, one can discern the major thematic preoccupations in the two stories. In *La tortue cite le léopard au tribunal de ancêtres*, Tortoise employs cunning and *savoir-faire* to survive. He deploys the full range of his considerable mental astuteness and imagination to defeat greed, covetousness and persecution. In *L'Orpheline et la vieille femme*, we see how villainy and wickedness are punished while kindness and humility are rewarded through the intervention of a supernatural being.

Linguistic Techniques of Oral Delivery

The expressive media of oral narrative-performance is language. Because of the presence of a live audience addressed directly, the bard has to ensure a verbal arrangement that would be pleasing and memorable. This section examines the different uses and adaptation of language for effect.

a. Use of Language

(i) Descriptive style

Ewondo bards use the protracted style for stories which is appropriate for the narrative sub-genre. Tales are supposed to be direct verbal discourse and as such words flow in an easy leisurely conversational style. The stories in Mfomo's *Au pays des initiés* are narrated in a diffused style and his bards practise the long winding style often attributed to African narrative artists. For example, this extract from *La tortue cite le léopard au tribunal des ancêtres* is a sumptuous cinematographic description of the Tortoise, after his return from the spirit land. He is dressed for effect: bizarre, colourful, flamboyant and regal:

> Jusqu' au soir les foules affluèrent. La tortue avait fait sa toilette. Un accoutrement haut en couleurs. Le torse nu, bariolé de rouge et de noir, les yeux cernés de blanc; sur la tête, une couronne de guerrier piquée de plumes multicolores de perroquet, de toucan, de pintade et de touraco bleu; autour des reins, un pagne flambant neuf et bouffant de part et d'autre de ses hanches. Elle avait ajusté sa besace en bandoulière et pris soin de la ganir d'un noeud de canne - à - sucre, d'un morceau de manioc et d'un gros os. La main gauche armée d'une lance étincelante, un chasse - mouches des plus touffus à la main droite: le héros s'apprêtait à sortir de sa cachette soigneusement dissimulée à l'entrée du village. Au total, un personnage si impressionnant qu'il semblait tout à fait digne d'un ambassadeur du royaume des ancêtres
> (*Initiés*, p. 84)

It should be noted that costume and dressing are extra-verbal devices in the communicative arts and speech performance. In contrast to the laborious descriptive style above some of the stories are narrated in an austere and laconic style. Some of the bards, like Theodore Fara Tsala in *Le jugement du Nguid, l'amulette magique*, are shrewd with words and the events are recounted in the briefest, starkest terms. Also, Cosmos

Awoumou's narration of *On meurt facilement du fétiche d'autrui* is pared to the bone. The aim is to arouse emotional response in the listener. Therein lies the affective power of the narrative.

(ii) Subjectivity in prose narratives

The subjective is very prominent and obvious in Ewondo oral prose narratives. The use of the first person subject pronoun shows that the bard is a solid presence before the audience. Mfomo's selected bards make profuse use of the exclamation: *Je vous dis* (*Initiés*, pp. 55, 66, 83, 109 and 166), which is a direct translation from the Ewondo: *Ma kat Foar Mina!* an exclamation of glee used before or after an extraordinary happening. It translates in English as "I tell you!" Variants of this exclamation are *Que vous dire!* (*Initiés*, pp. 41, 42, 59, 80, 108, etc) and *Que vous dirais-je* (*Initiés*, pp. 104, 115, etc). The use of 'I' by the bards here presents the bards as eye-witnesses to the events of the stories and so elicits credibility from the audience. To elicit belief from the audience, some bards like Gustave Beling' Onono use phrases like *croyez-moi* (Believe me!) (*Initiés*, p.103) as if the story were an eye-witness account of events. *Croyez-moi* is translated from Ewondo. *Wog ne I zom ma dzo!*.

Apart from conferring credibility, the subjective point of view sometimes heightens the appeal of the narrative. The aesthetic and ornamental roles of subjectivity in speech can be seen in the use of the phrase: *Pourquoi vais - je vous fatiguer les oreilles?* (*Initiés*, pp. 68, 69, 84, 135, 144, 145, 158).

(iii) Verbal Repetition

Verbal or stylistic repetition is a fundamental feature of Ewondo speech norms, carried over to storytelling. It is an oral form of emphasis and style employed by Mfomo's selected bards. In his collection, one can identify the use of ploche, formulaic and mimetic repetitions.

Ploche is repetition of words or sentences with or without variations. Ploche can be seen in the story *On ne casse pas le pattes à la perdrix sa voisine*. To emphasize the distance of Olinga's trek, Enyegue - Amvouna the bard bays: *Il marcha, il marcha, il marcha encore jusqu'à ce qu'il eut grand - faim* (*Initiés*, p.44). Exactly the same words are used by another bard Jacques Mbida to describe the distance covered by *Woa-le- Chimpanzé* in search of God, *Zamba-Dieu*, on page 142.

Formulaic repetition occurs usually in songs, in incantations, in praise epithets and in other fixed-phrase passages. Tortoise is an excellent town-crier and communicator in Ewondo folktales. Repetition is a speech device used by traditional messengers and tale-bearers. Tortoise uses it extensively while summoning other animals like in this instance:

— *Nobles rejetons de la race des quadrupèdes: accourez, accourez, accourez! Tous sans exception, sans exception, sans exception! Tout est d'échiqueté, déchiquété, déchiqueté. Tout en miettes, en miettes, en miettes! Keng! Keng! Keng! Keng! (Initiés, p. 80).*

Repetition used here is to ensure that the message is grasped, to convey the seriousness of the meeting and to prepare the audience psychologically for his very inciting address. Formulaic repetition can also be seen in this magical utterance spoken by the forest fairy: *Tout voum! Tu ne te moques que de toi-même!* (*Initiés*, pp. 115, 116, 117 and 118).

Mimetic repetition dramatically re-echoes an action or a behaviour of a particular character. For example, Bëmë, the wild boar, repeatedly performs silly acts in the first four tales of Mfomo's collection. In Ewondo oral tradition, Bëmë-le-Sanglier is the epitome of stupidity. This character trait can be seen in the first tale aptly captioned *Les sottises de Bëmë-le-Sanglier*, the wild boar indulges in foolish imitation. Firstly, to look like his friend the parrot who can stand on one foot, he attempts to cut off one of his feet. Result: he is seriously injured and is bedridden for three months. Secondly, he attempts to regurgitate food like Otana, the bat, when stricken. Result: he receives, in vain, a terrible flogging that takes him a week to recover from.

The wild boar in his silly braggadocio attempts to 'fly' from a palm tree like the sparrow-hawk in the tale. *Bëmë-le-Sanglier et l'epervier* Result: crippled and bedridden for three months. In *Bëmë et l'éléphant*, he attempts to extract oil from his hoof in imitation of the elephant. Result: scorched and bedridden for three months. In yet a fourth tale *Comment Bëmë manqua de cornes alors que son oncle en fabriquait*, his folly reaches its zenith. In his presumptuousness, he stays back in the fields, ravaging cassava farms while his uncle, Tortoise, was distributing horns and charms to other animals. Result: the horns are exhausted by the time he returns and so gets none. His repeated foolish behaviour is an instance of mimetic repetition.

Another example of mimetic repetition is found in Chameleon's self

-effacing and aloof attitude. Each time the animals assemble, the Chameleon is very conspicuous in absence: *il brillait par son absence* (*Initiés*, pp. 26,65). Each time we see Tortoise, he is either playing tricks or performing magical feats.

(iv.) *Scenic parallelism*
By parallelism, we mean the use of identical or completely different syntactic forms to describe the same scenario or picture. This adds variety or even complexity to the basic roles of repetition. Cases of scenic parallelism abound in Mfomo's collection of tales. For instance, the animal assemblies summoned by Tortoise are described in identical terms. At the distribution of horns and charms, the scenario is presented thus:

> *Au petit matin, la cour du féticheur fourmillait de monde, depuis la souris naine jusqu'à l'éléphant aux pieds ongulés. Sous les verandas, on reconnaissait tous les visages: mâles et femelles, petits et grands; ceux qui mâchent un interminable bol alimentaire ou frappent le sol de leurs sabots; ceux qui, furieusement, se grattent de leurs dents ou de leurs griffes, et ceux qui, de leur queue, se ventilent les flancs" (Initiés, p.26)*

The animal assembly described below uses different syntactic structures, but the scenery is strikingly similar to the first:

> *des foules commencèrent à prendre d'assaut le village de la tortue. Et au declin du jour, la place était noire de monde. Pas un visage que l'on ne reconnût dans la mêlée le lion au regard trompeur; le buffle intrépide; l'éléphant massif, le tragélaphe à robe fauve tachetée de blanc, le lièvre poltron; la souris naine. Bref, tous les représentants des grandes familles : griffes - gratteurs, sabotss - trotteurs et pieds - ongulés. (Initiés, p. 80).*

Another instance of scenic parallelism can be seen in these two extracts using different words and sentence structures but describing the same picture:

> *A leur arrivée: un scenario fantastique! Un village immense de polygame à quatre divisions. Rien que des belles cases. Mais seule était ouverte la maison de 'l'homme - du - village' ... un vieillard étendu sur sa longue chaise, une grosse pipe à la main (Initiés, p.115)*

A l'arivée: quel spectacle! Des troupeaux de moutons et de chèvres par centaines, un vaste village de polygame à deux divisions et, au milieu de ces richesses, 'l'homme - du - village' lui - même assis sous sa veranda, une longue pipe à la bouche (Initiés, p. 132)

The striking similarity of these two passages points to an instance of scenic parallelism. Wealth in the phallocratic and macho Ewondo society has many symbolic referents. The core referent is polygamy. A man's wealth is measured by the number of wives and children denoting virility and valour. Also possession of domestic animals is a mark of riches and prestige. The wealthy owner is considered as *l'homme - du - village* and the status symbol is a long pipe. This same image is painted on pages 39 and 100.

(v.) Use of ideophones

Ewondo bards make use of ideophones as a descriptive technique. Ideophones are some sort of echoes – descriptive sounds which add meaning and flair to words. On their own, ideophones are meaningless, but when attached to words they convey some impression. In this sense they are arbitrary formulations ingeniously attached to words to enhance meaning.

A wide and interesting range of ideophones appear in Mfomo's translations. For example *Koundoum - m - m - m - m* is used as an adjectival intensifier to dramatise and describe the crashing sound of Bëmë's fall from the palm tree (*Initiés*, p.23). The cry of the burnt Bëmë the wild boar is reproduced in an ideophone as : *Uïe! uïe! uïe! uïe! Aïe! aïe! aïe! Oh! Oh! Oh!* (*Initiés*, p.25). The appeal of ideophones lies in their phonological nature.

Response to Tortoise's greetings by other animals in both *Comment Bëmë manqua des cornes ...* and *La Tortue cite le léopard ...* is couched in an ideophone: *"Hé - é - é - é - é!* (*Inités*, pp. 26, 80). In the same vein, *Tcharrrrrrr* describes the noise made by the special cabalistic objects such as chains of shells or bone amulets thrown on the floor by Tortoise the diviner (*Initiés*, p. 34). Also, a descriptive sound echo of the resounding metal gong used by Tortoise the town crier is given ideophonically as: *Keng! keng! keng! keng!* (*Initiés*, p. 80).

Ideophones act as symbols of further identification. For instance, the chant of the cock, formulated from the echo of natural sound of its crowing is given as *kò - kò - kò - ò - ò - kò - ò - ò - ò -* (*Initiés*, p. 115). Similarly, *Héyé - é - é! Héyé - é - é! Héyé - é - é! Héyé - é - é!* (*Initiés*, p.14) describes sound echo of the owl's famous ominous warning cry.[31] Also ideophonised is the cry of the small river bleak: *Me ber' è - è - è - è! Me ber' è - è - è - è! Me souz è - è - è - è! Me souz è - è - è - è!* (*Initiés*, pp. 37, 50).

A notable feature of the ideophones cited above is the occurrence of melisma or vowel extensions. Melisma is a musical score derived from elongation of vowels. They seem to be entirely ornamental in function. But ideophones in Ewondo speech tradition are not only ornamental but they also sharpen meaning, increase memorability or mnemonic value and create emotional impressions in the communicative process.

b. Other Speech Devices

The Ewondo Nkat Minkana employs copiously other speech devices to enhance verbal communication and to sharpen meaning in speech performance. Such ingenious manipulation of words can yield fresh and compelling interpretation and meaning. In Ewondo folktales, the most commonly used speech devices are contrast and comparison, metaphor and personification.

(i) Contrast and Comparison

Contrast and comparison are used in stories to establish new and different meaning, in terms of affinities or disparities. Humans, animals and inanimate objects are used to establish a relationship of similitude or are contrasted to show dissimilitude in their appearances or in their actions.

In Ewondo folktales, contrast is used in portraiture of characters. For example, the leopard and the tortoise are contrasted in animal stories to draw out differences in their physical and mental make-ups. The leopard has strength and force, but is not so clever. It is contrasted with the weak and powerless but artful and clever tortoise. This can be seen in the stories *Concours de vitesse entre la tortue et le léopard* and *La tortue cite le léopard au tribunal des ancêtres*. Both characters are drawn into conflict.

The story *La tortue porte l'éléphant* draws attention to the body

---

[31] This forboding cry of the owl is object of superstition in Ferdinand Oyono's *Une vie de boy*

physique and intellectual traits of the tortoise in comparison with the elephant. The former is the trickster, powerless but cunning, whereas the latter is the dupe, big, powerful but gullible and clumsy. In the story *Bëmë - le - Sanglier et l'épervier*, contrast is used as a means of exposing the wild boar's congenital foolishness and the trickery of the sparrow-hawk. Through contrast, the dire consequences of imitation are communicated.

In the human tale *L'Orpheline et la vieille femme*, the ugly, masculine and villainous second wife contrasts with the beautiful virtuous and kind deceased first wife. This comparison brings out not only the body features of the two, but preference for the first wife is made more evident. The gigantic forest monster, *Emomodo, le gros - gros homme* is contrasted with the tiny adventurous hunter in *Un jeune enfant sauve l'humanité*. This hideous ogre is a symbol of death which dominates man.

(ii) Metaphor

There is pervasive use of metaphor in Ewondo oral narratives, especially in the form of proverbs. Metaphor is a "form of analogy where similarity between entities is given through inference and transference."[32] A metaphor has two separate parts, viz. *signan* and *signatum*.[33] And a metaphorical expression is created by transference of sense from *signan* to *signatum*, from the literal to the figurative. Taken literally, the metaphor would appear ludicrous and absurd. For instance, the following proverb can only be appreciated if interpreted on a figurative and associative level:

La sagesse est l'aînée et la force, cadette (Initiés, p. 67)

(Wisdom is the elder sister and force, the younger)

Analogy is drawn between wisdom and an elder sister while force is junior to it. The point in all of these is to stress the superiority of wisdom and tact over brute force.

A metaphor operates through a covert comparison between two items. For example, in this metaphorical expression, *Je tiens l'antilope*

---

[32] Helen Chukwuma, *Igbo Oral literature*, 1994, p.190.
[33] See C.W. Morris, "Foundations of the theory of signs", in *Encyclopaedia of Unified Science*, 1 & 2, University of Chicago Press, 1938. Cited by Helen Chukwuma, 1994, p.190.

naine par les cornes (*Initiés* pp. 28,83). As the story goes, the antelope chose very minute horns during the distribution of horns by the celestial emissary, the tortoise. Thus, when a situation is extremely delicate, it is compared to the act of holding on to the tiny infinitesimal horns of the antelope.

(iii) Personification

A preponderant figure of speech in oral narratives is personification. Here, non-human agents do things humans do while lifeless objects are animated and made to perform human activities. One such humanised objects in Mfomo's collection is the forest stone in *Comment la bouche de Nlo - Modo tua Nlo - Modo lui - même*. The mysterious killer stone is bearded, hears, thinks and kills.

In personification, objects are humanly active, they have sentiment and feeling. In *Le Soleil avait parlé* for instance, the Sun in the sky is always awake, hearing and seeing all things. It is the witness to all actions and it literally talks and reveals secrets.

On the whole, the selected bards by Mfomo have taken their audiences into consideration. They have carefully chosen their words and varied the diverse linguistic devices they employ. The language is the language of oratory. We cannot but marvel at the ingenuity with which these devices are manipulated. Thus listening to them narrating is sheer delight.

Conclusion

This chapter has sought to emphasise the fact that the oral narrative sub-genre is an alive art which depends entirely on speech performance for sustenance. The creativity and practice of storytelling depends also on the *Nkobo* or speech art. Storytelling in Ewondo is entertainment and this is brought about only through speech behaviour. The more artistic and talented the *Nkat Minkana* is, the more entertaining the tale would be.

The chapter also stresses the aestheticists' approaches in oral narrative performance. Storytelling is a process of communication involving the bard and his listeners. The bard has to pay attention to composition and delivery of the product to make listening to him a pleasurable experience.

The analysis and description of salient features of speech behaviour in the oral narrative sub-genre is a continuous venture by students of the verbal arts. Ours is just a modest contribution to this on-going enterprise. By way of conclusion, we recommend that more studies be carried out on verbal arts of French translations of tales to make for a fruitful understanding of the nature of speech behaviour in oral narrative performance in Francophone Africa.[34]

---

[34] We wish to acknowledge here our gratitude to Bertin Biem and Adolphe Gervais Essombo, both Ewondo indigenes - '*Bongo Bewondo*' - for their invaluable and enthusiastic help in translating certain Ewondo terms used in this study

References

Awouma, J.M. and Noah, J. I., *Contes et Fables du Cameroun*, Yaoundé: Clé, 1976.

Azuonye, Chukwuma, "Kalu Igrigiri: an Ohafia Igbo Singer of Tales" ed. Isidore Okpewho, *The Oral Performance in Africa*, Ibadan: Spectrum Books Ltd., 1990, pp. 42-79.

Bauman, Richard, *Verbal Art as Performance*, Masachusettes: Newbury House, 1977.

Binam Bikoi, Charles, "The Literary Dimension of Cameroon Cultural Identity" in *Cameroon Cultural Identity*, Yaoundé: Ministry of Information and Culture, 1982.

Bird, Charles, "Heroic Songs of the Mande Hunters", in *African Folklore*, ed. R. M. Dorson, Bloomington: Indiana University Press, 1972.

Cauvin, Jean, *Comprendre les Contes*, Paris: Les Classiques Africanes, 1992

Chevrier, Jacques, *Littérature nègre* (1975), Paris: Editions Armand Colin, 1995.

Chinweizu, Onwuchekwa, Jemie and Madubuike, Ihechukwu, *Towards the Decolonization of African Literature*, Enugu: Fourth Dimension Publisher, 1980.

Chukwuma, Helen, *Igbo Oral Literature: Theory Tradition*, Abak: Belpot, 1994.

Eno Belinga, S.M., *Chantestables du Cameroun*, Paris: Chant du monde, 1966.

─────────── *Comprendre la littérature orale africaine*, Paris: les classiques Africaines, 1978.

─────────── *Découverte des chantefables beti-bulu- fang du Cameroun*, Paris: Klincksieck, 1970.

─────────── *L'épopée camerounaise*, Yaoundé: CEPER, 1978.

─────────── and Minyono Nkodo, M.F., *Poésies Orales*, Paris: Editions Saint - Paul, 1978.

Finnegan, Ruth, *Oral Literature in Africa*, Oxford: Clarendon Press, 170.

Hymes, Dell, "The Ethnography of Speaking" in *Anthropology of Human Behaviour*, ed. T. Gladwin and W. C. Sturtevant, Washington; DC. : Anthropology Society of Washington, 1962.

Innes, Gordon, "Formulae in Mandinka Epic: the Problem of Translation", ed. Isidore Okpewho, *The Oral Performance in Africa*, Ibadan: Spectrum Press Ltd., 1990, pp. 101-110.

Kajubi, W. Senteza et al, *African Encyclopedia*, London: Oxford University Press, 1974

Kesteloot, Lilyan, *Mémento de la littérature Africaine et Antillaise*, Paris: Les Classiques Africaines, 1995.

Makward, Idris, "Two Griots of Contemporary Senegambia", ed. Isidore Okpewho, *The Oral Performance in Africa*, Ibadan: Spectrum Books Ltd., 1990, pp. 23-41.

Meva'a M' eboutou, M., *Les aventures de koulou la Tortue* Yaoundé: Clé, 1972.

Mfomo, Gabriel Evouna, *Au pays des initiés: Contes Ewondo du Cameroun* (Soirée au Village, tome II), Paris: Karthala, 1982.

Morris, C.W. 'Foundations of the Theory of Signs", in *Encyclopedia of Unified Science*, 1 &2, University of Chicago, 1938.

Milner, G., '*De l'armature des locutions proverbiales. Essai de taxonomie sémantique"*, in *L'Homme*, Vol.3, No. 11969.pp. 49-70.

Okpewho, Isidore, ed, *The Oral Performance in Africa*, Ibadan : Spectrum Books, Ltd., 1990.

——————— "Towards a Faithful Record: On Transcribing and Translating the Oral Narrative Performance", in *The Oral Performance in Africa*, Ibadan: Spectrum Books Ltd., 1990.

Oyono, Ferdinand, *Une Vie de Boy*, Benin City: Ethiope Publishing House, 1974

Oyono-Mbia, Guillaume, *Trois prétendants ... un mari,* Yaoundé: Clé. 1981.

Ricard, Alain, *Littératures d' Afrique noire*, Paris: Karthala, 1995.

Tedlock, Denis, "Dialogue" in Alchering *Ethnopoetics*, Vol.2, 1976.

Yondo, E.E., *La littérature orale douala*, Douala: Abbia, 1966.

4

THE MAJOR THEMES OF NEGRITUDE POETRY: PROTEST, REVOLT AND RECONCILIATION

Francis Angrey

Introduction

A critic may not find it an easy task to discuss the poetry of negritude without having to delve into what many critics before him have said. The field remains, in the words of Gerald Moore, a much-trodden one. What this entails is that the modern literary critic may find it quite difficult to find something new to say which will be different from what others have already said.

The critic may find himself in a kind of dilemma as he may not know where he should operate from and so make a useful contribution to the literary discourse as far as negritude poetry goes. But the dilemma so created is not deep-rooted. It is just in the mind of the literary theoretician who may feel that all the themes of the much-trodden field of negritude poetry have been exhaustively dealt with.

We believe that we still have a lot to say about this poetry in spite of the fact that many literary critics have dealt with its themes. It is this belief that has propelled us to attempt an analysis of some major themes of the rich and enriching poetry of the negritude philosophy.

Many critics before now have held the view that negritude poetry is not art for art's sake. It is poetry that seeks to place the black man in his right position. It is a response to certain socio-political stimuli that created it. It is not poetry that deals with matters of the heart that is to say it does not deal with romance *per se*. It is this much that Jean-Paul **Sartre** says when he avers:

> *Et la poésie noire n'a rien de commun avec les effusions*

> *du coeur: elle est fonctionnelle, elle répond à un besoin qui la définit exactement.*[1]

In the words of Sartre, negritude poetry is a response to a need that defines it. It is also meant to transmit an important message about the "black soul" not only to the white man but essentially to the black man himself. It is a means of the acceptance by the black man that he is "black". In other words, negritude poetry tasks the black man to rediscover himself and to teach him to see that his "black colour" is beautiful. Jean-Paul Sartre explains thus:

> *Le nègre ne peut nier qu'il soit nègre ni réclamer pour lui cette abstraite humanité incolore: il est noir. Ainsi est-il acculé à l' authenticité: insulté, asservi, il se redresse, il ramasse le mot de "nègre" qu'on lui a jeté comme une pierre, il se revendique comme noir, enface du blanc, dans la fierté.*[2]

Negritude poetry is essentially that of protest, conflict and revolt. It is also a poetry of pardon and reconciliation such as we see in the poetry of Léopold Sédar Senghor. In this chapter, an attempt is being made to survey these major themes through the analysis of some representative poems drawn from the poetry of well known negritude poets such as Senghor, Damas, Césaire, David Diop, Guy Tirolien, Dadié, Kossouho.

Our intention in the paper is not to attempt definitions of negritude and what it stands for. Many other critics like Jacques Chevrier, Bernard Lecherbonnier and Stanislas Adotevi have done enough justice to that already. Negritude itself is not a state, it is a certain attitude vis-à-vis the world. Hear Sartre:

> *On ne saurait mieux nous prévenir que la négritude n'est pas un état, ni un ensemble défini de vices et de vertus, de qualités intellectuelles et morales, mais une certaine attitude affective à l'égard du monde.*[3]

Our purpose is simply to show that the negritude poets, whose poems form the basis for our study here, use their poetry as an instrument of

---

[1] Sartre, J.P. *"Orphee noire"* in Senghor, L.S. *Anthologie de la nouvelle poésie négre et malgache.* Paris: PUF, 1948, p.x.v.
[2] *Ibid.* p.xiv.
[3] *Ibid.* p.xxix.

love, of struggle and of reconciliation and pardon. Some of the poets, like David Diop, also use their poetry to show their militancy.

Negritude Poetry as Protest

Negritude poetry has been variously described as poetry of refusal, poetry of rejection or poetry of repudiation. What this entails is that the negritude poet rejects a certain way of life, a certain condition which has been wittingly imposed on the African, and by extension on the black man in the diaspora. Negritude itself is a total repudiation of the unwholesome situation in which the European master kept the subdued black slave. Its poetry is a manifestation of the fact that the black man, hitherto considered ignorant, has regained his consciousness and, thus, he is now aware of the embarrassing situation in which he was kept for too long. Negritude poetry is an expression of this awareness. It is also a means by which the black man seeks to reclaim his freedom from the chains of slavery. Yves-Emmanuel Dogbé explains:

> De même, les Noirs se sont révoltés, réclamant, dans un premier temps, leur libération des chaînes de l'es-clavage, puis leur indépendance et la libre disposition de leur territoires respectifs, aussitôt qu'ils ont pris conscience des conditions de vie inhumaines dans lesquelles ils étaient maintenus.[4]

What these words imply is that negritude is primarily protest. It is a rejection of the attitude which the white man adopted vis-a-vis the black man. Its poetry is, in many ways, a means of rehabilitating the black man whose dignity has been lost and it is essentially, a protest against the white man who seeks to ignore the reality of the black man. It is this that L.V. Thomas explains when he says:

> tout d' abord la négritude impliqueune protestation contre l'attitude de l' Européen qui veut ignorer la réalité negre . . . Donc, à la base de la négritude nous trouvons unesituation historique plus ou moins douloureusement ressentie, celle dunègre paria, "assimilé", aliéné par la tutelle coloniale; puis un réelsouci d' indépendance et de

---
[4] Dogbé, Y-E. *Négritude, culture et civilisation.* Paris: Editions Akpagnon, 1980, p.15.

*promotion culturelles.*⁵

In the words of L. V. Thomas, negritude seeks both cultural independence and promotion. For this to be achieved, the negritude poet should first of all seek to accept himself the way he is. It is not by mimicking the white man that he will be able to get out of the rather embarrassing situation where he has been kept for centuries. It is, perhaps, in view of this that such poets as Bernard Dadié and Eugène Kossouho say that they are proud of their black colour. They accept, as Sartre would say, the term "Negro" which is thrown at them with arrogance.

Bernard Dadié says in one of his poems that he is grateful to God who thought it quite wise enough to make him a black man. To him, white is a circumstantial colour while the black colour is one that is permanent. To the poet, the black colour takes precedence over the so-called white colour. In the poem *Je vous remercie mon Dieu* he postulates:

Je vous remercie mon Dieu de m' avoir
créé noir d'avoir fait de moi
la somme de toutes les douleurs,
mis sur ma tête
Le Monde.
J' ai la livrée du centaure
Et je porte le Monde depuis le premier matin.
Le blanc est une couleur de circonstance,
Le Noir, la couleur de tous les jours
*Et je porte le monde depuis le premier soir.*⁶

Dadié's poem suggests that the black man's suffering is nothing to be worried about. The black man is just playing the role that nature assigned to him right from time. In other words the black man's head, shoulders and arms are made to carry the world. Rather than complain about his condition, the poet finds that he should be thankful to God who made him what he is. He is happy that God has made him bear all the pains:

Je vous remercie mon Dieu de m' avoir créé noir,

---

⁵ Thomas, L. V. *Les Idéologies négro-africaines d'aujourd'hui*. Paris: Nizet, p.22.
⁶ Vézinet, P. (ed.) *Poésie africaine*. Paris: Hatier, 1969, p.

> *d' avoir fait de moi*
> *la somme de toutes les douleurs.*
> *Trente-six épées ont transpercé mon coeur.*
> *Trente-six brasiers ont brûlé mon corps,*
> *Et mon sang sur tous les calvaires a rougi la neige*
> *Et mon sang à tous les levants a rougi la nature.*[7]

Bernard Dadié's poem is aimed at creating confidence in the black man and at making him feel that he has been made to contribute greatly to the growth of the world as a whole. He tends to make him feel that he is created to give the world its sense of direction and purpose. The black man should, thus, live above his condition and burdens. It is such words of encouragement that Gladys Casely-Hayford uses in her great poem "Rejoice":

> Rejoice and shout with laughter
> Throw all your burdens down,
> If God has been so gracious
> As to make you black or brown.
> For you are a great nation,
> A people of great birth
> For where would spring the flowers
> If God took away the earth?
> Rejoice and shout with laughter
> Throw all your burdens down
> Yours is a glorious heritage
> If you are black or brown.[8]

The black man will be unable to fight to ameliorate his condition if he does not first seek to understand who he is, if he does not learn to accept himself as he is. It is only by such acceptance of himself that he will be able to stand up and fight. The poet Eugène Kossouho, from Benin Republic, estimates that the black man should feel proud of his colour and accept it as such. In his poem *"Nègre, c'est mon mom"* he announces his acceptance of his colour without equivocation.

Eugène Kossouho may not, in the estimation of many literary critics, be seen as a core negritude poet. But what he says in his poem is no less

---

[7] *Ibid.* p.90.
[8] Nwoga, D. I. *West African Verse*. London: Longman, 1967, p.5.

a complete repudiation of all that the white people stand for. In the poem he says there is no colour better than the black one that is his own. In his acceptance of his natural black colour it does not matter to him what the whites may want to think about him and his blackness. He makes his stand very clear when he says:

> *Nègre, c'est ma race*
> *Nègre, c'est mon nom*
> *Si mon teint parfois bronzé*
> *T' induit en embarras*
> *D'autres traits peuvent justifier*
> *Ce que je suis.*

In the poem the poet goes on to enumerate all that he considers the good qualities of the black colour and, by extension, the richness of the African culture and civilisation. Kossouho feels that being black is a privilege; hence, he is proud to be a black African. He summarises his position thus and this is in spite of the fact that black Africans were treated as beasts of burden and as human cargoes in the obnoxious triangular trade perpetrated by the Europeans:

> *Les ambitieux émigrants qui ont*
> *Fait de nous des bêtes de somme*
> *Ne sont que méprisables négriers*
> *Mais, être Nègre, c' est un privilège,*
> *Et je suis heureux et je suis fier*
> *D'être un Nègre.*[10]

Guy Tirolien, the poet from Guadeloupe, adopts an approach that is peculiar to him. In form of a fervent prayer he says he is tired of all that the white man represents. Going to the modern school established by the white is a sure way of getting oneself enslaved. The school becomes, to the poet, a means for the white man to make the black man a carbon copy of himself. The school, thus, becomes a means through which the white man subjugates the negro by teaching him the white man's culture which is detrimental to the black man's progress in his natural environment. Tirolien's poem "*Prière d'un petit enfant nègre*" is a complete rejection and a repudiation of what black men are taught in the white man's school.

---

[9] Vézinet, P. (ed.) *Poésie africaine* Hatier, Paris. 1969, p 92.
[10] *Ibid.* pp.92-93.

Going to school is, therefore, a burden.

> *Et j'ai beaucoup marché depuis le chant du coq*
> *Et le morne est bien haut qui mène à leur école.*
> *Seigneur, je ne veux plus aller à leur école,*
> *Faites, je vous prie, que je n'y aille plus.*[11]

He prays God to make it possible for him to stop going to that school where he feels they teach things that are of no consequence to him. Rather than go to that school he would prefer a situation of freedom whereby he could follow his father to "fresh ravines" without anybody telling him what to do.

> *Je veux suivre mon père dans les ravines fraîches*
> *Quand la nuit flotte encore dans le mystère des bois*
> *Où glissent les esprits que l'aube vient chasser.*
> *Je veux aller pieds nus par les rouges sentiers*
> *Que cuisent les flammes de midi*
> *Je veux dormir ma sieste au pied des lourds*
> *Manguiers . . . . . .*
> *Comme un bateau ancré*
> *Vomit dans la compagne son équipage nègre . . .*[12]

The poet seems not to like the white man's school because its curricula, in his estimation, are not tailored towards catering for the needs of the black man. Such curricula are aimed at simply producing "fine gentlemen" who end up aping the white and his ways to the detriment of their own black background. The poet has no ambition to become the gentleman that they would want him to be in spite of himself. He would rather not go to that school at all.

> *Seigneur, je ne veux plus aller à leur école,*
> *Faites, je vous en prie, que je n'y aille plus.*
> *Ils racontent qu'il faut qu'un petit nègre y aille*
> *Pour qu'il devienne pareil*
> *Aux messieurs de la ville*
> *Aux messieurs comme il faut.*

---

[11] Senghor, L. S. *Anthologie de la nouvelle poésie nègre et malgache*. Paris: PUF, 1948, p. 86.
[12] *Ibid.* p.86.

> *Mais moi je ne veux pas*
> *Devenir, comme ils disent,*
> *Un monsieur de la ville,*
> *Un monsieur comme il faut.* [13]

Besides, what the black man is taught in the white man's school is not relevant to his background. He is taught lies that he is a descendant of the *Gaulois*. The poet extrapolates that the black man has been made to suffer indignities enough for him to spend his time studying irrelevancies.

> *Les nègres, vous le savez, n'ont que trop travaillé.*
> *Pourquoi fautil de plus apprendre dans des livres*
> *Qui nous parlent des choses qui ne sont point d'ici?* [14]

Those of the black men who followed the path of the white man's school are somewhat lost because they no longer have the *joie de vivre* for which the black man is known. They have become unhappy men who do not know how to dance, sing or tell folktales in the moonlight like in the days of old. In other words, those black men have lost the essence of their blackness having gone to *leur école triste* where they learnt selfishness and individualism as exemplified by *ces messieurs de la ville*.

> *Et puis elle est vraiment trop triste leur école,*
> *Triste comme*
> *Ces messieurs de la ville,*
> *Ces messieurs comme il faut*
> *Qui ne savent plus danser le soir au clair de lune*
> *Qui ne savent plus marcher sur la chair de leurs pieds*
> *Qui ne savent plus conter les contes aux veillées.* [15]

Two other renowned negritude poets, Léon Gontran Damas and David Diop, great exponents of the philosophy of repudiation of all that the white culture, via its education, symbolises, lament over the artificial and cosmetic life that the so-called civilised black man is made to live. In his great poem, "Limbé", Damas demands earnestly that his "black dolls" be returned to him. In the words of Daniel Racine, the black dolls referred to in the poem are the black ladies of his native Guadeloupe that his exile in France made him lose. In France, all around the *Quartier*

---
[13] *Ibid.* p.86.
[14] *Ibid.* p.87.
[15] *Ibid.*

Latin environment where he finds himself as a student he can see only white prostitutes who, in his estimation, are nothing compared to his Guadeloupean "black dolls." He, thus, compares his black dolls to the white ladies who are ever present in his little environment while his monotonous exile in Paris lasts. He begs:

> *Rendez-les-moi mes poupées noires*
> *qu' elles dissipent*
> *l' image des catins blêmes*
> *marchands d' amour qui s' en vont viennent*
> *sur le boulevard de mon ennui*
>
> *Rendez-les-moi mes poupées noires*
> *qu'elles dissipent*
> *l' image sempiternelle*
> *l' image hallucinante*
> *des fantôches empilés fessus*
> *dont le vent porte au nez*
> *la misère miséricorde.* [16]

The poem goes on to express the poet's desire to recover all the aspects of his original identity, of his original culture which have been wittingly and deliberately destroyed by the white man. More than this, the poem remains an important inventory of myriads of frustrations of which he is a victim. To Daniel Racine the poem is:

> *un véritable inventaire des frustrations dont le poète se sent victime parce qu' on lui a dérobé un certain nombre de biens précieux en l'enlevant de la Terre-Mère, tels la coutume, la chanson, le rythme, la case, la terre enfumée grise, la sagesse, les palabres, le sol . . .* [17]

In the poem "Hoquet" the poet virulently and violently attacks French cultural assimilation of which little black children are victims. The French culture is hereby represented by table manners, greetings and the language used either at home or at school. Like Tirolien, Damas seems to be condemning the type of education that is given to black children. Such education is usually not in line with these children's exposure and

---

[16] Racine, D. *L. G. Damas: l'homme et l'œuvre*. Paris: Présence Africaine, 1983, p.68.
[17] *Ibid.* p.70

experience. To the poet such education should be discountenanced. Such education is a caricature of the good education that black children should benefit from. Daniel Racine sees Damas's greatest poem in this light:

> *Ce poème représente, en effet, l' une des plus virulentes attaques contre l' assimilation culturelle imposée dès l'enfance par des parents bourgeois métissés imbus des valeurs occidentales. Damas dénonce ici l' éducation donnée au petit Guyanais de sa génération, car elle ne diffère en rien de celle de l' enfant européen et ne tient aucun compte de la part non gauloise de son héritage ancestral.*[18]

Such education as imposed upon the young Guyanese simply helps to depersonalise and alienate him from his people and his culture. It is in line with such thinking that David Diop sees the black man who, upon being educated, seeks to ape the white man, as a renegade. This is vividly demonstrated in his poem, *Le renégat*, in which he lambasts black men who think themselves civilised just because they dress and act like the white man. He feels some pity for such men because they are as good as lost. After describing how such men dress he goes on to say:

> *Tu nous fais pitié*
> *Le soleil de ton pays n'est plus qu'une ombre*
> *Sur ton front serein de civilisé*
> *Et la case de ta grand-mère*
> *Fait rougir un visage blanchi par les années*
> *d'humiliation et de Mea Culpa.*[19]

The poet suggests, as these lines show, that the educated black man has reneged on his African background which he now finds repugnant since he can no longer go even into his grandmother's hut in the village. The poet feels that all does not just end in Europe where the 'new' black man is domiciled. A sad experience awaits him at home where he will find it quite difficult to stamp his authority. Rather, he will be moving around with unsure steps because he will live steeped in fear, wittingly borne out of his stupid attitude, the poet warns, because all the educated black elite does in Europe is empty boast:

---

[18] *Ibid.* p.76.
[19] Diop, D. *Coups de pilon*. Paris: Présence Africaine, 1973, p.19.

> *Mais lorsque repu de mots sonores et vides*
> *Comme la caisse qui surmonte tes épaules*
> *Tu fouleras la terre amère et rouge d'Afrique*
> *Ces mots angoissés rythmeront alors ta marche inquiète.* [20]

In this section of our paper we have tried, through the analysis of some notable poems, to show that negritude poetry is one of protest. The protest in this case resides in the ability of the poet to accept his blackness with pride, to repudiate and to reject all that the white man represents.

Revolt as a Way Out

Many critics of negritude poetry are of the view that it is not just enough for this poetry to make an inventory of all the embarrassing situation in which the black man was held for too long by the white man. It is not just a poetry that sings the glory of blackness. It is poetry that seeks to change the poor condition of the black man. It is poetry that is combative and militant. It is poetry in which the poet seeks to transmute from creation of awareness to creation of struggle. Poetry becomes, in this case, an instrument of struggle. It is this much that Dogbé says when he remarks:

> *La poésie de la négritude doit donc évoluer, en passant de la prise de conscience de la condition des Noirs à l' appel à la lutte pour la reconquête de la dignité de l'homme noir, et, tout compte fait, à la reconciliation de l'asservi et l' asservisseur.* [21]

While negritude poetry seeks to make the black man aware of his uncomfortable and intolerable condition, it also seeks to restore his dignity. But this cannot be got on a platter of gold. The black man has to fight to change his condition. Thus, negritude poetry becomes a call to arms in spite of the fact that it has a thematic diversity. Negritude expresses the discontent and the disaffection of an oppressed people. Dogbé emphasises:

> *Malgré la diversité thématique de ce cri, la poésie nègre, globalement, exprime le mécontentement d'un peuple*

---

[20] *Ibid.* p.19.
[21] Dogbe, Y-E. *Négritude, culture et civilisation.* p.45.

> *opprimé, asservi, exploité, puis rejeté comme un sein nourricier.*[22]

In the vanguard of this revolt as seen in negritude poetry are the likes of Aimé Césaire, David Diop, Damas and, to some extent, Léopold Sédar Senghor. In his *Cahier d'un retour au pays natal*, Césaire does not just stop at making an inventory of the injustices suffered by the black man neither does he just stop at accepting the word "nègre" that was cast at his face like a stone. He goes a step further to assert his position as the leader of his subdued and oppressed people. Although he seeks to deliver himself from the chains of subjugation in the first instance, he thinks more about the overall deliverance of his people. He makes himself the spokesman for these people:

> *Ma bouche sera la bouche des malheurs qui...voix, la liberté de celles qui s'affaissent au cachot du désespoir.*[23]

Césaire is of the view that the black man should not just fold his arms and wait for divine intervention that may never come his way. He exhorts his people to avoid adopting the attitude of the beckettian characters, Vladimir and Estragon, two tramps, who just wallow in misery and want and think that it is when Godot comes that all their problems will receive attention. He warns that they should not just sit on the fence and watch what is being done to them because life itself is not a spectacle. In other words they should be part of the struggle.

> *Et surtout mon corps aussi bien que mon âme, gardez-vous de vous croiser les bras en l'attitude stérile du spectateur, car la vie n'est pas un spectacle, car une mer de douleurs n'est pas un proscenium, car un homme qui crie n'est pas un ours qui danse...*[24]

In the poem, the poet feels bad because he has to reintegrate his people who have remained inert. Their moral and physical degradation and their misery are repulsive and repugnant to the poet. In his seminal work, he goes on to take a retrospective look at the period marking slavery and colonialism. In spite of this reality, his people do not seem to react to the situation the way he would like it, hence he describes their heroism as

---
[22] *Ibid.* p.74.
[23] Césaire, A. *Cahier diun retour au pays natal*. Paris: Présence Africaine, 1983, p.22.
[24] *Ibid.* p.22

a "farce".

The attitude of the poet vis-a-vis his people who have remained inert is not surprising. Aimé Césaire has always identified with the surrealist literary movement that saw the light of day in France in the 1920s. Surrealism, as a literary and artistic movement, seeks to destroy all perceived automatisms in literature and in the arts. It also aims at liberating man from all constraints – social, economic, cultural and political. Ivonne Duplessis explains surrealism thus:

> Or le but des surréalistes est extralittéraire car il ne vise à rien moins qu'à libérer l'homme des contraintes d'une civilisation trop utilitaire. Pour le secouer de sa torpeur il fallait insister sur tout ce qui pouvait le dérouter, il fallait délibérément tourner le dos à l'intelligence et retrouver les forces vitales de l'être pour leurs flots tumultueux le soulèvent vers un horizon élargi.[25]

According to Duplessis, surrealism is a violent and nihilist movement that advocates very strongly that there should be a fundamental change in the social structure. Being a follower of this movement, Césaire conceives his own negritude as a movement that must lead the black man to a joyous end. His negritude philosophy seems to propose some action, a way of being black and of asserting oneself in one's blackness. He proposes an aggressive approach to effect this much-desired change. His poetry essentially is a call for the socio-political freedom of the black man. Césaire himself does not just preach from the pulpit. He is in the thick of political action and activism because it is only through his commitment to the total liberation of the black man that the much-needed change will come. For many years, Césaire was the deputy and mayor of Fort-de-France and chairman of the *Parti Progressiste Martiniquais* (PPM).

David Diop is a poet who has never claimed to be a follower of the surrealist movement. But like Césaire and other fiery negritude poets, Diop calls for a struggle for the betterment of the lives of the black people. In his poems, he is against the white colonialists, with their 'civilising' mission, who came and destroyed the culture and the unity of his Africa. His trenchant criticisms of the destruction occasioned by the

---

[25] Duplessis, I. *Le surréalisme*. Paris: PUF, 1950, p.3.

presence of the white men does not spare missionaries who are seen as collaborators of the perpetrators of slavery and colonialism. His poem *Les Vautours* is a clear demonstration of his intense loathing for the despicable activities of these white men he refers to as vultures, who came to pillage our village economies:

> *En ce temps-là*
> *A coups de gueule de civilisation*
> *A coups d'eau bénite sur les fronts domestiqués*
> *Les vautours constuisaient à l'ombre de leurs serres*
> *Le sanglant monument de l'ère tutélaire.* [26]

To the poet, the slave does not wait. A time comes when he decides to fight back to claim his liberty. It is this much that he expresses in the poem *Vagues*.

> *Les vagues furieuses de la liberté*
> *Claquent claquent sur la Béte affolée*
> *De l' esclave d' hier un combattant est né*
> *Et le docker de Suez et le coolie d' Hanoi*
> *Tous ceux qu'on intoxiqua de fatalité*
> *Lancent leur chant immense au milieu des vagues*
> *Les vagues furieuses de la liberté*
> *Qui claquent claquent sur la Béte affolée.* [27]

David Diop uses his poetry to call for action. He first of all, as Modum puts it, asks the black man to reject his position of a subdued and humiliated man. He exhorts the black man to stand up, face up to the challenge with defiance and say "No" to all that has the tendency to subjugate him and, thus, change the status quo. The poet's position is made manifest in the poem *Défi à la force*:

> *Toi qui plies toi qui pleures*
> *Toi qui meurs un jour comme ça sans savoir pourquoi*
> *Toi qui luttes qui veilles pour le repos de l' Autre*
> *Toi qui ne regardes plus avec le rire dans les yeux*
> *Toi mon frère au visage de peur et d'angoisse*
> *Relève-toi et crie: NON!*

---

[26] Diop, D. op.cit. p.10.
[27] *Ibid.* p.16.

This poem is perhaps the poem in which Diop does not pretend to have any semblance of finesse. He is just as brutal as the occasion demands. This is a direct call to the black man to reject in its totality the position of subaltern in which he has been held for too long a time.

In the poem *Afrique*, the poet takes a retrospective look at the Africa of old even though he never had an opportunity to know her. That does not, however, stop him from feeling the pains and tribulations her sons had gone through during many centuries of slavery. What preoccupies the poet is the fact that all hope is not lost. To him, liberty will come the way of the black man, but such liberty has to be of a bitter taste. He does not mince his words when he says in the last five lines of his poem:

> *Cet arbre là-bas*
> *Splendidement seul au milieu de fleurs blanches et fânées*
> *C'est l'Afrique ton Afrique qui repousse*
> *Qui repousse patiemment obstinément*
> *Et dont les fruits ont peu à peu*
> *L' amère saveur de la liberté.* [28]

Dogbé identifies the poem *Souffre pauvre nègre* as the poem in which he cries out the most; to him it is the poem in which he brings home the full meaning of what revolt the black man should embrace. By urging him to accept the whip on his back he is ironically calling on the black man not to accept such a humiliating situation in which he finds himself. The poet exhorts:

> *Le fouet siffle*
> *Siffle sur ton dos de sueur et de sang*
> *Souffre pauvre Nègre*
> *le jour est long*
> *Si long à porter l'ivoire blanc du Blanc,*
> *ton Maître*
> *Souffre pauvre Nègre*
> *Tes enfants ont faim*
> *Faim et ta case branlante est vide*
> *Vide de ta femme qui dort*
> *Qui dort sur la couche seigneuriale.* [29]

---

[28] *Ibid.* p.23.
[29] *Ibid.* p.36.

We see in these lines a deliberate evocation of all the tribulations of the black race in the hands of the white slave master. In the words of Dogbé, negritude poets use this style of exposing the ills perpetrated by the whites as a means of calling the black people to arms. Dogbé concludes:

> *En projetant dans l' esprit du peuple les*
> *malheurs de celui-ci, souvent en exa-*
> *gérant l' ampleur pour plus d'impression,*
> *le poète de la négritude convie à prendre*
> *les armes, à se révolter et à lutter contre*
> *l' emprise de l'asservisseur. L'évocation*
> *de la souffrance nègre est donc aux yeux*
> *du poète un instrument de subversion et de*
> *révolte pour ainsi dire, un instrument*
> *d' agitation de la conscience populaire.* [30]

Léon Gontran Damas, the poet who has always stood against assimilation, sounds a warning that things will not be the same for ever. That a change will come that will herald the victory of good over evil, the victory of the black man over the white man is a sure bet. He sounds prophetic in his poem *Pour sûr*:

> *Pour sûr j'en aurai marre*
> *sans même attendre qu'elles prennent*
> *les choses l'allure d'un camembert bien fait*
> *Alors je vous mettrai les pieds dans le plat*
> *ou bien tout simplement la main au collet*
> *de tout ce qui m'emmerde en gros caractères*
> *colonisation*
> *civilisation*
> *assimilation et la suite.* [31]

Léopold Sédar Senghor, the poet-politician, may not be ranked among revolutionary poets who call their fellow black men to take up arms and fight for the amelioration of their condition. Many critics, including Marcien Towa and Stanislas Adotevi, have even accused him of transforming

---

[30] Dogbe, Y-E. *Négritude, culture et civilisation.* p.80.
[31] Senghor, L. S. *Nouvelle poésie nègre et malgache.* p.12.

himself into a *"toubab"* through his scandalously close association with France. These critics see nothing revolutionary about Senghor's poetry. Jacques Chevrier holds a different view. To him Senghor's poetry, and indeed, his poem *Poème liminaire* in which he talks about the condition of the Senegalese *tirailleurs* is steeped in revolt. Jacques Chevrier considers this poem as one in which Senghor pours out the whole of himself because he takes it upon himself to solve the problems of the *tirailleurs* who seem to have no one to speak for them. He makes himself their spokesman as these lines attest:

> *je ne laisserai pas la parole aux ministres, et*
> *pas aux généraux*
> *je ne laisserai pas-non-les louanges de mépris*
> *vous enterrer furtivement*
> *vous n'êtes pas des pauvres aux poches vides sans*
> *honneurs*
> *Mais je déchirerai les rires BANANIA sur tous les*
> *murs de France.*[32]

These lines, which Chevrier considers a call to arms, sound like a promise that the poet makes to his black brothers who have found themselves fighting in the interest of France. He does not tell us how he intends to achieve his aim which is that of giving honour to the Senegalese *tirailleurs*. That is why many critics would rather see Senghor as the father of the poetry of reconciliation.

The Senghorian Reconciliation Perspectives

It has already been established that negritude poetry is that of protest and revolt. The revolutionary movement is made manifest in the works of nearly all the negritude poets. It cannot, thus, be said that the poetry of Senghor does not contain some elements of activism. But the critic of negritude poetry, Marcien Towa, sees Senghor's poetry in his own light. He feels that three important themes mark it. Towa explains:

> *on peut dire, pour donner une idée d'ensemble de chants d'ombre que troist hèmes fortement liés entre eux s'y révèlent dominants: la réhabilitation de la culture noire,*

---

[12] ————— *Poèmes*. Paris: Seuil, 1964, p.53.

le pardon, la réconciliation.[33]

Towa presents Senghor as a negritude poet who does not come out to call his black brothers to arms like Aimé Césaire or David Diop has done. His approach is essentially that of a man who seeks reconciliation among the races: his problem is not to revolutionise the world as such but to amend it so that it can accommodate everybody no matter one's race. As a man of faith, of piety, Senghor rather fits into the mould of a poet of reconciliation par excellence. Towa feels that his poetry does not seem to envisage any eventual victory for the black man. The only way out of the quagmire is to seek peace and reconciliation, which will benefit all the races. Towa sees his poetry thus:

> *La poésie de Senghor n'envisage pas l'éventualité d'une lutte victorieuse contre la domination étrangère. Sa perspective n'est pas la lutte, mais la négociation, voire le chantage, la prédication morale, et la prière. En ce sens sa poésie est en dernière analyse, moralisme et mysticisme.*[34]

Yves-Emmanuel Dogbé does not agree with Towa that there is no militancy in Senghor's poetry. He thinks Towa's position is extremist and erroneous because Towa himself, in his essay, recognises Senghor's poems *A l'appel de la race de Saba* and *Perceur de tam-tam* as revolutionary. That Senghor is not a fiery revolutionary poet *per se* does not preclude the fact that he has always remained sensitive to the plight of the black race. His approach to the situation springs from his own form of action, his temperament and understanding. Dogbé throws more light on this:

> *Bien qu'aucun de ses poèmes peut-être ne fasse état d'appel du peuple à la révolte, il est évident qu'il a choisi sa forme d'action, selon son tempérament et son entendement: une forme d'action qui ne diffère pas essentiellement de celle de ses confrères du mouvement.*[35]

While Senghor recognises that his black brothers have suffered all types of indignities and humiliation at the hands of the white man he feels

---

[33] Towa, M. *Négritude ou servitude?* Yaoundé: Editions Clé, 1971, p. 23.
[34] *Ibid.* p.14.

that the black man should pray for the white man. Senghor seems to obey the biblical injunction that we should love our enemy and pardon him. He tends to embrace the injunction that we should present the "other cheek" to be slapped. What Senghor seems to want and fight for is that the black man should learn to cultivate and sustain a good relationship with his white brothers. Senghor dreams of a world of peace and reconciliation in which every race is allowed to play the role that is assigned to it and to contribute its own quota to the edification of a world civilisation which Senghor himself refers to as *la civilisation de l'universel*.

We shall attempt an analysis of two poems to examine the poet's reconciliation perspectives. In these poems the poet adopts a somewhat liturgical tone to address his black brothers. He behaves like a preacher who mounts the pulpit to preach on what humanity stands to benefit from the principles of reconciliation and pardon. In the poem *Neige sur Paris* he presents himself to us as a pacifist who wants peace not only for his black continent or for Europe, but also for all mankind. Snow in the poem symbolises purification: it is a purifying element that is used to make Paris that had become *mesquin et mauvais* a pure and a peaceful place.

In the poem in question, the poet alludes to a troubled period in the history of Europe. It was the time when internecine wars tore the white continent apart. The poet then takes it upon himself to pray to God that this unwarranted barbarism should stop for peace to reign supreme:

> *L'Europe divisée*
> *A l'Espagne déchirée*
> ......
> *Et le Rebelle juif et catholique a tiré ses 1400*
> *canons contre les montagnes de votre paix.* [36]

The poet seems to tell God that he is quite different from these warlords whose activities threaten His peace. He has accepted God's own command by allowing his heart to melt like snow in the sun and as such *j'oublie*. What he says he has forgotten are all the exactions the white people committed against his black brothers:

> *Les mains blanches qui tirèrent les coups*

---

[35] Dogbé Y-E. *Négritude, culture et civilisation.* p.88.
[36] Irele, A. (ed.) *Poems of Senghor.* Cambridge University Press, 1977, p.45.

> *de fusils qui croulèrent les empires...*
> *Elles abattirent les forets d'Afrique*
> *pour sauver la civilisation*
> *parce qu'on manquait de matière première*
> *humaine.*[37]

In saying all this the poet has not, however, forgotten the destructive role that the white colonialists had played in the African continent. But as a man of God the black man, whom he symbolises, should pardon the white man all he did. He solemnly declares:

> *Seigneur, je ne sortirai pas ma réserve*
> *de haine, je le sais, pour les diplomates*
> *qui montrent leurs canines longues*
> *Et qui demain troqueront la chair noire.*
> *Mon coeur, Seigueur, s'est fondu comme*
> *neige sur les toits de Paris*
> *Au soleil de votre douceur.*
> *il est doux à mes ennemis, à mes frères aux mains*
> *blanches sans neige.*[38]

In *Prière de paix*, a rather long poem drawn from the collection, *Hosties noires*, we see the serene negritude of the poet, who sings the suffering of the black man. We also see in this poem an evocation of all the horrors that the black man was subjected to for over four hundred years. He even exposes what he considers France's hypocrisy. In spite of all the exactions as he enumerates in his poem, the poet says that Africa is ready to pray to God for his pardon, for peace and reconciliation:

> *Au pied de mon Afrique crucifiée depuis*
> *quatre cents ans et pourtant respirante*
> *laisse-moi Te dire Seigneur, sa*
> *priére de paix et de pardon.*[39]

In the third stanza of his poem, Senghor offers special prayers for France, which adopted an obnoxious assimilation policy which has remained detrimental to the total liberation of the black man, especially in Francophone black Africa. He asks that God should pardon France and

---

[37] *Ibid.* p.45.
[38] *Ibid.* pp.45-46.
[39] *Ibid.* p.68.

show her the right path to tread. His prayer runs thus:

> *Oui Seigneur, pardonne à la France qui*
> *dit bien la voie droite*
> *et chemine par les sentiers obliques*
> ......
> *Oui seigneur, pardonne à la France qui hait*
> *les occupants et*
> *m'impose l'occupation si gravement....*[40]

Through these two poems Senghor, no doubt, shows that he is preoccupied with pardon, peace and reconciliation. He is not disputing, with anybody, the fact that the exactions committed by the white man on the black continent are condemnable. He, however, calls upon the black man to have a forgiving heart that melts like snow in the sun. Senghor does not want fire to be returned for fire.

Marcien Towa, the fiery critic of the Senghorian school of thought, feels worried by such a disposition as adopted by the poet. Towa thinks that Senghor would do better as an outright preacher rather than a poet who should call out his people for a positive action. Towa is of the view that:

> *Les idées de Senghor sont très influencées par des préoccupations d'ordre religieux: il veut nous "gagner tous à Jésus-Christ".*[41]

Towa posits that the poet does not need to waste his precious time to teach the black man any lesson about Christ or about pardon and reconciliation. The black man already has all these principles entrenched in his own religion.

Conclusion

Negritude poetry uses a language that seeks to restore an ideal, noble and divine order. It also seeks to lead to a state of perfection and amelioration. It is this much that we have tried to demonstrate in this work. We undertook a long journey through this poetry by examining

---

[40] *Ibid.* p.70.
[41] Towa, M. *Négritude ou servitude?* p.101.

what are considered its major themes. A reading of this poetry, that remains rich and enriching, shows that its exponents talk about protest, revolt and reconciliation.

Negritude poets, as we have seen, base their writings on their temperament, their understanding and their world view. But the fact remains that their themes point to the same goal though they are varied. The theme of protest shows that the poets must first of all accept that they are what they are. They urge the black man not to be ashamed of his "blackness". Rather, he should embrace same and feel proud of it. To discuss this theme we analysed some poems by such poets of note as Damas, Diop, Kossouho, Dadié and Guy Tirolien.

In the poems analysed, these poets all tend to repudiate all that is white and put to the fore their blackness. Guy Tirolien and Damas even go to the extent of criticising the type of education that is given to the black man. They take a critical look at the curricula of the western type of school that do not take into consideration the background, experience and exposure of the black pupils. They repudiate such a school system and ask the black man to discountenance all that symbolises the white man and his culture.

The negritude poets do not only give an exposé of all the exactions that have been committed by the white man on the African continent. They use their poetry to call the black man to arms. Aimé Césaire, the poet-politician from Martinique, asks his peers to fight rather than stand and watch as if life were a spectacle. David Diop does not pretend to be diplomatic in his poetry as seen in his collection *Coups de pilon*. He throws a direct challenge to his peers and asks them to stand up and say "No" to all that the white man has done to them.

Léon Gontran Damas shows, in his poems *Pour sûr* and *Blanchi*, that the white man's victory cannot be forever. He states that he is sure that some day victory will be the black man's.

Senghor, the reconciliation poet par excellence, adds his own voice to the overall debate but he comes in as a pacifist who seeks to bring about peace, reconciliation and hope to a somewhat hopeless situation. Like his negritude counterparts, he exposes all the ugly deeds of the white man on the African continent. But he believes that, in spite of all that, the black man should learn to forgive the white man. This chapter has tried to illustrate this much by analysing Senghor's two most representative poems, "Neige sur Paris" and "Prière de paix."

It is our feeling that the three themes discussed in this paper complement one another. For there to be any revolt, there must be acceptance of what one is which comes as a result of awareness. After awareness, the next stage is for one to fight to ameliorate one's bad position. But, while fighting, one should not forget the tenets of forgiveness, peace and reconciliation because it will do nobody any good to maintain perpetual enmity with others. That is the useful conclusion that we can draw from Dogbe's seminal work, *Négritude, culture et civilisation*.

References

Poetic Works

Césaire, A. *Cahier d'un retour au pays natal*. Paris. Présence Africaine, 1983.
Diop, D. *Coups de pilon*. Paris: Présence Africaine, 1973.
Senghor, L. S. *Anthologie de la nouvelle poésie nègre et malgache*. Paris: PUF, 1948.
────────*Poèmes*. Paris: Seuil, 1964.
Vénizet, P. *Poésie africaine*. Paris: Hatier, 1969.

Other Works

Achode, Codjo S. *Crise et quête d'identité noire de l'Amérique à l'Afrique d'hier à demain*, CNPMS, Porto Novo. 1993.
Adotevi, S. *Négritude et négrologues*, 10/18, Paris. 1972.
Chevrier, J. *Littérature nègre*, Armand Colin, Paris. 1990.
Dogbe, Y.E. *Négritude, culture et civilisation*, Editions Akagnon, Paris.1980.
Irele, A. (ed.) *Selected Poems of Senghor*, Cambridge University Press, 1977.
Kesteloot,L. *Césaire*, Seghers, Paris. 1979.
────────*Les poèmes de Senghor*, Editions Saint-Paul, Paris, 1986.
Kesteloot, L. and Kotchy, B. *Aimé Césaire: l'homme et l'oeuvre*, Présence Africaine, Paris. 1993.
Lecherbonnier, B. *Initiation à la littérâture négro-africaine*, Editions Fernand Nathan, Paris. 1977.
Nkashama, P. Ngandu, *La littérature africaine écrite*, Editions Saint-Paul, 1979.
Ojo-Ade, F. (ed.) *Being Black Being Human*, OAU Press, Ile-Ife.1996.
Racine, D. *L. G. Damas: l'homme et l'oeuvre*, Présence africaine, Paris.1983.
Towa, M. *Négritude ou servitude?*, Editions Clé, Yaoundé. 1971.
Vaillant, A. *La poésie*, Editions Nathan, Paris. 1992.
Wellek, R. and Warren, A. *La théorie littéraire*, Seuil, Paris. 1971.

5

TALES FROM BIRAGO DIOP: TRANSLATION OF A TRADITION

Imeyen Noah

Introduction

Although Birago Diop featured early in the activities and in the circle of black students that created in Paris the movement known as Negritude, his role tends to differ from that played by Leopold Sédar Senghor and Aimé Césaire. Unlike these two, fiery and explicit denunciation of the woes of colonialism inflicted on the black race is not a significant trait in his major works. He distinguishes himself in the uniqueness and excellence that define his writings.

Renowned for his folktales, a genre which, unlike novels, poems and plays that are created by individual minds, is handed down already formulated, from generation to generation, by the community which remains its source and custodian, Birago Diop himself has never claimed to be the author of the *contes*. The anonymity of the tales thus raises questions as to the status of Birago Diop, the talented, incomparable artist that translated them into French.

Tradutore traditore (To translate is to betray – as it is said in Italian)! Can Diop therefore be taken seriously when he pretends to be absent from the tales? On the other hand, the transformation of the tales into a literary masterpiece in French implies a deviation from, if not a deformation of, the age-old norms of the transmission of oral texts. Has the authenticity of the ancient tradition of the Wolof survived the modern and alien codes of literalisation in Diop's work?

The peculiarity and grandeur of Diop's *contes* were first brought to the fore by Jean-Paul Sartre in his famous preface in Senghor's *Anthologie de la nouvelle poésie nègre et malgache de langue française*. According to Sartre:

> *Le centre calme de ce maelstrom de rythmés, de chants, de cris, c'est la poésie de Birago Diop, dans sa majesté naïve: elle seule est en repos parce qu'elle sort directement des récits de griots et de la tradition orale. Presque toutes les autres tentatives ont quelque chose de crispé, de tendu et de désespéré parce qu'elles visent à rejoindre la poésie folklorique plus qu'elles n'en émanent.*[1]

Two elements that need be underlined here are, first of all, that Diop's tales are poetry and, secondly, that they emanated directly from the oral tradition. The poetic dimension emphasises Diop's creativity while the oral tradition suggests the suppression of creativity in the texture of the stories. That out of this contradiction has emerged a work of great value that radiates its *majesté naïve* in Senghor's anthology speaks of the success of an encounter between African oral and Western literary traditions.

Birago Diop's work is therefore an invitation to examine the vision and the strategies that brought about, in the experience of the writer, the happy alliance between the ethnologist and the poet. In this regard, our study shall comprise three phases. First of all, we shall consider Birago Diop and his work. This will enable us to understand some of the influences that shaped the poet for his career. Then we shall observe Diop as a "transcriber" of folktales, how he has preserved the elements, the authenticity and the tradition in his work. And lastly, Diop's initiative, subjective disposition and creative skill will be assessed. Our conclusion shall assess the value of the work in the light of the two traditions that participate in its life.

Birago Diop and His Work

Birago Diop

Birago Diop was born in Ouakam on the outskirts of Dakar in December 1906. His childhood days were spent in the traditional socio-cultural set-up with koranic schools, which he attended, storytelling sessions in the

---

[1] Sartre, Jean-Paul in L.S. Senghor: *Anthologie de la Nouvelle Poésie Nègre et Malgache de langue française, précédée de "Orphée Noir" par Jean-Paul Sartre*, Paris, P.U.F. 1972, XXIV, XLIV, 227p.

family and traditional education in the values of the community.

Within the family where he grew up, the influence of his brother, Youssoufa, his elder by six years, on the young Diop was neither negligible nor transient. Later on, Birago will dedicate his *Contes et lavanes* to Youssoufa: *mon frère, mon ami, mon guide en tout, partout, de tout temps. Gardien de mémoire et berger de souvenirs*[2]. This dedication suggests the magnitude of Diop's indebtedness to his brother.

Another important influence that conditioned Diop's future literary career was his grandmother. The introduction to the first volume of his *contes* opens with a dialogue between Diop and his grandmother which reveals an event that remained a regular experience between the two: at bedtime, each night, little Diop would listen to tales from his grandmother until he slept off. At this stage in his life Diop's interest in and familiarity with folktales had already developed; he was a repertory of *contes*.

In 1916, Birago Diop commenced his education in the French school system and progressed into the Lycéc Faidherbe in Saint Louis, former capital of Senegal. It was a period of intense study where he read not only great masters of French literature but also serious works on Africa by such renowned scholars and writers like Hardy, Delafosse, Frobenius, Robert Delavignette and René Maran, author of *Batouala*. He thus not only became acquainted with the French literary tradition but also pondered the status and destiny of the black race. He dedicates his first book to his children with the admonition: *qu'elles apprennent et n'oublient pas que l'arbre ne s'élève qu'en enfonçant ses racines dans la terre nourricière*[3].

There was no scholarship for Birago Diop and so he was forced to mortgage the family house to finance his studies in France at the University of Toulouse where he studied veterinary medicine. He later left Toulouse for the Institute of Veterinary Studies in Paris where he completed the course. While in Paris, Diop met the group of African and West Indian students that produced the journal, *L'Etudiant noir* and took part in their deliberations. *L'Etudiant noir* is closely associated with the birth of Negritude. Much of the vision and aspirations of the movement had already

---

[2] Diop Birago, *Contes et Lavanes*, Paris, Présence Africaine, 1963, p.7.
[3] Diop, Birago, *Les Contes d'Amadou Koumba*, Paris, Fasquelle, Coll. *Ecrits Francais d'Outre-mer*, 1947, p. 7.

been articulated in the journal. It goes without saying that Diop's literary career has been influenced by the ideals and projects of Negritude.

On his return to Africa, Birago Diop was posted to Kayes in Niger as a veterinary officer. His territory comprised the whole of the then Western Sudan. He also worked in Ouagadoudou for some years. He went through these territories in all directions, using diverse means of transportation: car, canoe, foot, horseback etc. In "Sarzan", for example, Diop introduces the tale with a description of his journey across the villages; we see him changing from one mode of transportation to another.

These trips bring Diop into contact with the "bush", with people and cultures outside the influence of western tendencies. Diop draws abundant elements from his keen observation of these cultures to enrich his work. It was during one of these trips that he met Amadou Koumba, a "griot" from Sine Saloum, a descendant of his maternal family, to whom he attributes the *contes*.

His Work

Diop's major works include three volumes of folktales and one book of poems. Diop began writing the first collection of tales, *Les Contes d' Amadou Koumba* in Paris in 1942. The diffusion of the tales was done through journals and reviews until the book of nineteen stories was published by Fasquelle in 1947. The widest publicity came as a result of the inclusion of some of the *contes*, *Les Mammelles* and *Souffles*, from the collection in Senghor's anthology as well as, and perhaps more so, from Jean-Paul Sartre's highly favourable comments on the status and value of the texts in his preface to the anthology.

The first volume was followed, in 1958, by a second one: *Les Nouveaux Contes d'Amadou Koumba* published in Paris by Présence Africaine, with a preface by Léopold Sedar Senghor. The third book, *Leurres et lueurs*, containing poems, appeared in 1960, published by Présence Africaine. Next to be published was another collection of tales and folk stories, *Contes et lavanes*, in 1963.

An essential unity characterises the writings of Birago Diop, poetry or *contes*. The poem *Souffles* which concludes *Les Nouveaux Contes d'Amadou Koumba* is reproduced almost verbatim in *Leurres et lueurs*. This illustrates, first of all, the permanence of certain themes in all the works of Birago Diop, and, secondly, the preponderance of his poetic talent in his writings as is the case with *Les Mamelles* which is **a** *conte* supposedly written in prose form but which was ranged among poems in Senghor's anthology.

In 1964 *Contes et lavanes* was awarded the *Grand Prix littéraire de l'Afrique Noire d'expression française*.

Classification of the *Contes*

In his work, Birago Diop applies the term *contes* to all the stories. But a story like Petit-Mari, where most of the elements that constitute a *conte* are absent, which owes its life to the dexterity of style that orchestrates and proclaims fatality through its overwhelming rhythm, could be placed in a genre other than tales. Also, it is evident that the *contes* themselves do not all belong to the same family. In other words, to study the *contes* it is necessary to classify them according to types, then analyse each category in accordance with the factors that preside their nature.

But the question of the classification of the tales is a complex subject that cannot be undertaken here; first of all, because of space constraints in this short write-up, and, secondly, because, as Vladimir Propp has observed, it raises a fundamental question: that of the origin of the *contes*[4], a problem that Propp was unable to resolve in the *Morphologie du conte* and which took him eighteen years to address via a voluminous book, *Les Racines historiques du conte merveilleux*.[5]

Birago Diop himself does not propose any serious classification of his tales. The attempt by Senghor to group Diop's *contes* into two genres is far from convincing. Senghor writes in his preface to *Les Nouveaux Contes d'Amadou Koumba*:

> *Les contes que voici comprennent, en réalité deux genres, le conte proprement dit et la fable. Le conte est un récit dont les héros sont des génies et des hommes et qui est sans portée morale... La fable, elle, nous promène dans le monde réel des faits. les fables s'adressent aux enfants... Mais ce n'est là que simplification grossière.*[6]

---

[4] Propp, Vladimir, "*Morphologie du conte,*" Paris, Editions du Seuil, 1970, p. 11.
[5] Propp, Vladimir, "*Les Racines Historiques du conte merveilleux*", traduit du Russe par L. Gruel - Apert, Paris, Gallimard, 1983, xxii, 484p.
[6] Senghor in B. Diop, op. Cit. P. 8.

Senghor, having thus abandoned this excessive simplification of the issue, adopts a position which seems to be that of Birago Diop and of African artists. Senghor continues in the preface: *Il n'y a, en Afrique Noire, ni douaniers ni poteaux indicateurs aux frontières. Du mythe au proverbe, en passant par la légende le conte la fable il n'ya pas de fiontière.*[7] Bernard Dadié, another great writer of *contes*, considers the sticking of labels on human beings and things a distateful practice of western culture and warns against the division of tales into types in Africa because *dans l'esprit des peuples, du moins chez les Africains, il n'y a pas de différence entre la légende et le conte. La distinction doit provenir d'un souci récent de préciser les genres.*[8]

The question of the classification of the *contes* though an important one does not therefore fall within our preoccupation in this study.

Translation and Preservation of a Tradition

Folktales are the bulkiest part of the literature of a people without the tradition of writing. In every land, century after century, this literature is transmitted orally, from mouth to ear. The socio-cultural group that espouses the tales are the source and author of the oral texts. The community supervises the journey of the tales across time, to ensure that they are passed on, intact and unadulterated, to succeeding generations. In this respect, the role of the narrator is unlike that of the creator of fiction in western literary tradition. This is the role that Birago Diop set out to fulfil in translating the *contes* into French. We shall now examine some of the major aspects of this project.

Anonymity

Unlike written literature which carries the signature of the writer, oral literature is anonymous. The reason, as we know, is that oral literature is not attributed to any individual but originates from the socio-cultural group that remains its custodian. The fact that, according to Marie-Louis von Franz, "certain themes of tales go as far as back as 25,000 years before

---

[7] *Ibid.*
[8] Dadie, Bernard B., "*Le Role de la légende dans la Culture Populaire des Noirs d'Afrique*, contribution au premier Congrès des Ecrivains et Artistes Noirs", Paris, 1956, Présence Africaine, Numéro spécial, xiv - xv, 1957, p. 167.

Christ, practically unaltered"[9], is a testimony to the pleasant rigour with which each tradition or society protects the integrity of their tales from the ancient times. The audience participates actively in the unfoldment of the tales and censors any deformation, omission or extravagance in the narration. Thus, no performer can leave traces of individualism or of his personality on the structure, themes, symbols or chain of episodes in a tale.

Birago Diop, versed in the norms of the *contes* and faithful to the tradition of his race, did not perceive his role as that of the creator of the tales. In the words of Senghor:

Birago Diop ne prétend pas faire oeuvre originale, il se veut disciple du griot Amadou, fils de Koumba, dont il se contenterait de traduire les dits. [10]

Diop himself in *Fari l'Anesse*, which opens the first collection of tales, announced that his project is to relate the sayings of Amadou Koumba the "griot". A few lines down the page, Diop reveals the source of the sayings he set out to record; they are drawn from the memory of the "griot", a library of the *contes et les paroles de sagesse que le grand-père de son grand-père avait appris de son grand-père* (p.13). In other words, not even Amadou Koumba can be recognised as the author of the tales; everything goes back to the tradition, to the dim past. Thus Birago Diop himself advocates the anonymity of the *contes*, fulfilling a tradition that is crucial to the authenticity and preservation of the *contes*. He takes his place in the long line of faceless narrators – many griots, peasants, shepherds, Diop's grandmother etc.– who have recounted the tales across the ages. Whether or not Diop has succeeded in his intention to disappear from the *contes* will be discussed in the third part of this study.

Anarchy of Presentation in the *Contes*

The development of folktales does not normally follow any specified order or arrangement. One explanation for this is provided in the introduction to the first tale in the *Contes d'Amadou Koumba*. According

---

[9] Franz, Marie-Louis von, "An Introduction to the Psychology of Fairy Tales", Zurich, Spring Publications, 1975, p.3.
[10] Senghor, "*Préface*" in Birago Diop, *Op.Cit.*, p. 8.

to Birago Diop, Amadou Koumba is not guided by any plan in his release of tales. The griot brings out of his reservoir of knowledge, texts in response to circumstances: *un mot de l'un de nous... un homme qui passait... le geste d'une femme faisaient surgir de sa mémoire des contes et les paroles des sagesse* (p.13). Other narrators – peasants, old women, performers during storytelling sessions do not follow any established order or plan in their presentation.

Birago Diop does not adopt any scientific order of presentation of his *contes*. In this anarchy of presentation as in other aspects, he upholds the tradition of the art. In *Les Contes d'Amadou Koumba*, the four stories on "*Les Mauvaises compagnies*" are an example of what often occurs especially in storytelling sessions when a theme or a character can call up several stories to illustrate them. In *Contes et lavanes*, section two of the *Contes* seems to be progressing towards the end of Bouki the hyena who is in fact destroyed in the last story, *La Peau de Bouki*. But Bouki resurfaces in the last section of the collection with her perversity in *Le Tam-Tam de Lion*. Birago Diop thus refrains from the exercise of his organisational power to devise the order but adopts the traditional approach to the presentation of the *contes*.

The Land

The land, especially its geography and history, also features in the tales. These elements are not presented in a systematic manner as in schools, but featured within the legends, fables, myths and tales. Diop's work is dotted with many features of the geography and history of the land. The *Grand Fleuve,* wide stretches of sand, and the *vaste savane* all tend to anchor the stories in the real word. The villages are small, the professions include cattle rearing, farming and blacksmithing. Hunting and fishing are also practised. Diop hardly lets go the opportunity to describe with relish the appetising dishes of the land.

Elements of history are also numerous in the books; some of them are relatively recent while others are ancient. Thus we are shown events in *Contes et lavanes* before and after *la naissance du chemin de fer de Dakar à Saint-Louis* (p.194), and more frequently before and after the Islamic conquests. The last two stories in *Contes et Lavanes* introduce us into communities where western civilization has made inroads. Each of these two stories, unlike the others on traditional communities, represents the problem of stealing and robbery. It cannot however be concluded from this development that such a vice is an ingredient in the history of civilization.

Les Mamelles recounts a story that represents a special interest because of the way a natural and historical phenomenon functions in a *conte*. In *Les Contes d'Amadou Koumba*, the *mamelles* are two very modest "mountains" – *Le point culminant du Sénégal* (p.32). In the story, the origin of the two natural phenomena had nothing to do with geo-physics. They are the humps formerly on the backs of Khary and Koumba, the two hunch-backed wives of Momar. On account of her bad character, Khary, in addition to her own, earned the co-wife's hump. She drowned herself in the sea, but the waters, unwilling to bury her completely exposed the two humps. The *"contes"* thus integrate historical or geographical phenomena into their universe and use them to explain the why and the how of things.

African Cosmological Naturalism

In the tale, *Le Boli*, the shadows of an old ancestral statuette turns into a young man. The young man, on his part, transforms the bones of an old woman into a pretty young girl. In *Fari - L'Anesse*, a she-ass metamorphoses into a beautiful queen and marries a king. Commenting on such phenomena, Senghor writes:

> *que l'ombre de Boli.... se transforme en jeune homme... l'auditeur négro africain ne s'étonne de rien. Il sáttendait, naturellment, une solution surnaturelle. C'est dire que le surréalisme négro-africain est un naturalisme cosmologique, un surnaturalisme. Pour le negro-africain. les vivants les existents sont au centre du monde - d'où la place singulière qu'occupe la personne humaine ils ne sont pas les seuls êtres. Tout l'univers visible et invisible - depuis Dieu jusqu'au grain de sable en passant par les génies les ancêtres les animaux, les plantes les minéraux - est composé de "vases communicants" de forces vitales solidaires qui emanent toutes de Dieu.*[11]

These same ideas, Diop has expressed in his famous poem, *Souffles*. In *Samba de-la-muit*, a child not yet nine months old in the mother's womb

---
[11] Ibid. p.15-16.

gives an order to the would-be mother: *Mère, accouche de moi.* And the mother protests: *Et comment accoucher de toi, puisque tu n'es pas encore à terme?* In *Les Mauvaises compagnies* II, we see Fett the arrow in action, talking and carrying out assignments. The belief by Africans in the reality of the supernatural forces has been accorded attention in the *contes.*

Characters

Les contes evoke a universe teeming with adventure, where a gamut of actors from different races (Wolof, Maures, Peulh), religious affiliations, socio-cultural groups, political classes (kings, queens, courtiers) as well as shepherds, farmers, fishermen, peasants, children etc. exhibit themselves. It is a curious universe where non-human actors (dragons, inanimate objects, supernatural beings and, especially, animals) fulfil the same roles as those assumed by men.

Sometimes, even the physical portraits of the different species are confounded. It is Fari, queen of the asses, metamorphosed into a beautiful lady whom the king Bour makes his queen. This anomaly where an animal transforms itself into a human being is severely chastised in the story. In some cases, the travesty of identity is not as perfect as that of Fari. Thus, in *La Biche et les chasseurs,* an elephant metamorphoses into a beautiful lady to deceive and destroy a dangerous hunter; the mother of N'Dioumane, the hunter, signals to her son: *N'Dioumane, lui dit sa mère, tout ceci me fait peur. Regarde cette grosse femme au teint si noir, au nez si fort, elle ressemble à Nièye-l'Elephant.* A radical transformation of changing from animal to man cannot be sustained.

Each of the species maintains its physical traits yet, in this universe, the hyena attends the koranic school, the elephant uses an axe, the hare marries Anta, daughter of the king in *Tours de lièvre,* animals hunt other animals for food. Thus, beyond physical traits, at the level of action and behaviour, we witness in these characters a dimension other than that of normal animal comportment. In the words of Joyce A. Hutchinson: The animals are drawn with incomparable skill, covering the whole range of human psychology and yet ... somehow retaining a distinct identity as animals.[12]

---

[12] Hutchinson, Joyce A. "Introduction" in Birago Diop, *Contes Choisis*, Cambridge, Cambridge University Press, 1967, p.21.

A most colourful animal character in the *contes* is the hyena, which operates under the Wolof nickname of Bouki. He is cowardly, cupid and fraudulent, and opposes the main hero, the hare, who is cunning, malicious sometimes, but more humane. The elephant lacks intelligence but is inoffensive: the lion, king of the "brousse", despotic, intimidiating, is often benevolent. To enumerate here all the animals in the vast gallery of actors is not possible. Suffice it to observe, in the words of Senghor:

> *Chacun est dessiné de quelques traits vifs et pénétrants qui révèlent l'âme par-délà l'aspect sensible... car les animaux vivent, sentent, pensent, parlent comme les hommes, tout en gardant leur nature générique d'animal*[13.]

The animal form therefore serves as a mask for human nature.

The *contes* also represent men of diverse conditions. There is Bour the king, authoritative and bizarre, Narr the courtier who is indiscreet, Paulo the shepherd, lean and withdrawn, the Marabouts, wise, dedicated and knowledgeable, though one of their rank, Serigne Fall of *Le Prétexte* is a gluttonous hypocrite. The griots are loyal, pious and devoted. There are also the honest, peace-loving, hard-working peasants. The women are generally vividly sketched. Koumba in *Un Jugement* stands her ground in her rejection of a brutal though repentant husband and grabs the opportunity for excitement and a new alliance. The girls, in *Les Contes* seem too few for the numerous suitors. And, in *Les Mamelles*, Monar takes two hunch-backed wives, one after the other. Demba in *Un Jugement* is desperate after his wife left him. In marriage, the situation seems precarious for men.

Besides human and animal characters, there are also the supernatural beings. Through them one witnesses a direct manifestation of what Senghor calls *les forces cosmiques*. Such is *Le Boli*, the ancestral statuette whose shadow turns into a vigorous young man. In all cases, these actors – animal, human, supernatural – exemplify one aspect or another of man's nature. Birago Diop seems to have announced his intention to unveil human character when he declared in *Fari l'Anesse*, the *conte* that opens his entire work:

> *Quand l'homme dit à son caractère: "Attends-moi ici, à*

---

[13] Senghor. "Preface", *Op.Cit.* p.13.

peine a-t-il le dos tourné que le caractère marche sur ses talons. L'homme n'est pas le seul à souffrir de ce malheur (p. 16)

With such an impressive array of actors in their species, roles and characters, one is tempted to agree with Senghor that *tous les protagonistes de la comédie humaine*[14] have featured in *Les Contes*

Functions of *contes*

Les Contes, by being projected onto a wider milieu by Birago Diop, the narrator-translator, have been enhanced in their functions. One major function of tales is that of engendering a feast. A *conte* is the summoning of an audience and a narrator to a celebration of which the ingredients are words, rhythm and images. Diop's *contes* have not only introduced a wider public into the celebration but have also facilitated the participation of individuals in the experience as each reader, text in hand, plunges into the drama. Such a solitary participation is not the most exciting aspect of sharing in the manifestation of tales.

Within the context of the tradition itself, participation in the tales is usually lively and dramatic. The audience dialogues with the narrator; singing, clapping of hands and beating of drums are part of the event, while dancing is also a regular feature. In *Le Tam-tam de Lion*, the hare enacts the tale of the recalcitrant marabout so well, with clapping of hands, drumming and singing, that the king, Bour-Lion, is carried away to a point of *riant à perdre ses dernières dents*.

One other function of the *contes* in ancient cultures without the tradition of writing is their role as *nos seuls livres*. Bernard Dadie who used this expression explained that it is in the *contes* and legends that our ancestors deposited their science. In Dadie's words:

Contes et légendes sont pour nous des musées, des monuments, des plaques de rues, en somme nos seuls livres... Chaque soir, nous les feuilletons et nous aussi nous nous raccrochons chaque soir au passé[15]

The tales therefore serve as archives where Africa's past is stored. Their roots descend into the dim past which has left numerous traces in

---

[14] *Ibid.* p.10.
[15] Dadie, B. Op.Cit. p.165.

the *contes:* references to pre-Islamic ages, to archaic religious phenomena, to migrations involving the different races. Close to the function of archives is the role of *contes* as a source of history. In this case, it is history mixed with myths, legends and, sometimes, with fiction. Yet from the historical elements contained in some tales, a "scientific" history of a people or a nation can be formulated. Thus *Les Contes* are dotted with slices of genealogies and with indices of past and contemporary happenings. The soaking of historical data in the nature of tales renders them palatable at any age as they are assimilated with songs, dance and gaiety.

The *Contes* are also the vehicle of a function that can easily escape our attention, one that may be called an esoteric function. In many of the tales, it is a question of initiation that adolescents and adults have undergone. These rites are never described in detail in the stories; most of them are known to be secret, which means that below the surface of the tales, there are zones that are accessible only to the initiates, passages which only those "who have ears to hear" can apprehend. In *Contes et lavanes*, for example, a passage in *Bouki Orpheline* is suggestive; it relates curious behaviour by the "Bush":

Et toute la Brousse n'était plus tantôt qu'yeux, qu'oreilles et que jambes, pour voir, entendre et fuir Bouki - l'Hyène: tantôt que rugissements, hurlements, hululements pour terrifier et faire fuir Bouki - l'Hyène; tantôt que cris, rires et ricanements(p.93).

The personification of the *Brousse* and her strange behaviour cannot be explained solely by poetic devices. The *contes* veil the mysteries of the race, without sacrificing, to this measure, the interest of the tales.

One function of tales that has found remarkable expression in the works of Birago Diop is the use of other genres, particularly folk songs and proverbs, within the tales to enrich the stories or illustrate an idea. The tales are adorned by many forms of oral poetry:

Regarde-moi, mon Oncle! Regarde-moi!
Regarde l'arbre!
Regarde ton taureau!
Regarde surtout la lune
A-t-elle bougé celle-là?

The proverbs, in their illustration or exemplification of a truism, blend with the tales.

> *L'on ne connait l'utilité des fesses que quard vient l'heure de s'asseoir*
> *Quand il y a trop a ramasser, se baisser devient malaisé*
> *Point n'est besoin d'un gros appât pour attraper une grosse bête*
> *S'il n'est que de vous nourrir, une seule femme suffit.*
> *Secouer la tête doucement ou énergiquement n'a jamais débarrasé personne de ses oreilles, longues ou courtes.*

It is obvious that each of these proverbs, by itself, "can adequately, effectively and forcefully replace a lengthy discourse".[16] Their intervention and that of folk music in Diop's tales represent the comprehensive nature of the *contes* as a repository of elements of oral literature.

The mission of the tale as an instrument for teaching the people is also evident in *Les contes*. Hutchinson sums up this crucial function as follows:

> The obligation to respect traditions, to respect the ancestors and customary beliefs, and to pay attention to the teachings of one's parents and elders and the lessons drawn from *la sagesse du clan* figures as a *leitmotif* in many of Diop's stories.[17]

Severe punishment is the lot of the former sergeant in *Sarzan*, the young man in *Le Boli*, the hyena in *Le Tam-tam de Lion* for offences against the norms of the "clan".

In the functions of tales, as in other factors, Birago Diop demonstrates his avowed allegiance to the authenticity of the tradition of the *contes* in his work. His loyalty to his tradition is striking in his preference for Wolof words in certain expressions. In fact, the songs and poems in the work are first presented in Wolof, then translated into French and rendered finally in a mixture of both languages. While Diop thus plays the ethnologist in his projection of the tradition of Amadou Koumba, the artist in the translator as an amateur of French literary culture cannot be ignored.

---

[16] Noah, I.A., "Literature and Folklore" in S.W. Peters, E.R. Iwok, O.E. Uya: *Akwa Ibom State: The land of Promise*, Lagos: Gambuno Publishing Co. Ltd., 1994, p.65,

[17] Hutchison. Op.Cit., p.7

Tales as Written Literature in French

Introduction
Translation of the tales from oral versions to written literary work brought into play two conflicting factors: the realism of the oral phenomenon with its imperatives on the loyalty of the narrator to the heritage on the one hand, and on the other, the initiative of the translator and the exigencies of an alien system of communication with its literary culture. Faced with these options, Birago Diop preferred to adhere to the tradition of Amadou Koumba, that is, to reconstitute the tales as they were handed down from the distant past.

Diop's explicit intention does not seem to have fully materialised in *Les Contes*. Though he has been able to retain much of the elements of the tradition in his work, his personality has so pervaded the stories that the *contes* cannot readily be assigned to anonymity. In the words of Senghor:

> *Birago Diop ne se contente pas du mot à mot. Il a vécu comme seuls savent le faire les auditeurs négro-africains, les récits du griot, il les a repensés et écrits en artiste nègre et français en même temps*[18]

Birago Diop, with a double artistic vocation, has left a literary masterpiece. As an African artist, the narrator exercises some initiative in the proliferation of the tales. Responsibility for controlling this initiative remains, generally, that of the audience. It is to be expected that even while operating within the frontiers of the African patrimony, Diop's initiative and creative talent would still be perceptible in the translation of the tales. And, as an artist in the French literary tradition, Diop would exploit the resources that are most appropriate in the literary culture enlisted to serve his project. Therefore, Diop's initiative and creative disposition are an important factor in the three volumes of *contes* under consideration in this brief study. In this section, we shall examine the elements that betray the presence of Birago Diop in *Les Contes*.

Anonymity
Birago Diop does not claim to be the author of *Les Contes*. The name of

---
[18] Senghor. "Preface". *Op.Cit.*,p.7.

Amadou Koumba associated with the tales is intended to highlight the source of the stories; that is, the people whose tradition the "griot" transmits. But a writer is not always the best interpreter of his work or of his intentions. Diop's intention to attenuate his authorship of the tales and the silhouette of Amadou Koumba in *Les Contes* is not adequately reflected in the reality surrounding the publication. Amadou Koumba's name, conspicuously and permanently inscribed in the title of the first two volumes, constitutes a deviation from the tradition of anonymity, and veils the status of the owners of the texts.

The influence of Western culture where a piece of writing must bear a signature is evident right on the cover of *Les Contes d'Amadou Koumba* and *Les Noveaux Contes d'Amadou Koumba*. Charles Perrault did not include any name in his collection which bears the simple title of *Contes*. In Canada, Germain Lemieux is synonymous with authorship of the thirty volumes of tales he collected even though the title of the collection, *Les Vieux M'ont Conté*, has shown clearly that Lemieux attributes the tales to a generation and a people that preceded him. The profession of the "griots" includes recitation of important historical events, poetry, genealogies etc. These are never stamped with their names. By decorating the repertory with the name of Amadou Koumba, Diop's initiative perpetuates, not the ancestral authorship of his people, but individualism favoured by the literary tradition of the West.

Le Prétexte

Birago Diop, by the title of the collection and by his declaration, has shown that he borrowed his tales from Amadou Koumba. But this does not seem to be true of one tale *Le Prétexte*.

According to Senghor: *Le Prétexte est un chef-d'oeuvre du genre d'autant que Birago Diop ne l'a certainement pas emprunté a Amadou-Koumba, qu'il est de son cru, comme il arrive parfois*[19]. Thus, *Le Prétexte* was composed by Diop who exercised his individual creative talent. The issue here is not the literary quality of the tale which Senghor extols; the fact is that *Le Prétexte* was not bequeathed by the "griot". The creation of the tale is another initiative of Birago Diop that places some aspects of his work outside the current of tradition. His

---

[19] *Ibid*. p.19.

project has been to translate, faithfully, the tale of his culture; that programme does not accommodate creative writing by which Diop produced his story.

Suppression of the Incipit

Folktales all over the world are known to have an opening formula. The incipit, though a stereotyped expression, fulfils important functions in each tale. It signals the break with the real world that preludes the entrée into the *merveilleux*. By its conventional nature, the synthetic character of the text it introduces, and the closing formula that often concludes the stories the *contes* decisively ignore creativity. As in western, that is creative writing, the source of the text is reflected in the texture of the genre: the *contes*, like the tradition that for ages remains its source and custodian, is a faceless static immutable object.

The consequences, on the tales and on the native community, of the suppression of the incipit are perhaps more serious than those of any other creative measures that Birago Diop may have exercised. This can be seen in the criticism, the only one from Senghor, of the deletion of the opening and closing formulae, *Birago Diop supprime les formules initiale et finale parce que contraires, sans doute, au goût français, et c'est dommage.*[20] Senghor's remark shows Diop's intention to satisfy the literary taste of the West. The suppression of the formulae exposes the dilemma of Birago Diop trying to serve two masters: the tradition of his people and western literary culture. One consequence of this situation is that *Les Contes* no longer reckon with the traditional audience but focuses on western readership. Another consequence of this "crisis" is that, the formulae having been eliminated, other forms of opening were introduced for *Les Contes*.

Opening Formulae

The standard opening formulae having been discarded in Diop's tales, non-conventional devices made their appearance in the commencement of the stories. Consequently, many a *conte* in the collection took off without any form of prelude. (*Le Salaire, Le Boli, Bouki et ses tablettes*).

---

[20] *Ibid.* p.10.

In other cases, Birago Diop began the stories with an introduction as in *Fari-L'Anesse, Les Mamelles, Maman-Caiman*. Such an operation by Diop is not without consequences for the status of the genre, considering the strategic importance of the traditional opening formula, *il était une fois*.

We have discussed elsewhere the mechanisms and functions of the opening formula, the incipit. For instance:

> *Contrairement à ce qui se produit dans d'autres genres littéraires, l'incipit des contes est une formule stéréotypée. Il est donc, en quelque sorte, étranger à la fraicheur linguistique et aux innovations narratives propres à chaque conteur et à chaque version du récit. Autrenment dit, dans son aspect actif, l'incipit agit sur le conte; il joue dans le récit, le rôle de catalyseur.*[21]

A remarkable trait of folktales, not only within one culture, but from different cultures all over the world which Propp considered astounding is the similitude of their elements: structure, themes, *"personnages"*, functions etc. This singularity of the *"contes"* cannot find a more satisfactory manifestation than in the unity of all tales that the incipit proclaims.

This initial strategic declaration of the concord of features seems to have been waived in Diop's *contes*; the opening of each tale is peculiar to the particular story. We are reminded of short stories. Birago Diop, not the community, designs the beginning of each tale in *Les Contes*. The mechanical repetition of the opening formula implies the absence of an individual creator of a tale. By setting aside the incipit, Birago Diop allows the western literary tradition, which inspired his initiative, to prevail over the ancestral oral tradition.

We have also shown the rapport which the opening formula entertains with the semantic and stylistic elements within each tale. And so, *"la manifestation des incipit, par leur caractère rituel et incantatoire répond à la répétition des thèmes, schémas, actants et dénouements entre les divers contes."*[22] We have also shown, as have done Joseph

---

[21.] Noah, I.A. *Origine, Structure et Symbolisme des Contes*. Lagos: JBG Publishers, 1989, p.94.
[22.] *Ibid.* p.97.

Campbel[23], P. Saintyves[24], Miracea Eliade[25], James G.Frazer[26] and Mathe Robert[27], that the *contes* are remnants of ancient initiatic rites. Even in his *Morphologies du conte,* Propp had to affirm: *les formes définies pour telle ou telle raison comme fondamentales sont visiblement liées aux anciennes représentations religieuses.*[28]

Thus the *contes* are skeletons of archaic rituals. Diop's work is loaded with *le merveilleux*, the esoterism of *la sagesse*, elements of rites of passage etc. A uniform, invariable, opening formula handed down from antiquity with the tales perpetuates the ritualistic origin and nature of the *contes*; also, it repercutes the incantatory role of the elements: themes, actors, rythm etc in the tales. These dimensions of *les contes populaires* have been dimmed by the absence of the sacred formula in Diop's work.

It is not without reason that Senghor regretted the elimination of the incipit. The consequences of Diop's initiative, in this regard, hamper not only our perception of the legitimate verbal agent of manifestation of *les contes traditonnels*, but also of the style and destiny of the phenomenon.

Dialogues, Songs, Poems

Dialogues, songs and poems are essential ingredients in African folktales. Their intervention accentuates interest and heightens participation in the narration. The tradition of Amadou Koumba is delightfully garnished with dialogues, songs and poems. Diop's originality in the way he arranges these elements in the collections have enhanced the literary qualities of the *contes*.

In the stories, Diop has maintained some form of balance between dialogue and narration. This is important in these written versions of the *contes* where with neither a perceptible audience nor the theatricals of the narrator, a judicious dosage of dialogues interrupts the monotony of

---

[23] Campbel, Joseph. *The Hero With A thousand Faces.* Princeton: Princeton University Press, 1968, p.30.
[24] Saintyves, P. *Les contes de Perrault et les Récits Parallels.* Paris: Librairie Critique Emile Nourry, 1923, xxi.
[25] Eliade, Mircea. Initiations, rites, *Sociétés Secretés.* Paris: Gallimard, 1959, p.226-227.
[26] Frazer, James G. *Le Rameau d'or (Tomell). traduit de l'Anglais par P. Sayn,* L. Frazer et H. Peyrem. Paris: Robert Laffont, 1983, p.100.
[27] Robert, Marthe. "Préface" *dans Grimm:* Contes. Paris: Gallimard, Folio no. 840, 1976.p.13.
[28] Hutchinson, J.A. *Op.Cit.* p.28.

narration and vivifies the interest of the reader in the tales. The songs, by their rhythm and poetry enrich and sublimate the narration. A striking example of the use of songs is found in *Le Boli*:

> *Et ça tombe! Ça tombe!*
> *Et pourquoi ça ne tomberait-il pas?*
> *Ça tombe!*
> *- Quoi?!*
> *- Mais tout!*
> *Tout tombe!*
>
> ....
>
> *Oùi?*
> *Oùi?*
> *Oùi?*
> *Tout tombe!*
> *Vers la tombe!*

Hutchinson's comment on this poem is pertinent:

> The striking rhythm imitates the sound of the beats of the hammer on the anvil, followed by the sighing sound of the goat-skin bellows. Finally, the clever use of "tombe" as a verb, side by side with the noun "la tombe" adds to the effect of the song[29]

Diop's skill can be seen in the attention he accords the visual disposition of the words which is not possible in the oral version of the poem, but which, in this written form, intensifies the effect of the phonic and semantic elements.

Poetry remains the dominant feature of *Les Contes*. The fact that one of the stories, *Les Mamelles* is included in Senghor's anthology of *Poésie nègre* attests to the highly poetic nature of Diop's tales. Where, unlike *Les Mamelles*, the entire tale is not a poem, the poetic charge in many of its elements is nonetheless impressive. For instance, such beautiful sentences as *"Les oiseaux avaient vainement cherch sur la peau tendue et luisante du magnifique taureau, des poux ou des tiges à picorer"* from *Le Taureau de Bouki* abound in the tales.

Often, the influence of Stéphane Mallarmé who, according to Lilyan Kesteloot, had *trop marqué* Birago Diop[29] is perceptible, as in *Le Tam-*

---

[29]. Kesteloot, Lilyan. *Anthologie Négro-africaine La Litterature se 1918 a 1981*, Alleur (Belgique): Marabout, Coll. Marabout Service, 1987, p.142.

tam de Lion: "*La reine, morte depuis des lunes et des lunes, les enfants qui avaient grandi avaient trouvé, les filles des maris, les garçon des femmes...*". The effect is created, not through verbosity, but by the disposition of the words and the rhythm that results from it.

Diop's most popular poem, *Souffles*, is found in the tale "*Sarzan*" and concludes "*Les Contes d'Amadou Koumba*". It appears with little modificaitons in "*Leurres et Lueurs*". The literary qualities of this poem and the vision of "African cosmological naturalism" it advocates are too well known to be developed in this study. What we need point out is that this great poem is associated with insanity.

Already, in "*Dof-Diop*", we are told that *Le cerveau des grands à l'esprit plus sain* is incapable of apprehending the "*passines-devinettes*" and "*chants, initiatiques*" which "*le fou*", "*Dof-Diop*", registered easily because they "*frappaient plus facilement son cerveau plus simple par leur incoherence apparente*". Derangement is presented here as superior to a normal mental state in the appropriation of certain realities outside the rigid frontiers of sanity. And the mental derangement is considered to be merely *apparente*. This raises a question that has often been asked and which Edgar Poe expressed succinctly: "*La science ne nous a pas encore appris si la folie est ou n'est pas le sublime de l'intelligence*".[30]

In *Sarzan*, the ex-sergeant Keita treated with disrespect the traditions of his people. With insanity came his poetic verve; he had a revelation of the *Souffles*, the ancestral spirits and of their presence in both animate and inanimate objects, and went about screaming their reality. For Keita, an African who despises *la sagesse*, initiation, that is, transcendence from which poetry springs, can be brutal.

Conclusion

In writing the tales, Birago Diop was following a specific plan: to present to the world, the *contes* of his land of birth in the tradition in which his people narrated the stories. As we have seen in this study, he faithfully represented in the three volumes of tales, the major elements of the

---

[30] Poe, Edgar A. *Histoires grotresques et Sérieuses.* Paris: Garnier-Flammarion, 1966, p.95.

tradition. However, certain factors that intervened in the project caused, on the one hand, the introduction of elements that are not part of the tradition and, on the other, the omission or modification of some other elements that are part of the genre.

A conflict therefore arose between Birago Diop's profession of allegiance to the norms of the tradition and the constraints of his creative talents coloured by Western literary tendencies. In the centre of this struggle between African tradition and Western civilization, between anonymity and individual creative silhouette in the narration of the *contes*, is the role of the French language, the new vehicle for the tales.

The conflict subsides, perhaps dissolves in an attitude expressed in Senghor's words in answer to the question as to why he wrote his poems in French:

> *Parce que nous sommes des métis culturels, parce que, si nous nous sentons nègres, nous nous exprimons en français, parce que le français est une langue à vocation universelle.*[31]

At the heart of the *métissage culturel* is the adoption of French language by Francophone authors. As we have seen from the case of Birago Diop, the demands of the new language means a departure from the code of the oral indigenous text. But the *métis culturels* do not perceive the incongruity between the two traditions in terms of conflict but as a noble and profitable cross-breeding.

---

[31] Senghor, L.S. *Elégies Majeures suivi de Dialogue sur la Poésie francophone*. Paris: Le seuil, 1979, p.166.

References

Campbel, J., *"The Hero With a Thousand Faces"*, Princeton, Princeton University Press, 1968.

Dadie B. B., *"Le Role de la Légende dans la culture populaire des Noirs d'Afrique*, Contribution au Premier Congrès d' Ecrivains et Artistes Noirs", Paris, 1956, Présence Africaine, numéro spécial, xiv-xv, 1957.

Diop, B., *"Les Contes d'Amadou Koumba"*, Paris, Fasquelle, Coll. Ecrits français d'Outre-mer, 1947.

———— *"Les Nouveaux Contes d'Amadou-Koumba"*, Paris, Présence Africaine, 1958.

———— *"Leurres et Lueurs"*, Paris, Presence Africaine, 1960

———— *"Contes et Lavances"*, Paris, Presence Africaine, 1963.

Eliade, M., *"Initiations, Rites, Sociétés Secrètes,* Paris, Gallimard, 1959.

Franz, M.L. Von, *"An Introduction to the Psychology of Fairy Tales",* Zurich, Spring Publications, 1975.

Frazer, J.G., *"Le Rameau d'Or"*, T.II, traduit de l'anglais par P. Sayn, L. Frazeret H. Peyrem, Prais, Robert Laffont, 1983.

Hutchinson, J.A., "Introduction" in "Birago Diop: *Contes choisis*", Cambridge, Cambridge University Press, 1967.

Kesteloot, L., *"Anthologie Négro-Africaine: La Littérature de* 1918 à 1981", Alleur (Belgique), Marabout, Coll. Marabout Service, 1987.

Noah, I.A., *"Origine Structure et Symbolisme des Contes"*, Lagos, JBG Publishers, 1989.

———— "Literature and Folklore" in S.W. Peters, E.R. Iwok, O.E. Uya: *Akwa Ibom State: The Land of Promise*, Lagos, Gabumo Publishing Co. Ltd., 1994.

Poe, E., *"Histoires Grotesques et Sérieuses"*, Paris, Garnier-Flammarion, 1966.

Propp, V. *"Morphologie du Conte"*, Paris, Editions du Seuil, 1970.

———— *"Les Racines Historiques du conte Merveilleux"*, *traduit du Russe par* L. Gruel-Apert, Paris, Gallimard, 1983.

Robert, M., "Préface" in *"Grimm: Contes"*, Paris, Gallimard, Folio no. 840, 1976.

Sartre, J.P., in L.S. Senghor: *"Anthologie de La Nouvelle Poésie Nègre*

et *Malgache de Langue Française" Précédée de "Orphée Noir"
par Jean-Paul Sartre*, Paris, P.U.F., 1972.
Saintyves, P., *"Les Contes de Perrault et les Récits parallèls"*, Paris, Librairie Critique Emile Nourry, 1923.
Senghor, L.S., *"Elégies Majeures" suivi de "Dialogues sur la Poésie francophone"*, Paris, Le Seuil, 1979.
────── Préface" in *"Les Nouveaux Contes d'Amadou -Koumba"*, Paris, Présence Africaine, 1958.

6

THE LANGUAGE OF MODERN AFRICAN LITERATURE

Kester Echenim

Introduction

The use of language is indispensable in the execution of any work of literature. The traditional approach has always been to define the literary text on the basis of the interactions between the message and its expression (*le fond et la forme*). But this dichotomy, unfortunately, does not seem to stress the overriding importance of language as an indispensable tool in the literary text. It is practically impossible to think of literature without language. Indeed, the literary message revealed in the presentation of theme, the psychological make-up of characters etc. is essentially expressed through language. In other words, expressions and stylistic features are freely expressed and of necessity used so as to enhance the "literariness" and the message of the literary text. It is, therefore, obvious that the relationship between the message and its expression is not based on terms of equality but on the superiority of the latter over the former. In other words, without language, there is no text.[1]

In making this assertion, we should also bear in mind that the essential function of literature is to promote a situation of dialogue between the producer and the consumer of the text - a dialogue that is predicated on the existence of the fundamental functions of literature that are both aesthetic and didactic. Given that this communication process, in spite of

---

[1] Here, we are not making the distinction between the oral and written text. The concept of text implies any form of communication, oral or written, in which language is used.

the existence of both verbal and non-verbal forms, acquires its optimal significance through the use of language[2], it is clear that language is indeed a *sine qua non* for ensuring genuine communication amongst individuals sharing the same linguistic code, and a means of promoting mutual interaction and comprehension.

Another point of interest in this chapter is the use of the expression "Modern African Literature". Here it is vital to note that the operative word "modern" tends to create the impression that its essence and relevance derive from its opposition to non-modern, or in the perspective of African Literature, to the traditional. By extension this opposition between "modern" and "traditional" is sometimes reflected in the dichotomy between "oral" and "written". This dichotomous relationship may be valid in general terms as the study of African Literature is best perceived in its diachrony, i.e. as evolutionary, that is in the movement from the traditional to the modern, or from the oral to the written, with language use constituting an integral part of this evolutionary process, based, especially, on the historical, political and cultural evolution of the African society.

Consequently, it would appear that, as suggested by the title of this chapter, attention should be limited to the modern rather than traditional with the obvious implications of defining these concepts on the basis of a given time-frame, since the main thrust of our approach could be hinged on the necessary opposition between the traditional and the modern. But, as shall be seen, there is complementarity between oral and written means of expression depending largely on the perspective of the writer and the nature of his message, as the specific conditions of the evolution of the African society determine attitudes to the use of language. It is therefore vital to perceive language use in literature as a function of the historical evolution of African society. We, therefore, intend in this chapter to first present a historical overview of the relationship between language and literature and, secondly, to analyse some of the attitudes of writers to the language of African Literature.

---

[2] Although the distinction is made between the verbal and the non-verbal in the communication process, yet there is no doubt that in a situation of optimal communication, the non-verbal can reinforce the communication bid by the producer and the comprehension ability of the consumer.

Historical Overview:

The Relationship Between Language and Literature

There is no doubt that Western intervention and irruption in the history, life-style and destiny of the African people constitutes an important event in the evolution of African society. The transformations that subsequently took place underscore the importance of this intervention as an agent of upheaval and sometimes destruction of well-established practices, beliefs and habits.

One important area where this upheaval was profoundly felt was in the area of communication and social interactions. Hitherto, in the well-structured and ideologically protected environment of the traditional society, characterised by shared experience, beliefs and a holistic ideological world view, the interaction between members of the same social group was ensured through the use of an adequate and appropriate linguistic medium, whose denotative and connotative properties were accessible to members of the group. A genuine dialogue situation existed in which the informational value of any given message was practically understood by the receiver of such a message; where there was incomprehension and absence of dialogue, it then would be due to the esoteric and exclusive nature of the language used.

Literary and artistic expressions were essentially functional, fulfilling both aesthetic and didactic functions, with greater emphasis on the didactic. This situation was again possible because of the holistic perception of the relationship between man and society, where society is perceived both as a physical and metaphysical entity. It is therefore this reality of the interdependence of art and society that L. S. Senghor (1964) expresses in these terms: (Adebayo1983:367-368).

> *Le mérite de l'art nègre est de n'être ni jeu, ni pure jouissance esthétiqe. Parce que fonctionnels et collectifs, la littérature et l'art négro-africain sont engagés. Ils engagent la personne et non seulement l'individu par et dans la communauté en ce sens qu'ils sont des techniques d'essentialisation.*

It is this total view of art and society that confers a special status on language not only as an instrument of communication amongst individuals but as a means of communion between man and the natural and supernatural realms.

For the traditional literary artist, the use of language is not based on choice of individual idiosyncrasies. Language is an expression of totality and collective communion. Any attempt at personalisation of language can only be seen as a variation within accepted and unquestionable collective practice. This point acquires immediate relevance when due consideration is given to the basic inter-relationship between art and society. Thus, such literary forms as folktales, proverbs, myths and legends, songs, riddles etc. are an illustration of both the unifying role of language among members of the same community, and an instrument for forging a permanent link between the horizontal (social inter-relationships) and the vertical (religious and mystical interactions). It is therefore practically impossible to envisage a situation of creative autonomy of the artist in the closely-knit ideological structure of the traditional society. His role, his methods and his medium of expression are regulated and circumscribed within the identified exigencies of the community.

The point being made is that the relationship between language and literature, seen in terms of form and content, does not, in the traditional society, constitute an issue; there was a general agreement as to language use and relevance *vis-à-vis* literary forms.

But with the intervention of western civilisation and with the resulting restructuring of society and its coherence, language becomes an important factor in the discussion of modern African literature because of the obvious distortions in the status and role of the writer, his relationships with members of his community and his perception of his literary functions.

Western intervention brought with it western education, and subsequently the formation of a new class of individuals bound together by the use of the French language, a symbol of western domination in the Francophone African countries.

The establishment of schools and colleges, therefore, marked the beginning of a fundamental change and a distortion in the apparent quasi-deterministic structuring of society and social interactions with the holistic giving way to a fragmentary perception of human and social relationships. This new class of individuals, bound together by their ability to use the French language as a medium of communication, therefore constituted a privileged group, capable of piercing the mysteries and understanding the logic of Western civilisation. The use of the linguistic medium of expression of the colonial power became a sign of "cultural emancipation" and a symbol of a break with the established and well-structured practices of

It is especially in the area of literary expression and the conceptualisation of literature that the effect of this intervention is profoundly felt. As earlier mentioned, the existence of a common linguistic and cultural identity in the traditional society allowed for the total integration of literary production in the general preoccupation of the social group. Literature was seen as a means of promoting social cohesion and harmony within the group. The process of identification between the work and the societal norms was taken for granted. The literary text was seen as a collective creation and an expression of the collective will. There was no room for an individualistic approach to literature.

However, with the introduction of the French language as a medium of communication, literary production and conceptualisation acquired new relevance and significance. First, literature, instead of being an expression of group feeling and interpretation of reality, now becomes an expression of the creative resources of the individual. Secondly, the target audience of the literary text is no more the community as a whole but a group capable of deciphering the language of expression and the underlying significance of the work. Thirdly, in place of a language that is accessible to all, being indigenous to the community, the language of expression is primarily foreign to the community.

Thus, the issue of language becomes central to the definition of modern African literature. In terms of the immediate, the problem is not so much the ideological content of the linguistic medium, as that the French language constitutes simply a means of literary expression, chosen by this crop of the artists so as to give form to their literary creativity. And by so doing, they create a certain distance between them and their indigenous communities.

Another important aspect of the issue of the language of literary expression is that of the relationship between the artist and his audience. In the traditional setting, this language is exclusively oral. It is also characterised by its spontaneity and dynamism. Its use allows for genuine situation of dialogue among participants because of shared feelings, interests and ideological significance. On the other hand, the new linguistic medium does not take its origin from the indigenous community in which the writer finds himself. Except where verbalised in oral expression such as in theatre and, to a certain extent, in poetry, the written foreign language establishes a distance between the writer and an amorphous and heterogeneous audience bound together essentially by the use of that language. In other words, this new literary arrangement called "Modern African Literature," by its very nature would bring to the fore such basic issues in literature as the relationship between the writer (the producer) and the reader (the consumer), and between the writer and society. It would now become important to define these relationships on the basis of the interactions between the old set of literary values and practices, and the new one, as typified in the issue of language in modern African writing in French. As we shall see subsequently, these issues have become central in the overall problem of defining and assessing the appropriate linguistic medium for African literature.

It must also be noted that, in discussing the implications of the language choice in African literature, such factors as the ideological choice and the issue of linguistic competence have to be considered. As we are aware and as noted earlier, language is the expression of the sum total of the beliefs, practices and societal norms of a social group. It is therefore the cultural expression of the ideological option of a given community. Therefore considered along these terms, the use of a foreign language, vehicle of a foreign culture and ideology, to express and describe an indigenous culture and situation could create a fundamental distortion because of a contradiction in terms. Can a foreign language express an indigenous culture, especially because of the interrelationship between culture and language? Would such a situation be considered as not more than a mere approximation or a pale copy of what it could have been if there was perfect correspondence between language and culture, as would be the case in the use of an indigenous language in the traditional set-up? Can writers divorce themselves and be totally insulated from conscious or unconscious influences of their native tongue when using a foreign language to express their preoccupations and those of their community? Or would it rather be more convenient to envisage complementary roles of both the indigenous and the foreign in literary works? Can this dialectical relationship between the indigenous and the foreign give rise to a "new" language, which is neither completely foreign nor indigenous?

These interrogations constitute a vivid illustration of the fact that there is a genuine problem as regards the relationship between creativity and the language of its expression, a problem arising from the dichotomy between mother tongue and alien language in the process of literary creativity. As we shall see, the divergent opinions of writers and critics *vis-à-vis* the language of modern African literature constitute an expression of the reality of this problem and its importance in determining the nature of the evolution of African literature.

Attitudes to the Language of African Literature

Introduction

Before going into a detailed study of this topic, it is necessary to note that:
(i) modern African literature from its origins to the present is essentially a literature of protest;
(ii) the nature of the protest is determined by the historical context of the literary work;
(iii) there is a correlation between the nature of protest and the language of its expression;
(iv) although the French language is the medium of expression, there is a multifaceted approach to its use in the literary text;
(v) the attitude of the African writer/critic to the French language is determined by his ideological awareness of the implications of this choice.

Classification of Attitudes

J. Chevrier (1984:49) in his study, *"L'écrivain, sa conscience, son oeuvre"*, classifies these attitudes into three categories, equating each attitude to the chosen option of the writer/critic.[3] These are (a) *"les inconditionnels"*, (b) *"les réticents"*, and (c) *"les réalistes et les autres"*. We have also adopted these categories while adapting them to suit our purpose. For instance, in our classification, the category of *"les réticents"* is enlarged to become *"le camp du refus"*, characterised by a movement from an attitude of reluctance to outright rejection of the use of a foreign medium.

---

[3] It may be necessary to note here that emphasis is not on exhaustivity but on the representativity of examples of both writers and works cited in this study. In other words, these cases represent the general tendencies observable in a comprehensive study of African literature.

"Les inconditionnels"

These are writers/critics who consider and insist that the use of the French language cannot and should not be seen as an obstacle to literary creativity. As a matter of fact, such writers have consciously seen the foreign linguistic medium as the most convenient means to express their creative inspiration. Moreover, it would also appear that the problems of target audience and its exigencies are secondary, and have essentially been subsumed to the overall need for an adequate and appropriate instrument of literary expression. It is this overriding fact of the importance and appropriateness of the French language as literary medium that explains why the problem of *"mauvaise conscience"* or feeling of betrayal does not arise *vis-à-vis* the national language or culture.

Moreover, the writer feels very competent to use the French language, as he fully understands its intricacies and its connotative qualities as a medium of expression. Thus, Paulin Joachim (Chevrier, 1984:49) asserts that the French language is indeed *"évangile du jour"*: *"Je m'y suis enraciné loin pour pouvoir en explorer les profondeurs (...) et je peux affirmer aujourd'hui que je lui dois tout ce que je suis."* In other words, his status as a writer and literary artist is due essentially to his ability to use the French language.

The choice of the French language as an appropriate medium can also be explained by the inability of the writer to use his mother tongue as a means of literary expression. Senghor (1964:361) explains his choice of French in these terms: *"Je pense en français, je m'exprime mieux en français que dans ma langue maternelle"*. It is evident that what is important in this attitude is the appropriateness of the choice and not the relevance of this choice *vis-à-vis* such considerations as sociological, ideological and psychological factors which, as we shall see, could play a determining role in the attitudes of writers/critics towards the use of the French language.

It is therefore necessary to observe that for these writers, the language issue does not really constitute a problem, in the sense that not only is the linguistic competence already acquired, but there is also the belief that the need for literary "expressivity" transcends other considerations. The French language is a reality, and its use as a literary medium is also a reality. Consequently, it becomes unnecessary and unsatisfactory to reject its role as a means of literary communication. For instance, for Tchicaya U. Tamsi (Chevrier, 1984:50), the use of French is not a deliberate and conscious choice, it is essentially a *"situation de fait* and *"un phénomène naturel"*.

It is this self-assurance and positive attitude to the use of the French language which are reflected in the nature and quality of the literary production of these writers. Senghor's poetry, for instance, and as illustrated in the following except from *"Le Kaya-Magan"* is a demonstration of this uninhibited attitude *vis-à-vis* the French language. (Senghor, 1964:103)

KAYA-MAGAN je suis! La personne première
Roi de la nuit noire de la nuit d'argent, roi de la nuit de verre.
Paissez mes antilopes à l'abri des lions, distants au charme
de ma voix.

The underlying logic in this attitude is the firm conviction that the French language is apt and capable of reflecting the African consciousness and sensitivity, which are the motivating factors in literary creativity.

Indeed, it must be noted that the principle of uninhibited use of the French language does not necessarily imply that there is no attempt by these writers to tamper with both the denotative and the connotative values of the language as a means of expressing the "Africanness" of their writings. What indeed is primordial is ensuring that this language is adequate and apt to reflect and translate African realities and sensitivities which in essence would require the use of an African medium of expression. It is in recognition of this fact, and in order to justify his linguistic option that Tchicaya U. Tamsi (Chevrier, 1984:52) for instance states: *"la langue française me colonise; je la colonise à mon tour"*. The French language becomes therefore an instrument used to attain literary objectives.

However, although there is the professed intention to tamper with the structure and rhythms of the French language, yet it must be stated that in terms of actual realisation, such attempts by writers in this category remain timid. The degree of experimentation and de-structuring of language does not in any way attain the level, as we shall see in the category of "realist", of complete upheaval and of destruction of accepted syntactic and semantic norms.

This "timidity" in tampering with the French language can be explained by the historical situation of these works. As Chevrier (1984:51-52) noted:

Nul ne peut contester en effet qu'à l'époque coloniale, la
maîtrise de la langue française a constitué pour

> *l'intelligentsia africaine un atout de premier ordre, qui lui a permis à la fois d'exprimer sa révolte et de donner corps à une prise de conscience de sa situation politique, sociologique et culturelle.*

Moreover, because the target audience is essentially European, the use of French allowed for access to a large international public.

In the area of the novel, mention can be made of such works as *L'Enfant noir* and *Le Regard du roi* by Camara Laye, and *L'Aventure ambiguë* by Cheikh Hamidou Kane which, according to our classification would belong to the category of the *inconditionnels*. Their use of the French language is characterised by great "sobriété" and respect for the classical and unadulterated expression of the language.[4]

It is therefore obvious that this category of writers constitute the early apostles of African literature with emphasis on the absence or limited experimentation with the French language.

"Les réalistes"

The category covers a very broad spectrum of writers and critics whose attitude is characterised essentially by the need for a more explicit experimentation with the French language; an experimentation that spans different historical periods and represents as well a more audacious and "reckless" attitude *vis-à-vis* the French language. The bond that unites such a disparate group is the firm conviction of the need to transcend the constraints of the French language in the bid to impose a new linguistic form capable of reflecting their conception and perception of genuine African literature. It is in this vein that Aimé Césaire, commenting on the use of the French language in his literary work, in an interview accorded J. Leiner (Ngal, 1994:24) explains that *"mon effort a été d'infléchir le français, de le transformer pour exprimer, disons: ce moi, ce moi-nègre, ce moi-créole, ce moi-martiniquais, ce moi-antillais"* (Ngal, p.24)

The point here is that the writer sees the French language more as a simple tool and not an object of love and admiration as is the case with

---

[4] With Camara Laye and Cheikh Hamidou Kane, emphasis is on the use of an overtly purified classical expression of the French language. The "Africanness" of their texts is situated principally in the content of their works rather than in the medium of expressing this content.

Senghor. Aimé Césaire continues: *"Le français est pour moi un instrument mais il est tout à fait évident que mon souci a été de ne pas me laisser dominer par cet instrument, c'est-à-dire qu'il s'agissait moins de servir le français que de me servir du français pour exprimer nos problèmes antillais et exprimer notre 'moi' africain"* (Ngal, 1994:37)

This attitude of Césaire is indicative of the approach to the language problem as typified by this group of writers/critics. The issue is not that of choosing between one medium of expression and another, nor is it that of defining what attitude to adopt. Rather, there is a general agreement as to the utilitarian value of the French language as a means of communication and action.

Situated in the historical context of the movement from the anti-colonial reaction to the period of independence, the works of writers in this group constitute an expression of revolt against the political status quo, a revolt in which the choice of a means of expression becomes a reflection of the writer's ideological option. The important factor here is that the treatment meted out to the French language is then perceived as a means of denouncing the injustice and absence of respect for human dignity, which characterised the colonial period. It is therefore logical to state that there is a correlation between the evaluation of society and the evolution of attitudes *vis-à-vis* the medium of expression. And the "realistic" attitude of the writer stems from this interrelationship and correlation.

Thus, the perception of the issue of a medium of expression acquires significance both at the collective and the individual levels, as due consideration is now given not only to the production/creation of the text with its repercussions on the language used (the individual level) but also to the impact of the message on a target audience defined, on the basis of accessibility to the message through linguistic competence (collective level). It is the evolution of attitudes ranging from an improvement from the timid attempts made by the camp of the *"inconditionnels"* to more audacious experimentations with the medium of expression which gives its stamp to this group of *"réalistes"*.

Thus, the works of Oyono and Mongo Beti constitute an interesting improvement in the use of the French language as a medium of literary expression. Here, for instance, it is interesting to note the presence of words and expressions from the mother tongue introduced into the literary text. Such words as *"arki"* are therefore found in the text, but with footnotes to explain their meaning and relevance in the text. In *Le Vieux Nègre et la médaille*, F. Oyono explains that "arki" is *"alcool indigène"* (p.16). This is also true of some of the works of Mongo Beti, where footnotes are used to explain meanings because of their foreign value *vis-à-vis* the French language.

However, it should be noted that this approach, while constituting an improvement, is not really new. For instance in *L'Aventure ambiguë*, the word "tabala" is used and explained in a footnote as *"tambour annonciateur des grandes nouvelles"* (p.181) and *"chahâda", "une formule de la profession de foi musulmane"*. In *L'Enfant noir* Camara Laye introduces the song of "Coba" without providing any translation: *"Coba! Aye coba, lama!"* (this expression, which is like a refrain, is written in italics) (p.136-7).

But it must be noted that, in spite of this similarity in approach between the *inconditionnels* and the *réalistes*, there is a fundamental difference in the overall tonality and "atmosphere" of the works written by both groups. Indeed, the works of F. Oyono and Mongo Beti are expressed in a language of satire with *"nombreuses métaphores et comparaisons puisées dans la culture natale"* (Ngal, p.25). By so doing, an indirect appeal is made to an authentic traditional and oral source as a determining element in the presentation of their literary message with attention focussed on a target audience made up of both the colonisers and the colonised.

A step further in the "africanisation" of the French language is taken in some other works. This is in consonance with the remark by Léopold Sedar Senghor (Ngal, 1994:58) when he states that *"langue étrangère, le français ne peut, en effet, jouer le rôle d'une langue Africaine, mais il se colore et s'enrichit au contact des réalités Africaines ... Ainsi il emprunte aux langues africaines les mots dont il a besoin" (Postface à Ethiopiques).*

Here, instead of the sporadic appearances of mother tongue words and expressions, there is a conscious attempt to "africanise" by the massive injection of indigenous lexical items and the juxtaposition within the syntactic structure of sentences, or expressions of indigenous origins which are either translated within the sentence or as footnotes. This compromise solution reinforces the feeling of a conscious attempt by writers to make more daring incursions into the lexical and syntactic structure of the French language, and by so doing proposing a new dimension to the conception and production of the novel.

For instance, Sembène Ousmane, partisan of this attitude, uses the procedure of lexical and syntactic juxtaposition to express this approach:
(i) Titles of works are given in the autochthonous language - *Véhi Ciosane* (ou Blanche Genèse) and *Xala*
(ii) Lexical items are also introduced with either the juxtaposition of translation within the sentence or the items are explained as footnotes as in: *Gods Bits of Wood*
- juxtaposition: *"Kiô dieu n'da n'do?" "Qui veut m'acheter de l'eau?"* (p.94)
- lexical items translated as footnotes:
  "Karan" - *devoirs pour l'école* (p.16)
  Sabadord - *Tunique* (p.75)
  "n'gounou" - *Poulailler* (p.77).
  Kaye-Oui - (p.97)
- expressions, such as interjections, are not translated:
  "Asta - fourlah! Que Dieu te pardonne" (p.83).
  "Ouvaï, ouvaï fit-elle..." (p.86).

It should be noted that the distinctive feature of this inserted indigenous language is that its presence is characterised by the use of italics. Aminata Sow Fall in *La Grève des battù* uses the same procedure. For example:
- the translation is carried out by the character in the same sentence sequence where the word or expression in italics is the translation of the word or expression in juxtaposition. *"Tu deviendras dingue, rakaaj'u ba doylê"* (p.84).
- Translation of the word or expression in italics and given as a footnote. *A qu jigéén baaxul: Ceux qui maltraitent les femmes seront châtiés."* (p.42)
- However, sometimes, the lexical items in italics are not translated, although they are expressed in Wolof. These are, according to Ngal, interjections – *"ndeysan* (p. 31); *fi -i- iw! fi -i- iwo! fi -i- iw"* (p.144)

This again is a perfect illustration of the "africanisation" of the French language or the "integration" of an African language in a novel written in French. The logic of this integration in *La Grève des battù* becomes obvious when due consideration is given to the relationship between the theme *(Beggars' Strike)* and the linguistic characteristics of the discourse of the downtrodden, a relationship devoid of the niceties of perfect and untainted French expression. The linguistic realism expressed in these literary works is a confirmation of a move towards an unimpeded transformation of the form and language of a literary text.

It is however important to note that these moves in the modification of the nature of the medium of expression are also linked to the political and historical evolution of the African society. Situated after the 1960s and therefore in post-colonial Africa, such literary works express the need for a self-searching and inward-looking attitude in the appreciation of African problems. The aftermath of independence is characterised by disillusionment and betrayal. And the Africanisation of the literary discourse can be seen as a way of asserting autochthonous responsibility in Africa's predicament.

It is with the arrival on the literary scene of such writers as Ahmadou Kourouma and Sony Labou Tansi that the principle of Africanisation through a de-structuring of the French language attains a high level of experimentation with fundamental transformations of accepted and apparently intangible structural laws of the French language.

Ahmadou Kourouma, conscious of the need for an appropriate linguistic medium to convey not only his message but also his literary sensitivities, decides to write his first novel, *Les Soleils des indépendances* in the indigenous Malinké language but expressed in French. This *tour de force* creates a disturbing feeling in the reader, unaccustomed to this unsettling use of the French language. He is therefore implicitly requested to review his perception of the French language as an intangible model, and accept the principle of its malleability and transformation. As Makhily Gassama (1995:23) rightly points out, *"dans Les Soleils des indépendances, Ahmadou Kourouma asservit la **langue française** qu'il (...) interprète en malinké, pour rendre la **langue malinké** en supprimant toute frontière linguistique, à la grande surprise du lecteur."* (p.23)

This narrative "revolution" is made possible essentially because of the need to reconcile the French language (medium of written expression) with the Malinké language, which in its conception and realisation is, by nature, a medium of oral expression. Emphasis is no longer on grammaticality and stylistic finesse as dictated by a classical approach to literary expression. On the contrary, Kourouma provides a new type of writing based on the successful exploitation and application of the phenomenon of orature as a means of literary expression. For instance, the need to create concrete and accessible images is rendered by the use of nouns as substitutes for adverbs and adjectives:

- *"L'homme à son tour hurla le fauve, gronda le tonnerre"* (p.79). Here, emphasis on the "how" it is done is highlighted and reinforced by the use of images drawn from nature, i.e. *"le fauve"* and *"le tonnerre"*
- *C'était un court et rond comme une souche, cou, bras, poings et épaules ..." (p.14)*

In this example, the qualifiers, "court" and "rond" function as nouns, and render the impact of the message as palpable and effective as possible.

It is also in a bid to concretise concepts and abstractions that, just as in oral narration, the writer makes use of visual images drawn from the animal, vegetable and mineral kingdoms. For example, to express the concept of rapidity, the writer says – *"Rapides comme les pattes de la biche, les mains de Salimata allèrent et vinrent"* (p.59) and *"ils disparurent dans le marché comme une volée de mange-mil dans les fourrées."* (p.63)

Moreover, Kourouma uses proverbs abundantly as a means of illustrating his story, and reinforcing the impact of his message. It is interesting to note that proverbs can constitute the titles of chapters of his story:

- *"Les choses qui ne peuvent pas être dites ne méritent pas de noms"* (p.157). Or integrated within the context of the story:
- *"l'hyène a beau être édenté, sa bouche ne sera jamais un chemin de passage pour le cabrin"* (p.16).

The dominance of oral tradition in Kourouma's work is also illustrated in the structure of the plot. For instance, there is an extensive use of the narrative technique of "questions and answers", just like the storyteller in front of his audience -

"Maintenant, dites-le-moi! Le voyage de Fama dans la capitale (...), vraiment dites-le-moi, cela étai-il vraiment nécessaire, vraiment nécessaire? Non et non! (...)" (p.151).[5]

---

[5] Cf.my article "La structure narrative des *Soleils des Indépendances*", *Présence Africaine*, 107, 1978: pp.139-161.

Moreover, the entire plot is structured as the fulfilment of a prophecy, in which Fama's actions and the interactions between the natural and the supernatural work towards the fulfilment.

Kourouma's literary innovation is also expressed in the use of new words with unusual syntactic functions. For instance, *"viander – Les doux plus viandés et gras morceaux des Indépendances[6] sont sûrement le secrétariat..."* (p.23). It is thus obvious that Kourouma's literary strategy constitutes an entirely new approach to the use of language in African written literature. What seemed paramount for the writer is to ensure the adequacy of the linguistic medium *vis-à-vis* his ideological preoccupations. Indeed, as Georges Ngal has noted (Ngal, 1994:27)

> *(...) la politique des partis uniques et des dictateurs - Pères des nations a au moins un effet bénéfique sur les champs linguistique et littéraire. L'écrivain conquiert une plus grande liberté et se libère des carcans trop contraignants du classicisme. A. Kourouma en est le modèle (p.27).*

It is also in this perspective of reconciling ideological preoccupations with an appropriate linguistic medium that the Congolese writer, Sony Labou Tansi, carries out his onslaught on the French language. On the conceptual level, Sony Labou Tansi considers the French language, as it is presently, an inappropriate medium to convey his sensitivities and express his message. Since the French language is frigid, it becomes necessary *"de lui prêter la luxuriance et le pétillement de notre tempérament tropical, les respirations haletantes de nos langues et la chaleur folle de notre moi vital, vitré."* (Ngal, p.36). His objective is therefore to propose in his works a completely new perception of the French language: *"Je fais éclater les mots pour exprimer ma tropicalité: écrire mon livre me demandait d'inventer un lexique des noms capables par leur sonorité de rendre la situation tropicale* (Ngal, p.37). His works, such as *La Vie et demie* (1979), *L'Etat honteux* (1981) and *L'Antépeuple* (1983) constitute the forum of experimentation of this "tropicality" that is the total Africanisation of the French language.

The practice of *"tropicalité"* is, essentially, *"... un usage de la langue volontairement ambigu, éclaté, distendu, se référant à la*

---

[6] Cf. my article, *"Aspects de l'écriture dans le roman africain,"* Présence Africaine, 139, 1986: pp.88-114

polysémie (...) et à une luxuriance pour lesquels l'univers tropical lui fournit métaphores et symboles" (Ngal, p.38).

The different areas of operation of this "tropicalité" include the following:
(a) Formation of new words from existing ones -
   i. *geste > gester*
      "On se bat comme des choses. On geste, un point c'est tout" (*La ie et demie*, p.185)
   ii. Regard > regarder > *regardoir*
      "Jean-Oscar-Coeur-de-Père fit construire à tous les coins de rues des "regardoirs" des cuisses droites, toujours couplés (...)" (*La ie et demie, p.132*).
   iii. Excellence > *excellentiel*
      "drap excellentiel (La Vie et demie p.19); "chambre excellentielle" and "lit excellentiel" (La Vie..., p.21)
(b) Under the influence of the oral medium of expression emanating from local African languages, Sony Labou Tansi creates new syntactic associations:
   i. *"Mourir la mort"* (*La Vie...*, p.13).
   ii. *"Dormir la femme"* (*L'Etat honteux* p.52).
   iii. *"Les pas-tout-à-fait vivants"* (*La Vie...*, p.12).
   iv. *"Les près-de-mourir"* (*La Vie...*, p.40).
(c) The coinage of names reveals also the creative ability of Sony Labou Tansi in his bid to use the "new" French language as a means of creating an effective impact of his message on his reader. Thus, such coinages include: *"Jean-Coeur-de-Père, Jean-Coupe-Coupe"* which are the names of the nation's political leaders.

The objective of Sony Labou Tansi is to use language as a reflection of the decadent and cannibalistic leadership which has thrust itself on the African people. The society depicted is one characterised by total lack of respect for the individual, by ridiculous sexual aberrations, and an insatiable desire for blood through arbitrary and sadistic elimination of all forms of opposition. To attain such an objective requires a total destructuring of language and creation of a new medium made up of elements of oral expression and the formation of new semantic and syntactic structures. There is no doubt that Sony Labou Tansi has succeeded in indicating a new perspective on the use of language in literary works, thereby ensuring a successful alliance between his ideological preoccupations and the chosen medium of expression.

However, the questions that arise are: to what extent can it be argued that the identified experiments of Kourouma and Tansi have succeeded in indicating a new perspective on the use of language in literary works, thereby ensuring a successful alliance between his ideological preoccupations and the chosen medium of expression?

To what extent can it be argued that the identified experiments of Kourouma and Tansi have succeeded in resolving the issue of the language of modern African literature, especially in the real dichotomy between language (French) and civilisation (African), and indigenous African realities expressed in borrowed and totally alien languages? Are the experiments an adequate response or not?

Le Camp du Refus

In this category are mostly critics who consider that the French language cannot be an adequate medium not only for the creativity of the writer, but also for the effective appreciation of the literary works by the public. In other words, even if the writer has successfully created his work, how accessible is it to the African public, which in the first place, should constitute the target audience of the writer? These interrogations constitute the major preoccupations of members of this group.

The critic, Obi Wali, (Achebe, 1975:60) in 1963 predicted that "(...) until these writers and their Western midwives accept the fact that any true African literature must be written in African languages, they would be merely pursuing a dead end, which can only lead to sterility, uncreativity and frustration". This position is due essentially to the apparent impossibility of reconciling genuine African sensitivity surging forth from the depths of the African psyche and experience with the nature and exigencies of a foreign language. In his view, the foreign language, and in this case the French language, cannot be an adequate and appropriate medium. The most sensible and obvious option is for the African writer to express his creative ability in an African language.

This is also the point of view expressed by B. Z. Zaourou and C. Dailly in their paper *"Langue et critique en Afrique noire"*. They state clearly that:

> *L'inadéquation d'une langue à la civlisation d'un peuple est une entrave à la création littéraire et à une critique autonome et fructueuse. C'est que la langue de conquête,*

au lieu d'unifier, divise le corps social qu'elle prétend servir.[7]

In other words, what is it that is really African in the modern African literature when the authentic target audience (essentially African) is generally excluded from any form of consideration in the evaluation of a literary text? According to these critics, a large majority of Africans do not feel directly concerned by modern African literature because of the use of a foreign medium of expression, basically inaccessible to them.

This statement of fact is the reason for which critics in this group consider that a true and relevant modern African literature is one in which the medium of expression is an African language. Such a work would express the perfect merging between language and civilisation, and culture and experiences of the African people who should constitute both the subject and the target of the literary discourse. In their view, any attempt to express African realities and sensitivities in the French language, no matter how successful, is a mere approximation, a pale reflection of genuine African creativity.

According to the partisans of this position, it therefore behoves African writers to ensure the rapid development of literature in African languages so as to give full vent to the creative potential of the African. It is also possible to envisage the translation into a foreign language of these literary texts written in African languages so as to ensure their accessibility to both an indigenous and international audience.[8]

But as Tidjani Serpos (1989:67) has noted, the basic problem in the language question is that most of the exponents of the immediate use of an African language as medium of literary creativity are not creators, and, so, are not fully aware of the implications of literary creativity. As for the writers, *"ils avouent qu'ils ne peuvent pas s'en servir (c'est-à-dire des langues nationales) pour créer, puisque même quand ils peuvent les écrire ils ne les maîtrisent pas suffisamment pour en faire leur médium littéraire."* This is the crux of the matter.

Does the African writer, in terms of the immediate, have the choice between the indigenous and the foreign media of expression? If so, what

---

[7] *Le critique africain et son peuple comme producteur de civilisation, Colloque de Yaoundé, 16-20 avril 1973.* Paris: Présence Africaine, 1977, p.468.
[8] Alain Ricard in his article sees this option as a compromise solution. There is no doubt as to the inevitability of African creative writing in African languages, and its accessibility to an international audience is ensured through translation. Cf. *"Langues africaines et littérature"*, ASCALF Year Book, No.2, 1977: p.50.

are the factors that dictate his choice? Does this choice have any serious effect on his creative inspiration and ability? It would appear that, as far as the writers are concerned, the use of the French language does not seem to have seriously impeded their ability to create nor reduced the impact of their message on their public.

Conclusion

The language of modern African literature, as we have seen, is a crucial factor in assessing not only the creative ability of the African writer but also in determining the issue of writer-reader relationship. Considering the fact that there is a dialectical relationship between society and literature, it is not surprising that social and cultural evolution has also become a determining factor in the nature of language use to express this evolution in the literary work. Consequently, there has been a progressive movement from the timid Africanisation of the French language in the early texts to a more ambitious and creative approach in the handling of the process of "de-frenchifying" the French language. As has been observed, this process coincides with the movement from an attitude of creating political and cultural awareness *vis-à-vis* decolonisation to that of disenchantment and cynicism *vis-à-vis* the dictatorial tendencies characteristic of political leadership in Africa.

Language is therefore a political weapon used to translate the multiple responses to the issue of literary creation in Africa. Although the ultimate goal of creative writing in Africa would be the adoption of national languages as an effective means of ensuring total dialogue and complicity between the African writer and the vast majority of his potential African audience, the fact still remains that African writers have succeeded to a great extent in imposing an obvious African specificity on the use of the French language in their literary works. And until a more purposeful and politically aggressive language policy is put in place and pursued vigorously[9], the African literary audience may have to be contented with more audacious experimentation in the use of the French medium of expression in African creative writing.

---

[9] This is the opinion of Ngandu Nkashama in an interview accorded to B. Magnier in *Présence Africaine*, 133/134, 19—, pp.260-267. Abiola Irele expresses an identical opinion in his paper, "African literature and the language question", *Le Critique africain et son peuple comme producteur de civilisation, Colloque de Yaoundé: 16-20 avril, 1973*. Paris: *Présence Africaine*, 1977.

References

Creative Writing:
Beti, Mongo. *Mission Terminée*. Paris: Buchet/Chastel, 1957.
Fall, Aminata Sow. *La Grève des Battù*. Dakar: Nouvelles Editions Africaines, 1979.
Kane, Cheikh Hamidou. *L'Aventure ambiguë*. Paris: Ed. 10/18, 1972.
Kourouma, Ahmadou. *Les Soleils des Indépendances*. Paris: Seuil, 1970.
Camara, Laye *L'Enfant noir*. Paris: Ed. Julliard, 1956.
——— *Le Regard du roi*. Paris: Plon, 1954.
Oyono, Ferdinand. *Le Vieux nège et la médaille*. Paris: Ed. Julliard, 1956.
Sembéne, Ousmane. *Les Bouts de Bois de Dieu*. Paris: Press Pocket, 1971.
——— *Véhi-Ciosane ou Blanche Genèse suivi du Mandat*. Paris: Présence Africaine, 1965.
——— *Xala*. Paris: Présence Africaine, 1973.
Senghor, Léopold Sédar. *Poèmes*. Paris: Seuil, 1964.
Tansi, Sony Labou. *La Vie et demie*. Paris: Ed. Du Seuil, 1979.
———*L'Etat honteux*. Paris: Seuil, 1981.
———*L'Anté-peuple*. Paris: Seuil, 1983.

Critical Works:
Achebe, Chinua. *Morning Yet on Creation Day, Essays*. London: Heinemann, 1975.
Adebayo, Aduke, "Protest and Commitment in Black American and African Literature," *Comparative Poetics*, Journal of I.C.I, vol II, 1983, PP367-373.
Chévrier, Jacques. *"Grands écrivains d'Afrique noire et du Maghreb"*, *Jeune Afrique Plus*, No.7, Mai, 1984
Le Critique africain et son peuple comme producteur de civilisation, Colloque de Yaoundé, 19-20 avril, 1973 (Présence Africaine 107). Paris: Présence Africaine, 1978.
Echenim, Kester. *"La structure narrative des Soleils des Indépendances"*, *Présence Africaine*, 107: 1978.
——— *"Aspects de l'écriture dans le roman africain, Panorama de la littérature négro-africaine des années 80"*, *Présence*

Africaine, 139: 1986.

———— "*De l'Oralité dans le roman africain*", *Peuples noirs, Peuples Africains*, 24: 1981.

Gassama, Makhily. *La langue d'Ahmadou Kourouma ou le français sous le soleil d'Afrique*. Paris: ACCT-KARTHALA, 1965.

Irele, Abiola. "African Literature and the Language Question", Colloque de Yaoundé, 16-20 avril, 1973. Paris: Présence Africaine, 1977.

Ngal, Georges. *"Création et rupture en littérature africaine."* Paris: L'Harmattan, 1994.

Ngalasso, M. M. "*Le dilemne des langues africaines*", *Au-dela du prix Nobel, Notre Librairie*, No. 98: juillet/septembre, 1989.

Ngandu Nkashama. Interview by B. Magnier in *Présence Africaine*, 133/134, 1985: pp.260-267.2.

Ricard, Alain. "*Langues africaines et littérature*". *ASCALF Yearbook*, No.2: 1997.

Senghor, L. S. *Liberté I. Négritude et humanisme*. Paris: Seuil, 1964.

Tidjani-Serpos, N. "*L'Ecrivain africain: griot contemporain*". *Au-dela du Prix Nobel, Notre Librairie*, No. 98: juillet/septembre, 1989.

7

A PANORAMA OF THE FRANCOPHONE AFRICAN NOVEL FROM THE 1920s TO THE 1990s

Victor Aire

> *On ne peut vouloir le rayonnement de la culture africaine si l'on ne contribue pas concrètement à l'existence des conditions de cette culture, c'est-à-dire à la libération du continent.*
>
> (Frantz Fanon, p.165).

Prolegomenon

The itinerary of the Francophone African novel is reminiscent of the fate of fruits, such as mangoes, which are often prematurely picked and whose ripening process is hastened with heaps of ash: the novel had barely bloomed when it had to assume maturity; it had barely been imported when it had to take up arms to fight racism and colonialism and agitate for the dignity of the black man.

Indeed, soon after its birth, the Francophone African novel was saddled with an anti-racist battle because slavery and the racist prejudices which allowed it to endure for centuries had resulted in the institutionalised dehumanisation of the black man. The anti-colonial battle was also imperative because, despite the official abolition of slavery, the colonialists continued to dehumanise the inhabitants of the colonies from where they derived enormous wealth. This situation elicited from Frantz Fanon this scathing remark: *"L'Europe est littéralement la création du Tiers-monde. Les richesses qui l'étouffent sont celles qui ont été volées aux peuples sous développés" (Fanon, p.59).*

If we recall Jules Ferry's haughty remark that *"les Droits de l'homme ne sont pas faits pour les Nègres"* (quoted by Gourdeau, p.88), then we can understand why, in the face of the duplicitous and hypocritical stance of the colonisers, African writers had to resort to the power of the word in order to wrench those contested human rights. This is the cause to which the Francophone African novel, like the African novel in general, was committed from its inception. It can even be said, without fear of contradiction, that the novel owes its birth to politics, understood etymologically as the affairs of the city, meaning, in this context, the big city composed of the French colonies and their "mother country."

The Senegalese Bakary Diallo's *Force-Bonté*, generally regarded as the first Francophone African novel, was published in 1926. This is why the literary history of the novel usually starts from that year and is envisaged in three major periods: from 1926 to 1944 or the end of the second world war; from 1945 to 1960 (the year of independence) and from 1960 to the present. However, for the purpose of this diachronic study, I would like to adopt a six-part division: 1926-1944, 1945-1959, 1960-1969, 1970-1979, 1980-1989 and 1990 to the present.

1926 to 1944: The Novel between the two World Wars

The first Francophone African novel, Bakary Diallo's *Force-Bonté*, is an autobiography dealing with the author's childhood in Africa, his campaign with the French army in North Africa and his life as a demobilised soldier in France after the first world war. All through his narrative, Diallo undertakes a facile and rather irritating panegyric France, which incidentally explains the title *Strength and Benevolence*.

The second Francophone African novel was Ousmane Socé's *Karim, roman sénégalais*, published in 1935. In this work, the Senegalese writer uses the experiences of a young compatriot to dramatise the moral upheavals resulting from colonisation. Two years later, Socé picked up the same theme of acculturation in *Mirage de Paris*, but in a slightly different form: whereas, in *Karim*, the hero sows his wild oats in the city and returns duly edified to the traditional community, Fara, the bewildered hero of the second novel, cannot find the way back to his roots.

The fourth work of this period preceding the second world war is *Doguicimi*, the historical novel published in 1938 by Paul Hazoumé. This Beninois ethnologist presents the barely fictionalised chronicle of a

19th Century Dahomean kingdom. The work smirks a bit of the adulation of France already mentioned in respect of Bakary Diallo's novel. However, *Doguicimi* is, essentially, a subtle criticism of both colonisation and certain social customs such as human sacrifice. After these four works, the Francophone African novel was to go through a fifteen-years silence.

1945-1959: The Novel Before "The Suns of Independence"

This period is characterised by an increase in the number of published novels, an intensification of anti-colonial agitation and a flourishing of the theme of cultural conflict. In order to further illuminate these developments, it would be necessary to situate them in the political context of the period.

During the second world war, many African soldiers had the opportunity of meeting other black people from other parts of the world. They were thus able to compare their experiences and, in particular, to live with Europeans who, in the colonies, were their so-called "masters." They noticed a glaring contradiction: that, in Europe, France was fighting to resist Germany's colonialist intentions, whereas she herself possessed a colonial empire elsewhere. Having tasted of the fruit of freedom and, believing that, after the war, France would decolonise, Africans were full of hope as they fought side by side with their colonisers. The least that they expected was that there would be a reassessment of the relationship between France and her colonies.

The opportunity for such a reassessment presented itself in January 1944, that is even before the official end of the war, at the Brazzaville conference presided over by General Charles de Gaulle and convened to discuss the political, social and economic reforms demanded by Africans. But, apart from granting a few concessions (such as the termination of forced labour), France categorically refused to consider the eventual independence of the colonies. One of the resolutions taken at the conference declared vehemently:

> *Les fins de l'oeuvre de civilisation accomplie par la France dans les colonies écartent toute idée d'autonomie, toute idée d'évolution hors du bloc français de l'empire: la constitution éventuelle — même lointaine — de "self-*

governments" dans les colonies est à écarter (Soustelle, p. 36).

With the prospect of liberation having been thus postponed indefinitely, African intellectuals had no choice but to intensify their agitation. Novelists, in particular, did not spare any energy in attacking the colonial machine, using methods as diverse as biting satire and the direct description of the evils of colonialism as well as the social conflicts to which it gives rise.

The satirists are mainly the Cameroonians Mongo Beti and Ferdinand Oyono, who were part of the very first crop of writers of the post-war period. In *Une Vie de boy*, published in 1956, Oyono, using the personal diary format, tells the story of the houseboy of a colonial commandant. The indictment of colonisation is all the more biting in that the story is told by a naive narrator who reports everything with a disarming objectivity until he himself falls victim to colonial violence. Beaten to a pulp on the orders of the prison director, for a trumped-up charge, the hero-narrator dies from his wounds in a neighbouring country.

In *Le Vieux nègre et la médaille*, which Oyono published in the same year, the theme is similar, but the denouement is less tragic: an old man who has given all to France — his two sons to the war and his land to the Catholic mission — is decorated with a medal; and the satire lies mainly in the fact that he and his compatriots perceive this decoration as a sign of rapprochement between blacks and whites. They are disillusioned by the old man's misadventures after the decoration: he gets roughed up and thrown into jail. When he is released, he returns home, tired but rid of all his illusions about white men.

Mongo Beti [Alexandre Biyidi's second and definitive pseudonym], who resorts less to satire than humour, is more profound in his criticism of colonialism. In his first novel, *Ville cruelle* (published under his first pseudonym Eza Boto), he describes the disorientation and the tribulations of the peasant in the city, symbol of colonialism. In *Le pauvre Christ de Bomba*, Beti salutes the courage of the natives in holding on to their beliefs in the face of the assaults of colonial officers and missionaries. It is needless to recall that, in the colonial set-up, the mission always lent a helping hand to the colonial administration. The main focus of the novel is, however, the naivety of a missionary who takes twenty years to realise the failure of his evangelisation.

As for Ousmane Sembène, he denounces economic exploitation first in *Le Docker noir*, and then in *O Pays, mon beau peuple*. The former novel depicts the pitiful plight of African and Arab labourers in Marseille, while the latter dramatises the mobilisation of the masses against the economic exploitation meted out by foreign companies. This selfless concern for the masses is also the main characteristic of Sembène's masterpiece, *Les Bouts de bois de Dieu*.

Francophone African writers of the period also tackle the problem of acculturation experienced either, unwittingly, by a black schoolboy compelled to repeat "Our ancestors the Gauls", or by the adult who, on his return from Europe, can no longer identify with his society. The young hero of *Mission terminée* does not even need to go outside his country to realise the inadequacies of colonial education. All that he has to do is see himself through the eyes of the inhabitants of a remote village and the dilemma which he experiences encompasses not only colonial education but colonial life in general. Here is a key passage from this ironically titled novel:

> *Le drame dont souffre notre peuple, c'est celui d'un homme laissé à lui-même dans un monde qui ne lui appartient pas, un monde qu'il n'a pas fait, un monde où il ne comprend rien. C'est le drame d'un homme sans direction intellectuelle, d'un homme marchant à l'aveuglette, la nuit, dans un quelconque New York hostile* (Beti, *Mission*, pp.250-251).

The most harrowing example of this social conflict is the one described in Cheikh Hamidou Kane's *L'Aventure ambiguë*, a novel published in 1961, but which deals with the colonial period. The work adopts the three-tier structure very common at the time: in a first stage, the writer presents the often happy childhood of the hero; in the second phase, we see his arrival in France, where he experiences uprooting and alienation. Finally, on his return to Africa, he is so distraught that he can no longer adjust. Such is the itinerary followed by the hero of *L'Aventure ambiguë* before he falls victim to a homicide that has all the appearances of a suicide.

It would be quite incorrect to think that all the novelists of this period were overtly militant. Far from it. For example, *L'Enfant noir*, the very first novel published after the second world war, does not decry colonialism. The author, Camara Laye, deals with acculturation while celebrating African authenticity. But, as will be shown later, this celebration of traditional Africa had an equally militant objective.

Indeed, apart from the open militancy and commitment of the novelists, the most striking characteristic of the novel of this period was its sociological realism of which *L'Enfant noir* constitutes a perfect example. Some novelists set out to present a faithful picture of their society, thus transforming themselves, so to speak, into ethnologists. This sociological realism was motivated by the political and cultural commitment of the novelist who saw himself as the voice of subjugated people and the custodian of their cultural heritage.

Indeed, the novelist, as a mouthpiece, had as his first audience the public in the "mother country" and the liberal opinion whom he thought could bring pressure to bear on the architects of the colonial machine if only to alleviate the conditions. Unfortunately, the French public was quite ignorant of the real situation prevailing in the colonies. European travellers and lovers of the exotic brought back from there mostly anecdotes capable of justifying colonisation. Even French ethnology betrayed its scientific calling by wittingly or unwittingly endorsing the colonial enterprise, as is illustrated by Lucien Lévy-Bruhl's claim that "primitive people" did not have the same mental capability as Europeans. This was his thesis in works like *Fonctions mentales dans les sociétés inférieures*. In his posthumously published *Carnets*, Lévy-Bruhl renounced his thesis, but nobody paid any more attention to him.

Consequently, the African novelist saw it as his duty to demystify such wrong preconceptions about Africa. This explains the preponderance of novels depicting the African and attempting to show that he is a man like all other men and also illustrating the specificity of his culture as is evident from titles such as *Le Fils du fétiche*, *L'Enfant noir* and *Le Docker noir*.

Briefly then, in the 1950s, the African novelist, just like the historian, was under the moral obligation to put his pen at the service of his people, either by working for her liberation or by preserving her culture. All these factors contributed to making the novel of the period a social document with an easily verifiable sociological content.

As is to be expected, these exigences also left their mark on the formal aspect of the novel. Indeed, writers of the period had a predilection for real or fictionalised autobiography. This mode, which afforded the opportunity to talk about oneself and one's experiences, was no doubt most convenient for direct activism. This also explains the frequency of "fictional diaries" which facilitated criticism and satire through the viewpoint of a naive narrator.

Commitment and realism were thus some of the most striking characteristics of the Francophone West African novel of the 1950s. By courageously assuming their responsibility, the writers and, especially the novelists, thus contributed to the advent of independence.

1960-1969: The Francophone Novel in the Sixties

This third period of the history of the Francophone African novel can be subdivided into two stages: the first one runs from 1960 to 1965 and the second one, from 1965 to 1969 or thereabout. During the first five years after independence, very few novels were published. Some works, perhaps in press for years still deal with the colonial period. For instance, the Cameroonian Jacques Kuoh-Moukouri published *Doigts-noirs*, an autobiographical work based on his career as a writer/interpreter under the colonial administration; in *Le Rescapé de l'Ethylos*, finished in November 1952 but published in 1963, Mamadou Gologo narrates a real-life experience and warns against alcoholism, which he considers as a colonial heritage.

Some themes are still prevalent, like acculturation and generational conflict which we see in Seydou Badian's *Sous l'orage*. The social and progressive aspect is still prominent as is shown in Bhêly-Quénum's *Le Chant du lac* and the Togolese Félix Couchoro's *L'Héritage, cette peste*. Bernard Dadié displays his satirical and humorous talents in *Patron de New York*, a kind of American version of *Un Nègre à Paris*.

In some of the works published during the first half of the decade, one discerns a certain justified euphoria as well as a wait-and-see attitude. Writers, and novelists in particular, wait patiently to see what the new leaders will make of the vaunted independence, bloodily conquered in some countries, but handed over, in some others, on a platter of gold. Hopes were raised and expectations were high.

But, as a few writers were quick to perceive, it was futile expecting a genuine renewal because most of the new regimes had made a *faux pas* which could only lead to disaster. This false start consisted in the fact that the vestiges of the colonial system had not been completely extirpated. In too much haste to take off, we had not considered that the colonial structure which we inherited and maintained as such was designed for a situation of domination and so could not satisfy our democratic aspirations; we had not bothered to obliterate all signs of the past in order to make a fresh, new start. And as the refuse left under the carpet by a previous tenant surfaced intermittently and embarrassingly, so did the inadequacies and contradictions, on which we hoped to graft our democracy, corrupt and invalidate our efforts at nation building. That was why, all over the continent, a few armed men thought they could do better at statecraft, and thus, like a contagious epidemic, from country to country, most of Africa came to be governed from "the barrel of a gun".

And so the scene was set for the works published in the second half of the sixties, a period which saw African novelists reverting to their pre-independence stance of virulent, acrimonious denunciations of the *status quo* and of happenings in the African society. The main targets were different: writers, some of whom had spent time in jail, were now faced with black (African) leaders who, having pledged to lead their people from the colonial deserts into the independent and supposedly bountiful new-found land, betrayed that trust and sought only to line the pockets of their three-piece suits or long flowing robes. As the British historian, Basil Davidson, aptly puts it,

> "neo-colonialism" during the second half of the 1960s acquired a native dress and form, so that political independence, more often than not, remained little more than a facade for ideological and economic subservience (Davidson, p.148).

Indeed, some of the novels published between 1965 and 1969 testify to Davidson's assessment of the period. While some works such as Charles Nokan's *Violent était le vent* criticise the tyranny and oppressive character of the new oligarchy in shameless collaboration with their former masters, now operating from the backstage, others, like Ahmadou Kourouma's *Les Soleils des Indépendances*, decry the alarming incidence of single party systems and the acts of arbitrary arrests and imprisonments that these parties have to resort to in order to retain their grip on the oppressed masses. It is not surprising that these novels by Nokan and Kourouma end with the death of the main characters, for death became one of the instruments used by African writers to denounce the violence so prevalent in many African countries.

On balance then, the sixties were, both on the social and fictional levels, a period of light and darkness; and given the high hopes that had been raised at independence and the way these hopes were soon shattered, it is not surprising that the negative aspects of the period tend to linger more in people's minds, as is evident in this gloomy assessment by the Senegalese political scientist, Pathé Diagne :

> L'échec de ces dix années, inscrit dans le bilan des constructions politico-économiques, idéologico-culturelles de l'Afrique occidentale, traduit, avant tout, une incapacité à dégager une conscience et une force politique qui unissent les masses ouest-africaines, pour conquérir leur cadre naturel de vie (Diagne, p.36).

This balance-sheet of the sixties, drawn up with immediate reference to West Africa, is of course, applicable to the whole continent.

1970-1979: The Francophone Novel in the Seventies

As in previous decades, not all the works published in the seventies deal directly with that period. Some of the writers continue to assess the impact of independence in Africa, which means that most of the themes prevalent in the fifties and early sixties are still present in the seventies. In fact, quite a number of the novels bestride either the colonial and post-colonial eras or the sixties and the seventies. This tendency should not necessarily suggest that writers are obsessed with colonisation, although that could be true for certain novelists. I think that the intention of the writers is to place African independence in perspective, to recall the hopes and euphoria that had ushered in liberation and by so doing to further highlight the problems of the period. But, generally, the novel was more centripetal, more introspective than during the earlier periods, because its main preoccupations were now within Africa, although there is no doubt that neo-colonialism was still practised, not only by Africans alone, but also clandestinely by some of the former masters. Thus, as Jean-Pierre Makouta-Mboukou says, with reference to the African writer:

"*Il accuse encore parfois l'Occident ; mais il accuse aussi et surtout les responsables nègres. Dès lors l'enfer n'est plus seulement l'Occident, c'est aussi le monde nègre*" (Makouta-Mboukou, p.165).

And it was to that black world that the novel addressed itself above all, in contrast to the colonial period when African writers had Western audiences in mind much more than their fellow Africans. This tendency seems to have changed, somewhat, not only the content but also the form of the African novel. Whereas most novelists, writing under colonialism, often indulged in unwieldy sociological glosses, conscious as they were of addressing an uninitiated reading public, the writers of the seventies greatly reduced the long treatises on traditional practices. This may explain why some novelists, unable to make the required transition from sociological glosses to real fiction, fell by the wayside, having realised the folly of explaining to Africans their own traditional customs and beliefs. This does not, however, mean that the ideological content receded. Far from it, the novel was still generally as committed as it was at its inception.

This change in content brought about a corresponding change in style. Whereas during the fifties and the early sixties, most novels were quasi-autobiographies, narrating, in a more or less linear progression, the experiences of an individual, and leaving little room for introspection, the novel in the seventies was more akin to the twentieth century European novel in the sense that more attention was paid to the inner life, to the psychology of the protagonist. The storytelling was often less linear; the narrative voice broken and the genres rather mixed, with different techniques involved. The narrator, where there is one, is less omniscient and accords more independence to characters.

But, on the whole, taking theme and style into consideration, it would seem that the seventies did not bring too much of a change to the African Francophone novel. For instance, in the early sixties, it was customary to evoke neo-colonialism in African socio-political affairs. The same tendency is discernible in the seventies. Thus we read in Ousmane Sembène's 1973 novel *Xala* :

> *Nous voulons la place de l'ex-occupant.*
> *Nous y sommes (...) Quoi de changé, en général*
> *comme en particulier? Rien. Le colon est devenu*
> *plus fort, plus puissant, caché en nous... Il*
> *nous promet les restes du festin si nous sommes*
> *sages* (Sembène, *Xala*, p.139).

This auto-critical diatribe is, however, not born of a desire to see a change in the *status quo*. It is rather the selfish riposte of an individual abandoned by his peers, unleashing his last shots before accepting his lot. *Xala*, a novel replete with sexual symbols, and whose cinematographic adaptation was banned in Dakar in 1975, marks a departure from Sembène's previous fictional works. While pursuing as relentlessly as ever his two favourite themes - the oppression of the masses and the emancipation of women - Sembène this time attacks the man and the bourgeois through the prime instrument of his crime - his phallus ('xala' in Wolof means sexual impotence). It is the sexual impotence inflicted on a middle-class business man, already saddled with two wives and many children, who decides to take a young hot-blooded girl as a third wife. It is, by extension, the impotence, or castration, of an arrogant, domineering middle class which feeds on the masses, while pretending to be their benefactor.

However, sexual impotence is just one of the numerous themes treated by *Xala*. There are other more important ones such as polygamy and its nefarious social and psychological consequences; there is also the issue of the use of occult powers, for the protagonist's sexual impotence is attributed to the supernatural powers of a beggar, whose family was once despoiled by El Hadj Kader Bèye, the protagonist.

However, by far the most important theme, which the sexual impotence corroborates, is the problem of a political independence bedevilled and vitiated by economic dependence, for without the latter the former is impossible. Although this state of affairs can be attributed to the false start made at independence, the leaders of the period are usually held responsible as well. They are blamed, as in *Xala*, for their inability to lead the masses out of famine, indigence and illiteracy towards a cultural, economic, political, spiritual and moral revival

Although Sembène presents in *Xala* a pessimistic picture of Africa's evolution, as one would expect from the realist that he is, he, however, gives it an ideological twist at the end by seemingly giving the masses of the downtrodden and wretched the last say: in the final scene of the novel, the protagonist, completely ruined, is humiliated by beggars and lepers who make him strip down while they shower him with saliva. This is perhaps Sembène's way of subscribing to the popular Marxist belief that the masses are the ultimate repository of real power; that they alone, having suffered the most alienation, possess the means of bringing about a genuine and authentic liberation. It is perhaps in this light that one should interpret the fact that Kader Bèye's impotence is caused by a miserable beggar.

Ousmane Sembène may have been Africa's first feminist writer, but he has long since ceased to be alone in this category, for he was joined in the seventies by other female and male feminist writers, amongst whom is no less a novelist than Mongo Beti. At least that is the light in which this veteran Cameroonian writer appears in one of his novels of the seventies: *Perpétue et l'habitude du malheur*, published in 1974. Set in the Cameroons a decade after her independence, *Perpétue* takes up some of the now familiar themes, but above all it tackles two related issues: on the one hand, it decries the deplorable condition of the Cameroonian woman, as illustrated by the fate of the heroine, Perpétue. On the other hand, it carries out an 'autopsy' of the decolonisation of the Cameroons, while highlighting what the writer calls *"une colossale machine de despotisme sanguinaire agencée à la hâte dès la veille de l'indépendance"* (p.269).

On one level, *Perpétue* is the study of the martyrdom of a young girl destined by her education to succeed in life, but who is prematurely thrust, by an avaricious mother, into the arms of a mediocre civil servant. Thereafter, she suffers a slow moral and physical degradation; in order to rise in rank, her incompetent husband prostitutes her to a higher officer, who fathers her second child. Wanting, for once, to assert her independence, she takes a lover of her own free will. But during her third pregnancy, which results from this liaison, her jealous husband makes her life extremely miserable until death frees her from him forever.

In a way, *Perpétue* reads like a detective story, for it is long after her death that her brother reconstructs *"le chemin de croix parcouru de son vivant par sa soeur"* (p.48). At the end of his investigation, the self-appointed knight-errant commits a carefully meditated and coldly executed fratricide, a crime which provides the final proof of the decadence of the regime, for, although the criminal gives himself up, he goes unpunished.

Such then are the bare bones of *Perpétue et l'habitude du malheur*, whose tragic heroine is a symbolic figure. She is the symbol of the Cameroons in particular and of young Africa in general, an Africa opposed to the Africa of yesteryears, aptly represented by Perpétue's cruel mother. Perpétue's experiences in her short life are similar to those of Africa. Just as the girl is helpless in the face of her tyrannical mother, so also Africa had to succumb to a stronger force. Like Perpétue, Africa was later raped, raided, plundered and exploited mercilessly. For both Africa and the young woman, the only ray of hope soon turned out to be nothing but a mirage. For Africa, it was independence, for the woman it is her amorous affair with a popular soccer star, an affair which she justifies as follows:

> *Pour la premiere fois, j'ai envie de n'en faire qu'à ma tête. Jusqu'ici, j'ai fait tout ce qu'on me demandait de*

faire [...] Eh bien, je saurais pour une fois à quoi ressemble la saveur des choses qu'on accomplit de sa propre volonté (Perpétue, p.238).

Does this not remind one of the eve of independence in Africa, when African nations thought they were finally about to take their destiny in their own hands? Just as Perpétue's attempt at auto-determination fails and leads to her death after a brief period of euphoria, so African independence lost its meaning and became in many country a bloody tyranny. So, in both cases, the oppressive forces had only made a momentary withdrawal which the unsuspecting victim took for victory. But the scales have since fallen off all eyes : the real liberation is yet to come, while the young woman prefers the oblivion and invulnerability bestowed by death. Thus, beyond its rather melodramatic plot, Mongo Beti presents in *Perpétue* an indictment of a tyrannical and bloody regime. The same preoccupation is evident in *Remember Ruben*, also published in 1974. In fact, these two novels are like the fictional reproduction of Beti's socio-political treatise *Main basse sur le Cameroun* which was banned on its appearance in 1972. And, at the risk of flogging a near-dead horse, Beti continued his fictional history of the Cameroons in his 1979 novel, *La Ruine presque cocasse d'un polichinelle.*

The most representative of the novels of the seventies is perhaps Williams Sassine's *Wirriyamu* which appeared in 1976. Most representative in the sense that it deals with events situated directly within the decade, the most significant of which is the liberation of Lusophone African countries. Williams Sassine (whose first novel *Saint Monsieur Baly* appeared in 1973) does for these countries what others have done for Francophone and Anglophone countries, that is denouncing Portugal's so-called civilising mission in her overseas territories which she considered as an extension of the mother country. And in these territories, in the words of Salazar, quoted by one of the characters, *"il ne saurait...y avoir de nationalisme qui ne soit portugais* (p.147)". Fortunately, the march of history has since given the lie to these misguided colonialists.

Briefly, *Wirriyamu* deals with the experiences of a Francophone poet, Kabalango, when he makes a stop-over in the Portuguese-speaking village of Wirriyamu, around which resound echoes of the battle of liberation from Portuguese fascism. While waiting for the weekly bus that connects with his village, Kabalango gets to know what Sassine describes as *"ce petit village agonisant, dans cette colonie oubliée avec des hommes perdus"* (p. 65). That is the uninviting setting in which the tuberculous and downcast poet meets the small population of blacks and whites all at the end of their tether. It is as if, already bled white by the exploitation and tortures of the colonialist, rid of its able-bodied men, the village were merely waiting for the *coup de grâce*. This finishing stroke soon comes when two important strands of the plot are brought together in Wirriyamu: these are, on the one hand, the kidnapping by some freedom fighters, of Augustinho, son of the Portuguese commanding officer D'Arriaga, and, on the other, the latter's efforts to find his son and his kidnappers.

First to arrive in Wirriyamu with his forces, D'Arriaga orders the systematic torture, rape and execution of the villagers, in an attempt to make them reveal the hide-out of the freedom-fighters who, meanwhile, are heading for the same village. At the end of the inevitable battle that follows their arrival, all the villagers and Portuguese soldiers are dead, with the exception of four taken prisoner. One of the supreme and tragic ironies of this sad story is that the hostage, in whose name D'Arriaga massacres a village of sixty odd souls, is himself killed during the battle. This blood-bath is thus a morbid dramatisation of the atrocious and deadly fascism practised in Africa for five centuries by Portugal under its racist and hypocritical policy of Lusotropicalism.

Wirriyamu, constructed like a war diary, with hourly entries, and written in a felicitous and appealing style, can be considered as the best tribute so far paid to the valiant struggle of Lusophone freedom-fighters in Africa against their former colonial masters. But it closes on a disturbing note. Months after the Wirriyamu massacre, an attempt is made on the life of one of the leaders of the freedom-fighters by a rival faction. The would-be victim muses: *"les Portugais ne sont pas encore partis que deja on commence à s'entredéchirer pour le pouvoir"* (*Wirriyamu*, p. 199). This is perhaps a reference to the liberation war in Angola, where rival forces continued to fight one another long after the departure of the Portuguese.

Thus, one of the dominant themes of the novel of the seventies is violence, which was, no doubt, a reflection of the society itself. In the next section, devoted to the novel of the eighties, we shall see if this theme of violence is as prevalent.

1980-1989: The Francophone Novel in the Eighties

It should be pointed out from the onset of this section that the fiction of this period still bears a lot of resemblance to what it was in preceding decades. In fact, there are novels, which contain themes and stylistic devices prevalent in the seventies and even during the colonial period. Thus, the theme of colonialism is taken up again by *Bernard Dadié, Jean-Marie Adiaffi, Massa Makan Diabaté* and *Tchicaya U Tam'Si*. As I pointed out earlier, this return to the colonial period is motivated by the revaluation and correction of the false colonial history disseminated by the very architects of colonisation.

Other themes inherited from the colonial period include fictionalised ethnology and the generational gap. The former is evident in Okoumba-Nkoghe's *La Mouche et la glu* and Jean Christophe Casu's *La Force de l'amour*, while the latter theme is taken up by Ibrahim Sèye in *Un trou dans le miroir*, amongst others. There is, additionally, the theme of the fortunes and misfortunes of mixed marriages depicted in novels like Mongo Beti's *Les Deux mères de Guillaume Ismaël Dzewatama*, Jean Dodo's *Le Médiateur* and Elisabeth Delaygue's *Mestizo*.

Mention must also be made of the thematic of the city which takes on a particular colouration during the eighties. Thus, (the Senegalese) writer, Pape Pathé Diop, situates the action of *La Poubelle* not just in the city, but in a popular neighbourhood of Dakar. This is the Medina, with its communal tea sessions, its Muslim festivals and, in particular, the story of the eponymous dustbin overflowing with electrical appliances supposedly discarded by Camara, a mere civil servant. But his reputation slumps overnight when the neighbourhood learns that the dustbin actually belongs to an American couple. Camara leaves the neighbourhood and, at the end of the novel, he has become a tramp scavenging Dakar's biggest dustbin, a *deus ex machina* which adds very little to the rather scanty plot of *La Poubelle*.

Another important and recurrent theme of the novel of the eighties was that of political denunciation. Indeed, as in the sixties and seventies, writers continued to denounce the ineptitude of indigenous African regimes which, for more than thirty years, had been trying to effect self-rule. The pitiful and often bloody state of affairs is depicted in novels like Jean-Marie Adiaffi's *La Carte d'identité*, Sony Labou Tansi's *L'Etat honteux*, Yodi Karone's *Le Bal des caïmans*, Henri Lopes' *Le Pleurer-rire* and Okoumba-Nkoghe's *La Mouche et la glu*.

A new form of denunciation was political fiction introduced by a veteran of the African novel, Ousmane Sembene, author of the two-volume *Le Dernier de l'empire*. Despite the *incipit* in which the writer denies any resemblance between the work and reality, *Le Dernier de l'empire* is a fictionalised history – or "faction": fact and fiction – of Senegal from its birth to the date of publication of the work.

This stylisation of factual and often verifiable events leads us to another characteristic of the novel of the eighties. If we recall that African dictators take exception to any form of opposition, whether implicit or explicit, then we will appreciate why some novelists devised new forms of transgression. Some of their works give the impression that the creators deliberately set out to confuse the reader, perhaps in order to protect themselves from possible censorship. There is, for instance, the nebulous setting of *Le Pleurer-rire* which the narrator situates

Quelque part au nord ou au sud de l'Equateur... Semble-t-il en Afrique, mais pas forcément. Pourquoi pas en quelque autre continent de la planète, de nos rêves ou de nos cauchemars. A rechercher, je l'ai déjà dit beaucoup plus dans le temps et en nous-mêmes que sur les cartes de géographie (p.290).

Thus, by locating the stifling atmosphere of his novel in a kind of 'no man's land', Henri Lopes protects himself from the tyrants and also gives his work a universal outlook.

The escape through dreams which is evident in the passage just quoted is even more prevalent in some other novels. Thus, anyone reading Yodi Karone's *Nègre de paille* can easily be disconcerted by the alternation between dream and reality, an alternation reproduced typographically by the use of roman and italic scripts. Interrogated on this recourse to dream and fantasy, Yodi Karone replied:

"J'exprime la liberté par la juxtaposition du conte, de la fable, du rêve que fait mon personnage, avec la réalité de tous les jours, avec ses mesquineries et ses traîtrises" (Magnier, "Entretien avec Yodi Karone", p.11).

Similarly, Sony Labou Tansi claims never to establish a real division between reality and magic. Indeed, one of the abiding features of Tansi's craft of fiction is the recourse to the improbable and the grotesque, a technique which aptly renders the horror of the situation that he describes.

Finally, I would like to mention a theme that was more of a renewal than an innovation, namely drug addiction. As I mentioned under the section devoted to the novel of the sixties, in 1963, Mamadou Gologo's *Le Rescapé de l'éthylos* had condemned dipsomania. In 1984, the Senegalese Abasse Ndione attacked drug addiction in his novel *La Vie en spirale*. This is still a very relevant novel, considering how much modern youths are attracted to hallucinogenic drugs. It is no doubt the same urgency that led Abasse Ndione to publish a sequel *La Vie en spirale II* in 1988.

Out of more than 70 novels identified, only eight were written by women. These works include Mariama Bâ's posthumous *Un Chant écarlate*, Aminata Sow Fall's *L'Appel des arènes* and three works by Nafissatou Diallo. The Cameroonian writer Werewere Liking published two novels: *Orphée Dafric* and *Elle sera de jaspe et de corail*. The eighth novel listed is Elisabeth Delaygue's *Mestizo*.

Werewere Liking's *Elle sera de jaspe et de corail*, sub-titled *journal d'une misovire* and *chant-roman*, is unclassifiable and polyphonic in structure because it combines various genres: prose, poetry, theatre and song. The work is essentially an allegory of Africa nicknamed Lunai with two characters discussing diverse topics such as negritude, African independence and aesthetics. The female narrator concludes by preaching a balanced feminism, since her fundamental motivation is the search for positive humanism:

> Quand l'homme ne jouera plus au porc
> Quand la femme ne sera plus chienne en chaleur
> Quand je ne serai plus misovire et qu'il n'y aura plus de misogynes
> Quand il n'y aura plus que des Etres en quête d'un mieux devenir et d'un mieux Etre *(Elle sera de jaspe,* p.153*)*.

Although the composition is more traditional, Delaygue's *Mestizo* is no less disconcerting. A vast polyphonic work, started by the ancestor Jeferson Richard Ndiaye, continued and completed by his grand-daughter Kémi Jean de Lourès, the story depicts three generations of mulattoes and closely follows the history of the twentieth century in Africa, Europe and North and South America. On the whole, *Mestizo* is an often harrowing celebration of mycegenation as a preparation for the advent of a world where *il n'y aura plus bientôt de 'races pures* (p.140). And this is thanks to the intercontinental miscegenation which leads Kémi Jean de Lourès, mulatto grand-daughter of an African, to marry a Nicaraguayan and engender the "Mestizo."

Elle sera de jaspe et de corail and *Mestizo* are thus the only two novels written by women among the corpus studied. It would then seem that, in the eighties, fiction writing was still a preserve of men.

As we turn to the craft of fiction, it is gratifying to note that many of the works published in the eighties contribute to the aesthetic and linguistic renewal of the medium. Hence, the increasing frequency of such practices as intertextuality, metatextuality as well as linguistic and structural experimentation. This last phenomenon is present in the trilogy published during the decade by the late Congolese writer Tchicaya U. Tam'si, namely *Les Cancrelats, Les Méduses ou les orties de mer* and *Les Phalènes*. Indeed, the entomological, animalistic and vegetal titles of these novels can be subjected to interesting interpretations in the light of the characters and the events exploited.

The fairly new practice of metatextuality finds its best illustration in the work of yet another Congolese writer, Henri Lopes. His novel *Le Pleurer-rire* contains numerous corrective and auto-critical passages. Thus Lopes creates an alter ego who is supposed to read the chapters as they are written and who either praises or rebukes, as in this passage:

> *Vous me faites peur avec toutes ces scènes d'amour trop osées ... tel qu'évolue votre manuscrit, je crains que cédant trop à des souvenirs intimes, vous mêliez les genres et perdiez de vue l'objectif fondamental de tout écrit engagé (Le Pleurer-rire,* p.123).

The final feature of the novel of the eighties which I would like to mention is intertextuality. It will be recalled that in the seventies, the Malian writer Yambo Ouologuem had incurred the accusation of plagiarism because, according to him, he had borrowed bits of texts from other writers, without, however, giving them credit. And yet, during the 1980s, this practice, which was normally considered as a literary theft, was no longer frowned upon. For example, in *Le Pleurer-rire*, Henri Lopes borrows more than a page from Denis Diderot's *Jacques le fataliste*. The more traditional form of intertextuality is quite frequent in the works of Congolese writers of the period who often dedicated their novels to one another. Thus, Sony Labou Tansi dedicates *L'Etat honteux* to "H. Lopes et U.Tam'si" and *Les Sept solitudes de Lorsa Lopez* to the same Lopes and Sylvain Bemba. On his part, Bemba dedicates *Le Soleil est parti à M'Pemba* partly to two other Congolese, namely, Jean Malonga and Jean-Baptiste Tati-Loutard.

As can be surmised from the last few pages, the Francophone novel of the eighties was a rich heterogeneity of style and content, attesting to the accrued independence of African writers who manipulated the imported fictional mode in ways that were totally creative and original.

1990-1998: The Francophone Novel in the Nineties

As every painter or lover of painting knows, in order to fully appreciate a completed painting, the observer has to stand at a distance from it. Looking at the nineties from the year 1998 is tantamount to trying to assess the picture before it is fully completed. Nevertheless, one can venture to draw tentative conclusions, which can be modified subsequently as necessary. This section will therefore be devoted to a tentative examination of the Francophone novel published between 1990 and 1998.

A careful look at some of the novels so far published in this decade reveals that they are characterised by more or less the same tendencies as in the eighties. As for the writers themselves, a few old masters have retreated into silence (Ferdinand Oyono, Bernard Dadié), while some have actually broken a silence of one or more decades: in 1990, Ahmadou Kourouma published his second novel, *Monnè, outrages et défis*. Similarly, nearly thirty-five years after the appearance of *L'Aventure ambiguë*, Cheikh Hamidou Kane published *Les Gardiens du Temple*. The novelist and film maker, Ousmane Sembène, also converted a film scenario into the novel titled *Guelwaar*.

Amongst novelists of the second generation, two died within the present decade: the Congolese Sony Labou Tansi passed away in June 1995 and the Guinean Williams Sassine died in February 1997, but not without leaving a sort of swan song: Tansi's *Le Commencement des douleurs* came out in the year that he died, while Sassine's *Mémoire d'une peau* appeared after his death in 1998. Some other members of the second generation remained consistent in their publications. Henri Lopes published *Le Chercheur d'Afriques* in 1990, *Sur l'autre rive* in 1992 and *Le Lys et le flamboyant* in 1997. Francis Bebey's *L'Enfant-pluie* came out in 1994, while Tierno Monénembo published *Pelourinho* in 1995.

Apart from the writers of the first two generations, some others — much younger — discovered in the eighties blossomed fully in the current decade. The Senegalese Boubacar Boris Diop, whose first novel *Le Temps de Tamango* appeared in 1981, continued with his peculiar anachronistic and experimental narrative. The female novelists have also fared well in this decade. Aminata Sow Fall published *Le Jujubier du patriarche*. The Cameroonian, Calixthe Beyala, whose first novel *C'est le soleil qui m'a brûlée* appeared in 1988, has since published at least five more novels this decade.

Some other newcomers worth mentioning are Tita Mandeleau, author of *Signare Anna ou le voyage aux escales* (1991), Abdoulaye Elimane Kane who, in 1992, published *La Maison au figuier*, as well as the Malian Moussa Bissan, author of *Un Mariage de raison* (1996).

During the first few years of the nineties, one notices a frequency of novels that deal with not just the colonial period but also the period preceding the colonial experience. As I mentioned earlier while discussing the novel of the seventies, certain writers return to the past, especially the colonial past, in order to correct the inaccurate colonial historiography written and disseminated by the proponents of colonialism.

As for the writers that tend to resuscitate a past preceding even the colonial period, I think that two reasons can be found to justify the practice. First of all, there is the need to record as much of the oral tradition as possible before its main custodians — the elders — die off in the face of the encroachment of modern technology. Secondly, it would seem that, despite the use of the written medium, the modern African writer feels more at home in the oral medium. In fact, he would seem to want to be considered as a modern 'griot.'

That, then, is the context within which we can situate some recent novels which combine oral and written literature to produce what has come to be known as "oraliture." This syncretism is present in Ahmadou Kourouma's *Monnè, outrages et défis*, which revolves around the history of a Malinke dynasty spread over more than a century and having as its linchpin King Djigui who had to succumb to the superior power of French forces. The novel culminates in the single party system of the twentieth century. As in *Les Soleils des Indépendances*, the work is characterised by a multiplicity of narrative voices, frequency of flashbacks and numerous local proverbs. Kourouma also repeats the practice of using, as chapter headings, sentences drawn from each of the seventeen chapters.

Characterised also by frequent flashbacks and flash forwards, Aminata Sow Fall's *Le Jujubier du patriarche* is a typical example of the marriage of oral and written literature. In fact, the incursion into the oral tradition is so dominant that the reader is virtually bewildered. Although Cheikh Hamidou Kane's *Les Gardiens du temple* also starts in the distant past, it combines folklore, history and fiction and culminates in the political tension prevalent during the early years of independence. Early in the novel, Kane makes overt references to the hero of his first novel, *L'Aventure ambiguë*.

Tita Mandeleau's *Signare Anna ou le voyage aux escales* and Abdoulaye Elimane Kane's *La Maison au figuier* also combine colonial history and fiction, the difference being that Abdoulaye Kane adds the magical dimension to his novel. As is to be expected, this propensity for fictionalised history often vitiates the writers' craft. Such is the case with the works of Mandeleau and Abdoulaye Kane.

As for our final example, Moussa Bissan's *Un Mariage de raison*, set in an urban contemporary milieu, its numerous weaknesses can perhaps be attributed to poor editing and the greenness of the author himself. These few examples of novels published so far seem to point the way to the Francophone fiction of the future, and perhaps of the Twenty-First Century.

Conclusion

In this chapter, I have endeavoured to present a panorama of the Francophone African novel published since 1926. I have mentioned the committed nature of the fiction from its very inception; its major characteristics in terms of form and content as well as the promises that it holds out for the future. As the most recent works indicate, the novelists, concerned about the fast disappearing traditional African heritage, now seem to favour a mixture of oral and written literature, a combination which has now led to the neologism "*oraliture*." Whether, in the new millennium, this will turn out to be a dead end or a positive development, only time will tell.

References

Adiaffi, Jean-Marie. *La carte d'identité*. Abidjan: CEDA, 1980.1935.
Ananou, David. *Le Fils du fétiche*. 1955; reprint; Paris: Nouvelles éditions latines, 1971.
Bâ, Mariama. *Un Chant écarlate*. Dakar: Nouvelles Editions Africaines (N.E.A.), 1982.
——— *Une si longue lettre*. Dakar: N.E.A., 1979.
Badian, Seydou. *Sous l'orage*. Paris: Présence Africaine, 1963.
——— *Noces sacrés*. Paris: Présence Africaine, 1977.
Bebey, Francis. *L'Enfant-pluie*. Saint-Maur: Sepia, 1994.
——— *Le Roi Albert d'Effidi*. Yaoundé: Editions CLE, 1976.
Bemba, Sylvain. *Le Soleil est parti à M'Pemba*. Paris: Présence Africaine, 1982.
Beti, Mongo. *Les deux mères de Guillaume Ismaël Dzewatama*. Paris: Buchet/Chastel, 1982.
——— *Main basse sur le Cameroun*. 1972; reprint. Québec: Editions québécoises, 1974.
——— *Mission terminée*. Paris: Corrêa-Buchet-Chastel, 1957.
——— *Le Pauvre Christ de Bomba*. Paris: Laffont, 1956.
——— *Perpétue et l'habitude du malheur*. Paris: Buchet/Chastel, 1974.
——— *La Ruine presque cocasse d'un polichinelle*. Paris: Editions des peuples noirs,1979.
——— [Eza Boto]. *Ville cruelle* in *Présence Africaine*: "Trois écrivains noirs," 1954; reprint; Paris: Présence Africaine, 1971.
Beyala, Calixthe. *Assèze l'Africaine*. Paris: Albin Michel, 1994.
——— *C'est le soleil qui m'a brûlée*. Paris: Stock, 1987.
——— *Maman a un amant*. Paris: Albin Michel, 1993.
Bhêly-Quénum, Olympe. *Le Chant du lac*. Paris: Présence Africaine, 1965.
Bissan, Moussa. *Un Mariage de raison*. Bamako: Editions Jamana, 1996.
Casu, Jean-Christophe. *La force de l'amour*. Dakar: N.E.A. 1985.
Couchoro, Félix. *L'Héritage, cette peste*. Lomé: Editogo, 1963.
Dadié, Bernard. *Commandant Taureault et ses nègres*. Abidjan: CEDA, 1980.
——— *Un Nègre à Paris*. Paris: Présence Africaine, 1959.
——— *Patron de New York*. Paris: Présence Africaine, 1964.

Davidson, Basil. *Which Way Africa?* London: Penguin, 1971.
Delaygue, Elisabeth. *Mestizo.* Paris: Présence Africaine, 1986.
Diabaté, Massa Makan. *Le Boucher de Kouta.* Paris: Hatier, 1982.
————— *Le Coiffeur de Kouta.* Paris: Hatier, 1980.
————— *Le Lieutenant de Kouta.* Paris: Hatier, 1983.
Diagne, Pathé. *Pour l'unité africaine.* Paris: Editions Anthropos, 1972.
Diallo, Bakary. *Force-Bonté.* Paris: F. Rieder & Cie, 1926
Diallo, Nafissatou. *Le Destin de Fary.* Dakar: N.E.A., 1984.
————— *Le Fort maudit.* Paris: Hatier, 1984.
————— *La Princesse de Tiali.* Dakar: N.E.A., 1984.
Diop, Boubacar Boris. *Le Cavalier et son ombre.* Paris: L'Harmattan, 1997.
————— *Le Temps de Tamango.* Paris: L'Harmattan, 1981.
————— *Les Traces de la meute.* Paris: L'Harmattan, 1993.
Diop, Pape Pathé. *La Poubelle.* Paris: Présence Africaine, 1984.
Dodo, Jean. *Le Médiateur.* Dakar: N.E.A., 1984.
Fall, Aminata Sow. *L'Appel des arènes.* Dakar: N.E.A., 1982.
———. *Le Jujubier du patriarche.* Dakar: CAEC Khoudia Editions, 1993.
Fall, Malick. *La Plaie.* Paris: Albin Michel, 1967.
Fanon, Frantz. *Les Damnés de la terre.* Paris: F. Maspero, 1968.
Fantouré, Alioum. *Le Cercle des tropiques.* Paris: Présence Africaine, 1972.
————— *Le Voile ténébreux.* Paris: Présence Africaine, 1985.
Ferry, Jules. in *Journal Officiel,* 29 juillet 1885; quoted by J.P. Gourdeau, *La Littérature négro-africaine d'expression française.* Paris: Hatier, 1973.
Gologo, Mamadou. *Le Rescapé de l'Ethylos.* Paris: Présence Africaine, 1963.
Hazoumé, Paul. *Doguicimi.* Paris: Larose, 1938.
Kane, Cheikh Hamidou. *L'Aventure ambiguë.* Paris: Julliard, 1961.
————— *Les Gardiens du temple.* Paris: Editions Stock, 1995.
Kane, Abdoulaye Elimane. *La Maison au figuier.* Dakar: *Les Nouvelles Editions Africaines du Sénégal, 1992.*
Karone, Yodi. *Le Bal des caïmans.* Paris: Karthala, 1980.
————— *Nègre de paille.* Paris: Silex Editions, 1982.
Kourouma, Ahmadou. *Monnè, outrages et défis.* Paris: Eds. du Seuil, 1990.
————— *Les Soleils des indépendances.* Paris: Seuil, 1968.

Kuoh-Moukouri, Jacques. *Doigts-noirs*. Montréal: Eds. à la Page, 1963.
Laye, Camara. *L'Enfant noir*. Paris: Plon, 1953.
Lévy-Bruhl, Lucien. *Carnets*. Paris: P.U.F., 1949.
———— *Fonctions mentales dans les sociétés inférieures*. Paris: F. Alcan, 1910.
Liking, Werewere. *Elle sera de jaspe et de corail*. Paris: L'Harmattan, 1984.
———— *Orphée Dafric*. Paris: L'Harmattan, 1981.
Lopes, Henri. *Le Chercheur d'Afriques*. Paris: Eds. du Seuil, 1990.
———— *Le Lys et le flamboyant*. Paris: Eds. du Seuil, 1997.
———— *Sur l'autre rive*. Paris: Seuil, 1992.
Magnier, Bernard. "Entretien avec Sony Labou Tansi." *Notre Librairie*, No.79, avril-juin 1985.
———— "Entretien avec Yodi Karone." *Notre Librairie*, no.79, avril-juin 1985.
Makouta-Mboukou, J.P. "*La condition de l'écrivain négro-africain*." *Présence Francophone*, no.14, 1977.
Mandeleau, Tita. *Signare Anna ou le voyage aux escales*. Dakar: Les Nouvelles Editions Africaines du Sénégal, 1991.
Monénembo, Tierno. *Les Crapauds-brousse*. Paris: Seuil, 1979.
———— *Pelourinho*. Paris: Seuil, 1995.
Ndione, Abasse. *La Vie en spirale*. Dakar: N.E.A., 1984.
———— *La Vie en spirale II*. Dakar: N.E.A., 1988.
Nokan, Charles. *Violent était le vent*. Paris: Présence Africaine, 1966.
Okoumba-Nkoghe. *La mouche et la glu*. Paris: Présence Africaine, 1984.
Ouologuem, Yambo. *Le Devoir de violence*. Paris: Seuil, 1968.
Oyono, Ferdinand. *Le Vieux nègre et la médaille*. Paris: Julliard, 1956.
———— *Une Vie de boy*. Paris: Julliard, 1956.
Sassine, Williams. *Le Jeune homme de sable*. Paris: Présence Africaine, 1979.
———— *Mémoire d'une peau*. Paris: *Présence Africaine*, 1998.
———— *Saint Monsieur Baly*. Paris: *Présence Africaine*, 1973.
———— *Wirriyamu*. Paris: Présence Africaine, 1976.
———— *Le Zéhéros n'est pas n'importe qui*. Paris: Présence Africaine, 1985.
Sembène, Ousmane. *Les Bouts de bois de Dieu*. Paris: Le Livre contemporain, 1960.
———— *Le Dernier de l'empire*. Paris: L'Harmattan, 1981.

—————— *Le Docker noir.* Paris: Nouvelles éditions latines, 1956.
—————— *Guelwaar.* Paris: Présence Africaine, 1996.
—————— *O Pays, mon beau peuple.* Paris: Amiot-Dumont, 1957.
—————— *Xala.* Paris: Présence Africaine, 1973.
Sèye, Ibrahima. *Un trou dans le miroir.* Dakar: N.E.A., 1983.
Socé, Ousmane. *Karim, roman sénégalais.* Paris: Nouvelles éditions latines, 1935.
—————— *Mirages de Paris.* Nouvelles éditions latines, 1937.
Soustelle, Jacques. *Lettre ouverte aux victimes de la décolonisation.* Paris: Albin Michel, 1973.
Tansi, Sony Labou. *Le Commencement des douleurs.* Paris: Eds. du Seuil, 1995.
—————— *L'Etat honteux.* Paris: Seuil, 1981.
—————— *Les Sept solitudes de Lorsa Lopez.* Paris: Seuil, 1985.
U Tam'Si, Tchicaya. *Les Cancrelats.* Paris: Albin Michel, 1980.
—————— *Les Méduses ou les orties de mer.* Paris: Albin Michel, 1982.
—————— *Les Phalènes.* Paris: Albin Michel, 1984.

8

THE EARLIEST FRANCOPHONE AFRICAN NOVELS: FROM *FORCE-BONTE* TO *DOGUICIMI*

U. A. Ogike

Introduction

Western literary critics and their African adherents believe that the novel is not a traditional African genre.[1] Adrian Roscoe affirms that the novel, "unlike the story, is not a fact of the African past." His arguments can be summarised as follows: first, the story is oral while the novel is essentially of a written nature and consequently a European import; second, the story is short but the novel is a much longer narrative; and third, "...the complicated turns of plots, the minutiae of physical and scenic description of even a short novel would be an impossible burden for the African griot's memory." (74-76).

Roscoe's arguments could be examined in the same order. First, there is nothing in the etymology of the word 'novel' that identifies it inextricably with the written form. The Latin root of the word, *novus-nouvellus* simply means 'new', 'strange', or 'fiction'. Moreover, to say that the novel in its written form "is a literary import ... from Europe" is an over-simplification. Technically, the European writing systems originated in Africa, in ancient Egypt. In fact some hieroglyphic texts of ancient Egyptian stories are known. Second, there is no clear lengthwise demarcation between the story and the novel. Even in the European sense, none of the definitions of the two genres throws any light on this

---

[1] For a full discussion of the question whether the novel is a traditional African genre, see Cook (18), Roscoe (74-6) Dorson (9-10) and Chinweizu et al (7-10).

question. Third, Roscoe considers the novel and its complications too much for the memory of the African storyteller. He immediately contradicts himself by citing the example of *Soundjiata* and then tries to evade the contradiction by describing such novels as "being special, occasional, exceptions, belonging more to the category of historical texts, and in any case of fairly short length." Obviously, critics, Europeans for the most part, have been led into this erroneous view because of the paucity of African long stories, oral novels one may say, which have been translated into foreign languages.

In fact, there are myriads of unwritten novels, which a researcher has to take into consideration before denying the existence of the novel in traditional Africa. Among the Igbo, it takes days and even weeks to tell one single story like *Eze Idu na Oba,* a fiction of intrigue, love, adventure and marvel among the kings, queens, nobles, princes of the ancient fictitious kingdoms of *Idu* and *Oba*. This tale, like the old Celtic romances about King Arthur and his Round Table, is told in bits daily around fireplaces after dinner. Nobody doubts that romances are novels. Literary scholars like Henri Coulet include them in the definition of the novel (55-57).

A number of modern African novels have emerged due to the efforts that some African writers have made to collect, reconstruct and translate into written forms pieces of old stories. Besides Djibril Niane's *Soundjiata* and Thomas Mofolo's *Chaka*, Amos Tutuola's *The Palm-wine Drinkard* has come to us this way. It is known that many of the episodes in *The Palm-wine Drinkard* were popularly known among the Yorubas prior to their transcription and use in the novel. It is therefore not true, as Roscoe would have us believe, that the contents and mechanism of the novel are impossible for the traditional African memory. In fact, old people, storytellers and, especially, African griots are noted for their prodigious memory.

The above remarks are important if we are to put the African novel into its right perspective, establish its authenticity, specificity and originality. In fact, the aim of this chapter is to, as far as possible, extricate early Francophone novels from the disparaging stereotypes into which they have been thrown by Eurocentric critics like Janheinz Jahn (89-95) and Fredric Michelmen (7) who describe them as "apprentice", "missionary" and "pro-assimilationist" literature.

Early Francophone Novels: Language, Patronage and Publication

Judith Gleason rightly observes that African "novels often give the impression that there were generations of it", and goes on to attribute this to "intensive imposition of European authority and ideology on Africa ... which lasted only about sixty years"(3). In fact, within sixty years of colonisation, there appeared seven African novels written in French, namely *Les trois volontés de Malic,*[2] *Le réprouvé,*[3] *Force-Bonté,*[4] *L'esclave,*[5] *Karim,*[6] *Mirages de Paris and*[7] *Doguicimi.*[8] Of course, there are other publications in other domains by Africans, especially school teachers. With the founding of the *Bulletin de l'Afrique Occidentale française* in Dakar in 1913 and the *Bulletin du Comité d'études historiques et scientifiques de l'A.O.F.* in 1916, Africans wrote pieces on culture, folktales and legends for publication in these journals. Claude Wauthier and Robert Pageard have done extensive research on these early writings.

Gleason's remark on the 'intensity' of the imposition of the French colonial authority on African writing is borne out at several levels, first of all the language level. All the early Francophone publications were written in perfect French. The language of Vaugelas would not tolerate in its territory anything equivalent to Amos Tutuola's *Palm-wine Drinkard* in English. Pageard (9) points out that even though African students were comparatively very few in number, they received very sound education in the renowned Teacher Training Colleges of William Ponty and Edouard Renard. This education was of the same level as in metropolitan France. Black students side by side with their French counterparts read the same history books which began with "*nos ancêtres, les gaulois...*" Bernard

---

[2] Diagne, Ahmadou Mapaté (Senegalese). *Les trois volontés de Malic.* Paris: Larose, 1920
[3] Dion, Massyla (Senegalese). *Le réprouvé.* Dakar: "Revue africaine et littéraire", no.6, juillet, 1925.
[4] Diallo, Bakary (Senegalese). *Force-Bonté.* Paris: Rieder et Cie, 1926.
[5] Couchoro, Félix (Benin-Togo). *L'esclave.* Paris: Dépêche Africaine, 1929. I am unable to find a copy of this novel, so it will not be discussed here. If anyone knows how I can find a copy, he should please let me know.
[6] Socé, Ousmane (Senegalese). *Karim.* Paris: Nouvelles Editions Latines, 1935.
[7] Socé, Ousmane (Senegalese). *Mirages de Paris.* Paris: Nouvelles Editions Latines, 1973.
[8] Hazoumé, Paul (Benin). *Doguicimi.* Paris: Larose, 1938.

Dadié, in his *Climbié*, romanticises the shameful use of the *symbole* to punish a student who happens to speak a language other than French in the school premises.

Besides the imposition of high level French, the patronage of Frenchmen accounted for the speedy publication and diffusion of African writing. The Principals of Ecole William Ponty and Edouard Renard encouraged creative writings among their students. Bakary Diallo's manuscript, *Force-Bonté,* was collected by Lucie Cousturier and handed over to J.R. Bloch who prefaced and published it. Robert Delavignette, a former colonial Governor General, wrote the preface to Ousmane Socé's *Karim* and George Hardy, Recteur de l'Académie de Lille, chronicler of the European epic who held the chair of colonial history at the Sorbonne, prefaced Paul Hazoumé's *Doguicimi*. This patronage continued and, by their prefaces to Senghor's *Anthologie de la nouvelle poésie nègre et malgache* and Césaire's *Cahier d'un retour au pays natal,* French literary juggernauts like Jean Paul Sartre and André Breton introduced African writing to the European world.

Another factor that led to a speedy promotion of African writing in Europe was the craze for Negro art and exotism in France between 1905 and 1907 when, according to Jacques Chevrier, "a group of Parisian painters and artists ... for the first time discovered African statues and masks" (18). In the literary domain, Apollinaire evokes his *"fétiches d'Océanie et de Guinée".* In 1921 Blaise Cendrars published the first anthology of Negro poetry, and in 1928 his *Petits contes nègres pour les enfants blancs.* In 1927 Philippe Soupault published *Le Nègre blanc.*

The quality and success of early Francophone novels coupled with the proven existence of white literary cheats and fraudsters have led critics to cast doubts about their authorship. It has been claimed that *Force-Bonté* was actually written by Lucie Cousturier based on her conversation with Bakary Diallo[9]. This opinion is all the more plausible given the fact that Bakary Diallo was self-taught. But what about his more prolific self-taught successor, Ousmane Sembène? His own novels are not any less accomplished literature. Frenchmen have written novels

---

[9] Pageard (16) agrees with his predecessors in considering that Force-Bonté can only be counted with reserve among negro African literature. Until we can get a concrete proof of the contrary, we have to attribute authorship to Bakary Diallo.

with African pseudonyms. Janheinz Jahn analyses one such novel, *Kavwanga* by G. Bolombo, who was in fact a European missionary disguised under the African name Bolombo (92-93). Lilyan Kesteloot claims that Camara Laye told her in confidence before his death in 1980 that "*Le regard du roi avait été écrit par un blanc*" (468). Could it be that these European patrons arrogate to themselves the successes of their African wards?

Let us say for the moment that early African writing in French may have undergone tremendous editing by the French "patrons" in order to meet the rigorously high standard set by European publishers of literary works.

The Early Novels

Ahmadou Mpaté Diagne's *Les Trois Volontées de Malic* raises the problems of caste. His hero, Malic, enters a French technical school and learns the ironsmith trade in spite of opposition from his parents and relations. The trade is reserved for the lower caste in the society and it is a social anathema for a freeborn 'diambour' to forge iron! Eventually, Malic succeeds and his trade brings prosperity to his village.

Needless to say that the problem of the caste was a nagging one in traditional Africa. Members of castes were shunned, discriminated against and could not aspire to high social and political posts in the society. They are unjustly maltreated by their freeborn compatriots. But with the coming of the French ideals of 'liberté, égalité and fraternité' as well as technology, the emancipation of the members of the caste was at hand.

Bakary Diallo continues where Diagne leaves off. In his *Force-Bonté*, he tells us that during his military career, one of his companions and friends was a member of the Labbo (carpenter) caste. Acknowledging a good advice about military life from this Labbo, Bakary shamefully remarks:

> *Décidement, le monde est renversé.*
> *Maintenant ce sont les Labos qui ont plus*
> *d'esprit que les Peulhs* (35).

A later novelist, Camara Laye, takes the queue from his predecessors, Diagne and Diallo, and exploits the subject to his own advantage. Camara Laye is himself a member of this despicable caste of ironsmith. His ultimate aim in writing *L'Enfant noir* was to upgrade his caste. The aura, respect and quasi-priestly and prophetic powers that he attributes to his father, the glory and fascination of the smithy work, the family totem, the magical powers of his mother etc – all these are aimed at redeeming the members of his caste. In fact, both Alexandre Biyidi, who reprimands Camara Laye for not attacking colonialism, and Leopold, Senghor, who defends him miss the whole point and aim of *L'Enfant noir* (Blachere:55-58).

But Bakary Diallo's *Force-Bonté*, while prefiguring other forms of the African novel, deals with more socio-political, traditional and contemporary issues. The hero, a young Peulh, relates his early life in the rural Senegalese region of Fouta Toro. He then goes to the city of Saint-Louis where he enlists in the French Army and serves in Morocco and in Europe. He is wounded and is treated in a French hospital.

Thus, Diallo's *Force-Bonté* set the tone for subsequent autobiographical novels like Camara Laye's *L'Enfant noir* and Bernard Dadie's *Climbié*, city novels like Ousmane Soce's *Karim* and Abdulaye Sadji's *Maïmouna*, and novels of European discovery like Ousmane Soce's *Mirages de Paris* and Ake Loba's *Kocoumbo, L'étudiant noir.*

Like novelists before him, Bakary Diallo deals with the social evils of his time. Massyla Diop, in his *Le Réprouvé, roman d'une Sénégalaise*, had described marabouts as *"roublards et ingrats"* (37) and indicted the Moslem religion as an impediment to progress. Diallo in his turn condemns the fetish and quackery of the marabouts. To a wounded soldier, who experiences the advanced scientific medical care in a French hospital, indigenous medicine with its inherent fetishism would naturally prove despicable. In fact the *gris-gris* which the hero obtained from a marabout did not protect him *"à travers les maladies et les pluies de balles"* (51) after all.

Yet the whole point of the novel, as the title implies, is the author's acceptance of what he considers the two cardinal virtues of colonial France, namely *force* and *bonté*, the two recurrent themes in the novel. With her *force*, the colonisers brought an end to the internecine wars which plagued pre-colonial Africa. The *bonté* of France is illustrated by an episode. The author is taking a stroll in Parc Monceau, in Paris, and notices a beautiful young French lady feeding birds. He reflects on the incident and says to himself: "Ah, how sweet! This young woman is France and we, black people, are the birds. The birds are grateful to their benefactor. *Vive la force-bonté de la France!*" (108)

Although Bakary Diallo encounters racial discrimination in the French Army, he does not change his opinion about France. He feels that there is more for Africa to gain than lose in her association with France. In spite of his infatuation with France's *mission civilisatrice*, and condemnation of marabouts, he remains a devout Moslem and an African of culture. The publisher, J.R. Bloch, in the preface to the novel vindicates the author's *candeur, simplicité* and sincerity. *Force-Bonté*, therefore, can hardly be described as an apology for total assimilation.

The City Novel

For Bakary Diallo, the ancient Senegalese city of Saint-Louis is a setting for his hero to enlist in the French Army before proceeding to the metropolis. Earlier in his novel, *Le Réprouvé - roman d'une Sénégalaise*, Massyla Diop, had portrayed a seasoned African functionary, N'Diaye, "*taille bien prise sous ce costume colonial blanc*", making his way daily to the Government Building in Dakar, "*C'était un homme sérieux, d'une sincérité à toute épreuve, fort estimé de tous les Européens.*" But Ousmane Socé prefers to use the two cities side by side, as the setting for his *Karim, un roman sénégalais* and chooses as his hero not a mature colonial civil servant, but a young employee, who is only 22 years old.

In the ancient town of Saint-Louis, young Karim lives a life typical of his Ouolof ancestors, the great Lingueres. Like them he is hospitable, generous and amiable; he loves feasting, nobility and heroic deeds. With his meagre salary, Karim embarks on his first amorous conquest, a young woman named Marieme. He gives generously to her and to the griots and griotess who continually sing his ancestral exploits. He borrows too much money to maintain his prestige and generosity and soon he is broke. Worse for him, Badara, a richer rival wins the heart of his girlfriend, Marieme. Karim leaves for Dakar.

With the help of his uncle, Karim gets a job. He shares a room with young intellectuals, Ibrou, a philosophy major at a Lycée, Abdoulaye, a school teacher and a graduate of the Ecole Normale de Gorée, and Ibrahima, his cousin. He now dresses in suit like a Frenchman. For three months he sends money to his poor parents at home. At a "sabil", Karim meets the beautiful dancer Aminata, a widow, and falls in love with her. He also courts Marie, a Catholic, whom he could not marry because of religious differences. Once again, he returns to extravagant living. He loses his job, suffers from malaria; he gets a letter from a friend informing him that his rival Badara has been disgraced. He returns home, reconciles with Marieme and the couple finally get married.

Ousmane Soce describes the two cities. Saint-Louis is a *"vieille ville française, centre d'élégance et de bon gout sénégalais"* (p. 18). According to Karim's father, *"Dakar est une ville ou l'on se trouve facilement vers le mal..."* (64). He admonishes his son to shun the company of dishonest men, avoid alcohol, say his daily prayers and maintain the family reputation. Throughout his work, the author maintains the tone of a moralist and advises Africans on how to meet the challenges of cultural exchange with the West. He advises Africans to *"prendre en example ces pays de vieille civilisation"*. Hard work is necessary for *"un pays qui ne veut pas travailler, qui se complait dans la mollesse et le plaisir, va à sa perte"* (121). Young men should learn to adapt to bureaucracy by enduring the insults of their bosses. Religious differences should not debar marriage between a Moslem and a Catholic: *"En Europe ou en Amérique, ils passeraient sans doute, outre les religions et l'opinion"* (129). He pleads with his society to lift the primitive ban on the education of women and to support the efforts of the French in this domain.

It is evident that Ousmane Socé wants Africa to borrow a leaf from America and the West for her cultural enrichment but this does not at all imply that the novelist "admits unconditionally the supremacy of European civilisation" as Chevrier would have us believe (29).

Ousmane Socé's second novel, *Mirages de Paris*, launches the hero into the French metropolis. Fara, his principal character leaves his village, Niane, for his dreamland, France, whose language, history and geography he had learned, with love, in school. He is fascinated by Paris with its crowd, cars, buildings, boulevards, parks and monuments. He meets Jacqueline, an attractive young blonde and falls in love with her. Soon, the couple get married despite strong opposition from Jacqueline's parents. Jacqueline gets pregnant and delivers a baby boy but dies of sudden haemorrhage. Fara is overwhelmed with grief. His friend convinces him to return to Africa. Three days before his proposed departure his grief returns. As he strolls along the deep waters Jacqueline's ghost appears from the deep waters and invites Fara to join her. Delirious with happiness, he plunges into the river.

Thus, Ousmane Soce prefigures the *"roman d'enchantement et de désenchantement*" or, as some critics would say, the novel of mystification and demystification. Early in the novel, while his hero Fara is still on the ship sailing to his enchanted city, the author introduces the germs of disenchantment. Fara is shocked when he overhears a conversation between two Frenchmen and a Syrian, who have been to Africa on various missions:

> *Je vous assure que les Noirs sont capables d'assimiler notre culture aussi bien scienttifique que littéraire ....*
> *......... l'Administration français à tort de pousser l'instruction des indigènes ....*
> *- Il faut laisser les Noirs dans l'ignorance* (21-23)
>
> (I assure you that Black people are capable of assimilating our scientific as well as our literary culture.
> - It is wrong for the French Administration to hasten the education of indigenes;
> - Black people should be left in their ignorance.)

In the ship, the Africans are segregated and crowded under the deck and are made to eat hastily and in silence. At a conference in Paris, Fara is further stunned by the ignorance, misconceptions, exotic and stereotyped ideas that even the most informed Frenchman has about Africa. He deplores the situation of black Africans living a jobless life of outcasts in misery and poverty. This is another source of disenchantment. He himself has to seek a menial job, which he cannot get, and he finally settles as a "*petit commenrcant*" of African artifacts.

The author reiterates his earlier stand that Africans should work hard in order to develop. He now pushes his pleas for cultural *métissage* to the biological level. "*Tout est métis, (says Fara), il n'y a pas sur la terre une race pure, une civilisation qui ne soit pas métisse*" (148) .

Perhaps the most significant aspect of the novelist's work is his treatment of the theme of love. The love between Fara and Jacqueline surpasses all previous love affairs, withstands all opposition, transgresses geographical and racial frontiers and finally, like the proverbial Shakespearian love between Romeo and Juliet, unites the lovers inseparably in life and in death. It is rare to find subsequent novelists who treat the theme of love with such tenderness and profundity as Ousmane Soce, not even Paul Hazoume whose heroine, Doguicimi, loves her husband so much that she chooses to be buried alive with him.

The Epic Novel

Paul Hazoume's *Doguicimi* published in 1938, is a landmark in the history of the Francophone novel. It is not only the most voluminous novel (510 pages) written by an African till date, it is also the precursor of epic and historical novels in Francophone West Africa.

The plot is simple. Gueze, king of Agbome, undertakes a war against the Mahinous to avenge the massacre of his white friends. The king suffers a humiliating defeat and one of the Agbome princes, Toffa, is taken captive. Doguicimi, the beloved wife of Toffa successfully resists the amorous advances of Vidaho, heir to the throne and remains faithful to her absent husband. After a long delay marked by national festivals, the king at last undertakes a second war to deliver the prisoners of the Manihou. This time victory is on the side of Agbome but only Toffa's skull is recovered and Doguicimi chooses to be buried with it.

The supreme import of Paul Hazoumé's novel is unquestionably the Africanity of expression. One is never left in doubt at any stage that it is an African who is writing. Hazoumé translates, transliterates, interprets and weaves into perfect French the African palaver.

The African palaver is manifested in meaningful greeting names, titles, epithets, riddles, conundrums, maxims, anecdotes, parables - all of which are regarded as 'proverbs' described by Achebe as "the oil with which words are eaten". One would have had to quote the whole work to give all the good examples. However, here are some taken at random. 'Doguicimi' means 'distinguish me'. King Agaja is '*le Conqérant-des-navires*' because he conquered and annexed the coastal regions to the Kingdom of Dahomey. Houegbaja is '*l'ananas qui s'est rit de la colère de la Foudre*' and Weho, with a small army, defeated the choleric, boastful Dan and built his kingdom over his ruins. King Gueze is '*Maître de l'Aurore*' because his daily human sacrifices make the sun rise; *Maître de la vie*' because he has power of life and death over his subjects; '*Père de richesses*' for he is the sole dispenser of gifts to the people. He is also '*Roi de l'Univers*' and '*Roil prédestiné*' and so on. Side by side with these panegyric titles, three are disparaging ones; women are referred to as 'êtres à sept paires de côtés' and white men are '*immondes bêtes de mer*'. There are about 150 proverbs in *Doguicimi*, a novel of 510 pages, that is to say more than one proverb in every three pages. The proverbs are in no way evenly distributed across the novel: there are, for example, two proverbs on page 19, four on page 20, five on page 21, **six** on page 22 and none on page 23.

Some proverbs are first of all illustrated by an anecdote. During one of King Guezo's council meetings, Migan, the prime minister, desiring to get the members to seek the right solution to the problem posed by the presence of arrogant white men in their midst, tells the members the story of Awliponouwe who lost his horse and went to look for it in a bird's cage. Then he gives the conclusion which is the proverb: "*L'affolement n'a jamais rien fait d'intelligent*" (355).

Sometimes, the anecdote is expanded into a parable. When the Mahinou youths rebelled and turned a deaf ear to the prediction of Elder Dee that the unnatural misfortune which plagued the country was a portent of an impending attack by the enemy, the old man told them this parable. De-Messe, the king of Porto-Novo, ordered the youths to kill off all the old men of the kingdom because they were a nuisance. The young men obeyed except one of them who hid his old father. Later, the same King commanded the young men to bring to him within two days, a hundred rolls of unbreakable cord made of clay, otherwise they would all be executed. The deadline was almost at hand and they risked death, when the young man who hid his father brought him out and the old man taught them the ancient art of making an earthen cord (435-444).

Another aspect of the palaver is the use of songs, mimics, gestures and gesticulations as means of communication. Most of these are uniquely African in form and meaning. Paul Hazoume exploits this vein. Instead of stating that Doguicimi perceived the bad odour of the prison, Hazoume writes: "*De sa lèvre supérieure, elle forma les narines*" (323). Physiologically an African's lips are enormous and elastic, and the upper lip is easily stretched up and expanded at will to cover his flat nose. By snapping her two fingers, the thumb and the middle finger, Doguicimi signifies that she has taken a firm decision. But most majestic, most awe-inspiring and most sublime are the gestures of an elder delivering his words of advice, suggestion, command or consolation either directly or indirectly in the form of a story, anecdote or parable. Old Dee, addressing the youths of Dahomey, sometimes interrupts his words to look up as if to seek divine inspiration or to give his words the force of a prophecy. He shrugs his shoulders as if struck by instant danger; he sneezes or looks towards the family shrine to invoke his ancestors. The author carefully records all these gesticulations which Africans employ as language or as support for spoken words.

Hazoume also introduces into the novel the traditional African oral technique of the *Chantefable*. *Doguicimi* is punctuated by poems and songs of all sorts and appropriate to different occasions. War songs, dirges, griot's praises, songs to disparage the enemy of the kingdom, people's songs to incite the king to vengeance or mercy, and songs of complaint appear at their appropriate occasions. Songs are so important as a means of communication between the ruler and the ruled, that King Guezo thus advises the heir to his throne:

Recherche les chancons qui courent dans le peuple.
Le chanson est la meilleure arme du faible. (215)

Throughout the novel, Hazoume uses the traditional African calendar and metric systems. Time is marked by the crow of the cock, the position of the sun and, in the evening, by the extent of the visibility of the marks on the palm. Each of the eight days of the week is named after the god of the market that sits on that day. The month follows the detailed phases of the moon and the year is marked by seasons and national festivals. Distance is measured by the average length of a bamboo stem or the time it takes a messenger to travel from one village to another. There are other literary devices emanating from African culture which Hazoume introduces into the art of the novel. Omens and totems based on local animist beliefs and superstitions are used to arouse suspense, anticipation, prophecy and apocalypse (Ogike: 87-100).

Like his predecessors, Hazoume deals with some of the gnawing problems of his time; he condemns inter-ethnic wars often undertaken for flimsy reasons: Guezo declares war on the Manihous in order to a avenge the killing of his white friends. Under the kings of Agbome, wars provide victims for human sacrifices and merchandise for slave trade. Many passages abound where Hazoume describes with stark realism, lugubriously, shocking scenes of human sacrifices and wanton immolations of young maidens. Gleason rightly observes that Hazoume "is rather skilled in the description of immolations" which he portrays in a "straightforward manner" (50), but she interprets this as the author's way of giving his assent to "outrageous or extravagant behaviour". On the contrary, by abandoning the traditional African *sagesse* and adapting a direct language, he not only disassociates himself from these hideous practices but also exposes them in a manner to shock both the African and European readers.

Furthermore, Hazoume denounces the 'chosification' of women.

Women are among the choiciest rewards made by the kingdom. During wars, newly delivered mothers are sent to offer their breasts to the fetishes of the enemy country so that they remain asleep and silent when consulted. The author goes on to execrate fetichism, oracles, and other forms of superstition. He questions the validity of trial by ordeal, an art learned from an enemy country and which is easily manipulated by corrupt jurors.

Hazoume suggests that it is impossible to eradicate these barbarous aspects of custom because of the socio-political set-up of the Agbome kingdom. Power is concentrated in the hands of the king, who rules by divine right. He is protected against any from of rebellion or *coup d'état* by summary divine sanction of calamity. Princes are excluded from political offices in order to keep them away from the temptation of treason. Ministers are chosen from among the common people. The masses are described as sedentary, incapable of political thought or action and completely subjugated and mystified by the daily incantations of the royal '*crieur*'. All loyalty is thus centered on the king's person.

However, above the king and people, custom reigns supreme. Kings are bound to fulfil to the letter all aspects of the custom. They may introduce new elements to it: King Tegbessou initiated the trial by ordeal and King Agaja the sacrifice of human beings. But the king cannot, omit, eradicte nor modify any part of custom upon which depends his kingship and power. All efforts from within, including the attempts by the "constitutionally temperate" King Guezo, to eradicate the most dreadful aspects of custom, prove abortive.

Hazoume therefore opines that only external forces can intervene to eliminate the barbarous elements in the Agbome custom. Colonial powers are already present. The author feverishly prays for the least evil among them: the *Agoudas* (Portuguese) are "*négriers féroces*" and are likely to perpetuate slavery; the *Glincis* (English) are snobish and out for material exploitation and gain. He therefore chooses the French whom he describes as *sympathiques* and are most likely to practise their ideals- of *liberté, égalité et fraternité*. It is pertinent to emphasise that Hazoume does not advocate the destruction of the magnificently constituted society of Agbome, but the eradication of the inhuman aspects of the custom. It is therefore an exaggeration to state that the author "shows the African society as a world unconditionally hungering for Christian salvation and French freedom and humanity" (Jahn:95).

Conclusion

The impression spread by literary critics, mostly Europeans, is that the novel is purely a European import and that early Francophone novelists, under the influence of European paternalism are docile apprentices and apologists of the French assimilation policy and *"mission civilatrice"*. These stereotyped judgements have biased many a critic who would have delved into an objective study of early African novels. The novel in Africa is as old as orality. By introducing their languages and graphics, Europeans have turned African orature into literature. African writers, in their turn, have enriched literary European languages by introducing African vocabulary, expressions, cultural elements and style into the art of novel writing.

Early Francophone novelists dealt with the social problems posed by the European colonial presence. Some, like Bakary Diallo, sincerely acknowledged the benefits of colonialism ending internecine wars, establishing schools, buildings, roads and railways and so on. Some like Ousmane envisaged a society of cultural and even biological *metissage*. Others, like Paul Hazoume, saw the coming of the French as an opportunity to eradicate evil customs from the African society. But all of them sensed the lurking danger of colonialism and none was prepared to sacrifice Africanity on the altar of total assimilation.

The pre-negritude novelists, as early Francophone novelists are sometimes called, laid solid foundations for the post-war negritude and revolutionary novels. They have sown the seeds of autobiographical, epic and city novels, novels of culture conflict, enchantment and disenchantment, mystification and demystification, traditionalism versus modernism, politically and socially committed novels. These forms and themes are to be harvested by their militant successors in their war of independence.

References

Achebe, Chinua. "The Duty and Involvement of the African Writer." *The African Reader*: Independent Africa. Eds. Wilfred Cartey & Martin Kilson. New York: Vintage Book.1970.
Biyidi, Aledxandre. *"L'Enfant noir."* Paris: *Présence Africaine*, Ed. 1953.
Blanchere, *Jean-Claude et al. Les Genres littéraires par les textes.* Dakar: Nouvelles Editions Africaines.1977.
Boni, Nazi. *Crépuscule des temps anciens.* Paris: Présence Africaine, 1962.
Chevrier, Jacques, *Littérature nègre.* Paris: Armand Colin, 1984.
Chinweizu *et al. Toward the Decolonisation of African Literature.* Vol.I. Enugu: Fourth Dimension Publishers, 1980.
Cook, Mercer. *The Militant Black Writer in Africa and the United States.* Madison: the University of Wisconsin Press, 1967.
Coulet, Henri. *Le Roman jusqu'à la Révolution.* New York: Versity Press, 1971.
Dorson, Charles. *The Emergence of African Fiction.* Bloomington: Indiana University Press, 1971.
Gleason, Judith Illsley. *This Africa: Novels by West Africans in English and French.* Evanston: Northwestern University Press, 1965.
Jahn, Janheinz. *Neo-African Literature.* New York: Grove Press, 1968.
Kesteloot, Lilyan. *Anthologie nègro-africaine.* Verviers: Marabout University, 1981.
Malonga, Jean. *La légende de M'Pfoumou ma Mazono.* Paris: Présence Africaine, 1954.
Michelman, Fredric. "The Beginning of French-African Fiction". *Research in African Literatures* Vol. II No 1 (1971): p.5-17.
Midiohouan, Guy Ossito. *Biliographie Chronologique de la littérature nègro-africaine d'expression française.* Cotonou: UNB, 1984.
Mofolo, Thomas. *Chaka: an Historical Romance.* Trans. from the Sesuto by F.H. Dutton. Oxford University press, 1967.
Niane, Djibril. *Soudjata: l'épopée mandingue.* Paris: Présence Africaine, 1964.
Ogike, Uche A. "The Aesthetics of Time, Omen and Totem in West African Novels in French", *Literature and Black Aesthetics.* Ed. Emenyonu Ernest N. Ibadan: Heinemann Educational Books, 1990.

Ouologem, Yambo. *Le devoir de violence*. Paris: Seuil, 1968.
Pageard, Robert. *Littérature négro-africaine*. Paris: Livre Africain, 1966.
Tutuola, Amos. *The Palm-Wine Drinkard*. London: Faber, 1952.

9

THE RADICAL PERSPECTIVE IN THE EARLY AFRICAN NOVELS

Elerius John

The thematic concerns of African literature and the need for the literature to transcend the ephemeral present while still identifying itself with it has been of interest to the critic of African literature. Clive Wake, for instance, in commenting on African literary creations has observed their oneness in terms of political, social and literary preoccupations and has noted the extent to which African creative writing has been motivated by political and social revolution.[1]

In essence, literature in general has come a long way from being seen as a source of distraction produced by and for a small group of cultivated people to being valued as a cultural phenomenon that can give information about society and also help to bring about social change. Literature thus plays the role of depicting reality and passing on social experience, and, above all, of influencing the formation of the political, economic, and socio-aesthetic ideals of the society that produces it. It has by its nature become a specific form of social consciousness to which the artist and the critic cannot be indifferent.

In apprehending observable reality and reflecting the findings in his literary creation, the African writer is not unaware of the real nature and objective of good literature which he sees as being largely determined by the needs of the society. His literary output is therefore a response to the needs of his time, needs which to a large extent are politically, economically and socially determined. When he masks himself therefore with the cloak of objectivity in his representation of human experiences, he is,

---

[1] cf. Clive Wake: "The Political and Cultural Revolution" in *Protest and Conflict in African Literature* edited by Pieterse, C. and Munro, D., New York, Africana Publishing Corporation 1970 p.47.

nevertheless, guided by a critical sense of social responsibility. This predisposition is easily discernible in his ideological perspective as made manifest in his literary creation.

The perspective of the writer in the reflection of the dialectical movement of reality in its individuality, varied forms and typicality is therefore worth critical examination for a better understanding of a literary piece, the preoccupations of the writer and his ultimate world view.

The present study which is an attempt to highlight the radical perspective in the early African novels is inspired by such considerations. Its area of coverage is the African novel of French expression of the pre-independence period. It focuses primarily on the early novels of two authors: Mongo Beti and Sembène Ousmane, novels published during the colonial period and which, by their forms, structures, and revolutionary ideological perspectives succeed in touching the general human condition and in transcending their actual settings. Eza Boto's *Ville Cruelle* (The Cruel City), Mongo Beti's *Le Pauvre Christ de Bomba* (The Poor Christ of Bomba) and Sembène Ousmane's *Les bouts de bois de Dieu* (God's Bits of Wood) fall under this category of novels. These creative works are those marked by progressive postures of the writers towards the multifarious nature of reality depicted, and by conscious attempts, made in them to restructure the realities interpreted along revolutionary lines, reflecting as it were, a felt need for a significant social or political change in the society portrayed.

The dialectics of radical consciousness in the works cited above is examined here under the following broad headings: thematic concerns of the novels and their relevance; authors' dominant ideological perspectives, characterisation, narrative structure and the perceived world view of the artists themselves.

Thematic Concerns of the Novels

Products of society, the early African literary creations appeared naturally as direct reactions to Europeans incursions on the African scene. The literary artists in their loyalty to observable reality were conscious of the disruptive role of European intrusion in their depiction of the colonial world. The successful representation of the crises of culture and the dislodgement of the systems and structures of thought of the African by Ferdinand Oyono in *Une Vie de Boy* (House Boy) and *Le Vieux Nègre et la Médaille* (The Old Man and the Medal) for instance is not only a reflection of the dominant theme of African literary creations of the period, but also an indication of the competence of the author in grasping effectively the characteristic phenomena of life of the time and interpreting and typifying them.

While cultural conflict between Africa and Europe determined to a large extent the literary interest of the early African writers, there was, all the same, a growing awareness of the need to introduce new themes that could serve as vehicles for conveying social and democratic ideas and proposing positive trends which could bring about permanent values of society such as love, justice and human dignity. Consequently, creative works which were aesthetically challenging and ideologically committed having themes which encompass cultural, social and political affairs came into being on the literary arena. The new development marked a radical departure from the literary preoccupations of the period in favour of literary themes infused with revolutionary humanism and ideals, such as those to be highlighted in the novels within the purview of the present study.

Eza Boto's *Ville Cruelle* (The Cruel City), published in 1954, figures among the early African novels purveying revolutionary sensibility in Africa. Mongo Beti, the author, whose pen name then was Eza Boto, was conscious of his responsibility as a writer and of the need to produce creative works which were socially and historically relevant. He was guided by the knowledge of the historical experiences of his country. A German protectorate, which was later divided into two League of Nations' mandate, and which became thereafter two United Nations territories before the final unification in an independent Federal Republic in 1961, Cameroon found itself having to pass through two successive systems of colonial administration - German and French.

It is in this whirling and seething stream of historical reality that the destinies of the characters in his *Ville Cruelle* (The Cruel City) are decided.

Set in the southern part of Cameroon of the colonial period, the novel offers the reader the vicissitudes of life in a colonial territory. He is introduced to Banda, central character of the novel, through whose adventure the economic structures of the society, prevailing norms, injustice, exploitation, conflict and revolt are seen as the creative artist's field of investigation. It is not by chance that the plot of the novel centres on two events of economic significance. It is a reflection of the preoccupations of the colonial masters and an indication of Eza Boto's loyalty to reality in all its ramifications. The author is committed to depicting the unsung, though the most crucial aspect of the colonial civilising mission in Africa.

Both events mentioned are closely related. The reader is informed of the planned attack of a colonial employer of labour by a mechanic, Koumé, and his team of workmen. The cause of the violence is not far-fetched: M.T., the white employer, arbitrarily refuses to pay the salaries of the workers.

The second incident centres on the confiscation of cocoa belonging to Banda, a young village farmer, by produce inspectors, who are agents of colonial masters. Their excuse is that the produce was not sufficiently dried. But the reader knows the real cause of Banda's misfortune. He can separate the facts from fiction. Banda was yet to appreciate the strange realities and survival strategies of urban life in colonial Africa. He did not bribe the produce inspectors. Unknowingly, he was giving these agents the opportunity to sell his cocoa, put the money in their pockets and pretend that is was burnt since it was not suitable for export.

Later in the narrative, Banda meets Koumé who is pursued by the colonial police for his participation in the attack which led to the death of his employer. He offers him and his sister, Odilia, asylum in his village. Unfortunately, en route, Koumé dies accidentally. Banda discovers the money which the deceased had forcefully collected from the employer and hands it over to the sister, Odilia. The reader is told later of a handsome reward received by Banda for finding a missing suitcase belonging to a Greek trader.

The novel ends on a note of hope. Banda gets reconciled with his mother. The marriage between him and Odilia takes place before the departure of the couple to settle in the town of Fort-Nègre. One may conclude from here that the essence of the peasants' struggles for survival and justice and their attempts to actualise their potentials constitute the overriding themes explored by Eza Boto in his *Ville Cruelle* (The Cruel City).

With Mongo Beti's *Le Pauvre Christ de Bomba* (The Poor Christ of Bomba), published in 1956, the themes of injustice, racial and ethical incompatibility, protest, conflicts and their resolution come to light and determine the perspective and form of the novel itself. The story centres on a conscientious missionary, Reverend Father Superior Drumont who, after spending twenty years in Africa spreading the Gospel, decides to visit Tala, one of the small stations attached to the central mission of Bomba. He had neglected this station for three years on account of the parishioners' lukewarm attitude towards the Christian religion. On arriving at Tala, he discovers much to his dismay that his converts had abandoned their faith and had gladly returned to their traditional practices. The disappointed priest returns to the central mission in a state of confusion to reappraise the nature of his missionary work in colonial Africa. Through a sustained conversation with a young colonial administrator, M.Vidal, it becomes clearer to him that he has, all along, been playing an indispensable and complementary role in the colonial scheme.

The realisation that he, a man of good intention and of outstanding zeal in evangelism, could serve as an agent of colonial domination was disturbing. In utter disillusionment, he closes down the mission at Bomba and abandons his missionary vocation.

Set in a remote district in Cameroon of the late nineteen thirties, and written in the form of a diary of a boy, Denis, Reverend Father Drumont's acolyte, *The Poor Christ of Bomba* examines critically the missionary activities of Father Drumont as seen through the young, naive and unsuspecting eyes of the priest's acolyte. It is thanks to the recorded information of the latter in his diary that we appreciate the missionary zeal of the priest and the scandalous activities of the churchmen at the centre set up by Father Drumont for the preparation of girls for Christian marriage. The incompatibility of African and European moral values and Father Drumont's uncompromising attitude towards African tradition are equally taken note of in the document.

Other aspects of missionary experiences highlighted in the diary include the sad discovery by Father Drumont of the link between his missionary activities and the colonial mission; the people of Tala, their consciousness of their cultural identity and their collective rejection of an imposed religion. Denis' book of events also contains reports of Father Dumont's disheartening awareness of the fruitlessness of his missionary work in Africa. The presentation ends on an upbeat note with the Tala peasants' joy and consciousness of their total freedom from the yoke of a culturally-disturbing religion whose controlling force they could hardly distinguish from that of colonialism.

This optimistic perception of history is indeed an indication of the author's radical penchant. The happy mood of the Tala people is predicated on their consciousness that there is a change and for the better.

Sembène Ousmane's epoch making novel, *Les bouts de bois de Dieu* (God's Bits of Wood) appeared in 1960 with radical features in form and content. Published though on the eve of independence of many African nations, the preoccupations of the novel are the socio-economic realities of the days of colonial imperialism. The seat of action is the Senegalese colonial society of the early forties.

A socio-historical novel dealing with the colonial period and identifiable events, *God's Bits of Wood* strikes the reader by the ideological maturity of its characters, who actualise their potentials within a well planned socio-historical framework. Set against the background of an actual historical event, viz. the concerted resistance of railway workers on the Dakar-Bamako line from October 1947 to March 1948, the novel manifests itself as a radical literary piece that is seriously grounded in the mechanics of revolutionary thought. The striking workers, from whom the fictional characters take their inspiration, were protesting against exploitation, oppression and inhuman conditions of service perpetuated by colonial employers of labour.

Sembène Ousmane's artistic response to this reality and to the challenges of social change takes a serious radical form of which the following resounding themes are pertinent determinants: trade unionism and labour agitation, injustice, oppression, resistance and revolutionary struggle. The prevalence of such themes in a literary creation leaves no one in doubt concerning the artist's ideological penchant.

To depict these themes objectively and show the extent to which they determine individual and collective destinies, attempts are made to create a convincing feeling of verisimilitude by fixing the exact historical locale which, in this case, is colonial Senegal. The reportage of the actual dates, time and place of the historical event which forms the framework of the novel, is made with the authenticity of a historian. The striking workers and their demands for better conditions of service, individual and collective sacrifices, the women's great march, and the spirit of solidarity binding the workers together receive bold strokes of the pen. The whole panorama of the worker's life is shown from a historical and socio-economic perspective.

This novel which the author dedicates to "God's bits of wood" and to his comrades in the unions opens with the workers having full consciousness of the precarious nature of their material means of existence and of the need for solidarity and concerted effort in their struggles to establish a new socio-economic order based on justice. Specific demands are therefore made to their employer. They include "equal pay" for "equal work", old age pension, proper housing and family allowances[2] – benefits

---

[2] Ousmane Sembène: *God's Bits of Wood*, London, Heinemann 1960 p.290.

already enjoyed by their European counterparts. The request is turned down.

Following this insensitivity of the employer to the workers' grievances, a decisive confrontation, a strike action, becomes imperative. This is followed by the long march of women in support of the men's cause.

In the presentation of the ensuing events, attempts are made to represent the two parties in the conflict and their cherished positions objectively. But the discerning reader knows on whose side the author is and whose aspirations he identifies himself with.

The struggle takes its course concertedly and resolutely. Even at moments of shattering grief, the strikers still display solidarity and consciousness of their collective strength. This will-power has a potentially explosive force. It accounts for the fierce and uncompromising nature of the workers' struggle. Finally, the battle is won. A new socio-economic formation comes to being in line with the collective radical perspective of the masses with whom the author is in sympathetic link.

It seems that Sembène Ousmane shares Frantz Fanon's militant views in his projected solution to socio-economic problems. According to Frantz Fanon, the use of "rightful violence" is necessary for a return to the straight path ahead.[3]

By portraying in his novel themes which are revolutionary in nature, by offering through his moral vision of the reconstituted realities radical and positive alternatives available, and adopting in his literary creation working class perspective in his desire to see the socio-economic order radically restructured, Sembène Ousmane stands shoulder-high among the radical writers of the continent. A close examination of the ideological stance of these authors could help to determine the direction of their literary message.

Dominant Ideological Perspective

The ideological position of the literary artist is easily noticeable in his interests, sympathies, disposition and general posture towards the reality depicted. It is the author's dominant ideological disposition which, in the

---

[3] Opinion shared by Hugh Webb in his article "The African Historical Novel and the Way Forward" in *African Literature Today* no. 11, edited by Eldred Jones, London, Heinemann 1980 p.36.

final analysis, influences his interpretation of reality and the course and content of his work. This ideological disposition is indicative of the artist's sense of social responsibility, knowing too well that literature, being a product of society, has a normative influence on the society that produces it.

In *Ville Cruelle* (The Cruel City), Eza Boto projects himself as a writer with revolutionary sympathy. Both Banda and Koumé, principal characters in the novel, are the oppressed peasants who are conscious of the injustice which they are victims of and who show in their determined reactions their resentment of the socio-economic system that encourages it. Banda protests against the confiscation of his cocoa by the agents of colonial administration and struggles for his rights which, in the colonial situation, is seen by the oppressed peasants as unattainable ideals.[4] Koumé on his side adopts a more radical approach in solving the problem of the non-payment of his salary. He fights for his rights and forcefully collects more than his due from the employer who, unfortunately, dies in the encounter.

Through the struggles of these peasants to change their situation for the better, the author's interest, sympathy and general attitude towards the realities depicted leave no one in doubt with regards to the ideological direction of the novel. From the reactions of the fictional characters, one sees the positive alternatives proposed in the place of existing realities.

In the *Poor Christ of Bomba*, Mongo Beti attributes the failure of Reverend Father Superior Drumont to establish a lasting Christian Mission in Bomba to the priest's obvious misconceptions and his incomprehension of the mentality and the value system of his parishioners. Racial and ethical incompatibility between Africa and Europe portrayed in the novel are indicative of the author's consciousness of the need to radically replace the structures of the Christian religion in Africa with those which are genuinely African-oriented, in line with the spirit of nationalism of the period. Mongo Beti appears to champion the cause of the Tala people who are seen gradually reasserting their African identity and moving consciously into a position of hardened maturity. He identifies himself with the Talans who, being advanced in their consciousness of the real nature of the colonialists' cultural imperialism, seek refuge in their traditional religion.

The same progressive radical posture towards observable reality is

---

[4] Boto, Eza: *Ville Cruelle*, Paris; Présence Africaine.

seen in the choice of themes, creation of characters, their perceptions and behaviour and in the overall narrative movement of Sembène Ousmane's *God's Bits of Wood*. The author is seen taking a clear, decisive and radical stance in his interpretation of objective reality. The historical locale of the novel is presented as real. The characters are seen in their particularity and typicality. They are identifiable human beings. A pleasant harmony of literary form is achieved, thanks to an artistic design which unites structure, meaning and ideology

Positive alternatives to the depicted oppressive happenings are offered and are rooted to particular social and historical situations, sometimes at the expense of transcendental references. The heroic dimension of the activities of the workers engaged in the struggle to change their lot under the stress of oppression is celebrated with sympathetic understanding. The workers' consciousness of the real cause and nature of their deplorable social conditions, the spirit of brotherliness, reminiscent of the traditional African solidarity, and the collective resolve to succeed, do echo throughout the duration of the strike and the long solidarity march of the women. These are presented by the author with discernable concern as constituting the main force which exploiting capitalism has got to grapple with.

The need for an immediate establishment of a new socio-economic order to replace the existing one that is based on injustice and exploitation appears to be the overriding concern of Sembène Ousmane's *God's Bits of Wood.*

In the three novels surveyed, the recognised repositors of radical ideals (particularly in Sembène Ousmane's novel) are those who are fully conscious of the need for social change and are actively agitating for the realisation of this noble objective. They are the workers, the masses, whose aspirations the literary artists have identified themselves with and whose ideological perspectives they have endorsed and adopted as positive alternatives to the depicted oppressive reality. This interest in the masses as agents of social change is illustrated in the artists' choice of characters for their novels.

Characterisation

The role and nature of fictional characters in any literature that has direct correspondence to observable reality cannot be underestimated. Good characterisation gives the novel its very essence. Conscious of this fact therefore, Eza Boto and Mongo Beti who, incidentally, are one and the same person, create characters that come alive in *Ville Cruelle* (The Cruel City) and in *Le Pauvre Christ de Bomba* (The Poor Christ of Bomba) respectively. Banda and Koumé in *Ville Cruelle* (The Cruel City) remain in the reader's mind because of their resilience and their refusal to be changed by circumstances. They are real, dynamic and recognisable as human beings who act on their respective environments to produce radical changes. Banda is a plausible and convincing character in his role as a cocoa farmer whose labour is rewarded. He has 200kg of cocoa for sale. His anger, following the confiscation of his cocoa by dishonest produce inspectors, is human and understandable.

Koumé's portrait is equally vivid and compelling. Sturdily built as a local wrestler and revolutionary agent, he responds positively to the design of his creator. His violent show of force, occasioned by the unfair treatment meted out to him by his employer, is indicative of his courage and revolutionary potential. His consequent flight from home to escape from the invading forces of law and order and his eventual accidental death are believable human experiences. Both Banda and Koumé are presented to us at turning points in their lives. Their perception of the world and their reactions to events are sharpened by their experiences which help to raise their level of consciousness. They are positive heroes who achieve their missions. Both heroes hate injustice but have visions of brotherliness and justice. Despite his apparent despair arising from the confiscation of his cocoa, his obsession about travelling and the wandering nature of his existence, Banda still dreams of greatness and happiness. He strongly believes that he can still make it. This optimism in effect determines his departure to settle in the town of Fort-Nègre where self actualisation appears to him realisable.

In the *Poor Christ of Bomba,* Reverend Father Superior Drumont, the Bomba Christians and the Tala neophytes are graphically portrayed as active participants in the Christian religious scheme. They are human beings who can display grit, stand up to adversity and challenge circumstances. Denis, the priest's acolyte, acquires individuality and typicality because of his sincerity, devotion and open mindedness. M. Vidal, the young colonial administrator, appears in a characteristic social and historical environment as a good example of an exploiting class. These fictional characters are embedded in total reality - social, economic and political. Each section of a portrayed totality is placed in a well determined and concrete social context and historical situation. These are all devices which the author skillfully employs to ensure credibility.

The systematic exploration of the psychology of the striking workers in Sembène Ousmane's *God's Bits of Wood* is a contributive factor in the great success of the novel. The literary piece is also significant due to its historical originality, and the behaviour, strength, integrity, talent and resourcefulness of its characters. Their creator has highlighted these noble qualities of his creatures in their general perception of the world. Their innermost qualities are thoroughly explored against the background of the sacrifices that they make during the strike in the interest of their collective ideals. They are presented as simple people who believe in their collective strength and in the nobility of their cause. Such is the impression given by Penda, the transformed prostitute who becomes the heroine of the novel; Tiemoko, Bakayoko and Maïmouna the activists who, though socially motivated, do not in any way lose their identity as individuals. Their depths of feeling, forthrightness and integrity make them artistic types of considerable strength.

Of particular significance is the positive and new role which Sembène Ousmane assigns to female characters who, hitherto, were confined to the traditional role of mothers and housekeepers. The new woman represented by Penda is articulate and politically conscious. She participates freely in public affairs. The author recognises women as an essential factor of socio-economic transformation of the African continent. Their historic march in Dakar reported in the novel makes manifest their revolutionary potential.

The presentation of these vivid characters has enabled Sembène Ousmane to depict social relations and their determinants in colonial Senegal Of equal concern are the contradictions, conflicts and their resolutions in the society. His representation of these phenomena in the novel is in tune with his ideological perspective as a radical artist. One notes for instance that the participants in the strike are all workers committed to the task of improving their existence through an uncompromising struggle. They have proposed radical changes of viewpoints, changes of relationships between man and woman, employer and employee and a significant restructuring of the socio-economic order. Their radical approach to social change reflects the ideological perspective of the masses who find in Sembène Ousmane a reliable ally.

By making striking workers the purveyors of progressive and democratic ideals, Sembène Ousmane articulates the concerns of the African masses for freedom and justice. The promotion of the workers as radical agents of socio-economic transformation and the depiction of the nature of their ideological perspective call for an appropriate narrative technique that can also respond satisfactorily to the exigencies of the workers' collective potential.

Narrative Structure

The form and structure of a novel often reflect the attention which the literary artist gives to such considerations as appropriateness of characters and situations, relevance of the subject and the underlying themes, verbal structure, ideological thrust and the reading public. As Georg Lukacs rightly observes:

> The genuine categories of literary forms are not simply literary in essence. They are forms of life especially adapted to the articulation of great alternatives in a practical and effective manner—.[6]

By implication, it is the content of a literary piece that determines the form and the narrative structure of the work concerned. The narrative, of course, must adequately meet the demands of significance and the story perceived as narratable.

The story in Eza Boto's *Ville Cruelle* (The Cruel City) has a strong sense of place and a plethora of incidents. The narrative rises to the level of the author's concerns. Also plausible and convincing is the sensation of life that the novel creates. The author is deliberately realistic in his narrative. He wants his story to be believed as real. The reader is led to examine the economic motives of the colonial civilising mission in Cameroon. The two events presented to him in this exercise are of economic nature, viz. the confiscation of Banda's cocoa and an employer's refusal to pay his workers their salary.

Right from the opening of the plot, the devices designed to give shape to the author's perception of reality are made evident through a faithful portrayal of details, plausibility of characters and authenticity of the setting. The story starts with a dialogue which has a tone that is appropriate to the characters. The novel itself consists of thirteen chapters comprising many narrative units which, in a way, represent different aspects of human

---

[6] Lukacs Georg: *Writer and Critic and Other Essays* ed. and trans. A Kahn, London, Merlin Press, 1970 p.21.

experiences by which the central character is meant to benefit.

The first chapter opens with the lamentations of Banda's girlfriend over her lover's indecision concerning their plan to get married. From the ensuing dialogue, the reader is informed of the real reason for the marriage and is not surprised by the news of the cancellation of the marriage proposal and the consequent uneasy relationship between Banda and his mother. The use of the dialogue makes it easy for the author to stress with noticeable detachment the genuineness of the feeling, thought and behaviour of his characters, and to outline the essential elements of the novel which are to be fully developed in the accompanying chapters.

Notably in this regard are considerations bordering on Banda's mother's wish for her son to get married; the imperatives of the bride price; Banda's contact with the colonial school and the Christian religion, the attraction of the city and the hero's decision to go there to sell his cocoa. From the beginning of the chapter, the narrative reveals the dialectics of life which is seen not only as a struggle but as a forward movement. Banda is travelling out of the quiet Bamila village in response to economic exigencies.

Chapter two of the novel starts with a rhetorical question, decidedly to advance the narrative situation and build up tension "What has become of Tanga since the period of the events reported here?"[7] This prepares the mind of the reader for an appreciation of the characteristic features of colonial domination since the city to be visited by Banda symbolises the point of contact between Europe and Africa.

The writer's radical response to the appropriateness of colonial city as a literary theme necessitated a change of narrative technique. A third-person narrator whose omniscience is tempered with a strong dose of irony and satire emerges and takes over control. He provides detailed information on the major characters mentioned in the plot, their state of mind, and their preoccupations. He also touches on the determinants of social relations in the city. Tanga, the colonial town, is divided into two sections: North and South. Tanga South is inhabited by Europeans while the North is for Africans. A clear line of demarcation between good and evil is drawn. Tanga South with good houses and roads is the epitome of comfort whereas Tanga North is made prominent by the absence of the basic necessities of life which characterises its very existence.

Although the continued existence of a conducive environment for

---

[7] Boto, Eza, *Op. Cit.* p.16 (the translation is ours)

self actualisation in Tanga South is assured, thanks to the cheap labour provided by the inhabitants of Tanga North, there is no reciprocal gesture from the colonial masters to alleviate the sufferings of these workers.

From the detailed information on the two incompatible cities, the reader has a fair impression of the author's concerns and his social stance as made manifest in the description of the motives, acts, thoughts and feelings of the inhabitants. There is a noticeable condemnation of the existing reality in the overall depiction of the antagonistic social relations between the two cities.

As the plot progresses in the third chapter, the realistic elements in the narrative gain more strength. The description of events and historical circumstances becomes more precise. The opening phrase of the first sentence of the chapter is indicative of this near documentary style in the reflection of reality: "One morning in the month of February 193..."[8]. The issues to be depicted call for historical accuracy: A European M.T. has arbitrarily refused to pay his workers on a particular day in the history of Cameroon. Koumé, one of the affected members of staff plans with his colleagues to collect the money from him by force. The chapter which follows presents another scene of injustice. Banda's cocoa is unjustly confiscated by produce inspectors. Banda protests vehemently. He is arrested but later discharged. His case receives no sympathetic consideration. The knell of injustice tolled louder and louder.

Chapter five reports of the realisation of Koumé's plan and the actualisation of his potential. M.T., the cruel employer, is attacked and money is collected from him. He dies in the process. Eza Boto subtly signals here that oppressive socio-economic conditions give rise to revolutionary actions.

The same commitment to socio-historical and psychological truth, in describing events, characteristic features, characters' perception and behaviour which mark the narrative of these early chapters of the novel, also condition the presentation of the remaining eight chapters. The reader's interest in the novel is skillfully sustained through the spiralling composition of the plot, the power of the narrative and the author's lucid and incisive capturing of life in a colonial city.

With *The Poor Christ of Bomba,* Mongo Beti shows clearly how character, coincidence and environment can converge to make lives and

---

[8] *Ibid.* p. 27

their plots. It is the pathetic story of Reverend Father Superior Drumont's inability to evangelise Africans despite his sincerity and commitment to his assignment. The use of an all-seeing first-person narrator allows the author to range over a wide horizon and to place the historical locale convincingly. This device tends towards a unity of point of view and coherence. It is therefore not a surprise that this story told by Denis, the narrator endowed with certain omniscient powers, has a rigid structural coherence. Each episode is satisfactorily fitted within the overall structural pattern and precipitates another. Satire remains the dominant tone of the novel while the artistic method adopted is realism. With the authorial ordering of events, the novel is assured the necessary spatial and temporal features that make for a comprehensive representation of the observable reality.

Action in the novel begins on Sunday the 1st of February 193...[9], and terminates also on a Sunday the 23rd of the same month.[10] Divided into three sections with each recording the events of each week, the novel presents the experiences and activities of Reverend Father Drumont during his routine visits to all the stations in his parish.

During the first week, the narrator's focus is on Father Drumont and the parishioners in seven stations from Bomba to Ekokot. The reader is conducted into the houses of some of the parishioners to appreciate the conflicts and contradictions occasioned by the priest's mode of evangelism. He is allowed reasonable insight into the inner conflicts that beset the characters. From their reactions, a consciousness of the positive alternative values available to them is sensed.

The second week takes the reader to seven other stations from Ndimi to Bomba where there is a marked shift in the narrative from a psychological portrayal of the life of Father Drumont to a broader vision of the parishioners in their social, moral and economic relationships.

The incompatibility of European and African values, illustrated through the negligence and indifference of the parishioners towards the Christian religion, defines the structure of the narrative in the final section of the novel and reinforces its radical thrust. There is a felt need for the new religion to be restructured in line with African realities.

---

[9] Beti, Mongo: *Le Pauvre Christ de Bomba*, Paris; Présence Africaine 1976 p.11
[10] *Ibid.* p.272

From the station of Bomba to Sogolo, the last station visited by the Reverend Father, the general mood of the parishioners reflects an uncomfortable mixture of indifference, sorrow and joy. While the majority of the people rejoice over the departure of the priest since they are now going to be left to worship God their own way, others exhibit total indifference towards the priest's activities since, in their opinion, his mission was unnecessary. They were already worshipping God before his arrival in their territory.

By portraying this honest and conscientious priest's sorrow and the abandonment of his missionary vocation as a psychological reaction to a deep feeling of failure and awareness of his complicity in the colonial mission, is the author not unwittingly whipping up the sympathy of the reader for him, sympathy which is rooted in shared human experience of failure and disappointment? As for Reverend Father Superior Drumont himself, his sorrow and disappointment have opened his eyes to new vistas of experience as a result of which he is more conscious of African realities.

The narrative structure of Sembène Ousmane's *God's Bits of Wood* is equally exciting. The pertinent features which have given it significant characteristics that lend credence to the author's radical ideological stance are the frequent coming together of the characters and their having to share common experiences and tales together. Also noticeable as determinants of the narrative is the author's conscious consideration given to such moral values as group participation solidarity; mutual understanding, communal endeavours and positive thinking. All these aspects of the plot constitute the narrative technique which is destined to reflect and strengthen the ideological thrust of the novel. The plot itself is tight and has organic unity.

God's Bits of Wood is epic in sweep. It is historically concrete, tense and dynamic in its succession of scenes and psychological intensity. The striking workers are seen as authentic human beings working together and constituting a formidable force that determines the destiny of the collectivity.

The novel which opens with a depiction of the harsh socio-economic realities of the Senegalese society of the colonial period also portrays the growing consciousness of the workers of their potential and their resolve to take the road of collective struggle to better their lot. The narrative flows with a satisfying intensity and reveals the author's attachment to reveal the inner meanings of facts and situations. This explains his attempt to examine the observable phenomena from all sides, describe them in all their complexity and contradictions without neglecting their historical implications.

With the strike action and the great march of the women, the interest of the reader shifts to Bamako, Thiès and Dakar where the characters, throbbing with life and determination, are seen expressing positive and radical views which the thrust of the narrative ably sustains. Such optimistic disposition is what echoes in this song extemporised by the women led by their leader, Penda, in support of the striking men:

> The morning light is in the east;
> It is daybreak of a day of history.
> (..)
> On the 10th of October, fateful day
> We swore before the world
> To support you to the end.
> You have lit the torch of hope
> And victory is near.
> The morning light is in the east;
> It is daybreak of history.[12]

Having the truth as his principal guide in the portrayal of the colonial milieu which is seething with passions and explosive contradictions, *Sembène Ousmane* presents the two antagonistic forces at work - the employers and the employed. The strike is shown from its developing stage to when it is full-blown. The protagonists of the strike action such as Bakayoko, Ramatoulaye and Penda are painted in bold touches. Those who oppose it are in no way ignored. They include *El Hadji Mabigué, Bachirou and Dejean*. The novel depicts the positions and characters of the principal actors put on stage. It is an impressive literary piece with satiric overtones. The author overtly promotes Penda – his major feminine character whose radical views are of general significance within the historical sweep of the narrative – to a position of great importance. For Penda, success is certain and the future bright once the workers are united in their struggle against injustice. And so it was at the end.

A survey of these early novels of Mongo Beti and Sembène Ousmane reveals the general ideas of the authors about the basic phenomena of life and their understanding of the historical process. Through careful

---

[12] Ousmane, Sembène: *Op. cit.* pp 237-238.

selections of literary themes, fictional characters and a good mastery of the narrative technique, the writers have created works having social problems as fields of creative investigation. These creations advocate radical restructuring of the socio-economic realities in response to the demands of justice and democracy. They also celebrate the growing consciousness of the masses of their potential, and depict their relentless struggles to bring about change in the society. The novels are infused with radical ideals and a feeling of fortitude arising from the workers' awareness of their collective strength.

One may therefore posit that Mongo Beti and Sembène Ousmane recognise the common people, the masses, as agents of progress and the purveyors of radical ideals. They have accordingly adopted the working class ideological perspective in their depiction of colonial realities in their respective countries. In their loyalty to observable truth, both authors have presented literary creations that tend to have direct correspondence to reality.

Everett Knight was probably expressing the opinion of these artist when he remarked that:

> ... the world is no longer interpreted to the masses by the church and the throne; and the newspapers that have taken their place are inevitably either tendentious or simple organs of propaganda. How is the truth to be made known if not by literature? In the face of the increasingly efficient methods for the dissemination of lies, literature is one hope that will not eventually swallow up the facts.[13]

---

[13] Knight, Everett: *Literature Considered as Philosophy: The French Example.* New York, Collier Books 1957 p. 94.

References

Boto, Eza. *Ville Cruelle*. Paris Présence Africaine 1971.
Beti, Mongo. *Le Pauvre Christ de Bomba*. Paris, Présence Africaine, 1976.
Eagleton, Terry. *Criticism and Ideology*. London, Verso 1976.
Fishcher, Ernest. *The Necessity of Art*. Harmonds Worth, Penguin Books 1963.
John, Elerius E. *Literature and Development: The West African Experience*, Calabar, Paico Press Ltd, 1986.
John, Elerius E. *Creative Responses of Mongo Beti and Ferdinand Oyono*. Calabar, Paico Press Ltd., 1986.
Jones, Eldred (ed.) *African Literature Today*. No. 11, London, Heinemann 1980.
Knight, Everett W. *Literature Considered as Philosophy: The French Example*, New York, Collier Books 1957.
Lukacs, Georg. *The Meaning of Contemporary Realism*. London, Merlin Press 1963.
Lukacs, Georg. *Writer and Critic and Other Essays* (ed. and trans. A Kahn) London, Merlin Press 1970.
Mbock, Charly-Gabriel. *Comprendre Ville Cruelle d'Eza Boto*. Paris, Les Classiques Africains 1992.
Ngara, Emmanuel. *Art and Ideology in the African Novel*. London, Heinemann 1985.
Nwoga, D.I. (ed.) *Literature and Modern West African Culture*. Benin, Ethiopc Publishers, 1978.
Ousmane, Sembène. *God's Bits of Wood*. London, Heinemann 1960.
Pieterse, Cosmo and Munro D. (eds.) *Protest and Conflict in African Literature*. New York, Africana Publishing Corporation 1970.
Slaughter, Cliff. *Marxism, Ideology and Literature*. London, Macmillan 1980.
Udenta O. Udenta. *Revolutionary Aesthetics and the African Literary Process*. Enugu, Fourth Dimension Publishing Co. Ltd. 1993.
Vassily Novikov. *Artistic Truth and Dialectics of Creative Work*, Moscow, Progress Publishers 1981.
Vladimir, Baskakov. "Mass Art and the Popular Spirit in Art" in *Problems of Contemporary Aesthetics*. Moscow, Raduga Publishers 1984.
Young, Robert. *Untying the Text: A Post-Structuralist Reader*. London, Routledge and Kegan Paul 1981.

10

MODERN AFRICAN LITERATURE AS ILLUSIONS OF AFRICAN REALITY: THE CASE OF THE FRANCOPHONE NOVEL

Olusola Oke

Introduction

Modern African literature, that is that literature that has emerged since the beginning of the modern era in Africa and which is written both in foreign and African languages, has sought relentlessly to portray the socio-political reality of traditional and contemporary Africa. It has done so by painting a series of images (illusions) of that reality. Illusion, which constitutes one of the key elements of fictional literature, is a predominant element of modern African literature, especially of the African novel and of modern African theatre.

In the particular case of fiction and especially when it seeks to portray society and socio-political reality, the world of literature is sometimes the world of illusion, the world of imaginative reality, the world "in which the imagination of the author shapes the material." It is the world of distorted reality, distorted to the extent that "fiction is opposed to fact, as being not actual but an invention, to deceive, to entertain, or by its suggestions of reality to teach."[1]

The persistent reference to modern African literature as committed literature, *littérature engagée*, is no doubt a reflection of the commitment of the African writer to the referential aspect of his works. The relationship

---

[1] J. T. Shipley. *Dictionary of World Literary Terms*. London: George Allen & Unwin, 1970, p.119.

between authentic reality and its fictional version, which the African writer paints in his works, cannot be ignored without doing untold damage to the true import of the literature. It has often appeared that he, the African writer, hardly respects the inevitable difference between authentic reality and fictional reality. He loads his image of socio-political reality, with obvious references to authentic reality; he deliberately intrudes in the unfolding scenario of his stories.[2]

The vitality of modern African literature seems primarily to be more a function of the relevance of the image of reality (the illusion) to authentic reality than of the literary attributes of the works in which this illusion is purveyed. It is more of the former than the latter not only because the writers wish it to be so but also and, perhaps, more significantly, because it is the only way that the socio-political issues that concern the writers would be put in proper focus.[3] The significance of literary images to modern African literature is reflected both in the writers' unflinching commitment to the closeness of the image to authentic reality and in their visions of reality that reflect ideological and philosophical positions and principles. Negritude, African personality, socialism and even, nowadays, Western modernist and post modernist psychologism and feminism have shaped the image of Africa that appears in modern African literature. The illusions of reality that bear the influence of these ideologies and angles of vision present diversified images of Africa and thus confer on African literature a significant status. These images constitute alternative visions of authentic reality that invite the more discerning minds to reflect on the latter. Initially, they helped to raise African literature to the status of a weapon in the struggle against colonisation. They have provided an effective medium for reflecting on the aftermath of African independence and have even started to raise the issues of modernism and feminism that were not anticipated by

---

[2] See Eza Boto. *Ville cruelle*. Paris: Présence Africaine, 1954; Camara Laye. *L'enfant noir* Paris: Plon. 1953; Ferdinand Oyono. *Le vieux nègre et la médaille*. Paris: Julliard, 1956.

[3] Modern African literature was written initially partly against the background of the conscience-awakening that led Africans to counter the disparaging images of Africa and Africans that appeared in European and colonial literature. Modern African literature was partly written too as part of the natural development of an African literary tradition that predated colonisation. In that tradition, literature always gave priority attention to authentic reality. Literature existed largely for the edification of society. Art for art's sake was not part of the primary considerations of pre-colonial African literary tradition and it enjoys perhaps only minimal attention among the individual African artists and writers who succeeded the collective creators of traditional communal art and literature.

the enervating protest against colonisation and neo-colonialism.

The necessary concomitant of the above is the significance of the illusion of reality that is contained in African literature to African (or any) society. Given especially the preoccupation of society with immediate and authentic reality, fictional reality is usually disdained but only so by the less sensitive societies or by those societies in which there is an acceptable concurrence between the preferred values and ideology and the ones that literature projects. By reflecting imaginatively on reality, literature projects the latter to the realm of ideas. It extends authentic reality through this imaginative projection and is thus able to point up societal values, both positive and negative, that may not be easily or immediately visible. In addition, literature helps in sustaining moral principles and reinforcing ideology partly by increasing society's awareness of them and partly too by the direct didactic conclusions and messages that it projects through literary illusions.

The Illusion-of-Reality Dimension in Modern African Literature

Illusions of reality and their connectedness to authentic reality cannot be taken away from the centre of literature without shutting modern African literature away from the limelight. The circumstances of its birth were such that it was required to serve as a medium through which Africans would be able to respond to the need to define African cultural heritage. Modern African literature drew its inspiration, initially, partly from the need to mobilise all the avenues that were available to the African intellectual for a life-and-death struggle against colonial and racist prejudices that threatened to relegate the African (negro, black, sub-Saharan) man to the level of a savage half-human. All aspects of the superstructure in the African universe including all the political, social and cultural practices and institutions and, indeed, all the African languages were given little or no recognition as valid contributions to human civilisation. The colonising Europeans in order to justify their pernicious white-man's-burden conception of their invasion of black Africa had denigrated and relegated African philosophies of life, religions, art, music, dance, marriage and family system, etc. to a despicable status from which they are still to be fully rehabilitated.

Modern African literature particularly in the negritude era played a significant role in redressing the situation in which African culture was banished to the status of a pre-rational culture. Africa was given the central role in negritude literature and African men and women were ascribed principal roles in the images of African reality that were projected in the literature.[4] The white colonialists began to be relegated to the negative role that they had ascribed to the Africans in their colonial literature.[5] This was achieved first in negritude poetry, which, without painting a full image of African social reality (hardly the role of poetry), drew positive attention to the denigrated and rejected African culture.

The massive poetry that negritude generated contributed significantly to the rehabilitation not only of African culture but also and more importantly, perhaps, of the African man. In this respect, negritude poetry is perhaps less dependable than post-negritude fiction. This is because the attention that it has drawn to traditional Africa and African culture has proved to be rather unrealistic since it glossed over areas of conflict and contradictions that may have been responsible in the first place for the failure of Africa to evolve into modernity.

This role would be played later and quite responsibly by prose literature. In the images of Africa and African reality that would be depicted in post-negritude fiction, traditional and post-colonial Africa would be projected both negatively and positively. The scepticism of post-negritude African writers towards traditional African culture confers on the images of African society and culture that they paint in their works a higher degree of reliability than is found in the negritude images of Africa.

The illusion-of-reality element in literature can hardly be discussed without paying some attention to realism, that is to that element of perception of literary image that leads the reader of literature to recognise the world within the novel, in particular, and its explicit and implicit relation to the world without. As the ideological extrapolation from the representativeness of the illusion and which characterises the degree and state of its *mimesis*

---

[4] The images of Africa and Africans that are painted in Senghor's *Chaka*, Camara's *L'enfant noir* and Beti's *Mission terminée*, etc. are a follow-up to René Maran's *Batouala*. As early as 1922, the West Indian colonial administrator had painted the African not merely as a man, whose image is to be reflected through the eyes of benevolent or malevolent missionaries or colonial administrators, but as an independent entity in himself even if a rather pathetic one at that.

[5] In the novels that Mongo Beti and Ferdinand Oyono wrote after the Second World War and until independence around 1960, the white missionaries and colonial administrators come out as misguided and naïve evangelists collaborating even if reluctantly with whimsical, arbitrary and sometimes plainly wicked administrators. The combination of the two makes their African dependants rather sorry figures to behold.

or imitativeness, realism may serve as a yardstick for measuring literary reality's relevance or mere relatedness to authentic reality. In the specific context of modern African literature, which, at the inception, was a literature of revolt, a literature that had to have direct relevance to authentic socio-political reality which it seeks to indict, a literature of illusion that would subsequently have to cope with disillusionment, realism must assume a significance that it does not assume in those other literatures that have more literary than socio-political motivation and goals.

The Varying Degrees and Different Types of Illusion

For various significant reasons, the images of authentic African reality that modern African literature projects are varied. This is, most obviously, because they emanate from different individual imaginations and experiences. But it is also because they are the reflections of differing perceptions and ideological viewpoints that could come even from the same individual imagination at different points of maturation.[6] The varying illusions may also reflect the effects of literary conventions that can never be avoided totally even by the most politically committed literature. The influence of French romantic literature on modern African literature and on negritude poetry in particular coupled with the influence of surrealism on African writers and the image of Africa that they project in their works can hardly be overlooked without taking something away from the literature. The different types of illusions are amply represented in various African novels of the colonial and post-colonial eras, in negritude and neo-negritude novels as well as in the novels of the radical and modernist

---

[6] The images of colonial and neo-colonial reality that Mongo Beti paints in his novels from *Ville cruelle* through *Mission terminée* to *Remember Ruben* are a case in point. The manichean world of Tanga Nord and Tanga Sud as painted in *Ville cruelle* emanates from a sensitive imagination that seeks to draw attention to the plight of hapless Africans, who enjoy maximum sympathy from the writer.

The role of Jean-Marie Medza in *Mission terminée* reveals a more subtle relationship between him and the author's convictions and/or ideology. The writer refuses to connive at the hero's *naïve* arrogance during his confrontation with the Kala peasants. But this is a far cry from the Marxian perspective from which he wrote *Remember Ruben*. Here, the plight of the African is depicted in the life of an unwilling revolutionary who discovers his revolutionary potentials during a series of harrowing experiences in neo-colonial Africa. He accepts the need to fight for his people's liberation in a struggle that is narrated in a subsequent novel, *La ruine presque cocasse d'un polichinelle*.

perspectives.

Negritude literature articulated what was regarded as the essence of the Negro philosophy of life, the true values of the African way of life; it puts forward articulate illusions of traditional Africa that the Western detractors of Africa were invited to contemplate, reflect upon and help to validate in preference to the denigrating images of Africa that they propagated. The young African *évolués* from the French colonies in Africa and the West Indies, who found themselves imprisoned in qualified Frenchness in the metropolis, rejected hollow French citizenship – hollow in terms of its paradoxes and ambiguities – and re-assumed their Africanness which it became necessary to define and articulate. Their choice of the literary medium for the articulation of the essence and values of African existence, cultural values and practice is no doubt because literature provided the most appropriate medium for reaching out to both fellow Africans and to the French society. Africa and the Africans had been so deliberately denied the right to the status of human beings by their European colonisers, including the French, that any and all avenues of countering their insidious propaganda became acceptable.

Literature assumes a significant role in this respect, for it provides a medium for the popularisation of ideas, a role that has been passed on in the last third of the last century to radio and television. In addition, emotive issues like the relative value and virtue of culture are more suited to literature than to history and philosophy, which purvey more systematic and rational versions of reality.

African literature in French concerned itself initially not only with the articulation of the values of African existence, it also gave considerable attention and space to the presentation and description of concrete African qualities and also to the African philosophy of life. It was a disseminator of the ideas relating to the political, economic and social reality of African life before the white coloniser appeared on the scene and during his unpleasant and unfortunate intervention. It is inevitably and closely linked to authentic reality at this stage; its references and relationship to authentic reality is such that literary criticism can only ignore this dimension at the risk of becoming a mere intellectual exercise which nobody would take seriously. The negritude preoccupation with the affirmation of Africanness and African values has remained a continuous trait in Francophone African literature but it was only dominant until the early sixties. Before then, new perspectives had started to emerge that contested the "negritudist" assumptions about traditional African culture and this perspective was well-documented in literature.

The Reality of Our Illusions

Negritude and post-Negritude Francophone African literature presents images of Africa, African society and socio-political reality that confront us with moral and political implications some of which have been fully understood and appreciated. In most cases, however, the capabilities of literature as a tool for the affirmation and redefinition of cultural and social reality, values and ideology have not been properly harnessed and utilised in most African countries to date. Three tendencies dominate the image of African society that emerges from Francophone African fiction. All the three tendencies have co-existed since the emergence of modern African literature between the two world wars but each has been more prevalent at one time than the others. Each of the tendencies seems to tally with the level of cynicism of the writers coupled with their preparedness or otherwise to point the way forward through the literary medium to political and other non-political activists in the continent's social, political and economic life. It is also true that the dominant world view dictated by African socio-political reality, viewed against the background of African aspirations and priorities at any given period, has been reflected in the tendency that is dominant in the literature of the time. The tendencies are "mimetic" realism, "cynical" realism and "experimental" realism.

Mimetic Realism

The most visible tendency at the inception of Francophone African literature is that of the depiction of African reality in images that come as close as possible to the "authentic" source of literary inspiration. This we shall characterise as "mimetic realism". The term mimetic has been adopted in full awareness of its all-inclusive connotation in prose fiction where it covers the explicit or oblique "imitation of (society and its) actions" (mimesis). But we would like to anchor it here on the high degree of closeness between the imitation and the imitated thing in a situation where the imitator (the writer/novelist, in this case) has no room for cynicism nor is involved in any attempt to project reality beyond its visible characteristics. His main concern is to represent observable reality in such a way that more of its qualities than its defects, more of its strength than its weaknesses, more of its beauty than its ugliness, is revealed. The protagonists of this phase in Francophone fiction are Camara Laye in *L'Enfant noir*[7] and *Le Regard du Roi*,[8] Cheikh Hamidou Kane in *L'Aventure ambigüe*[9] and O. Bhêly-Quénum in *Le Chant du lac*.[10] These do not exhaust the list of works in the category but they provide some of its substantial examples.

L'Enfant noir was written (or was it?) by Camara Laye the Guinean engineer in 1953. However, more recently, a French girlfriend of his was said to be the real author of the novel. The lady's name has not been revealed and a Parisian girl could not have written the details about life in Guinea that appear in the novel. Indeed, the copyright of the novel has not been altered; we must continue to associate the book with the late Camara Laye. Like all négritude literature, African society is depicted here in its most serenely peaceful, positive and culturally stable form. The African child, Fatoman, knows parental love, lives in a happy agrarian society which is hardly influenced by Islam or Christianity and where traditional African beliefs and modes of worship are virtually intact. He passes through the rites of initiation, participates in the tedious but highly poetic life of the rice farmers and learns to respect the family's totem, the serpent. His journey through this "pure" African reality does not prevent, indeed it seems to enhance, his success in the French school in Conakry to which he transfers from Tindican, his native village. He finishes his studies in Conakry, qualifies for studies in France and crosses over only to find that his apprenticeship in the French factory, where he undergoes industrial training, offers little in comparison to his spiritually enriched life in Guinea. Indeed, it is his nostalgia for that life that leads to the writing of *l'Enfant noir*. Fatoman recaptures his African childhood, albeit imaginatively, in an effort to neutralise the pangs of his new technological and unpoetic "French" life.

In another and more symbolic novel, *Le Regard du roi*, Camara inverts the role of Africa in the Euro-African saga by creating a French neophyte who engages in an intriguing search for the blessing of an African

---

[7] Camara Laye. *Op. Cit.*
[8] *Ibid. Le Regard du roi.* Paris: Plon, 1954.
[9] C. H. Kane. *L'Aventure ambigüe.* Paris: Julliard, 1961.
[10] O. Bhêly-Quénum. *Le Chant du lac.* Paris: Présence Africaine, 1965.

king. This hankering takes the French man, who has been ostracised by the French community in the African colony in which he lives, on a journey to the south of the country on the trail of the young African king who is accompanied by two enigmatic servants, "Noaga" and "Nagoa." The latter turn the journey almost into a nightmare for the hapless Frenchman. At the end he has been turned into a stud that impregnates many African girls in order to produce Afro-French mulattoes; the French man is received by the African king and thus fulfils his life-dream.

The validation and valorisation of African cultural values that are involved in these novels is reflected not arbitrarily but in well articulated fictional realities that are engaging in their uncomplicated plot in the case of *L'Enfant noir*, and in the enigmatic quest in *Le Regard du roi*. Both Fatoman and Clarence are imbued with an overpowering hankering after redeeming African values: the expatriate African is thirsty for the cultural water that France cannot provide and the rejected French man is looking for African salvation in colonial Africa. He has lost all his bearing and cannot return to France.

It is obvious that the thirst of the French man for African culture in *Le Regard du roi* cannot seriously be said to be close to the real French experience in colonial Africa nor can his destitution find much parallel in the plight of the French sojourner in French African colonies. Nevertheless, the aura that is created around the young African king who symbolises Africa in the novel is quite close to the enigma that African cultural values, and particularly the values of kingship and mysticism, constituted for the secularly minded republican Frenchmen imbued with Cartesian logic and post-war cynicism.

The values of African kingship and happy communal and agrarian life of spiritualism and totems are not only depicted in positive light, the European is enriched by them and the African recaptures them even in the midst of European civilisation and Christian values. And the works are quite engaging and convincing.

The case of Cheikh Hamidou Kane's *L'Aventure ambiguë* introduces a new dimension into the novels of the "mimetic mode". The image of Africa as represented in this novel becomes a counterpoint in a kind of musical arrangement in which Africa is juxtaposed with Europe. The contrasting cultures of Europe and Africa are pitched against each other in the mystico-philosophical adventures of Samba Diallo, the hero of the novel. Islam provides the cultural values that delineate African culture and the African world view in *L'Aventure ambiguë*; for it is the scientific-materialist cultural values of post-industrial modern Europe that provide the cultural underpinnings of the materialist philosophy of life that is so well articulated by the French colonial civil servant who shares the same office with *le chevalier*, Samba Diallo's father. The latter projects the Islamic mysticism of his African society as a more humanistic and more reassuring philosophy of life and one which prevents the African and Muslim world from descending into the anti-human belief and that the relationship between man and the universe is one of unremitted absurdity.

Samba Diallo crosses from Afro-Islamic mysticism to Western materialism when he proceeds from Africa to France to study philosophy at a French university. He resists every temptation to be consumed by materialism and scientific logic even as he pursues his university degree programme in Western philosophy. Rather, he delves into the new insights that he acquires in order to find parallels to Afro-Islamic mysticism. On his return to Africa and after successfully completing his studies in France, Samba Diallo can no longer carry out the role that had been reserved for him as the new leader of the Muslim faith in *Diallobé*. This is to his chagrin and to that of his African society. Urged on by "the mad man" (*le fou*), the prop that accompanies him to the praying ground, Samba Diallo tries but fails to regain the spiritual inspiration and Islamic devotion that he requires to assume the role of *maître*, the Imam. Indeed, Samba Diallo, by failing to find peace with the spiritual role that was cut out for him in the society forfeits the right to life. With the help of "the mad man" he commits suicide, as if to say, "If I can no longer live as a true African, life as a whole has become meaningless and must be given up."

This is a rather pessimistic depiction of the value of African culture for Africans but which, nevertheless, stoutly demonstrates the preoccupation of African writers with the direct and implicit implications of the impact of foreign cultures. It is the indispensability of an unalloyed commitment by African spiritualist and temporal leaders to African culture in its purest form that becomes the issue in *L'Aventure ambiguë*. Samba Diallo's formidable defence of the culture against opposing philosophies proves inadequate in spite of its relentlessness.

In *L'Etrange destin de Wangrin ou les roueries d'un interprète africain*,[11] a novel that was written by Hampate Bâ, one of the foremost

---

[11] A. Hampâté Bâ. *L'Etrange destin de Wangrin*. Paris: Union Générale d'Editions, 1973.

promoters of negritude, especially of its historical dimensions, the image of traditional Africa is rather skewed. *L'Etrange destin de Wangrin* is the story of an enigmatic African employee of the colonial administration, an interpreter, a man, who through repeated acts of heartless betrayal of trust engineered by an overbearing ambition causes the downfall of fellow African employees and colonial administrators alike. By their number, the petulance of the executor and the sheer skill with which Wangrin carries out his acts of betrayal, he is nothing less than an evil genius. He is like the tortoise in the Yoruba folktales or the spider in Ashanti stories. He is practically inimitable. After ruining his friends and foes alike, African compatriots, benefactors and close associates, French colonisers and, indeed, anybody through whom he could further his quest for power and wealth, nemesis catches up with Wangrin, alias Gongoloma-Sooké. He loses the protection of the god whose name he has acquired as alias. Gongoloma-Sooké, the protector of Wangrin, forsakes him following the loss of the talisman that he acquired on adopting the protector-god.

The former master of his art, the accomplished rogue and traitor par excellence meets his waterloo, quite paradoxically, in the hands of a French couple who become his associates in the booming import-export business that he has set up. Wangrin becomes Madame Terreau's concubine after the latter practically seduces him. The amorous relationship lulls his sixth sense; he drops his guards, becomes less attentive to the financial transactions that the Terreaus carry out on his behalf and finds out too late that the French couple has transferred half of the company's capital to France. The woman and her husband disappear without any trace before Wangrin discovers his bankruptcy. What remains of the company's funds is not even enough to pay for its liabilities. In his ruin, Wangrin recognises the hand of the gods, refuses to request or accept help in cash or in kind even from his former beneficiaries, he becomes a *clochard*, a tramp, and dies a miserable death, drowned in a deep gutter in Dioussoula after a heavy downpour. Wangrin was in his last days and from the beginning of his amorous affair with Mrs Terreau a hopeless drunkard, who robbed women on their way to the market to pay for his alcohol.

Placed side by side with *L'Enfant noir*, *L'Aventure ambiguë* and the other novels that are meant to validate the authentic traditional African way of life, the negritude works that demonstrate mimetic realism, *L'Etrange destin de Wangrin* looks like a deliberate and rather unpleasant distortion of traditional Africa in the face of colonisation. It seems to do so little credit to our ancestral values and virtues that include basic honesty, hospitality and the fear of retribution, especially for deliberate acts of disloyalty. However, it has been recognised, and quite rightly so, that:

> *Le récit, à travers la carrière poursuivie par Wangrin, met*
> ....
> *en lumière les tensions dont la société coloniale est le théâtre* [12]
>
> [The story reveals, through Wangrin's adventures, the tensions that characterise the colonial society]

Such tensions do not however obliterate the more familiar preoccupations of traditional African society.

> *On peut....voir dans le récit de Hampâté Bâ l'histoire d'un homme qui vit conformément à la culture qui est la sienne, dans un univers marqué par le destin et les forces surnaturelles* [13]
>
> [One can ... see in Hampâté Bâ's story the life of a man who lives, as is normal in his culture, in a universe that accommodates the idea of destiny and of supernatural forces].

The *naïve* display of Negritude values in *L'Enfant noir* and *Le Regard du roi* is complemented by the not-so-simplistic portrayal in *L'Aventure ambiguë*. Whatever questions are raised therein about the not-so-rosy image of traditional Africa are amplified in *L'Etrange destin de Wangrin*. In our literary illusions, even of the most accommodating nature, our complacency is not total.

Cynical Realism

It is, however, in the next category of novels, that is those that we shall classify under the rubric of "cynical realism", that our cynicism comes to the surface. Our cynicism in the face of the disturbing contradictions of traditional African culture and which have been compounded by the intervention of the coloniser is fully expressed in these novels. The novels do not depict traditional African society on a one-to-one basis. The image

---

[12] B. Mouralis. "Le problématique de la liberté dans Wangrin", in Lecture de l'oeuvre d'Hampâté Bâ. Paris: l'Harmattan, 1992.

[13] *Ibid.*

of African society that emerges from the novels of Mongo Beti,[14] Ferdinand Oyono,[15] Ahmadou Kourouma,[16] Henri Lopès,[17] Mariama Bâ,[18] etc, results from a deliberate depiction, even enlargement, of the debilitating factors that explain the obvious backwardness in which the African society finds itself. Unlike in the novels of the first category, the image of African society is here distorted, albeit with a lot of cynical humour, which allows it to jolt the consciousness not only of the Africans themselves, particularly the more complacent ones that are ever so ready to swallow the negritude clichés, but also of their foreign friends who are only too ready to reduce African reality to what is easy to handle by friendly and condescending anthropologists.

The most incisive of these novels include *Le Pauvre Christ de Bomba, Le Roi miraculé, Le Vieux nègre et la médaille,* and *Le Pleurer-Rire.* The illusion of African reality that emerges from these novels is, in its totality, rather cynical.

In *Le pauvre Christ de Bomba*, Drumond, the enthusiastic, rather overzealous leader of the Catholic mission in Bomba, leads a "crusade" to upbraid his African congregation whose Christianity is waning. He is fully convinced that all that is needed to rouse the "sleeping" Africans from their slumber is a crusade that would reawaken their interest in Christianity and in its good values. He upbraids them publicly and right in their own homes, reminding them of the inevitable price that they were bound to pay for their neglect of the Lord's ways. He humiliates their dignitaries and chiefs who have deviated from the Christian ways by taking more than one wife. He refuses to understand why the poor people find it practically impossible to pay the tithes in their churches even though they complain that they can hardly feed well. He stops their festivals especially when the celebration involves drumming on Friday since Friday is the day of abstinence and fasting for Catholics. Above all, he insists on preparing their young women, who are about to be married, for a Christian

---

[14] Mongo Beti. *Le pauvre Christ de Bomba.* Paris: Laffont. 1953; *Le roi miraculé.* ibid., 1955
[15] Ferdinand Oyono. op. cit.
[16] Ahmadou Kourouma. *Les Soleils des indépendances.* Paris: Seuil, 1970.
[17] Henri Lopès. *Le Pleurer-Rire.* Paris: Seuil, 1982.
[18] Mariâma Bâ *Une si longue lettre.* Dakar: N.E.A., 1983.

marriage. This preparation, which involves separating the women from their families, exposes them to a risk that life in their private African homes does not involve.

He sets up a special boarding house for these future brides, where they are required to stay for a while, before entering into married life. The rigorous preparation for Christian marriage that the young brides are supposed to be engaged in during the period and under the priest's supervision turns to something else; the young women are sexually abused by the priest's assistants and catechists, including his cooks and stewards. Indeed, an open fight breaks out between the priest's cook and the suitor of one of the young brides, who has been smuggled into the priest's entourage during his "crusade".

The priest organises an inquiry into the mission's activities after the scandalous fight between his cook and the aggrieved suitor and particularly into the goings-on in the "sixa", that is the hostel from which his cook has smuggled a young bride into his touring party. It is discovered that the young brides are sources of sexual pleasure for the mission's African male staff; it is also confirmed and after medical examination that most of them have contacted venereal diseases from those who have been exploiting them sexually. The scandal is fully exposed and attracts the attention not only of the Catholic church in the colony but also beyond the local colonial administration. The Catholic priest accepts the blame for the scandal and returns to France.

The image of Africa that emerges from the novel is far from impressive in spite of the priest's acceptance of blame for the failure of his mission as well as for the scandal that brings it about. The image of the inhabitants of Bomba, who are depicted in the novel, is far from reassuring. Their naïve attachment to Christianity and to the Christian priest is quite intriguing viewed against the background of the utter contempt in which he holds their customs and traditions. They seem ever so ready to be trampled upon and brutalised all in the search for membership of the Christian fold.

The same goes for the hapless King Lazarus in *Le Roi miraculé*, who, in misguided submission to Christian demands, attempts to "sanitise" his palace by renouncing polygamy. The attempt to "discharge" twenty-two of his twenty-three wives in favour of the one "Christian" that the Catholic church allows its adherents is met with violent resistance by his subjects. Each of the twenty-three clans of the kingdom insists on having their part of the kingdom represented in the king's palace. They refuse to withdraw their daughters from the palace nor would they consent to the king unilaterally repudiating wives that he had to marry according to their tradition. Indeed, the stability of the kingdom seems to depend on this rather democratic royal marriage system. The near calamity that would have been caused by the ill-advised repudiation of the royal wives is averted by the intervention of the colonial administration that virtually expels the head of the Catholic mission from the kingdom and the colony. The king's court remains intact and catholicism learns its hard lesson in another novel that reminds us vividly of the Bomba imbroglio.

Africa comes off rather ingloriously here again and in spite of the embarrassing situation in which the Catholic priest has to withdraw from King Lazarus' troubled kingdom. The humiliated wives of an insincere "monogamist" king and husband, who for one pretext or another would have married new wives even after repudiating previous ones, are direct victims of a certain naivety and insensitivity on the part of an African ruler of his own principality. The readiness and apparent levity with which he agrees with the Catholic mission that he should repudiate his wives in order to conform to the tenets of Catholicism does little credit to the respect that the African ruler has for the traditions of his people and kingdom. The fact that he reabsorbs all the "repudiated" wives without having to openly repudiate Catholicism does not show that King Lazarus realises either that the new religion does not easily mix with the kind of "democratic polygamy" that his kingdom has institutionalised.

In *Le Pleurer-rire*, President Bwakamabé Na Sakkadé (Tonton Hannibal-Ideloy) is the modern ruler of an imaginary African country, where he has overthrown the democratically elected civilian ruler, President Polépolé. He settles down to a most arbitrary and whimsical rulership that comes out very cynically in the novel. He enjoys unlimited power and exercises it absolutely cynically with the support of a French man, Monsieur Gourdain, who runs his security service. Rather than engage in the reorganisation of the country, the president preoccupies himself with making political speeches in which he lashes out at his enemies, visible and invisible, dead and living with the most unbecoming vulgarity. He organises elaborate state receptions during which the most expensive French champagne and Scottish whisky are served lavishly. He returns to his tribal roots to perform traditional rites that are meant to strengthen him against his detractors and enemies particularly the supporters of the overthrown Polépolé. He neglects his wife, who finds solace in the arms of the chief cook at the presidential palace. He prefers the company of school girls and young virgins who are recruited for his pleasure during his many tours of his constituency. He seems to derive special joy from the use of violence against the offenders that are arrested and reported to him.

It is instructive that the narrator through whom this very appalling image of the president is revealed to the reader is a member of the president's tribe, the Djabotama tribe. He is the chief cook in the presidential palace, the one who sleeps with the first lady. The Moundié populace is submissive and quite prepared to live with the president's excesses in spite of their rather unhappy economic situation. All in all, Moundié under President Hannibal-Ideloy Bwakamabé Na Sakkadé is a rather undesirable country that cannot survive for much longer unless something happens to change the president. From the look of things, that possibility seems quite remote. There is no redeeming feature in the image.

This inglorious image of Africa, albeit a literary image, has prompted a scathing review of the novel by a group known as *Association interafricaine des censeurs francophones*, a non-governmental organisation.[19] But the image is not too different from the general image of the African world that is painted in the other novels of the cynical realism bent.

The impression that the image of the African society, which emerges from these novels, is that of a rather unstable and superficial society that foreign missionaries of all shades can destabilise with impunity. It is one of a continent, which, after independence is totally incapable of ruling itself. The Africans that are depicted in them are often hapless and confused if not patently stupid or simply incorrigible. They appear as mere deserters, who have abandoned traditional Africa but for whom very little exists to show that the African values, which they have tried to escape from, are any more reprehensible than the new and ill-digested modern values.

Much is lost but only little has been gained: the novels in the cynical realism category paint a fuller picture of the African situation, which, in essence, is a clear departure from the naïve serenity of the image of

---

[19] Henri Lopès. *Op.Cit.* p. 9-12

Africa that the negritude movement encouraged and endorsed. The Africans are no longer the simple and poetic people that are depicted in *L'Enfant noir* but they are hardly yet the type of people to engage in any meaningful struggle against the forces that put them at the awful disadvantage in which they find themselves. The "new" novels hardly look beyond a liberal preoccupation with a changing consciousness, which has not yet quite identified the truly viable alternatives to traditional African values. The flirtation with Christian values leads them into a cul-de-sac from which they retrace their steps not into any more viable option but rather into the unsatisfactory African situation from which they had been lured away by the Christian apostates.

Radical Realism

It is in the last category of novels, that is the novels of the radical realism category, that a vision of a possible alternative to the disoriented colonial society is developed. *Les Bouts de bois de dieu*[20] by Ousmane Sembène and *Le Cercle des tropiques*[21] by Alioum Fantouré present us with an African reality that possesses not only aspects of the naïve serenity of the negritude image, the unsatisfactory mediocrity of the African situation that is painted in the "cynical novels", but they also point to a clear and visible alternative to the African situation that the other novelists have only celebrated or merely indicted. They do not only "distort" the complacent image of Africa of the negritude persuasion but they offer an alternative that draws its inspiration from an ideological modern consciousness that has not yet taken firm root on the African soil.

In *Le Cercle des tropiques,* the dominant aspect of the illusion of reality that appears lies in the almost tragic situation in which *la République* populaire des Marigots du Sud finds itself under the rule of Baré-Koulé to whom the departing colonisers bequeath independence. He is totally arbitrary and whimsical, more concerned about his post as president than about the welfare and happiness of his subjects. He institutes a one-party state and wipes out all vestiges of opposition including, particularly, the well-established *Club des Travailleurs* (the Trade Union) which thrived with little interference under the colonial regime. The union

---

[20] Ousmane Sembène. *Les Bouts de bois de Dieu.* Paris: Le Livre Contemporain, 1960.
[21] Alioum Fantouré. *Le Cercle des tropiques.* Paris: Présence Africaine, 1972.

leaders are arrested and imprisoned without trial; their headquarters that houses many unemployed unionists including their families is occupied by the national army following the forceful ejection and relocation of the occupants.

But, unlike in *Le Pleurer-rire*, there is the convincing and very visible presence of the underprivileged, represented by the *Club des Travailleurs*, who constitute a force that *Baré-Koulé* and the *Parti Social de l'Espoir* are unable to suppress completely. Indeed, the tone of the narrative, particularly the dialogues, is dictated by the ideological position of the unionists, who engage the colonial police and the succeeding national army in an exchange of points of view from which their own position comes out more forcefully and more convincingly. For example, this conversation between a unionist and Le Commissaire Sept-Saint Siss, the chief of the colonial police:

> *- Et vous croyez que Baré-Koulé croisera les bras devant vos tentatives de lui barrer la voie?*
> *- C'est vous qui dites cela Commissaire? Alors que les pouvoirs métropolitain et territorial ont formément soutenu Baré Koulé et fermé les yeux sur les assassinats commis par ses hommes de main? Répondit la voie de Mellé Houré. Personne n'a impose Baré Koulé, il a tracé lui-même sa voie. Si vous voulez vous en prendre à quelqu'un, surtout pas à nous. Notre rôle se termine et nous tenons à faire une bonne passation de pouvoirs. Vous vous entretuerez ensuite si cela vous chante, mais seulement après l'indépendance, pas sous notre arbitrage.*
> *Surtout prenez garde que notre sang ne vous éclabousse pas et que nous reprochez-vous? Ce n'est tout de même pas notre faute si vous êtes incapables de vous entendre, de bâtir, de gouverner! Gouverner suppose un apprentissage.*
> *Vous nous donnez l'indépendance parpersonne interposées, car notre indépendance ressemble à ce jeu de marionnettes qui tout en jouant Shakespeare, Molière ou Tchekov, ne doivent leurs mots, leurs actes et leurs décisions qu'à l'invisible et adroit manipulateur caché dans les coulisses...*[22]

---

[22] *Ibid.*

And this, between Baré Koulé's soldiers and a unionist:

- *Le chef de la délégation sortit un papier qu'il met sur la table en disant: pour l'intérêt du peuple signez votre affiliation au parti, vous serez immédiatement libérés par le Messie-koi*

- *Je ne comprends rien à ce texte, il ne veut rien dire, c'est un leurre. Vous savez bien que vous avez liquidé tout opposition au nom de votre bon droit de disposer du peuple. Il n'y a plus rien à approuver, dit Mellé Houré*

- *Vous êtes décidés à nous tenir tête, mais vous en creverez, cria un des Kois.*

- *Où en est à présent le peuple? Dans la félicité peut-être? répliqua Mellé Houré. Vous êtes trop stupides pour comprendre. Toi, ton prochain repas sera la terre, dit le commissaire Sognai.*

- *Tôt ou tard vous mourrez aussi, ce n'est qu'une question de temps.*[23]

But, perhaps, the more important difference lies between the end of this novel and those of the novels of the cynical-realism bent. At the end of *Le Cercle des tropiques,* the situation is not closed nor is it left open without a visible direction. Here, Baré Koulé is toppled and replaced by a leader, who will most probably be more ideologically tuned to the development of the masses of his country. The disastrous prospects of a badly governed neo-colonial society and the necessity for a radical change in order to avoid these prospects seem to be the main message of the novel.

In *Les Bouts de bois de Dieu*, the illusion of reality that is created is deliberately given an ideological bent. The overriding impression that emerges from the strike of the *cheminots* of the Dakar-Niger railway is that of a class struggle in which colonised Africans are pitched against the insensitive and exploitative colonial administration. The exploited colonials include remarkably lucid and bold individuals who, rather than succumb to the overwhelming odds that they face and, perhaps, seek

---

[23] *Ibid.* p.160.

refuge in religious fatalism and negritudist self-exoneration, prefer to confront the situation in spite of all the risks that are involved in that choice. Prominent among the unionists are Bakayoko, Tiémoko, Lahbib and others, who pose the problems of the striking unionists in clear ideological terms; they point out the deplorable disadvantages which they have confronted since the introduction of the railway. Mamadou Kéita, for example,

> *évoqua la pose des premiers rails... puis il parla des épidémies, des famines de l'annexion des terres tribales par l'administration du chemin de fer.*[24]

He assesses the supposed advantages that they may have derived from the system by way of jobs and salaries:

> *Nous avons notre metier, mais il ne nous rapporte pas ce qu'il devrait, on nous vole. Il n'y a plus de différence entre les bêtes et nous tant nos salaires sont bas.*[25]

Tiemoko attacks the economic exploitation to which the underprivileged Africans have been subjected:

> *C'est nous qui faisons le boulot, rugit-il et c'est le même que celui des Blancs. Alors pourquoi ont-ils le droit de gagner plus? Parce qu'ils sont des Blancs?*[26]

The racial undertone of the situation is put in its proper perspective by Lahbib, who prefers to see the struggle through the ideological perspective. Rather than see it as a struggle between the black and white races, he points out that it is the class interests that override the racial ones. When Dejean, the French Managing Director of the Dakar-Niger railway, warns the Africans not to insult France, which is *"une nation, une race qui vaut cent fois la vôtre"*, Lahbib corrects his perspective immediately:

> *Vous ne représentez ici, ni une nation, ni une race: une classe. Et nous aussi nous représentons une classe dont les intérêts sont différents de ceux de la vôtre.*[27]

---

[24] *Ibid.* p.24.
[25] *Ibid.*
[26] *Ibid.* p.24.
[27] *Ibid.*, p.281.

But, perhaps, the most exciting aspect of the situation is the enhanced role of women that the union of railway workers' strike involves. The women are drawn into the strike action to play roles that they do not usually play in the society. True, they are not as prominent as their sons, fathers, husbands and friends, who constitute the main actors in the struggle, they are, however, involved in the strike to a higher degree than is usual in an African society of the pre-independence era. This could be explained by the fact that the railway workers' community does not truly belong in the fold of the traditional African society being as it is housed in the railway quarters and subjected to the alienating effects of the cold rails and silent wagons. But the more important reason is that the impoverishment by way of inadequate salaries that the menfolk are protesting against affects the women as much as the men and perhaps the women even more than the men. It is the women who have to ensure that the children do not go hungry by borrowing money and food from those who can spare some and by imploring the Arabs and Mauritanians, who sell local and imported foodstuff, to sell to them on credit pending the termination of the strike. The women do not simply sit at home bemoaning their lot, they join their menfolk in the organisation and management of the strike action.

Assitan, Ramatoulaye and Penda all constitute forces that are harnessed in the prosecution of the struggle for a better society. The underprivileged and particularly the womenfolk who are doubly affected can look forward to justice and a better socio-economic life in a society in which they are no longer the victims of class, racial and sexual discrimination. That goal seems to be one of the main preoccupations of the Africans of *Les Bouts de bois de Dieu*.

The Bakayokos [28] and Bohi Dis [29] take us into a future African reality that exists only in the imagination of the writers and socialists.

Iconoclastic Realism

Beyond the novels of the radical perspective, there exists already a new generation of novels in which what we would like to call iconoclastic

---

[28] Bakayoko is the indomitable leader of the famous railway workers' strike and the hero of *Les Bouts de bois de Dieu*.
[29] Bohi Di is the hero of Fantouré's *Le Cercle des tropiques*.

realism, the kind that was already visible in Yambo Ouologuem's *Le Devoir de violence* [30] has re-emerged. Calixthe Beyala, the avant-garde writer of *Tu t'appelleras Tanga*,[31] while reminding us of the morbid and gory details in the works of Yambo Ouologuem, takes the illusions of African reality to an almost surrealistic preoccupation with the sexual exploitation of Tanga, the heroine of the novel. But, while Ouologuem is preoccupied in his novel with the demystification of Africa's pre-colonial world of morbid rituals and primitive subjugation of the human society, Beyala is concerned in hers with the exposure of the ignoble role to which the woman has been reduced in a male-dominated African society.

Conclusion

We regard literature as being, in essence, illusions of reality with all the implications that this may have for our conception of literature and of its inevitable relationship with society. In addition to religion and politics, literature is probably the single most important contributor to the soul and collective image of the society. History and sociology deal mainly with life as it has been and is being lived while literature has the advantage of being used to portray life as it could be lived, but not necessarily as it should be lived, which is the domain of religion. The image of society that literature purveys is, at all times and in most situations, of visible relevance to society itself even if this relevance is not realised or is deliberately ignored by the latter.

The different levels of image-making that we have highlighted above, while attesting to the literary preoccupations of African novelists, constitute important angles of vision through which colonial Africa in particular was viewed and could still be viewed in retrospect. As literary artefacts, the works, which are referred to above, may not have been monumental in their contributions to the socio-political image of Africa. These works demonstrate, however, the intellectual and imaginative capability of African novelists as they introspect on contemporary Africa. The range and categories of images that we have highlighted above have continued to dominate African novelists' consciousness even if the images of *the*

---

[30] Yambo Ouologuem. *Le Devoir de violence*. Paris: Seuil, 1968.
[31] Calixthe Beyala. *Tu t'appelleras Tanga*. Paris: Editions J'ai lu/Stock, 1988.

mimetic realism mode have gone largely out of fashion. The tendency may not be yet to prick Africa's consciousness with the kind of image of Africa that dominates the novels of Calixthe Beyala; the kind of images that are purveyed by the *radical realists* and the *cynical realists* have, however, continued to dominate the consciousness of Francophone African novelists.

References

Adiaffi, J.M. *La Carte d'identité*. Paris: Monde Noir, 1989.
Auerbach, E. *Mimesis*. Princeton: P.U.P., 1968.
Bâ, A.H. *L'Etrange destin de Wangrin*. Paris: Union Générale d'Editions, 1973.
Beti, Mongo. *Le pauvre Christ de Bomba*. Paris: Laffont, 1953.
─────── *Mission terminée*. Paris: Buchet/Chastel, 1957.
─────── *Le Roi miraculé*. Paris: Buchet/Chastel, 1958.
─────── *Remember Ruben*. Paris: Union Générale d'Editions, 1974.
─────── *La Ruine presque cocasse d'un polichinelle*. Paris: Editions des Peuples Noirs, 1979.
Beyala, C. *Tu t'appellera Tanga*. Paris: Editions J'ai lu/Stock, 1988.
Camara, Laye. *L'Enfant noir*. Paris: Plon, 1953.
─────── *Le Regard du roi*. Paris: Plon, 1954.
─────── *Dramouss*. Paris: Plon, 1966.
Césaire, A. *Discours sur le colonialisme*. Paris: Présence Africaine, 1955.
Diop, B. *Les contes d'Amadou Koumba*. Paris: Présence Africaine, 1961.
Fantouré, A. *Le cercle des tropiques*. Paris: Présence Africaine, 1972.
Frye, N. *Anatomy of Criticism*. Princeton N.J: Princeton University Press, 1987.
Girard, R. *Mensonge romantique, vérité romanesque*. Paris: Grasset, 1961.
Goldmann, L. *Pour une sociologie du roman*. Paris: Gallimard, 1964.
Jouanny, R.(dir.) *Lecture de l'oeuvre d'Hampaté Bâ*. Paris: L'Harmattan. 1972.
Kane, A. *L'aventure ambiguë*. Paris: Julliard, 1961.
Kourouma, A. *Les soleils des indépendances*. Paris: Seuil, 1970.
Litré, E. *Dictionaire de la langue Française*. Paris: 1983.
Lopès, H. *Le pleurer-rire*. Paris: Seuil, 1982.
Ouologuem, Y. *Le devoir de violence*. Paris: Seuil, 1968.
Oyono, F. *Une vie de boy*. Paris: Julliard, 1956.
─────── *Le vieux nègre et la médaille*. Paris: Julliard, 1956.
Sembène, Ousmane. *Les bouts de bois de Dieu*. Paris: Le Livre Contemporain. 1960.
Shipley, J.T. *Dictionary of World Literary Terms*. London: George Allen & Unwin, 1970.
Tadié, J-Y. *La critique littéraire au xxe siècle*. Paris: P.U.F., 1987.

11

REVOLT AND REVOLUTION IN THE FRANCOPHONE AFRICAN NOVEL OF THE COLONIAL PERIOD

Olalere Oladitan

Revolt and Revolution Distinguished

We have always distinguished between revolt and revolution[1]. It is a distinction of fact as well as of interpretation, which finds itself substantiated as events in actual life as well as incidents in works of fiction. As a matter of interpretation, it is possible to propose or suggest that a revolt is an attempt to effect a change without success, an opposition to oppression or unwarranted situation, which is quickly dealt with. Many times too, a revolt terminates in its being abandoned by the person in revolt and the action quickly evaporates. But such an interpretation is limited in validity, for a revolt that succeeds does not necessarily become a revolution. Indeed, a revolution aims more at a fundamental change of the situation of deprivation, whereas a revolt is more restricted in its objectives, processes and scope. And the distinction does not reside in the outcome or result of action. For a revolution which is well conceived may in fact fail in the course of the execution, but that does not reduce it to a mere revolt. It could be an abortive revolution, certainly. Nor does a successful revolt, solely on account of the success and without more, graduate to a revolution.

On the Threshold of Revolution

Works, which deal with incidents of revolt, dominate the Francophone African novels of the colonial period. The themes are varied, the tones

---

[1] See O. Oladitan. *The Theme of Violence in the African Novel of French Expression* (Ph.D Thesis). University of Ibadan: 1975, pp.179-246 and O. Oladitan. "Suicide in African Literature: An Obtuse Revolution" in *Ife Journal of Foreign Languages*, No 1 April 1993: pp.1-10.

are different and the fate of the heroes is of a diverse nature. So also are the outcomes or conclusions of the stories. The revolt in Camara Laye's *L'Enfant noir*[2] for example, is subtle and sober. A serious tone is assumed. The reaction of the family to the distress resulting from the colonial situation is one of pragmatic or strategic acceptance of Western education, allowing the child to continue with his study abroad. This results not only in a separation of the child from the family but particularly in the alienation of the African *évolué* from his roots. A similar trauma is experienced by Samba Diallo in *L'Aventure ambiguë*.[3] This ends in the death of the brilliant, princely and spiritual leader, learned also in Western philosophy. Defeat, alienation, confusion and disorder mark the fate of the characters of Mongo Beti who engage in revolt. Jean-Marie Medza in *Mission terminée*[4] is lost to Western education - he fails his *baccalauérat* examination but he is also maladjusted to the traditions of his people. His predecessor, Banda, who appears in the novel, *Ville cruelle*,[5] loses his battle against the agents of the whites, that is the produce inspectors of Tanga; and his co-hero in the same novel, Koumé, the apprentice mechanic, meets his own death after murdering his white master.

Revolt in the Francophone novel has even ended in suicide for some of the heroes. We recall, for example, the fate of Bakary in *Un piège sans fin*[6] who commits suicide for the disgrace he suffers in the hands of the white commandant. So also did Diouana in Sembène Ousmane's short story *La noire de* who drowns herself in a bath tub in France where she is taken to live virtually as a prisoner when she has always looked forward to a life of enjoyment in Europe.

In some other works, revolt is handled in a light mood and the reader is well entertained, even though he knows that the subject is that of suffering and persecution in the colonial situation. In this respect, Ferdinand Oyono is the master. Toundi, the hero of *Une vie de boy*[7] and all the other African characters in the novel are reduced to mere slaves for the whites. Toundi, in particular, loses his life for serving his masters too

---

[2] Camara Laye. *L'enfant noir.* Paris: Plon, 1952/53.
[3] Cheikh Hamidou Kane. *L'aventure ambiguë.* Paris: Julliard, 1963.
[4] Mongo Beti. *Mission terminée.* Paris: Correa 1957 and Paris: Buchet/Chastel, 1972.
[5] Mongo Beti (Eza Boto, pseud). *Ville cruelle.* Paris: Eds Africaines 16 (Trois ecrivains noirs), 1954 and Paris: Présence Africaine, 1971.
[6] Olympe Bhely-Quénum. *Un piège sans fin.* Paris: Stock, 1960.
[7] Ferdinand Oyono. *Une vie de boy.* Paris: Julliard, 1956.

diligently. For knowing too much, for sweeping into the open the convicting evidence of the unfaithfulness of the commandant's wife from under the marital bed, he is persecuted unto death. However, his indomitable spirit enables him to escape from prison and from Cameroon to die in Spanish Guinea. There is the belated revolt of Meka, the old man who is awarded a bogus medal in the novel *Le vieux nègre et la médaille*[8]. The medal which Meka wins for giving his land to the church and for sacrificing his two sons for the French nation is thoroughly worthless afterall, for, on the same day of his decoration, he is arrested by the French police. He is severely beaten and detained overnight. He learns in a bitter way that there can be no sincere or true friendship or brotherhood between the whites and the blacks. He therefore rejects everything and anything white, including their Christianity, the religion to which he has given so much.

More significantly, the stories that involve revolt end in defeat and, in many cases, in submission for the African "revolutionaries". In the last novel, *Le vieux nègre et la médaille,* for example, all the Africans join in the revolt against the whites and colonisation generally, but they all disperse on a note of frustration and pessimism. They seem virtually resigned to their fate as if the lot of the colonised Africans were unchangeable.

> *Que les femmes aillent au marigot et que les hommes retournent à leurs occupations... Nous ne pouvons rien sur ce qui est fait, les Blancs sont toujours les Blancs..., dit Meka en jetant un regard attendri autour de lui. Peut-être qu'un jour...*
> *Par ma mère! Répondit Engamba. Le rat de nuit ne raconte pas les aventures qui lui arrivent dans l'obscurité! Les hommes naissent et meurent.. Par ma mère! Comment finira le monde avec ces Blancs? (p.221)*

The story reflects a certain level of despair and fatalism. In fact, the novel closes on a note of utter helplessness in the face of the whites' presumed invincibility.

Certainly, all the stories involving the Africans in revolt depict different forms of rejection of colonisation without actually ending in any visible change in the physical situation. Meanwhile, it is the removal of the

---

[8] Ferdinand Oyono. *Le vieux nègre et la médaille*. Paris: Julliard, 1956.

untenable and abhorrent situation and its replacement with an acceptable alternative that is designed by the revolutionaries themselves that true revolution is all about. This is the stage that is never reached in the revolt of the Africans against the colonial regime. It could even be suggested that, even as mere revolt, the efforts of the colonised Africans that are depicted in these novels are rather timid.

The Early Rumblings

A number of novels come within the category of the revolutionary described above. Of particular relevance here are the works of Sembène Ousmane, the renowned Senegalese Marxist novelist. Reference can be made here to his *Le docker noir, O pays, mon beau peuple!, L'harmattan I (Référendum)* and *Les bouts de bois de Dieu*,[9] all of them set in the colonial period. These works, arranged as they are in the order of the contexts treated in them, approximate a progression from revolt, through a rising tempo of revolutionary action, including an abortive revolution, culminating in the successful popular movement in *Les bouts de bois de Dieu*.

The first work, *Le Docker noir*, is a story of an individual's revolt ending in the defeat of the hero. And as in final suffering and even the death of many other heroes, great sympathy is whipped up for the colonised, and the racist instigators are firmly indicted. Unfortunately, no follow-up action is taken to sustain the interest of the hero. Indeed not much action in solidarity can be taken in *Le Docker noir*, for the event takes place in far away Marseilles, France.

In the second novel, however, some full-fledged revolutionary action begins. The hero, Oumar Faye, returns from abroad on a boat and right from the port he commences the action of avenging and liberating his people. He fights those who put excessive load on African porters who load and off-load the vessel. On arriving on the mainland, he organises his people - the farmers - into a co-operative to countermand the exploitative actions of the whites who dominate the economic life of the

---

[9] Ousmane, Sembène. *Le docker noir.* Paris: Nouvelles éditions Debresse, 1956.
────────── *O pays, mon beau peuple!* Paris: Amiot Dumont, 1957.
────────── *L'harmattan 1. (Référendum).* Paris: Présence Africaine, 1964.
────────── *Les bouts de bois de Dieu.* Paris: Les Livres Contemporains, 1960.

land to their own advantage. He suffers with the people to combat the invading pests and forcibly secures the intervention of the colonial administration for the farmers. Consistently, he presents his demands on the administration as well as organising the people economically as matters of fundamental rights. He insists that it is part of the responsibility of the colonial administration in the colony to protect the interest of the colonised people, even in such matters as the invasion of their farms by locusts. Similarly, he confronts the economic exploiters by asserting the rights of the people to the freedom of association, and the right to organise themselves so as to control the marketing of their farm produce.

This second novel of Sembène Ousmane can be seen as a transitional phase between the isolated, individual and defeat actions of revolt on the one hand and revolution on the other, in literary works. We can see that group action is involved but the leader and motivator is still too far ahead of the people. The revolutionary ideas are like grains of mustard seed being sown. They have taken root but the farmer is eliminated too soon. It must be said however, and this is very encouraging, that the seeds have fallen on fertile grounds. The people appreciate what Oumar Faye stands for and there is the indication that his ideas and his struggles need to be continued after him. This is how the old man, Papa Gomis, puts it:

> *Vous savez tous que Faye voulait que vous vous unissiez. Et c'est pour cela qu'il a été tué ...Il faut que nous tous nous unissions nos forces. La terre est à nous, c'est l'héritage de nos ancêtres. Il nous appartient de l'arracher à ceux qui veulent s'en emparer. Car souvenez-vous de ceci: "que le roi prenne tes fils pour aller faire la guerre ailleurs, ta femme t'en donnera; qu'il prenne ton troupeau, avec le temps, tu finiras par l'oublier, mais, qu'il s'approprie tes terres, c'est qu'il veut ta mort ... et celui qui veut ta mort ne se soucie pas de tes peines. (p.232)*

An Abortive Revolution

This kind of militant acceptance of revolutionary pursuit even in the face of a temporary setback is what one observes in another novel of Sembène Ousmane, *L'harmattan (Référendum)*, which is set in a purely political context, based on the 1958 (September 28) Referendum in the French colonial territories of Africa.

The story takes off as if it were a private vengeance or individual revolt of a few hunters who have suffered privation in their professional means of livelihood. But we soon discover that the novel deals mainly with the activities of a group of young men and women who campaign for the *"Non"* vote in the referendum. Their struggle implies immediate independence for the colonies and the youths see this as a vote of dignity, a vote for the rebirth of Africa. Against them is the "*Oui*" vote, which is the position of the conservatives and reactionaries, sustaining the position of the status quo. The partisans here include the colonial overlords as well as the new African leaders who have been assuming power since the transitional period of the Loi-Cadre.

The youths have a rallying point, in the Front for independence which also publishes a paper *The Front*. It is an alliance for all organisations voting *Non* and seeking independence. These include the Democratic Union of Women, Student Union, Trade Union, section of the UGTAN and PAI (Parti africain pour l'indépendance). Another remarkable point is the extent to which the youths are committed to action, so much so that they represent great changes from the past, and high hope for the future.

> *Ce n'était plus l'homme noir, passif, répandu ailleurs : c'était la semence de l'homme de demain. Ils sortaient des canons de la passivité, pour conquérir leur moi. Ils écoutèrent comme tous les matins, depuis la création du Front, les différentes interventions en langue du pays. Ils étaient jeunes. Il leur fallait l'étendue de l'Afrique, pour assouvir leur soif de créer. (pp.88-89)*

Their personal conveniences, interests, professional aggrandisement and emotional attachments are subjected to and made secondary to the revolutionary cause. Thus, Koffi the doctor sacrifices his private time and all his earnings from the medical employment for the cause. In particular, the deep and sincere love between Tioumbé, the school mistress, and Sori, the cycle repairer, is sacrificed for the struggle and they separate. However, they continue the struggle as Sori returns to his independent Guinea whilst Tioumbé remains to fight on at home in the composite country of the novel.

Employers watch their workers in private and especially public sectors. Termination of appointment and punitive transfers are imposed at the slightest suspicion of links with *Non*.

> *Les forces conservatrices avaient décuplé leurs efforts. Elles avaient mobilisé les militaires, la police, les institutions*

religieuses, - églises et mosquées - la presse. Rien n'était plus à l'ombre. Leurs tentacules adhéraient à toutes les parties vives du pays; les forces administratives on révoquait, mutait les fonctionnaires. La démocratie n'avait qu'un visage: celui de la force.(p.149)

Thus, even the politically non-committal position of Doctor Tangara cannot save him, in spite of the national and international recognition of his professional accomplishments and administrative competence. Similarly, Tioumbé, the school teacher, is subjected to torture by her father, a lay catechist. The family breaks up on account of the referendum. More importantly, the conservatives dispose of money and material to bribe. And so, the day before the voting, the people are entertained, gifts of all kinds are distributed, yards and yards of clothes, with the picture of De Gaule and the local leader printed on them, are measured out to women. And, in any case, they vote for all households. By the next day, the voting pattern was already predictable. Only in Guinea of Sékou Toure does the *"Non"* vote win.

The Revolutionary Masterpiece

The climax of revolutionary action in the colonial situation is found in a masterpiece of Sembène Ousmane's, *Les bouts de bois de Dieu*. This novel is a transformation of the 1947 heroic struggle of the railway workers on the Dakar-Niger line in the French West African territory. In this novel, the defeat of the historical strike is re-created from a Marxist-socialist point of view to end in the victory of the workers who are essentially blacks. The novel is a modern epic based on a past which was certainly not as glorious as it is now fashioned.

The processes of the revolutionary action include the propaganda machinery, the organisation, the leadership and the evolution of the characters. Compared to other works examined so far, we find that in this novel, more than anywhere else, there is a deliberate effort to explain the cause of action to people. The workers convince and convert others to their cause. This is particularly so among the Africans. Of particular significance here is the role of Bakayoko who goes from one place to another, seeking support for the strike. The management knows this and because of the potency of the action, the whites regard him as very dangerous, particularly because he is known to be a persuasive person.

> *Savez-vous que Bakayoko, leur meneur, à réussi a collecter plus de cinquante mille francs quand il a pris la parole dans un meeting à Saint-Louis*
> *Je le croyais à Kayes, dit Victor.*
> *Il y a été puis il est venu tout près de vous, à Diourbel, de là il est remonté sur Saint-Louis, il va revenir ici.*
> *C'est un homme dangereux, dit Isnard.(p.262).*

It is in fact largely on his power of oratory that the strike becomes a general strike towards the end of the novel where groups of workers moved by him declare support for the strike. He says:

> *Et maintenant vous maçons, menuisiers, ajusteurs, pêcheurs, dockers, fonctionnaires, agents de police, miliciens, employés du secteur public et du secteur privé, comprenez que cette grève est aussi la vôtre comme l'ont déjà compris ceux du Dahomey, de la Côte d'Ivoire, de la Guinée et de France. Il dépend de vous travailleurs de Dakar, que nos femmes et nos enfants connaissent des jours meilleurs. Nous avons un rocher qui se dresse sur notre route, tous ensemble nous pouvons le déplacer. En tout cas, les cheminots ne reprendront le travail que lorsque satisfaction leur sera donnée.(p.338).*

And the various groups reply thus:

> *Nous, les maçons, nous sommes pour la grève ! ...Nous, les ouvriers du port, nous sommes pour la grève. Nous les métallos ... Nous, les ... (p.338).*

The general declaration of support and the sustenance of general strike for ten days partly account for the ultimate success of the strike, and the demands are granted without any pre-condition.

The Women and the Mass Movement

Another major feature of this novel is the role of women in the revolutionary struggle. In the Francophone novel of the colonial period, a number of women play significant roles. Such women include the mothers of Camara Laye in *L'Enfant noir* and of Toundi in *Une vie de boy*, the several women in the *sixa* in *Le Pauvre Christ de Bomba*, as well as the wife and mother of Oumar Faye. Significant as their roles may be, they remain secondary in the works in which they appear. The personality of Tioumbé in *L'harmattan* represents some new beginning, but she still remains isolated. In *Les bouts de bois de Dieu*, however, the women not only contribute to the revolutionary action in the strike, they virtually take over the strike action. In fact, the determined struggle at various points along the rail line becomes more sharpened as soon as the women get involved. Even the management becomes jittery as soon as they learn of the involvement of the women. A white guard admits and warns on the likely dramatic turn that the intervention of the women may bring to the whole affair:

> *Si vous bousculez trop les femmes. Ç' va faire du grabuge. Ça fait dix ans que je connais ce quartier, je ne pense pas qu'elles comprennent grand-chose à la grève, mais si elles s'en mêlent, si elles font bloc avec les ouvriers, je me demande ou ça finira. (p.186)*

This is soon confirmed by the resoluteness with which the women act, since, for them, the struggle has to do with all areas of livelihood, especially feeding. It is remarkable, in fact, that the very idea of the epic march of the strikers on Dakar is an idea of the women, and they pursue it with such vigour and determination, that the men have no choice but to support and participate in it.

Arising from the role of the women *en masse*, we should emphasise here the multitude of participation in the revolutionary action. In effect, credit for the success of action in this modern epic has to be widely spread, unlike in the antique epic where the king, the prince or some other singular hero is held up far above others, as in D. T. Niane's *Soundjata*.[10] In *Les bouts de bois de Dieu*, we have an array of leaders and therefore a multitude of heroes. If it can be so said, the hero of the novel may very well be the strike itself, the revolutionary action, or the people as a whole. As for specific human beings, it is observed that each phase of the strike, each area of action, props up its own leadership. In the early stages of the story, even the old woman Niakoro and her grand daughter Adjibidji are important characters. As for the organisation of the workers, important leaders include Lahbib and Tiémoko. Among the women, the initial stages of deprivation at home bring to the forefront the character of Ramatoulaye who kills the ram of a big chief and relation.

---

[10] D. T. Niane. *Soundjata ou l'épopée mandingue*. Paris: Présence Africaine, 3ème Edition, 1969.

The event of the strike and the evolving role of the women make Penda the harlot and Maimuna the blind beggar important. Even, the dead child, one of the twins of Maimuna, assumes significance in whipping up emotion in support of the strike, as an illustration of the calamities suffered in the course of the strike. At the end, with the strike becoming general, the various groups and their leadership become relevant. What is important in this multiplicity of heroes - individuals and groups alike - is the fact that the strike relies not just on a singular character but on a wide base, making it impossible to terminate the action by the elimination of one leader or another. It is then certain that whatever happens to an individual, as in the tragic end of Penda, there are successors to take over and continue the struggle.

In spite of all the above qualifications as to the diminished position of the sole hero in *Les bouts de bois de Dieu*, we cannot but single out for a special mention, the import of Bakayoko. This character is portrayed as the very soul of the strike. He is the errant ideologue preaching the gospel of the strike from one place to the other. He presents the most sharply focused analysis of the reasons and the processes for pursuing the strike. He canvasses for and secures material support for the strike. Although he is not visible for the greater part of the novel, his name is on every one's lip. When finally he appears, he is seen as the very embodiment of the essence of the struggle. His appearance at the negotiation table ensures that the main objectives of the strike are not compromised. And with his oratory in the public addresses, he is able not only to sustain the position of the strikers but also to counter and argue convincingly against the management and the whole of the colonial administration. By the time he ends his speech, the strike not only becomes a general one, it assumes symbolic dimensions as a rallying movement for the total liberation of all the colonised people, all "the wretched of the earth."[11]

Revolutionary Consciousness Beyond Class and Colonisation

Perhaps the role of the women affords any reader the opportunity to observe and illustrate a major aspect of revolutionary action. Revolutions

---

[11] English translation of Frantz Fanon's tiltle Les damnés de la terre. Paris: Maspero, 1961 (Cahiers Libres, no 27/28), 1970 (Petite collection Maspero, 20).

have the effect of serving as therapy, a healing, in many areas of life. An individualisation of the therapeutic effects of revolutionary action is found in Penda, a notorious harlot, who, by going through the various stages of the action finally becomes an acclaimed revolutionary, a leader of the women and a model of discipline and dignity. Unguarded references to her past become an absurdity that is not tolerated even in the leadership of the strike. Penda in fact becomes a leader not only of the women but also of the whole strike. She is so committed to achieving the goals of the strike that she readily lays down her life in the course of action. With the certainty that other women and other revolutionaries will continue the struggle after her, her life is not a waste.

The truth is that the revolutionary action creates the new man, a new world. Old ideas are shelved and new ideas are born. There is a new perception of men and events. Phenomena like violence are re-considered. For example, on the specific issue of violence, the revolutionary experience teaches that it cannot by itself be seen as positive or negative. The perception of it has to depend on the end to be achieved. It is only a weapon, a means of action and, if action becomes necessary, it has to be undertaken, even if violence has to be involved. As we learn:

> *Il ne sert à rien de contempler nos feuilles de paie et dire que nos salaires sont insuffisants; si nous voulons vivre décemment, il faut lutter.(p.25).*
>
> ...
>
> *celui qui a peur du sang n'est pas capable d'égorger et si on veut de la viande, il faut égorger.(p.38).*

If Sembène Ousmane were a non-African French or Soviet novelist, we would adequately situate and summarise his work within the leftist ideological literary scheme of socialist realism. His works certainly have features of class struggle, the brutality of capitalist oppression against some masses of the society seeking liberty. In the European context, such oppressors would be from within the same society as the oppressed. In that kind of content, it would be easy to see his work as a laudable or even perfect illustration of the broad sense of socialist realism as "the realism of men who transform or and rebuild the world", with these details:

> Socialist realism firmly supports the view of existence as action, as a creation whose aim is the continual development of the most precious individual capabilities of man to ensure his victory

over the forces of nature, his health and long life, the great happiness of being able to live on this earth, which in answer to his ever-increasing needs he wishes to make over, entirely, into a magnificent home for all mankind united in a single family.[12]

Perhaps Sembène Ousmane himself, by reason of his ideological leaning, would concede close affinity to those who see writers as engineers of souls, having their two feet firmly planted in real life, a life of class struggle, for the building of a classless society. He would then be agreeing with some other writers that the literature he is engaged in is biased, and would be proud of it, on the ground that the bias is to liberate the workers and other men from the yoke of capitalist slavery.

Certainly too, Sembène Ousmane may have shared the spirit of the statutes adopted at the end of the first Congress of Soviet Writers, 1934, stating partly:

Socialist Realism [...] demands of the artist a truthful, historically concrete representation of reality in its revolutionary development. Moreover, he must contribute to the ideological transformation and the education of workers in the spirit of socialism.[13]

One thing is however certain. Sembène Ousmane has not written as a mere ideologue of a party, or as a foreign experimentalist of Marxism on the African soil. What we have in the stories of revolution by him is a deep social consciousness of the African situation. He takes extreme care in avoiding gratuitous party or ideological labelling outside clearly political discourse. What has been paramount to him has been the reinterpretation of the concrete historical reality of colonisation with a view of liberating all his people, not workers or party members alone – although these groups constitute the starting point. And the struggle concerns not just the issues of workforce and mere livelihood, or the mere struggle against a known enemy outside the self. There is in fact a struggle against the self. To him, the creation of the new African world

---

[12] Gorki, cited by Henri Arvon in *Marxist Esthetics* (translated from the French by Helen Lane with an introduction by Fredic Jameson). Ithaca and London: Cornell University Press, Cornell Paperbacks, 1973, p.85.
[13] Cited in *Marxist Esthetics* at p.86.

requires victory over the self before, and even as a condition for, attaining victory over the colonialist enemy. The fear of defeat is gone, the thoughts of easy victories are abandoned, the women and the generality of the people far outside the rail working group rise in action and in solidarity, to win. Old war songs, tales, dances and epic saga of the past are revived and adapted to the modern struggle, proudly.

In reality, Frantz Fanon appears to offer a perspective more adapted on the African revolutionary literature of the colonial period. It is for him the third and final phase of the evolution of the literature of the colonised people. After the assimilationist writings and the pre-combat literature comes this culminating point;

> *Enfin, dans une troisième période dite de combat, le colonisé, après avoir tenté de se perdre avec le peuple, va, au contraire, secouer le peuple. Au lieu de privilégier la léthargie du peuple, il se transforme en réveilleur de peuple. Littérature de combat, littérature révolutionnaire, littérature nationale.[14]*

What strikes one, however, at the end of *Les bouts de bois de Dieu* is a new life, a new world that goes beyond the immediate anti-colonialist victory. It is certainly a changed world in which one holds the head high, a world in which victory fills the heart. But more importantly, it is a world fully consummated in a renewal and a re-birth, in which there will never, ever more, return the initial disgrace, hurt or hate which had caused the revolutionary action to be inevitable in the first instance. This is dramatically and philosophically formulated by the old man, Fa Keita:

> *Tout à l'heure, poursuivit Fa Keita, j'ai entendu Konaté et Tiémoko qui parlaient de tuer le "gendarme". Mais s'il faut le tuer, il faudra aussi tuer les Noirs qui lui obéissaient et les Blancs à qui il obéissait et où cela finira-t-il? Si l'on tue un homme comme celui-ci, il y en a un autre pour prendre sa place. Ce n'est pas là ce qui est important. Mais faire qu'un homme n'ose pas vous gifler parce que de votre bouche sort la vérité, faire que vous ne puissiez*

---

[14] Frantz Fanon. *Les damnés de la terre* (préface de Jean-Paul Sartre). Paris: Maspero, 1961 (Cahiers Libres, no 27/28), 1970 (Petite collection Maspero, 20) p.154

> *plus être arrêtés parce que vous demandez à vivre, faire que tout cela cesse ici ou ailleurs, voilà quelle doit être votre occupation, voilà ce que vous devez expliquer aux autres afin que vous n'ayez plus à plier devant quelqu'un, mais aussi que personne n'ait à plier devant vous. C'est pour vous dire cela que je vous ai demandé de venir, car il ne faut pas que la haine vous habite.* (p.367)

It is on this note of victory devoid of hate that the novel ends. The concluding poem reaffirms the theme and moral of the struggle. It however shifts the relevance beyond the immediate social, political and economic contexts of colonisation. It invests the message of the revolutionary combat and victory with timelessness and eternal validity:

> *Pendant des soleils et des soleils,*
> *Le combat dura.*
> *Goumba, sans haine, transperçait ses ennemis,*
> *Il était tout de sang couvert.*
> *Mais heureux est celui qui combat sans haine.* (p 379)

12

THE DEVELOPMENT OF NATIONAL THEATRES IN FRANCOPHONE AFRICA

Raufu Adebisi

Introduction

The word theatre has been variously defined and we consider it necessary to look at some of these meanings if only to give indication of the direction of our discussion. Theatre has been defined as a *"lieu ou lon représente des ouvrages dramatiques"*.[1] This implies any building or area reserved for the performance of plays. The term also refers to textual plays and may connote the entire dramatic works of an author or a country. Yet, "theatre" also means *"la profession d'axteur"*, that is, one whose vocation is play-acting. However, it needs to be stressed that these definitions are not mutually exclusive. For a playwright can also be an actor or vice-versa. It is not even impossible that a theatre-designer will turn into a dramatist or an actor some day. Thus, theatre is a loaded word of closely inter-related fields, each complementing the other towards a common goal, to entertain and also to instruct. Thus, when we talk about the development of theatre, we are thinking of plays, where they are acted and those involved in acting them. In other words, we are dealing with the administration of the theatre, which at one level is limited to the director and his troupe and which at the level of policy relates to the relationship between political authority and the theatre industry of the country.

If theatre as a notion is easy to explain, the same cannot be said of theatrical forms. This is because what is considered by some scholars and practitioners as integral components of the art may not be so regarded

---

[1] A theatre in *Petit Larousse*, 1963 ed. All subsequent definitions of this term are taken from this edition.

by others. Indeed, this is the root of the controversy as to the origin of theatre in Francophone black Africa. This problem must be tackled at this point as settling it will assist us in delimiting the field of our study and in understanding the roles of individuals and groups found in this sector in Francophone African states. While this controversy cannot be denied and even rages on, it is significant that most theoreticians and practitioners of the theatre in Francophone Africa endorse a wider conception of the art. Wrote the Beninois Bienvenu Koudjo:

> *Une analyse minutieuse des productions des multiples troupes qui portent de région en région le message et les préoccupations quotidiennes de leur terroir suffirait à les [critics of a wider definition of theatre] convaincre.*[2]

The message Koudjo has in mind is at once ritual, cultural, economic and political. In the same vein, writes the Nigerien dramatist, Chaibou Dan Inna:

> *Il y a en effet une variété de formes artistiques ne correspondant pas toujours aux critères strictement admis par les critiques pour définir le théâtre mais qu'on ne saurait ignorer.*[3]

This broad interpretation enables experts to include all local elements having affinity with the theatre as is practised in all cultural environments. Hence, it is possible to include the *guelede* mask outings and the diurnal of the Kouvitos in the Republic of Benin and the puppet shows for which the Togolese Danaye Kanlanfei is universally known. Thanks to this wider conception of the theatre, practitioners in Francophone African countries have been able to bring to public awareness the multifarious aspects of the traditional and modern lives of their people.

For the purpose of our discussion we shall go in the following direction. We shall look first, at the state of *the theatre during the colonial era,* starting with the William Ponty School experiment up to the time of independence. The accession to independence by most French speaking African territories in 1960 also meant the attainment of political autonomy. This is the time one could seriously talk about *national theatres* and one

---

[2] Bienvenu Koudjo. *"La Pratique théâtrale au Bénin"*, Notre Librairie, No.128, Oct-Dec. 1995, p.133.
[3] Chaibu Dan Inna, *Le Théâtre*, Notre Librairie, No.107, Oct-Dec, 1991, p.63.

would want to know the relationship between the governments and the industries and the extent to which this affected the fortune of the latter in the various territories. Of course, not all segments of the sector enjoyed a good relationship with governments. Some of the aggravations and difficult relationship with the authority were reflected in what may be called *the theatre of disillusionment* and we should know how this fared under the post independence government. This is to be followed by reflections on the material and *infrastructural inadequacies* hindering the growth of the theatres in Francophone African states and what should be done about them. It is in this portion that we look at *the role of France* and the implications of her involvement in the development of the theatres of French speaking African countries.

The Theatre During the Colonial Era

Much has been said about the origin of the theatre in Francophone black Africa. Following the studies by Bakary Traore in his book *Le Théâtre négro-africain et ses fonctions sociales* and R. Cornevin's *Le Théâtre en Afrique noire et à Madagascar*, it is now generally agreed that communities in Francophone Africa had one form of theatrical expression or another before the advent of the Europeans. Indeed, the Nigerian playwright, Ola Balogun, incidentally the only Anglophone West African to write in French, who tried to argue that "there is no theatrical tradition in Africa... Contact with western civilisation revealed the theatre to Africa as a means of artistic expression"[4], has had to abandon this thinking. Even with this revelation, one still cannot seriously talk about conscious efforts towards developing the theatre of this time as what was considered as theatre were mere ritual or cultural celebrations limited most of the time to the village level. This was the situation before the white men came.

Much has also been said about the contribution of Europeans to the rise of dramatic art in Francophone Africa. According to Jacques Chevrier, *"D'abord introduit par les pères missionnaires, le théâtre indigène d'expression française connait à partir de 1930 un développment rapide."*[5] But it is now known that the first European missionaries not

---

[4] Quoted in Dorothy S. Blair. *African Literature in French*. Cambridge: Cambridge University Press, 1976, p.84.
[5] Jacques Chevrier, *Littérature nègre*. Paris: Armand Colin, 1974, p.167.

only failed to promote African arts, they even impeded their progress as is manifested in the attitude of one of them who stated: *"Alors, me moquant de leurs superstitions, je pris leur fétiche que je rompis en mille pièces."*⁶ The European missionaries were opposed to traditional celebrations by Africans because they regarded them as paganistic and therefore obstructive to the progress of evangelism. It was only after the missionaries had realised Africans' taste for the theatre that they started to exploit it for religious ends. As a matter of fact this experience was not limited to the French speaking territories alone. In Nigeria for instance, particularly in the Abeokuta-Ibadan area, cultural festivals came under the hammer of the Christian missionary fathers and it was much later that "traditional masquerade songs were re-worked into church songs as a means of winning over converts from traditional religions."⁷ Even Islam was unfavourable to local festivities, but it was less violent as it did not frown directly at African traditions.⁸ Thus, to some extent, the two religions, Christianity and Islam, slowed down the pace of development of indigenous African theatres in the precolonial era - even if the latter did not do so with the intensity of the former. However, the face of theatre was soon to change and the William Ponty School was a major factor in this direction.

The William Ponty School situated at Goree in Senegal has gone down in history as the birthplace of modern theatre in Francophone Africa. When in 1933, Charles Béart, just posted from the Ecole Primaire Supérieure at Bingerville in Côte d'Ivoire to the Ecole Normale Supérieure William Ponty, he asked his pupils to collect materials for plays *"au plus près du goût européen"*,⁹ little did he know he was sowing the seed of a business which would soon spread to all corners of French-speaking Africa. It is noteworthy that the first theatre group from French black Africa to perform in France is a troupe from the William Ponty School and it appeared at the Theatre des Champs Elysées on 12th and 17th August, 1937, under the direction of Governée Labouret. Kafewo reveals

---

⁶ See Bakary Traore, *Le Théâtre négro-africain et ses fonctions sociales* (Paris: Présence Africaine, 1958), p.45.
⁷ Yemi Ogunbiyi, *Nigeria Theatre and Drama: A Critical Profile*; *Theatre in Nigeria: A Critical Source Book* (Bath: Nigeria Magazine, 1981) p.19.
⁸ Traore, *Le Theatre*, p.46.
⁹ Quoted by Françoise Ligier, *"Lettre ouverte à Monique Blin à l'occasion d'un anniversaire,"* Notre Librairie, No. Hors Série, Sept. 1993, p.12.

that among the plays presented were *Sokame* in which farmers were at war with drought and *Prétendants rivaux*, a subtle and pungent comedy in the Molière tradition.[10] It is remarkable that today most of the experienced and prolific playwrights in Francophone Africa including the multi-talented Bernard Dadié are direct or indirect products of the William Ponty School.

After 1948, the new system of education introduced in French West Africa under the pressure of events which had started shaking the colonial empires, also affected the structures of William Ponty. However, even with the political stir, the idea of an indigenous theatre of French expression was not completely abandoned for, as from 1954, the "Centres Culturels" established by Bernard Cornut-Gentil in the territories not only encouraged but also supported the production and performance of dramatic works.

However, even at this dawn of the independence of most French speaking African territories, and even after more than a decade of the founding and outings of Fodeba Keita's *Ballets Africains de Guinée*, one could still not seriously talk of national theatres. Authority still reposed with the French colonial administration, with the enterprise still being referred to as the Theatre of the French Community.[11]

Independence and National Theatres

The attainment of political independence by the majority of French African territories in 1960 marked a turning point in the evolution of the theatre in French black Africa. For, since the outset, the dramatic arts of Francophone Africa were intricately linked to the lives of the people. So, a major occurrence like independence was bound to exert considerable influence on their nature and direction. The colonial authorities, having departed, at least officially, the nationalist fervour peaked in all Francophone African countries with the leaders demonstrating zeal and determination to protect their national sovereignty. Each new state had a national flag and an anthem expressing the collective aspiration while ministries, hitherto manned by the Europeans, now came under the control of Africans.

---

[10] See Samuel Kafewo, "The Development of Theatre in Francophone and Anglophone West Africa," Post Graduate Seminar Series, University of Jos, May 1990, p.9.
[11] This name is used by the Malian dramatist Gaoussou Diawara in an interview *A. Propos du théâtre au Mali, Notre Librairie*, No.102, Juillet-aout 1990, p.38.

In spite of these changes, it is remarkable that independence could not alter fundamentally the structures of Francophone African societies. The traditional and cultural activities binding tribes together across the artificial boundaries imposed by colonialism remained the same as they had been at the beginning of the colonial era. This common identity of the peoples certainly led Bakary Traore to declare that: *"ce qu'on a vu au Soudan et en Côte d'Ivoire s'observe aussi en Casamance, Guinée, au Nigéria, au Dahomey, à quelques variantes près."*[12] The situation remains basically unchanged today, four decades after the independence of French-speaking African countries.

Thus, when we talk of the national theatres of Francophone African countries, we are more concerned with their management within their geo-political boundaries than with their themes. Of course, few playwrights and script writers may have treated peculiar national problems here and there, but generally, issues addressed by the writers are common to practically all Francophone African societies of the post-independence era. It is rewarding to think also that even in the administration of the national theatres, there are several areas of convergence in policies, perhaps more points of convergence than divergence, and this is without prejudice to efforts made by regimes and private individuals to chart a course for the theatres of their respective countries. Implicit here is that a nation by nation approach to the study of the theatres of post-colonial Francophone black Africa is bound to lead to repetitions, hence we adopt the thematic approach, a step which also facilitates the simultaneous citation of the widest number of examples from the countries under study.

Our starting point here is a reflection on the state of the entertainment industry in the immediate post independence era, and a common observation is that there were only few theatre groups in Francophone black African countries generally at this period. Some critics even note the quantitative superiority of dramatic works over the number of performing groups. R. Cornevin, one of such critics, attributes this to the *"préoccupations des nouveanx chefs d'Etat (qui) ne furent pas immédiatement orientéees vers le théâtre."*[13] To some extent, this is true, but it is also true that the drought of the stage was provoked by the

---

[12] Traore, *Le Théâtre*, p.23.
[13] R. Cornevin, *Le Théâtre en Afrique noire et à Madagascar* (Paris: Le Livre Africain, 1970), p.116.

dramatists themselves. In the colonial era, most of the playwrights were also nationalists; once independence was achieved they found it more rewarding to join the new regimes and therefore turned their backs on theatre. Only the writing of plays was possible for them in their new roles and this they did with commitment and, expectedly, in support of the nascent regimes of their various countries. Commenting on the paucity of scenic activities in comparison with dramatic works, the Burkinabe playwright and dramatist Jean-Pierre Guingane wrote:

> *Alors que la production du texte théâtral a évolué en Afrique francophone, en fonction surtout de la conjoncture économique dans les pays et aussi de la volonté politique des autorités, on peut dire que celle des représentations sur scène a beaucoup plus été tributaire des circonstances socio-politiques.*[14]

Among former dramatists absorbed by the post independence regimes is the Malian Dr. Seydou Kouyate, alias Seydou Badian, who, on his appointment as Minister of Planning into Modibo Keita's cabinet, published *La Mort de Chaka*. In this play, he berates disloyalty to authority and the danger of political dissension to the existence of a nation.

The fortune of the stage in Francophone African countries, however, changed dramatically when the new leaders realised its pertinence to their mass mobilisation endeavours. One country in which the craft was put to maximum use is Guinea under the leadership of late President Ahmed Sékou Touré. The circumstances in which Guinea attained her independence, especially with Sekou Toure's historic declaration of *"Nous préférons la pauvreté à la richesse dans l'esclavage"*[15] and Guinea's subsequent *Non* vote, in the de Gaulle sponsored referendum of 1957, meant that the Parti Démocratique de Guinée (PDG) administration had to look for alternative ways of going about national development. Kwame Nkrumah's socialist option in Ghana attracted the Guinean leaders, who also saw it as the only viable way of rehabilitating an economy debilitated by more than half a century of colonial plunder.

In this journey, Sékou Touré concluded that, in the profoundly rural

---

[14] Jean-Pierre Guingane, *De Ponty à Sony: representations théâtrales en Afrique*, *Notre Librairie*, No.102, juillet-aout 1990, p.6.

[15] See Bernard Charles, *Atlas des voyages: Guinée* (Lausanne: Editions Rencontre, 1963), p.53.

environment that Guinea was, the theatre was the only means of instilling in the members, in a painless but effective manner, the motto of the party. The leaders were quick to understand that if this measure was to succeed then there had to be state monopoly of the nation's theatre. Thus from 1958 when freedom was achieved, all existing private theatre groups crumbled, giving way to the establishment of a conscious political theatre outfit, the *Jeunesse du Rassemblement Democratique Africain* (JRDA) which came into existence in 1959.

Even though some aspects of the PDG policies regarding the theatre were to be relaxed later, from 1959 the Guinean entertainment scene was to witness a strict regimentation perhaps unsurpassed in the history of the theatre in Francophone black Africa. The government itself set up theatre troupes and ordered the setting up of same nationwide along the lines of the PDG party structure. The administration determined the number of persons to be in each troupe, the length of time to be spent on stage, with fines imposed on the recalcitrants. The administration was in full control of competitions from the party's base (PRL) level to the national level. The government went to the extent of regulating the production of theatrical instruments.

That the PDG leaders used the theatre to promote party interest became all too glaring at the second National Festival of Arts and Culture held in March 1973, an occasion during which the official speech reaffirmed:

> *La certitude de la justesse de la ligne politique du PDG et l'assurance et l'inéluctabilité de la victoire de la Révolution Socialiste dans tous les domaines des activités du peuple guinéen et des peuples progressistes contre l'ennemi de classe, contre l'impérialisme, le colonialisme, le capitalisme exploiteur.*[16]

In spite of such rhetorics, an art in which President Ahmed Sékou Touré himself excelled, the PDG regime has gone down in history as one of the most repressive administrations in Africa. However, recourse to the theatre for partisan pursuits was not limited to Guinea. More recently, the numerous pro-government or government-controlled theatre

---

[16] Quoted by Jean-Marie Toure, *A Mobiliser,· informer, éduquer' Notre Librairie*, No.88/89, juillet - Sept. 1987, P.90.

organisations include the one that performed Barthelémy Sawadoge's *Révolution*, a play published in 1983 and in which the author extols the noble achievements of the Thomas Sankara regime in Burkina Faso. In the same country, the group that staged Ousmane Omer Ouedrago's *Et le peuple lava son linge* should also be seen in the same light.

As we shall see later in our discussion, the takeover of the theatre by some Francophone African leaders has some merit; but the problems created by such a measure are weighty and deserve attention. Theatre, whether it is the written script or a stage performance, is a product of imagination. Thus, when it is subjected to administrative regimentation, it loses its essential ingredient which is the freedom to produce according to the artist's personal taste. In short, governmental control stifles imagination and weakens all true art. This is a point Andre Gide emphasised when he was invited to join the Association of Revolutionary Authors and Artistes in 1932. Wrote Gide in response to Henri Barbusse's invitation.

> *Ecrire désormais d'après les principes d'une charte (je reprends les expressions de votre circulaire) cela ferait perdre toute valeur réelle à ce que je pourrais écrire désormais; ou plus exactement, ce serait pour moi la stérilité.*[17]

Exactly the refusal to compose according to the provisions of a charter provoked this declaration by Jean-Paul Sartre:

> *Je dis que la littérature d'une époque est aliénée lorsqu'elle n'est pas parvenue à la conscience explicite de son autonomie et qu'elle se soumet aux puissances temporelles ou à une idéologie, en un mot, lorsqu'elle se considère comme un moyen et non comme une fin inconditionnée.*[18]

Government policies that constitute an impediment to the progress of the printed word are equally inhibitive to the expansion of theatre practice. This is because what both require to thrive is an atmosphere free of restrictions and constrictions. Once they are denied this condition, they

---

[17] See Yvonne Davet, André Gide: *Littérature engagée* 11th ed. (Paris: Gallimard, 1950), P.9.juillet - Sept. 1987, P.90.
[18] Jean-Paul Sartre, *Qu'est que la littérature?* (Paris: Gallimard, 1947), P.186.

become artificial and stand the risk of falling quickly into oblivion once the government or ideology they promote collapses. The lot of the Guinean theatre under the PDG administration of Sékou Touré is an eloquent testimony of this reality.

The Theatre of Disillusionment

Even as governments of Francophone African countries continue to perfect the art of controlling the performing theatres, there has emerged in these countries and in full force what may be termed the theatre of disillusionment. The cause of this is not far-fetched; with the passing of years, especially as from the second decade of independence, it became obvious that the one-party regimes put in place in most countries, preoccupied with power and plagued by corruption, no longer represented the collective aspiration of the people. In Guinea, the PDG administration had eliminated all opposition. This was also the experience in Cote d'Ivoire where the *Parti Democratique de Côte d'Ivoire (PDCI)* was in firm control. Not even in Senegal, where the *Parti Socialiste* regime under the poet-President Léopold Sédar Senghor presented a semblance of tolerance, was serious opposition tolerated.

Generally, in Francophone Africa, the form and *modus operandi* of the theatre of disenchantment depended on the political climate in each country at a particular time. In Guinea under President Ahmed Sékou Touré where intolerance peaked, it was impossible for opposition theatre to develop in the country. Most critics fled the country and limited their activity to writing. Wrote Djibril Tamsir Niane: *"Si jai quitté la Guinée c'est qu'il y a quelque chose qui ne tourne vraiment pas rond."*[19]
Even then, the Government banned Niane's play *Sikasso,* portrayed by the leaders as being pernicious to national interests. It is significant that the only play critical of the government *La Face de l'empire* by Abdoulaye Fanye Touré could be performed in 1985 only after Sékou Touré's death and the overthrow of his administration by Colonel Lansana Konté. The situation in Cote d'Ivoire was not different. There, if Bernard Dadié's *Monsieur Thogo-gnini* was too veiled to be understood, so avoiding being hammered by the Felix-Houphouet Boigny's regime, Charles

---

[19] Quoted by Lilyan Kesteloot, *Ade Baro Bairo: Djibril Tamsir Niane,* Notre Librairie, No. 88/89, P.99

Nokan's *Les Malheurs de Tchako* was not. However, Côte d'Ivoire witnessed its real theatre of denunciation even in Boigny's time. This was Zadi Zaourou Bernard's *Compagnie Didiga* of Abidjan. Formed in 1980, Didiga's major performances include *l'Oeil*, a stinging political play which was banned in Abidjan only after three performances and *Le Secret des dieux*, a dramatic work generally considered to be less violent and less classical in the denunciation of dictatorship.

Since independence, theatre groups focussing on violence comparable to or even surpassing the ruthlessness on the political scene have proliferated all over Francophone black Africa. Among them is the *Théâtre Daniel Sorano* of Dakar, reputed for its successful adaptation of Aminata Sow Fall's *La Grève des battu* in 1985. In the same year, Senouvo Agbota Zinsou, leading the *Troupe Nationale du Togo* performed *La Tortue qui chante*, while in Burkina Faso, Jean-Pierre Guingane's troupe *Théâtre de la Fraternité* put on stage his own play *La Savane en transe* in 1990. In Francophone Equatorial Africa, Sony Labou Tansi's Rocado Zulu Theatre of Brazzaville, with its two major performances *La Rue des mouches* (1985) and *Antoine m'a vendu son destin* (1986) is unrivalled in the area of the theatre of violence. These performing organisations and many more, of unequal quality, and even with their limited means, have succeeded in highlighting the ironic situation of citizens, who not long ago rejoiced over the departure of European colonialists only to find themselves in the jaws of more vicious leaders.

However, not all the troupes are preoccupied with violence. Corruption is a favourite subject and is a special area of the *Atelier Théâtre Burkinabe*, known for its adaptation of Chinua Achebe's *No Longer at Ease* in 1984 and Jean-Pierre Guingane's *Théâtre de la Fraternité* of Ouagadougou. Some have tried to sensitise their compatriots and Africans in general to the dangers of cultural complacency; one of those leading in the area being the Camerounian Guillaume Oyono-Mbia who also brings to the fore the efficacy of music and dance in treating traditional African problems.

Playwrights and theatre directors in Francophone African countries have, on the whole, proved imaginative and enterprising. They have varied their themes and forms and, constantly, have been in search of effective means of reaching their audience. At the beginning of this chapter, we hinted at the status of the puppet show in the theatres of Francophone African countries. Apart from the Togolese Danaye Kanlanfei for whom this is a speciality, theatre troupes like the Nyogolon Group of Bamako and the Ki-Yi Mbock Theatre of the Camerounian born Abidjan-based Were-Were Liking have also made puppet theatre an area of great interest. It is gratifying to note that the Puppet Festival held at Charleville-Mezieres in 1988 witnessed *"une participation très importante de groupes venus principalement d'Afrique."*[20]

Some groups, such as the *Troupe du Lycée Municipal*, later transformed into the *Théâtre de la Fraternité* in Burkina Faso, have been academic-oriented and have endeavoured to adapt their techniques to the tastes of their targeted audience. There are troupes that have specialised in the use of local languages. Among these are the *Théâtre Kimpavita* of Mabieto Laadi and Josué Ndamba in the Congo and the *Troupe Daniel Ouézzin Coulibaly* in Burkina Faso. Many national theatres, especially in Mali and Cameroun, where censorship constitutes a serious impediment, have exploited tales and legends and their techniques for popular plays. In Benin Republic, there was once an exclusively feminine theatre called *Qui dit mieux*. Further researches into subject matters and forms will definitely yield encouraging results.

In this regard, closer attention should also be paid to those that have tried and continue to experiment with the use of local languages. The director of Mali's *Troupe Kotéba*, Ousmane Sow, demanded that more respect be accorded *"the dramaturges qui écrivent en langues nationales."*[21] Undoubtedly, the use of local tongues has its own limitations, especially, that of inability to reach a wider audience. However, local languages should not be dismissed in so far as they are a guarantee against the pitfalls emanating from the shaky mastery of the French language by actors and actresses from Francophone African countries. Indeed, not even playwrights are immune to these snares. Besides, there is ample evidence that plays performed in African tongues are very popular with African audiences. In Mauritania, when a group of young artistes called *Les Aristocrates* mounted a play entitled *La Jalousie du Barbouille* in *Hassanya* in 1966, a blend of Arabic and a national language

---

[20] Philippe Dauchez, *Acharleville - Mezieres: Festival de la marionnette, théâtre Sud* (Paris:L'Harmattan, 1989), P.132.
[21] See Ousmane Sow; Interview, *A Propos du theatre au Mali*, Notre Librairie, No. 102 juillet - aout, 1990, P.42.

was used. The show was well received. In Benin Republic, the *Fon* translation of Jean Pliya's *Kondo le requin* was performed 36 times between 1966 and 1968; while in Niger Republic, Boubou Hama's adapted work, *Sonni Ali Ber,* staged at the Festival of Arts and Culture in Lagos in 1977, was later translated into Hausa and performed in many towns in Niger and Northern Nigeria. True, a play staged in a local language can and does indeed limit its audience to its linguistic boundaries, but evidence also abounds in Francophone African countries that a script in indigenous tongue when properly written and put on stage by an experienced troupe can win international acceptability. Such is the case of *Fatouma ou la machine à créer des enfants* staged by the *Atelier Théâtre Burkinabe* at the France Forum in 1988. Similarly the *Théâtre Nyogolon* of Bamako has successfully dramatised plays in Bambara.

Infrastructural Inadequacies and the Growth of Francophone Theatre

We are now going to look at the material and infrastructural problems that have constituted a stumbling block in the way of dynamic and sustainable theatre industries in Francophone African countries. In every Francophone African country, theatre experts have bemoaned the dearth of financial resources to support their efforts. Congo's Sony Labou Tansi sums up their predicament this way. *"Je ne crois pas connatre un seul pays Africain qui prévoie des subventions pour le théâtre."*[22] The government-controlled theatres are hit, but worse affected are the private initiatives.

The popular argument of poor funding relates to competing demands on the lean resources of the individual countries. Yet, recent experience in at least one Francophone African country, Guinea under President Ahmed Sékou Touré, shows that even with the present level of their resources, these countries can still make provision for entertainment and achieve impressive results. That the PDG leaders used arts to foster party and personal interests is an issue which we have discussed earlier in this chapter. Indeed, the PDG's leaders' commitment to the establishment and sustenance of viable national theatres is a reality which

---

[22] See Sony Labou Tansi; Interview, *Le théâtre de 'utilité publique*, Notre Librairie, No. Hors Série, Sept. 1993, P.48.

even critics of the administration cannot deny. The results achieved are quite impressive: Guinea's national theatres, represented by *Ballets Africains de la République de Guinée*, *Ballet Djoliba* and *Troupe Théâtrale Nationale* have contributed to Guinea's fame worldwide in the area of arts and culture. They have travelled widely and won laurels in all parts of the world. One of such trophies was a gold medal won by the *Ballet Djoliba* at the first Folklore Festival at Agrezinto in Italy in 1967. Another gold awarded to the same organisation for the best spectacles was at Bucharest in 1978.

The adverse effect of poor funding on the theatre of the nations of French-speaking Africa has been tremendous. For financial reasons, once promising troupes have disappeared, two of them being the *Cerveaux noirs* and *Towakonou* both in the Republic of Benin while even in Guinea, the *Ballets Africains de Guinée* could sometimes not move all its troupe on account of financial difficulties. In this case of Guinea, members that could be moved were forced to learn the dances of the diverse ethnic groups and this hindered specialisation. Since funding is a problem, artists have had to look for other sources for their survival. The Burkinabe Jean-Pierre Guingane whose plays have won prizes within and outside the country is, for instance, a school teacher. This impedes professionalism and the achievement of concrete results in the theatre sector. Bogged down by this official lethargy, the Congolese Sony Labou Tansi asked rhetorically. *"Je me demande pourquoi on subventionnerait l'école et non pas le théâtre?"*[23] This indifference can be traced to the deliberate refusal of political authorities to appreciate the social functions of the theatre, and until there is a change of attitude, the stage will continue to play a second rate role in the struggle of Francophone African countries for real independence.

Faced with the stark reality of neglect, artists have been in constant search of ways for survival. One of these is by producing socially relevant plays: *"théâtre d'intervention sociale"*. When in Mali, Teneman Sanogo and his troupe turned to this form of theatre they became eligible for assistance from NGOs. Sometimes, troupes with similar inclination have even worked in collaboration with the NGOs, which could also commission them to produce plays for specific purposes. As a result of this sort of

---

[23] *Ibid.*, P.48.

collaboration, the *Koteba National* in Mali has staged micro programmes commissioned by UNICEF. Such mini-plays focus on AIDS, diarrhoea and immunisation. By the same token, the Rocado Zulu Theatre in the Congo has gone into partnership with international agencies to produce plays. While these agreements between the theatre groups and extra-governmental bodies have assisted the former in overcoming some of their material difficulties, they have not, in reality, boosted the status of theatre practice in Francophone African countries – for, the assistance they render is isolated and too scattered to have any significant effect on the sector in these countries. To some extent, this help can even be said to have, and indeed does really have, a negative effect on the management of the entertainment business in these countries as it encourages official lethargy while it does not itself solve any serious cultural problem. In some countries, it has been noted that the lack of a coherent and enduring cultural policy is attributable to these agencies. Even from the angle of the theatre troupes themselves, the "deal" with NGOs and international agencies has its problem which the Malian artist Moussa Konate explains this way:

> Sans subvention, vous ne pouvez pas tourner, et quand on vous en accorde c'est pour des pièces d'intervention sociale, du théâtre utile. Or, pour moi, vous êtes avant tout des comédiens. Vous avez un talent à parfaire (...) Comment pouvez-vous parfaire votre talent en n'exécutant que du théâtre sur commande?[24]

In spite of the clauses in the various agreement guaranteeing the freedom of the theatre organisations, in reality, no company is given absolute liberty by the sponsoring NGOs and international bodies. Actually, instructions issued by NGOs and multinational organisations to artistes to produce to meet the taste of a particular public constitute a violation of the latter's freedom, a value which all great artistes cherish and struggle to protect.

The Role of France and its Agencies

Our reflections on the contributions of foreign sources to the growth of

---

[24] See Moussa Konate, Interview, *Les troupes et le théâtre d'intervention sociale*, Notre Librairie No. 102, juillet-aout 1990, P.96.

the theatres of Francophone African countries will be incomplete without mentioning the role of France and its various pertinent agencies. France's interest in the theatres of Francophone African countries did not die with independence. Through direct grants and thanks to the efforts of her various agencies, the former metropolis continues to make contribution to the progress of the cultural sectors in the countries. The involvement of France has been remarkable, using Radio France International (RFI) and the Inter-African Theatre Competition which was instituted in 1967. Another channel is the *Festival International des Franco-phonies* founded by Pierre Debauche in 1983. Many Francophone African playwrights including the Ivorien Bernard Dadie, the Beninois Jean Pliya and Sony Labou Tansi were brought to limelight through the RFI competitions. A survey conducted at the end of the 70s revealed that 80 per cent of the Francophone plays staged in Africa came from the *Concours Théâtral Inter-africain* organised by RFI.[25] These competitions have encouraged dialogue between the North-South and South-South professionals and enhanced the confidence of African practitioners. Even then, the co-operation between the former metropolis and theatre experts in Francophone African countries is not without problems. In these competitions, a standard play that stands the chance of winning a prize is one that meets the tastes of judges based mainly in Europe. This has in most cases led to indifference to the sensibilities of African theatre-goers. This is what Francoise Ligier tried to emphasise when she wrote *"Il est urgent d'accorder la priorité au théâtre africain réalisé en Afrique pour l'Afrique."*[26] This is of course not to undermine the contribution of France, which also continues to make available its *centres culturels* to theatre organisations in Francophone African countries.

Implicit here is the lack of or inadequacy of theatres for rehearsals and actual performance in most Francophone African countries. In the Republic of Benin for instance, there are very few theatres even in the big towns and these are mostly multi-purpose halls constructed in cultural centres, *Maisons de Jeunesse et de la Culture*, assembly halls of academic institutions and more recently the *Maison du Peuple*. Lack of

---

[25] Francoíse Ligier, *Lettre ouverte à Monique Blin à l'occasion d'un anniversaire*, Notre Librairie, No. Hors Série, Sept. 1993, P.11.
[26] *Ibid.*, P.13.

space has forced artists to jostle for places at the *Centres Culturels Français* in Cotonou and Parakou, which have the best facilities. In Cotonou, plays are performed increasingly at Ciné Vog, a poorly equipped place and at the Chinese Cultural Centre (CCC). The situation in Brazzaville and Yaounde is not different. In Brazzaville, the *Centre Culturel Français* has been flooded with requests for assistance by various theatre groups. Overwhelmed, the centre has made it clear that it cannot substitute itself for local cultural structures.

A major difficulty confronting artistes in Francophone African countries is publishing. This problem, which is also the dilemma of all authors in Africa, has a crippling effect not only on the growth of the theatre but also on the struggle for the promotion of a sustainable reading culture on the continent. Albert Issa, the Managing Director of *Editions du Sahel* in Niger, traces the problem of the publishing industry to capital, stressing *"Notre problème principal est celui de fonds."*[27] The problem is attributable to capital but also to the poor attitude of the African to the printed word. A Central African critic observed that: *"Le livre n'est pas en Centrafrique un objet courant. Son nom est rarement associé à la notion de celle de manque, d'obligation ou du prix."*[28]

In a country in which the people are traumatised daily by illnesses and lack of basic needs, the book cannot but be considered as a forgettable luxury. The situation is not different in other African countries. It is a vicious cycle in which even publishers, who manage to secure the means to publish, produce for an indifferent audience, resulting in the loss of their meagre capital.

Yet, the publishing sector must arise if the theatre in Africa must grow. This is because, as aptly pointed out by Alain Ricard, theatre is *"une affaire de pratique mais aussi de théorie."*[29] A lasting theatre is more than one that limits itself to spontaneous improvisation and stage shows, it must be available to all for practical and academic purposes and this implies the existence of printing and publishing facilities. Even

---

[27] Albert Issa, *Ales Problemes de l'edition au Niger, Notre Librairie*, No. 97, avril-mai 1989, P.96.

[28] Jacqueline Saint-Dizier, *AVendre, acheter, lire, Notre Libairie*, No. 97, avril-mai 1989, P.96 e *d'Afrique noire, Notre Librairie*, No.119, oct-dec. 1994; P.140.

[29] Alain Ricard, "Notre Librairie et le theatre d'Afrique noire", *Notre Librairie*, No. 119, oct- dec. 1994, p.140.

within their short span of existence, theatres of many Francophone African nations have suffered losses due to lack of proper documentation and dissemination facilities. Many writers have also had to publish at their own cost. Such is the fate of Julien Alapini, author of *Les Acteurs noirs* and even of Guy Menga who wrote *La Marmite de Koka Mbala*. For those who do not have the means, and they are in the majority, they simply have to wait. This explains why most of the Burkinabe plays that have won prizes even at international encounters are yet to be published. This also means that these works cannot be made available for scholarship purposes. When a new history of Francophone African theatre comes to be written, all these hidden or vanished works and many more to come will pose serious problems to chroniclers.

With the inability of local publishers to cope with the avalanche of manuscripts they receive annually, many playwrights from Francophone African countries have had to turn to European publishers for consideration. For those whose works scale through the conditionalities, they still have to wait, and when their works finally appear on the shelves, they are versions tailored in conformity with European rather than African tastes and aspirations.

This is not to deny or undermine the countributions of publishing houses like the *Centre de Littérature Evangélique* (CLE) based in Yaoundé and which, since its establishment in 1963, has been of tremendous assistance to budding playwrights and artistes including Guillaume Oyono-Mbia, author of *Trois prétendants..... un mari*. But in the circumstances in which African writers find themselves, the way out is not solely through private initiatives; rather there has to be coherent national government policies aimed at helping those in this specialisation out of their present predicament.

Conclusion

The question of institutions where artistes can be trained in the individual Francophone African countries also needs to be looked into with all seriousness – for, many are the theatre troupes in these states that parade 'stars', who, actually, are ignorant of what theatre is all about. Admittedly, efforts have been made by a number of states; among them are the Republic of Benin, which, under the first regime of President Mathieu Kerekou, established the *Societés d'Exploitation des Centres de Spectacles* in all its provinces and Côte d'Ivoire, which has an *Ecole*

Nationale d'Art Dramatique and an *Institut National des Arts*. However, these are not enough. Drama in Francophone African nations should not continue to be a mere academic exercise in colleges and universities; rather it should be a concrete practical event geared towards mobilising all sections of the society in these countries.

From their humble beginning at *Ponty* in the 30s, the theatres of Francophone African countries have come a long way, passing through various regimes, and have continued to move on even if most of them are still wobbling. Considering the weak economic base of African countries generally and the pervasive poverty of Africans, only the governments of the individual states can provide funds towards energising the theatre industry. But this can happen only when the leaders cease to equate pro-government theatres with good theatres and to stop accusing theatres critical of government with plots to overthrow the government. There must be free and constant dialogue between political authorities and theatre experts towards improving the standard of living of the citizens. The circumstances in which Africans find themselves demand that there should be no gratuitous plays; theatre must talk, it must act as the conscience of society, keeping within bounds the excessive inclinations of political authorities as well as those of the followership. The theatres of Francophone African countries are doing just this even if with some difficulties and unequal success. To this extent, these theatres deserve the support of all.

References

Amon D'Aby, François Joseph. *"Des origines au Théâtre de Bingervile"*: *Notre Librairie*, No.86, janvier mars 1987: 94-97.

Bernard, Charles. *Atlas des voyages*. Guinée, Lausanne. Editions Rencontre, 1963.

Bienvenu, Koudjo. *"La pratique théâtrale au Bénin" Notre Librairie:* No.128, Oct - Déc 1995, pp.132-136.

Blair, Dorothy S. *African Littérature in French.* Cambridge: Cambridge University Press, 1976.

Chevrier, Jacques. *Litérature nègre*. Paris: Armand Colin, 1974.

Clarke, Peter B. *West Africa and Islam*. London: Edward Arnold, 1982.

Cornevin, R. Le *Théâtre en Afrique noire et à Madagascar*. Paris: Le Livre Africain, 1970.

Davet, Yvonne. *André Gide: Littérature engagée*. Paris: Gallimard, 1950.

Deffontaines, Thérèse-Marie. *"Théâtre forum au Burkina Faso et au Mali,"* Notre Librairie, No.102, juillet-aout 1990: 90-95.

Diawara, Gaoussou. Interview, *A Propos du théâtre au Mali, Notre Librairie*, No.102, juillet-aout 1990: 38-43.

Fayolle, Royer. *"Quelle Critique pour les littératures africaines?"* Notre Librairie, No.119, oct-dec. 1994.

Gomes, Aldonio and Cavacas, Fernanda. *"Vers une littérature nationale...,"* Notre Librairie, No.112, janvier-mars 1993: 101-106.

Griind, Françoise. *"La parole lourde des théâtres en Afrique,"* Notre Librairie, No.102, juillet-août 1990: 12-17.

Guennoun, Ezzedine. *"L'autre malaise du théâtre privé"*, Notre Librairie, No.102, juillet-aout 1990:73.

Guingane, Jean-Pierre. *"De Ponty à Sony..,"* Notre Librairie, No.102, juillet-aout 1990: 6-11.

_____. Interview. *"Jean-Pierre Guingane un fou de théâtre au Burkina Faso,"* Notre Librairie, No.102, juillet-août 1990: 48-53.

_____. *"Du Manuscrit à la scène, panorama du théâtre,"* Notre Librairie, No.101, avril-juin 1990:67-72.

Hornby, A.S. *Oxford Advanced Learner's Dictionary of Current English*. 16th ed. Oxford University Press, 1984.

Hounnou, Adrien, *"Notre Librairie et le problème des littératures nationales,"* Notre Librairie, No.119, oct-dec, 1994: 55-58.

Hourantier, Marie-Jose. *"La parole poétique du Didiga de Zadi Zaourou,"* Notre Librairie, No.86, jan-mars 1987: 84-89.

_____. *Théâtre-Sud No.1*, Paris: Editions L'Harmattan, 1989.

Inna, Chaibou Dan. *"Le Théâtre,"* Notre Librairie, No.107, Oct-Dec. 1991: 63-69.

Issa, Albert, *"Les problèmes de l'édition au Niger,"* Notre Librairie, No.1843-1844, /er-14 mai 1996: 45-95

Kafewo, Samuel, "The Development of Theatre in Francophone and Anglophone West Africa." University of Jos Post-Graduate Seminar Series, 1990.

Kampaore, Prosper. Interview. *"Prosper Kampaore et l'atelier théâtre burkinabe,"* Notre Librairie, No.101, avril-juin 1990: 79-81.

Kesteloot, Lilyan. *"De Baro à Boiro: Djibril Tamsir Niane,"* Notre Librairie, No.88/89, juillet-sept 1987: 97-99.

Koly, Souleymane. Interview. *"L'auteur et l'interprète,"* Notre Librairie, No.Hors série, sept. 1993:53-54.

Ligier, Francoise, *"Lettre ouverte à Monique Blin"*, Notre Librairie. No. Hors série, Sept 1993: 10-13.

Midiohouan, Guy Ossito, "Jean Pliya ou le bonheur au présent," *Notre Librairie*, No.124, oct-dec 1995: 143-148.

Midiohouan, Guy Ossito. *"Théâtres en ébullition," Notre Librairie*, No. 124, Oct-Dec 1995: 137-142.

Mignot, Daniel et Penel, Jean-Dominique. *"Le Niger dans la littérature française"* 1863-1991, Notre Librairie, No. 107, Oct - Dec 1991: 24-30.

Ogunbiyi, Yemi (Ed.) Drama and Theatre in Nigeria: A Critical Source Book. Bath: Nigeria Magazine, *Petit Larousse*. Paris: Librairie Larousse, 1963.

Pliya, Jean. Interview. *"Entretien avec Jean Pliya,"* Présence Francophone, No.23: 177-186.:

Ricard, Alain. *"Notre Librairie et le théâtre d'Afrique noire"*, Notre Librairie, No 119 Oct - Dec. 1994: 139-140.

Sartre, Jean - Paul. Qu'est-ce que la littérature? Paris: Gallimard, 1947.

Tansi, Sony Labou. Interview. *Le théâtre d'utilité publique, Notre Librairie*. No Hors Série, Sept. 1993, 48-49.

Toure, Jean-Marie. *Mobiliser, informer éduquer le théâtre, Notre Librairie*, No 88/89, juillet-Sept. 1987: 86-96.

Taore, Bakary. *Le Théâtre en Afrique noire et ses fonctions sociales.* Paris: Présence Africaine, 1958.
U'Tamsi, Tchicaya. Interview. *Dialogue sud-sud: Tchicaya U'Tamsi,* Notre Libraire, No.95, Oct - Dec. 1988: 56-59.
Werewere, Liking. Interview. *"Une nouvelle exigence", Notre librairie,* No. Hors Série, Sept. 1993: 52.
Zadi, Zaourou Bottey. Interview. *Lart comme équilibre de vie, Notre Librairie,* Hors Série, Sept. 1993: 50-51.
Zingou, Senouvo Agbota. Interview. *"Senouvo Agbota Zinsou, de Lomé à Limoges", Notre Librairie,* No.102, juillet-août 1990: 61-63.

13

FEMINISM IN FRANCOPHONE AFRICAN LITERATURE: FROM LIBERALISM TO MILITANCY

Aduke Adebayo

Introduction

It was not until the late 1970s that women's presence in African literature as literary writers and characters made their debut. A first and second generation of Francophone African male writers had by then established a solid base for the existence of African literature so that by the 1970s, a decade after African independence, Francophone African literature was already a force to be reckoned with in world literature. Names like Leopold Sedar Senghor, Aimé Césaire and Léon Damas had become famous because of the Negritude Movement while Camara Laye, Mongo Beti, Ferdinand Oyono, Sembène Ousmane, Tchicaya U'tamsi, Jean-Joseph Rabiarivelo among others had left indelible footprints on the different literary genres they engaged in. Many of the authors had even had their works translated into other European languages like English, Russian and German.

The prolonged debate about the validity of an African literature written in a foreign language did not reverberate on the Francophone divide. The Francophone writer had always taken the use of the French language for granted. For him, using the language of the Gauls to convey his experiences was not anomalous. In fact, he saw it as a matter or right having striven to equal or even outpace the French man in the use of the French language. What was at stake was how to prove the humanity of the black man in general and the African in particular; which was done abundantly in the Negritude poetry.

It is not known that any female author featured in the Negritude enterprise as a creative writer. At best we have learnt that Paulette

Nardal's salon served as the rallying point for the Negritude writers and allowed them a convenient location to debate their ideas. The first known published literary work authored by a woman in Francophone Africa was that of the Cameroonian, Thérèse Kuoh-Moukoury, titled *Rencontres Essentielles* (1969). The novel was easily overlooked by all anthologies and critical works of the time while those of her male compatriots, Mongo Beti, Ferdinand Oyono, Rene Philombe, and Francis Bébey were being praised to the high heavens. It was possible that in the face of the fervent nationalist and anti-imperialist writings of the period, a novel describing a woman's struggle to save her home, as *Rencontres Essentielles* did, was of no consequence.

Almost a decade separates Thérèse Moukoury's novel and the next. In 1977, the Cameroonian Lydie Dooh-Bunya's *La Brise du Jour* was published. The history of women's literature everywhere has involved the slow response of critics, who are largely male, to female-authored texts. The case of Francophone African literature written by women was therefore no exception.

Why then did the African woman in general and the Francophone woman in particular come late into the literary arena? Whereas the first female writer on the Anglophone divide, Flora Nwapa, published her first novel, *Efuru*, in 1966 and received instant acclaim from critics, her Francophone counterpart was still marginalised by critics even when she finally found her voice.

Lack of equal access to Western education the boy-child had deprived the African girl-child of the early opportunity for social, economic, political, and literary advancement for several decades in the pre-colonial and colonial times. In general, between the home, the farm, the brook, and the market-place, the woman had no time to go to the white man's school. The narrator of Tsitsi Dangaranba's *Nervous Conditions* puts the problem of the woman's condition in proper perspective when she described the woman's tasks as follows:

> *Twenty-four stomachs to fill three times a day. Twenty-four bodies to which water had to be fetched from Nyamorira daily. Twenty-four people's laundry to wash as often as possible... Now, this was women's work.* [1]

---

[1] Dangeranba. *Nervous Conditions*. 1988, p.133.

Besides, the parents were not favorably disposed to the education of the girl-child except when she came from an elitist home like the Senegalese Aoua Keita whose autobiographical and political account *Femmes d'Afrique: la vie d'Aoua Keita racontée par elle-même (1975)* remains the only one of its kind by an African woman. The story is told that when in 1935 Mariama Bâ was to be registered at the Western school, her grandmother opposed the move vehemently and that it was only by sheer luck that she finally went to school. After obtaining her Primary School Leaving Certificate with flying colours (she was first in the class of 1943), her grandmother expressed her reservation about further education for Mariama. She feared she would lose her head and mind to Western education. Such was the fear during the post-war years in Senegal of the educated woman, the *évoluée*, with her taste for modern comfort like a villa, a car, a refrigerator, a radio and modern utensils, that the generality of the people started to question a French education which fabricated women who were alienated from their immediate surroundings. Such prejudices further retarded women's education in the Francophone Africa.

Aoua Keita's book is instructive in that it told of the intense opposition of African men towards female political aspirants in a society where women and politics were and are still opposed because politics is power and power is the traditional domain of the men. In the Islam dominated areas of Africa, the religion imposed strict codes of conduct on women, which prevented them from going to school. Besides, the colonial administration put less emphasis on the education of girls than that of the boys since the latter were more needed to serve the colonial administrative structure. Where the girls went to school they were orientated towards "feminine" careers like nursing, teaching, domestic science and secretarial work – all totally absorbing works which left no time for creative writing especially when coupled with motherhood.

Moreover, cultural myths as well as the Christian and Islamic religions emphasised the main roles of women as maternity and domesticity. Within these contexts, female education consisted mainly of teaching obedience and submission to male authority. Women were not to speak in public, never to speak first to a male or to stare him right in the eyes or raise their voices against men's. Like Mama Ida in *Philomène Bassek's La Tâche du Sang* (1990), the good woman is the good wife and a good mother of a horde of children for whom she slaves all her life. Moreover, while the society emphasised achievement in male role, it put premium on conformity and domesticity in female role.

It is therefore safe to posit that the culture of silence imposed on the African woman was for long responsible for her lack of participation in all public domains. For example, whereas the universal franchise was granted in the French colonies in 1956, notable women politicians did not emerge until the 1980s. It was therefore not surprising that African women and particularly Francophone African women came very late to creative writing. The preconditions for such an enterprise (education, and especially leisure and time) were simply not available. In short, the various reasons we have adduced so far for the tardiness of African women's appearance on the literary scene can be put at the doors of the patriarchal arrangement of the society which suppressed and disempowered women especially since the colonial times.

The Francophone African women who first broke the silence performed a revolutionary act. Writing in itself is a deconstructive act since the written word was considered the exclusive preserve of the male, the father of logos. Women's writing was therefore first considered a deconstruction of the patriarchal order. This explains the general apathy, scepticism and at worst suspicion that greeted and still greets African women's writings by critics. Clear examples are Werewere Liking and Calixthe Beyala. While the former was simply consigned to the limbo of literary criticism, the latter was accused of plagiarism in her *C'est le soleil qui m'a brulée* (1987), an accusation which she loudly denied. She has had to prove herself over and over again to be accepted by the male-dominated field of African critical discourse.

The first Francophone female novels, *Rencontres Essentielles* (1969) and *La Brise du Jour* (1977) were largely ignored by critics. Werewere Liking protested against her marginality when she complained that she still remained relatively unknown even though she had published at least two books a year since 1977. Listen to her:

> *Je constate qu' il y a des gens qui m'ignorent alors que j'ai publié depuis 1977 environ deux livres par an et qu'ils sont tous disponibles en librairies, Je ne peux que m'étonner.*[2] (*Notre Librairie* No 79)

---

[2] Quoted in Notre Librairie, No 118, p.7.

While it is possible to blame the generally poor diffusion of African creative works for Liking's problems, one cannot overlook the tentacles of that vile octopus called male prejudice in this matter.

Writing and especially writing oneself is an act of liberation. It is "killing the emptiness" as Calixthe Beyala once put it. In the traditional society, only the female praise singer (*la griotte*) had the right of public speech in her chants which were basically historical. Passing from orality to writing is therefore a revolutionary act which the Francophone female writer has taken full advantage of to make her voice heard, to make her presence felt and to write herself into history (her story).

By the 1980s when Francophone African women stormed the literary scene, another problem arose. They did not speak with the same voice concerning the inherent problems of the female condition, unlike their male counterparts who were united in their effort to combat colonialism in their literature. Nor did the women overtly adhere to the feminist ideology even when their writings were eminently feminist. Their lack of courage to admit to a sound ideological base to their enterprise, even when they were free to adapt feminism to their African experience, robbed African women's creative writing of an identity for a long time.

African women's conservatism made them publicly denounce feminism in order to be accepted. However, towards the end of the decade, there developed a group of younger women who identified closely and publicly with feminism. 1980-1995 can be conveniently termed the golden age of women's writing in Francophone Africa, giving birth to the majority of writers, who are well-known today: Mariama Bâ, Ken Bugul and Aminata Sow Fall on the one hand and Calixthe Beyala, Delphine Zanga Tsogo, Philomène Bassek, Werewere Liking, Tanella Boni, Evelyne Mpoudi Ngolle and Angela Rawiri among many on the other hand. The trickles of the 1970s has today become a steady and formidable stream of Francophone African women's writing.

The Private Sphere in Francophone African Women's Writing: The Autobiographical Novel

Of all the literary genres, the autobiography is the most privileged by the female Francophone African writers whose thinly veiled personal story (her story) is often told as being representative of the female condition in

Africa[3]. The hallmark of the autobiographical mode is its "sincerity" and its restitution of memory. It is an introspective analysis which serves as a catharsis as well as a grand opportunity for the socio-political appraisal of the society in which the protagonist, who is now a female, evolves.

In order to fulfill its function, the autobiographical novel adopts both the realist and the romantic modes. In other words, there is a mixture of the objective and the subjective in the right proportion to create the effect of verissimilitude. Mariama Ba's *Une Si Longue Lettre,* (translated as *So Long a Letter*), remains the *chef-d'-oeuvre* of this sub-genre of the novel form in Francophone African women's writing.

In this part of our essay, we shall dwell mostly on *So Long a Letter* because its didactic and aesthetic import is further enhanced by its use of the epistolary sub-genre. The letter is the principal source of information and facts about everyday lives of women and their own perceptions about themselves and their lives: in other words it is a source of both objective and subjective information just like the autobiography to which it serves as a complement.

Despite the subjectiveness (now doubled) of the autobiographical novel, it is still the quintessential genre for capturing the cadences of the human being's life as well as his deepest aspirations. It is in the autobiography that the reader confronts the African woman as a person, as a presence, as Jean Paul Sartre's *'l'être-pour-soi',* as an autonomous being-in-society.

The first woman writer, Aoua Keita, as we earlier noted, had dwelt at length on her personal experiences in politics alongside male politicians. She however did not delve into the private sphere. Despite her close contact with women through her profession as a mid-wife, Aoua Keita was not interested in the private fortunes of other women or in what we otherwise would call the female condition in Africa. In the words of Catherine Mazauric:

> *On pourra regretter qu'Aoua Keita n'ait pas accordé une place plus large à son expérience et à ses réflexions de sage-femme ayant pu observer pendant des années, la*

---

[3] Since *So Long A Letter*, many autobiographical novels have been published. Véronique Tadjo's *A Vol d'Oiseau* and Nafissatou Diallo's *De Tilène au Plateau* are good examples.

> *rude condition, faite aux femmes en milieu traditionnel. Ainsi, on ne trouvera dans l'ouvrage aucune allusion aux mutilations traditionnelles qui ont pourtant une part considérable dans les souffrances et les difficultés endurées lors des accouchements.*[4]

In general we have noted that the Francophone female writer is much less concerned with her sisters in the bush than with her sisters in the cosmopolitan centres.

Whether she lived in the bush or in the city, however, the African woman was and is still doubly oppressed. Firstly, she is oppressed by colonialism and neo-colonialism like her male counterpart and, secondly, she is oppressed by the patriarchal arrangement whereby the women and the children belong to the minority group in the sense that they are denied some privileges and freedom, which society normally allows for the dominant group. In this case, the dominant group is the male. It is this destiny of the subaltern, of the minority group, which becomes the focus of many Francophone women's writings. For the modern woman, educated to respect traditions and at the same time to adapt to the norms of the Western world, a social and psychological problem is posed which Anne Oakley (1987) has described as "the double bind". This consists of:

> The clash between the consequences of women's status as a minority group and the democratic egalitarian ideology of our society which superficially, at least, encourages women to achieve as much as men and to be equal with them at significant points in their lives, particularly during formal education. Women are thus being given two contrary directions at the same time—be equal (be masculine) and be unequal (because you are).[5]

The trauma inherent in this double bind situation is what Mariama Bâ describes in her autobiographical novel *Une Si Longue Lettre (usll)*. Here we see a clear presentation of the female version of the African man-between-two-worlds. The difference however is that the African

---

[4] Catherine Mazauvic, "*Aoua Keita, Femme d'Afrique*", *Notre Librairie*: No 75-76, juillet-octobre, 1984, pp.184-186.

[5] Ann Oakley. *Sex, Gender, and Society*. London: Gower Publishing Company, 1972, p.75.

woman is torn in reality between three worlds: tradition, Western civilisation and patriarchy. Mariama Bâ's writing marks significantly the transition from orality to the written word in the history of Francophone women's literature. She spoke for the colonised woman who was battling with her need for emancipation from the three-pronged assault on her personality so that she could take her destiny in her two hands.

Mariama Bâ's novel is set in the Senegal of the 1950s and early 1960s, a period that witnessed fervent nationalist, political activities. True it was that she witnessed all the nationalist struggles and the advent of pan-national sorority in the then "French West Africa" during this period but she quickly abandons this public sphere in her novel to dwell squarely on the private, the intimate and the domestic as if to confirm the gendering of roles in the society whereby the public sphere belongs to men and the private to women.

The main thrust of Bâ's novel is the description of how yesterday's hopes are negated by today's reality in the life of the modern African woman. Yesterday's romance has become today's disillusionment, divorce, hate and death, depending on the character being considered in the novel. Ramatoulaye, in the opening of her long letter to Aissatou, her friend and foil, declares:

> If over the years, and passing through the realities of life dreams die, I still keep intact my memories, the salt of remembrance.[6]

For Ramatoulaye the promises of a happy long-lasting, married life had turned into a nightmare long before her husband died. In a pathetic and nostalgic tone, she reminds her friend of their past that was obviously very pregnant with hopes:

> Because being the first pioneers of the promotion of African women, there were very few of us. How many dreams did we nourish hopelessly that could have been fulfilled as lasting happiness and that we abandoned to embrace others, that have burst miserably like soap bubbles, leaving us empty-handed.[7]

---

[6] *So Long A Letter.* (trans) Modupe Bode-Thomas. Ibadan: New Horn Press, 1981, p.1. All references are to this edition.
[7] *Ibid.* p.14-15.

Ramatoulaye's reminiscences are made up of the educated, modern African woman's travails, products of the sexist norms in the society. Like her illiterate fore-mother, she is "first up in the morning, last to go to bed, always working."[8] Bâ's women are seeking liberation from conventional gender roles to be able to face their careers as a form of empowerment. Aissatou does precisely this when after her marital disappointment, she divorces her husband and faces her children and work squarely. Her solution is an aberration in the African society which fears that the empowered woman will be masculinised, aggressive and anti-family. Within this context therefore her choice is a courageous if not a revolutionary one.

The novel subtly denounces the intrusion of the collectivity into the private choice of a marriage partner and how one may wish to lead one's life. This point is especially crucial in a society like the Senegalese society which still puts premium on the caste system. Mawdo Ba loved his wife Aissatou and was satisfied with her until he began to receive external prodding as to how best to manage his marriage. The intrusions of the traditional caste and the extended family systems combine to ruin Aissatou's and Ramatoulaye's marriages. Ramatoulaye regrettably remembers: "We suffered the social constraints and heavy burden of custom.[9] Aissatou's mother-in-law could not reconcile herself to her son's choice of a marriage partner of low social origins:

> She bore a glorious name in the Sine: Diouf. She is a descendant of Bour-Sine. She lived in the past, unaware of the changing world. She clung to old beliefs. Being strongly attached to her privileged origins, she believed that the blood carried with it virtues, and nodding her head, she would repeat that humble birth would always show in a person's bearing.[10]

With the examples of the two husbands here (Ramatoulaye's Modou Fall and Aissatou's Mawdo Ba), the writer gives the impression that the educated African man is helpless when he is confronted by choices sanctioned by tradition. Mawdo Ba pleads tradition as an excuse for abandoning his first love for his mother's choice. The narrator asks rhetorically as if to exonerate him:

---

[8] *Ibid.* p.20.
[9] *Ibid.* p.19.
[10] *Ibid.* p.26.

> Faced with this rigid mother, moulded by the old morality, burning with the fierce ardour of antiquated laws, what could Mawdo Ba do?[11]

The choices could have been radically different if Mawdo had remained sincere to his wife of many years. But Mawdo did not display such courage. Rather he chooses the uneasy compromise between tradition and modernity represented by geographical polygyny whereby the wives live separately and the husband struts, like a proud cock, between different geographical locations. Aissatou on the other hand refuses such bastardisation of love. She confidently announces with finality, her decision to be on her own:

> I am stripping myself of your love, your name. Clothed in my dignity, the only worthy garment, my way.[12]

With her exposure to Western education, the educated African woman has been able to imbibe some aspects of the value systems of the Western world, most especially its individualism and democratic spirit. In the African society in which the heroines have their being, to think of an individual destiny based on individual values is considered abnormal. The society places value on collectively building norms, which are invariably determined by the males. Paradoxically, a woman could experience intense solitude simply because she is educated and despite the common claim that her society puts premium on solidarity. This African solidarity, to our mind, is meant for the individual woman who stays where the society consigned her gender: at home or at best behind the man.

The "transgressing woman", the rebel, the likes of Aissatou, who seeks autonomy and Ramatoulaye, who refuses levirate, is quickly isolated even by her own kind. Aissatou's demand for a divorce is against the practice among "other women". When faced with the inevitable polygamous fact, the stereotypical reaction of the African woman is to succumb to social blackmail. Platitudes, like the need for a father figure and a provider for the children, are advanced as arguments, even where these functions are not in any way being performed by the man. These commonplace truths had lowered the heads of many wives as they raised them in revolt.[13]

---

[11] *Ibid.* p.30.
[12] *Ibid.* p.32.
[13] *Ibid.* p.31.

The two women find further solace in listening to the radio, going to the cinema and sustaining a closer relationship with their children and friends. By these new preoccupations, they gain new spaces of freedom and self confidence but they continue to bewilder others.

So long a letter goes on to broach other social problems like the mother's anxiety for her children, the mother-daughter conflict, abortion and drug abuse among the youths but it largely shuns issues of sexuality and the serious problems of sexism in the society. Where they are broached at all as in the case of contraception and abortion, they are quickly glossed over and moralised into side attractions. Yet these issues are as important as polygyny which is the overwhelming issue in the novel.

The contradictions inherent in the double bind situation are echoed in the apparently contradictory stands in the novel. Aissatou and Ramatoulaye are poles apart as far as their choices are concerned, yet none of the positions is condemned or adjudged preferable. The same ambiguity is noted in the treatment of polygyny, which is never outrightly condemned even though its negative effects are highlighted. However, a feminist must take a stand on important issues as these. Mariama Bâ's discourse like Aoua Keita's is inscribed within the dominant male discourse as well as a nascent liberal feminist tradition that will be taken up by a section of the next generation of writers. The discourse seeks a compromise within the existing socio-political arrangement while respecting tradition and religion. Every act, every speech is measured so as not to rock the boat.

So Long a Letter is a powerful artistic statement about the Francophone African woman's quest for love and understanding from her male partner and this to our mind is its peculiarly African dimension to universal feminism. In her interview with Rolf Solberg in 1980, Bâ affirms that she is not a feminist, at least not in the Western sense of the word:

> Not in the western sense. No. Because our problem is beyond feminism. Now, I think our men have an excuse to oppress us because they are not free themselves, even in the so-called independent states. They cannot see that they are being used. So until they are free, you can't really claim to be a feminist.[14]

---

[14] Quoted by Samba Gadjigo "L'oeuvre litteraire d'Aminata Sow Fall" *Notre Librairie* 118, p. 28.

Mariama Bâ's Daughters

Between 1970 and 1980 more Francophone female writers towed Marima Bâ's footsteps by adopting the autobiographical mode. The Senegalese Nafissatou Diallo in *De Tilene au Plateau* (1975), the Ivorien Simone Kaya in *Les Danseuses d'Impa Eyai: jeune fille d' Abidjan* (1976), the Senegalese Ken Bugul in *Le Baobab Fou* as well as Fatou Bolli in Djigbo (1977) are some examples. In *De Tilene au Plateau,* we witness growing up as an African girl in Senegal. The heroine is caught in the tripartite cross-fire of male prejudice, female powerlessness and peer jealousy. As she moves from childhood innocence to adult awareness, she battles against the instruments of suppression of the female like religion and tradition which tend to rationalise the subaltern position of the female in the society.

Aminata Sow Fall's Political Commitment

Between 1976 and 1993, this prolific Senegalese writer published five novels: *Le Revenant* (1976), *La Grève des Battu* (1979), *L' Appel des Arènes* (1982), *L' Ex-Pere de La Nation* (1987) and *Le Jujubier du Patriarche* (1993). In general, this writer is concerned with the socio-political, and cultural transformation in Senegal after the colonial experience. In her view, Senegal's fortunes have changed for the worse with African culture suffering from the severe blows received during its confrontation with the West. In *Le Revenant*, the political, economic and cultural orientation of the people have changed due to the influence of monetarised economy. In *La Greve*, an apparently harmless strike embarked upon by beggars who are protesting the government's inhuman treatment meted out to them provides an opportunity to castigate the political class for its insensitivity to the problems of the masses and its generalised ineptitude and opportunism.

L'Appel des Arènes is a critique of the negative influence of Western education on the youth. The young Nalla becomes disorientated. Sow Fall indirectly posits that education must be embedded in the culture of the people to be of any value at all. *L' Ex- Pere* returns to the political arena in the tradition of the post-colonial novel, taking up the issues of neo-colonialism, nepotism, dictatorship and corruption in a post-independent situation. *Le Jujubier* is a nostalgic return to the heroic African past in this beautifully crafted epic.

Aminata Sow Fall's writings have no feminist strain in them. In fact she has been called anti-feminist. She once declared her stand thus:

Je ne suis pas féministe dans le sens où les gens l'entendent. Je ne suis pas une féministe militante et la conférence internationale de 1975 n'a rien à voir avec le fait que je me suis mise à écrire. L'écriture est un acte de témoignage, une façon de filtrer la réalité sociale du moment.[15]

(I am not a feminist in the general sense of the word. I am not a militant feminist and the 1975 Women's Conference had nothing to do with my starting to write. Writing is a form of witnessing, a way of filtering the social reality of the moment).

Sow Fall's preoccupation is politically rather than gender motivated. It is political in the sense that she is committed to the general problems agitating both sexes in the society and not those problems which are circumscribed by gender. She stands up for respect of tradition, religion and the collective values in the society rather than for modernism and individualism. Should her lack of concern for women's issues be held against her, the critic would be guilty of prescriptivism and dogmatism?

If we have touched upon Sow Fall's work even though her concerns are not feminist, it is to underline the fact that we raised earlier: that female writers did not speak with one voice. Sow fall's discourse is easily assimilated into the male dominant discourse, even more easily than Mariama Ba's. Some critics see this as a privilege in that the same criteria could be used to judge her works as the male-authored texts rather than be subjected to unnecessary rigours or a certain paternalism reserved for feminist writings.

When Sow Fall's female characters are examined (Yama in *Le Revenant*, Diattou in *L'Appel*, Sine in *La Gréve* and Yande in *L'Ex-Pére*), they are so unprogressive that they do no credit to any society whether matriarchal or patriarchal. They advocate a return to an idyllic past; which is neither practicable nor desirable. Like her male counterparts, Sow Fall's views are those of a social realist and liberal critic, who denounces a contemporary African situation, characterised by injustices, inhumanity, and corrupt practices.

---

[15] See Athleen Ellingtois, "Aminata Sow Fall's Demon Women: An Anti-Feminist Cocial Vision" *Contribution in Black Studies* 9\10: 1991- 92, pp.132-146. Samba Gadjigo," *L'oeuvre d' Aminata Sow Fall face à la critique*", *Notre Librairie* 118, p.28. See also Adrien Huanou, "*Entretien avec Aminata Sow Fall*", *Afrique Nouvelle*, No.1710, (16-22) juin, 1982.

Deconstructing Patriarchy: Revolutionary Post-Colonial Women's Writing

After 1985, new tendencies began to emerge in the Francophone women's writings. The first manifestation of a new orientation can be seen in the choice of new strategies for confronting and deconstructing patriarchy. Forging a new relationship with the female body, redefining maternity and appropriating language for self-identity are some of these strategies. Those who are now writing are truly post-colonial in that they did not experience colonialism which formed the backdrop of their elders' education and of their creative writings. For this reason, most of the inhibitions and the contradictory stances of the Mariama Bas had disappeared.

Reappropriating the Body

In the traditional African context, the female body is an object, purchased with the dowry. Virginity is demanded to ascertain the integrity of the bought item. Besides, there are several sexual mutilations like the clitoridotomy to prepare the woman for her roles as a receptive and passive receptacle of the man's pleasure. (See Awa Thiam's *La parole aux négresses*).

The first generation of writers in Nigeria dwelt at length on these issues of sexuality. Flora Nwapa in her *Efuru* and Buchi Emecheta in *The Bride Price* are salient examples. The contemporary changes in the society and the relative gains achieved in these areas are described by the new writings. Calixthe Beyala's heroine Letitia protests and symbolically snatches her body back with a *"Je veux mon corps"*[16] (I want my body). She proceeds further to claim for the entire womanhood what has for long been appropriated by men, *"Notre corps nous appartient"*[17] (our body is ours). Unlike Ramatoulaye, these new ones will jettison polygyny and large families without any hesitation:

> *Il faudra absolument interdire la polygamie: un homme aussi intelligent soit-il ne devrait pas avoir plusieurs femmes. A mon avis, une, c' est déja trop. Il faut reclamer*

---

[16] Calixthe Beyala. *Seul le diable le savait.* p.115.
[17] Ibid. p.115.

> *la pilule. Ensuite l'avortement libre. Ne plus être boursouflées d' enfants. Ce n'est pas aux hommes de nous faire un enfant. Notre corps nous appartient.*[18]

(Polygamy must be banished entirely. No matter how intelligent a man may be, he should not have many wives. In my opinion, one is already too much. We should ask for the pill. Then free abortion. Men should not force us to make babies. Our bodies belong to us.)

Calixthe Beyala has an intense regard for the body. The personhood of the woman, her body, is closely and jealously guarded because it is the only thing she owns. For Calixthe Beyala reappropriating the body is a condition *sine qua non* for woman's emancipation. To achieve this, Beyala says some categories of people must be discarded: the compromising mothers, the aunties who also assume motherly roles and of course the male. All these characters aid in the perpetuation of female oppression. Tanga in *Tu t'appellera Tanga* severs all umbilical links with her mother who sold her into prostitution, a new form of slavery, to provide livelihood for the entire family:

> *Je destructure ma mére. C'est un acte de naissance. Folie de croire à l'indestructibilite du lieu de sang. Bétise de croire que l'acte d'exister dans le clan implique une garantie d'appelation controlee...Comme le temps, comme l'oracle, je suis immobile malgré le désir de la vieille ma mére de m'imposer les repéres pour mieux me dévorer.*[19]

(I destructure my mother. It is an accident of birth. Madness to believe that blood links are indestructible. Stupid to think that belonging to a clan is a trademark. Like time, like the oracle, I am immobile despite my old mother's desire to guide my way in order to devour me better).

Within Beyala's new social context, there is no space at all for the man. The reader watches with amusement as the traditional patriarchal system turns into rubbles in the female imagination. The first casualty in this combat is marriage, which is the major mode of appropriating the

---

[18] *Ibid.* p.197.
[19] Calixthe Beyala. *Tu t'appeleras Tanga.* p.64.

woman's body by men. In *Seul Le Diable le savait*, Bertha refuses marriage as laid down by Western tradition and opts for polyandry. Monogamy, she avers is signing a slave pact.

> *Signer le pacte de l'esclavage: Porter l' eau.. Cuisiner. Repasser. Ouvrir son corps au male. Donner son ventre à la maternité.*[20]

> (You sign a pact of slavery. Carry water. Do the cooking. Do the ironing. Open your body to the male. Give your belly to maternity).

Along with marriage, maternity and fertility are thrown out of the window. These are prized elements within the patriarchal system as a means of perpetuating the lineage. Calixthe Beyala decries the negative effects of maternity on the female body which she describes with disgust:

> *Ventre épuisée par la maternité ou ventre prête ou donner à la maternité; seins et mamelles dégoulinants, corps ouvert à l'homme.*[21]

> (Bellies worn out by maternity or bellies ready or given to maternity; dripping breasts, body open up to the male).

What the author refuses is seeing the female body solely as a pleasure object and a baby-making factory.

In *C'est le soleil qui m'a brulée*, prostitution when consciously chosen is portrayed as a means of emancipating the body and exercising control over it. Ekassi, the prostitute withholds herself and dominates the men during the sexual act. The use of the impersonal third person reinforces the impersonality of the sexual act here:

> *Le ventre s'offrait, accueillait leur sexe imbécile, puis rejetait dans le vide ou elle s'était retirée, leur sève inutile. Elle se soumettait à tous les désirs mais tenait son ventre dans l'absence*[22]

> (The belly offered itself, welcomed their stupid manhood; then poured out their useless sperm into the empty space where she retired. She submitted herself to all desires but

---

[20] Calixthe Beyala. *Seul le diable le savait.* p.130.
[21] *Ibid.* p.130.
[22] Calixthe Beyala, *C'est le soleil qui m'a brulée.* p.62.

held her belly in absence.)

Tanga objectifies the sexual act by describing it as something that occurs outside her real self in a non-participatory act:

> *Je portais mon corps sur le lit; sous ses muscles. Il s'ébrouait, l'homme continue à s'ébrouer. Je ne sentais rien. Mon corps à mon insu s'était transformé en chair de pierre.*[23]

For this heroine, prostitution is one possible response to the dictatorship of the male. To compensate for her lack of power, the woman obtains vicarious, emotional satisfaction from her exercising control over the powerful male when she uses her sexuality to attract the male. In actual fact, the choice of prostitution is unfortunate and counter-productive. The woman who responds this way distorts her own personality since she must still submit her own desires and needs to those of the male.[24] She is therefore not emancipated in the real sense of controlling her body.

Calixthe Beyala's girls could even go to the extent of murdering their male verbally and physically. Her most violent novel so far, *C'est le soleil qui m'a brulée,* is replete with concrete examples. Ateba vows that she would arrest history, which is in favour of men *"en arrachant leur sexe d'un coup de dents"* (by yanking off their sex with her teeth). She kills her male aggressor, pleading *"légitime défense".*

The Misovire

Two incompatible beings: this is Calixthe Beyala's view of the male and female. And she is not alone. Werewere Liking coined the neologism "misovire" to describe the woman who is uncomfortable with men. In this way, she claims she has filled a yawning gap in logocentric language which has no female equivalent to the " misanthrope" and "misogynist". According to her:

> *Une misovire est une femme qui n' arrive pas à trouver l' homme admirable.. Elle se sent entourée par des larves uniquement préoccupées par leurs pensées et leurs bas-*

---

[23] *Tu t'appeleras Tanga,* pp.30-31.
[24] Coquery-Vidrovitch. *Les Africaines: Histoire des femmes d'Afrique Noire du 19e au 20e siècle.* p.121.

> *ventres et incapables d'une aspiration plus haute que leur tête; incapables de lui inspirer les grands sentiments qui agrandissent, alors elle devient misovire*[25]
>
> *(A misovire is a woman who finds men unadmirable. She feels surrounded by the larvae who are solely preoccupied by their thoughts and their underbellies and are incapable of any aspirations higher than their heads. Unable to find the noble elements which agrandise the man, she becomes a misovire).*

Liking goes beyond the essentialism of Beyala who divides the society into two distinct antagonistic groups of male and the female. Werewere Liking's grouse with men is because of their ineptitude. The long term desire of the misovire is for a better society of responsible men and women. As Veronique Tadjo puts it:

> *il faut dire aux hommes d'arrêter; les tenir à bout de bras et leur apprendre l'alphabet*[26]
>
> *(Men must be told to stop. We must hold them at arm's length and teach them the alphabet).*

Calixthe Beyala's violent and extremist attitudes are those of the Western world where she lives. Her stance is aptly described by C. Coquery Vidrovitch when she described the Western feminist as a woman whose main preoccupation is safeguarding her autonomy:

> *C'est le droit pour la femme, c'est-à-dire pour chaque femme en particulier de revendiquer son autonomie, voire son indépendance, de décider pour elle-même en son âme et conscience en qualité d'individu à part entière, d'exercer le choix de son corps, de ses désirs et de ses aspirations.*[27]
>
> *(For the European feminist, it is the woman's right to demand her autonomy, her independence; to decide for herself, in her mind and conscience, in her capacity as a full-fledged individual; to exercise control over her body, her desires and aspirations).*

---

[25] Bernard Magnier *"A la rencontre de Werewere Liking"* Notre Librairie No.79, 1985, p.2.
[26] Veronique Tadjo. *A vol d' Oiseau,* p.54.
[27] *Coquery-Vidrovitch. Op.cit.* p.359.

Refusal of Maternity

Some other writers, while not being as militant as Beyala are nonetheless anti-patriarchy. Zanga Tsogo, in her *Une vie des Femmes*, refuses maternity. This is a way of affirming ones autonomy. Angele Rawiri creates a character, Emilienno, who states that motherhood is only a choice among many other choices in *Fureur et cris de Femmes*. "*La maternité et les enfants ne représentent pas le bonheur absolu.*"[28] Maternity and child bearing are not the prized trophies of a marriage but experiences that are consciously desired and chosen by women. In other words, the woman should be loved and appreciated for her numan qualities (love, kindness) and not for her fertility.

Such views as are held by the writers we have just examined have come under acerbic criticisms as being anti-social, immoral, unlady-like and unfeminine. In the African societies, femininity is partly a lack of overt sexual behaviour. Active sexuality as dictated by these writers, especially Beyala, is deviant behaviour and an evidence of the woman assuming aggressive, masculine roles. It is therefore not surprising that Beyala especially has come under fire in recent times for her crude sex-ridden language.

New Realities, New Forms

The new writers have experimented with new forms in their writings. Beyala has successfully experimented with multiple or dialogic points of view instead of the undimensional or monologist narrative perspective of the classical novel. This is so in *C'est le soleil* where an invisible voice doubles the heroine's so that the reader has the benefit of a double interpretation. In T*u T"appelleras Tanga*, the story unfolds through two female voices who are engaged in a dialogue, a dying African prostitute, "*fesses publiques*", and the European Jew, Anna Claude. In *Seul le diable le savait*, it is a demonic voice which doubles that of Negri, the female protagonist, while the voice in *Le petit Prince de Belleville*, located in the bowels of Paris where the immigrants live, is multifaceted embracing voices as far away as in Africa in Tanella Boni's *Une Vie de Crabbe*, three voices alternate but the author achieves a symphony consisting of Niyous, her father's and her step-mother's voices.

---

[28] Angele Rawiri. *Fureurs et cris de femmes.* p. 92.

It is by far the most audacious experimentation with language as far as Beyala is concerned. She presents a mixture of *beur* and Parisian *titi* as well as vulgarisms. Language, we know "conveys a certain power. It is an instrument of domination. Ultimately, a revolutoinary movement has to break the hold of the dominant group. We cannot just occupy the existing words. We have to change the meaning of words even before we take them over."[29] Beyala does take the French language over and destructures it. She shocks the bourgeois sensibility with her sexual references. Such speeches when uttered by men would be considered bold (Ahmadou Kourouma for example) but from a woman they become immoral and indecent and brazen because the language a woman is allowed to use is the simple, clear, depoliticised speech like Mariama Ba's and Sow Fall's.

But then one must ask a pertinent question: Is Beyala's language emancipatory? Is frank, openly vulgar speech necessarily emancipatory because it now talks freely about subjects that are previously tabooed? The answer is negative. Beyala's language is defensive, reactionary and incapable of emancipating anyone. In actual fact, such a solution underestimates the magnitude of the problems inherent in the female condition in Africa. This is one area where Beyala fails the feminist test because it is very important within the feminist context that every innovation should be emancipatory and not gratuitous if it is to be reckoned with.

Werewere Liking has created new theatre forms and the *chant-roman* (song-novel) as a new sub-genre. Her test case is *L' Amour Cent Vies*. Even the conservative Sow Fall tries her hands on the epic in *Le Jujubier du Patriache*. She also deconstructs the traditional image of the father in *L' Ex-père de la nation*. Serious experimentation and attention to form is a characteristic of the "new writers". This is a happy development for African creative writing in general.

Conclusion

The Francophone African women have made very substantial contributions to African literature, so much as to alter the face of this literature. There

---

[29] Elshtain Jean-Bethke, "Feminist Discourse and its Discontents: Language, Power and Meaning", in *Feminist Theory: A critique of ideology*. Ed. Keohane et al. The University of Chicago Press, 1982. pp.127-145.

is a specific femaleness in the choice of characters, themes and sometimes in the use of language. Female writers have enriched literature with a special knowledge of their lives and experiences which is quite different from the portrayal of the same by the men. The women writers have successfully freed themselves from the psychological strictures imposed by the society and by the subaltern role assigned to them. Their images in the male authored texts are today both inadequate and unrecognisable and they have accepted the duty of correcting them continuously.

The female writers have introduced the dimension of feeling or the human angle into African literature as we have demonstrated with the autobiographies here. Open exhibition of ones feeling by men is frowned at by Africans and this may explain why the male authors have not paid much attention, if any at all, to the dimension of feeling in their works.

Like their male counterparts however, the female writers wish to be agents of social change through the portrayal of their African background and the uniqueness of their experiences as African women. Concerning the female thrust of their works, we have seen that various trends abound. Some writers have refused to accept the male dominance of the society and instead they seek equality (the Tadjos for example). Some refuse to confront the problems of sexism, insist on protecting their males and seek to play complementary roles in the social set-up (the Bas and the Falls) while others are combat-ready to confront patriarchy (the Beyalas and the Likings).

In the area of characterisation, three types of women have emerged: the physically and psychologically abused woman who is torn between tradition and modernity, the "new woman who is bold, assertive and ever-ready to recreate herself, and finally the so-called traditional woman whose profile is fast losing its contours as we see less and less of her in the female Francophone writings which are basically cosmopolitan.

Definitely there is today a tradition of Francophone women's writings and of African feminism that continuously enrich themselves like all emergent literatures do by defining themselves in their creation of new meanings and new values and new practices as the writers become more aware of the realities of the female condition in Africa and the need to change this condition if the society must move forward. If Africa must get itself out of the woods in the new millenium, it cannot afford to keep its women who constitute half of its population away from any aspect of human development. The female writer's duty therefore will be to continuously highlight the stumbling block to full development which are cultural and not biological. The African feminist has an urgent duty to change the mentality of the society, the mentality of both men and women towards the achievement of these goals. The feminist writer, who does not have to be a woman, will achieve this aim by invading the forbidden zones, challenging the status quo, presenting new, emancipatory options at the thematic and stylistic levels.

References

Selected novels written by Francophone women

Adiaffi, Anne - Marie. *Une vie hypothéquée.* Abidjan: NEA, 1984.
────── *La ligne brisée.* Abidjan: NEA, 1988.
Ba, Mariama. *Un chant écarlate.* Dakar: NEA, 1981.
────── *Une si longue lettre.* Dakar: NEA, 1979.
Bassek, Philoméne. *La tâche de sang.* Paris: L'Harmattan, 1990.
Beyala, Calixthe. *C'est le soleil qui m'a brulée.* Paris: Stock, 1987.
────── *Tu t'appelleras Tanga* Paris: Stock, 1988.
────── *Seul le diable le savait.* Paris Le Préaux Clercs, 1990.
────── *Le petit prince de Belleville.* Paris: Albin Michel, 1992.
────── *Maman a un amant.* Paris, Albin Michel, 1993
Boni, Tanella. *Une vie de crabe,* Dakar: NEA, 1990.
Diallo, Nafissatou. Niang. *La princesse de Tiali.* Dakar: NEA, 1987.
Kaya, Simone. *Le Prix d'une vie.* Abidjan: CEDA, 1984.
Ken Bugul. *Le baobab fou.* Dakar: NEA, 1984.
Kouadio Akissi. *Un impossible Amour: une Ivoirienne raconte.* Abidjan: Inadesse, 1983.
Liking, Werewere. *Elle sera de jaspe et de coraille: journal d'un misovire.* Paris: L'Harmattan, 1983.
────── *L'Amour cent vies.* Paris: Publisud, 1988.
Maiga ka, Aminatta. *La voie du salut suivi de Mirroir de la vie.* Paris: Présence Africaine, 1985.
────── *En votre nom et au mien.* Dakar: NEA, 1989.
Mpoudi, Ngolle Evelyne. *Sous la cendre le feu.* Paris: L' Harmattan, 1990.
NdiayeDja. *Collier de cheville.* Dakar: NEA, 1983.
Sow-Fall, Aminata. *L'Appel des Arenes*: Dakar: NEA, 1982.
────── *L'Ex-père de la nation.* Paris: L'Harmattan, 1987.
────── *Le jujubier du patriache.* Dakar: Edo Khoudia, 1993.
Tadjo, Véronique. *A vol d'oiseau.* Paris: Nathan, 1986.
────── *Le royaume aveugle.* Paris: L' Harmattan, 1990.
Warner-Vieyra, Myriam. *Juletane.* Paris: Présence Africaine, 1982.
────── *Femmes échouées.* Paris: Présence Africaine, 1988.
Zanga Tsogo, Delphine. *Vies de femmes.* Yaoundé: Clé, 1983.

General Works

Boyce, Davis Carole and Anne Adams Graves. Ngambika: *Studies of Women in African Literature*. Treton: Africa World Press, 1986.

Coquery-Vidrovitch, C. *Les Africaines: histoire des femmes d'Afrique noire du 19e et 20e siecles*. Paris: ed de Jonqueres, 1994.

Jamews, Adeola. *In Their Own Voices*. London: James Curry/Heinemann, 1990.

Lionnel, Françoise. *Autobiographical Voices, Race, Gender, Self-Portraiture*. Ithaca: Cornell University Press, 1989.

Mudimbe-Boyi, Elizabeth. "Anglophone and Francophone Women's Writings": Callaloo 16:1 (Winter 1993).

——————————"Post-colonial Women's Writing" *L'Esprit créateur* 33:2 (Summer 1993).

Oakley, Ann. *Sex, Gender and Society*. London: Gower Publishing Co., 1972.

Paume, Denise. *La mère dévorante*. Paris: Gallimard, 1976.

Peterson, Holst Kirsten."First Things First: Problems of a Feminist Approach to African Literature" In Ashcroft *et al The Post-Colonial Reader*. London: Routeledge, 1995.

Smith, Sudonie. *A Politics of Women's Autobiography: Marginality and the Fiction of Self-Representation*. Bloomington: Indiana University Press, 1987.

Smith, Sudonie and Julia Watson. (eds), *Decolonising the subject*. Minneapolis: University of Minnesota Press, 1992.

Thiam, Awa. *La Parole aux Négresses*. Paris: Danoel, 1987.

Index

Abstract-pattern sentences, 53
Achebe, Chinua, 11, 58, 148, 188
Adjuvants, 37
Adotevi, Stanislas, 99
African
— artists, 112, 121
— arts, 256
— background, 92
— Cosmological Naturalism, 115-120, 127
— creative works, 279
— creative writing, 150, 195
— cultural heritage, 217
— culture, 47
— epics, 9
— feminism, 295
— Folktales, 7, 125
— griots, 180
— heritage, 2
— Independence, 161, 165
— languages, 5, 13, 147, 217
— literacy creations, 195
— Literature, 2-4, 8, 15, 132, 275
— critics of, 195
— novelists, 236
— oral genres, 7
— Oral Literature, 1, 3, 7, 10, 18
survival of, 3
— oral poetry, 9
— oral tradition, 17, 108
— palaver, 188
— patrimony, 121
— philosophy of life, 220
— pseudonyms, 183
— revolutionary literature, 251
— society, 132-133, 144, 160, 192, 217, 221-222, 224, 227, 230, 236, 283, 293
— tales, 65
— theatre-goers, 268
— tradition, 128, 256
— traditional societies, 9
— vocabulary, 192
— writers, 150, 197, 216, 224, 270
Africanisation of French Language, 143, 146, 150
Afro-Islamic mysticism, 224

Agrarian environment, 14
Alien language, 136, 148
Analogy, 78
Ancestral
— authorship, 122
— oral tradition, 124
— spirits, 127
Anglophone world, 45
Animal
— character, 117
— imagery, 7
— tales, 7
Anti-colonial battle, 153
Artistic expression, 255
Ashanti stories, 225
Association of Revolutionary Authors and Artistes, 261
Attitudes
— classification of, 137
Authentic reality, 216-220
Autobiographical mode, 280, 286
Autochthonous language, 143

Ba, Mariama, 279-283, 285-287, 294
Balogun, Ola, 255
Barbarian invasions, 5
Battle of liberation, 165
Berlin Conference, 1885, 12
Beti, Mongo, 196-198, 202-203, 208, 211-212, 227, 240, 275-276
Black
— diaspora, 2
— man, 84, 86-91, 93-98, 100-104
— race, 107, 109
— students, 107
Boigny, Felix-Houphonet, 262-263
Burkinabe Jean-Pierre Guingare, 266

Camerounian oralists, 47
Caste system, 283
Centre de Littérature Evangelique (CLE), 270
Cesaire, Aime, 94-96, 100, 104, 107, 275
Chadwick, N.A., 4
Charles de Gaulle, 155
Chevrier, Jacques, 99
Chinese Cultural Centre (CCC), 269
Chronicles, 9

Colonial
— education, 14
— imperialism, 200
— police, 232
Communication system, 48
Communicative arts, 72
Contes, 113, 115-116, 118, 121, 123-125, 127-128
— anarchy of presentation, 113-114
— characters, 116-118
— classification of, 111-112
— functions of, 118-120
Contrast and comparison, 77-78
Conventional gender roles, 283
Constume and dressing, 72
Creative
— works, 196-197
— writings, 182, 277-279, 288
Cultural
— centres, 268
— conflict, 155
— emancipation, 134
— enrichment, 186
— environments, 254
— exchange, 186
— festivals, 256
— heritage, 6, 158
— identity, 134, 199
— myths, 277
— zones, 7
Culture conflict, 192, 197
Cynical
— Realism, 221, 226-231
— realists, 237

Dadie, Bernad, 17, 85-87, 181-182, 184, 257, 262, 268
Dance steps, 52
Dark continent, 3
Democratic Union of Women, Student Union, Trade Union, 244
Dialogue, 63
— and narration, 125
Dialogues, Songs, Poems, 125
Diop, Birago, 17, 107-128
— and his work, 108-111
Diop, Cheikh Anta, 5
Diop, David, 85, 90, 92, 94, 95, 96, 100, 104
Direct Speech, 63
Dirges, 190
Dogbes, Yves-Emmanuel, 97-98, 100
Dramatic works, 258-259
Drug addiction, 169

Early Rumblings, 242-243
Epic
— heroes, 36
— tales, 37, 39
— tradition, 36
Esoteric Incantations, 55-57
Ethnic
— culture, 34
— groups, 2, 6, 266
Eurocentric critics, 180
European fables, 7
European literature, 15
Ewondo
— animal tales, 65-66
structure of, 67-69
— belief system, 63
— folktales, 74, 77
— oral narratives, 54, 62, 78
— Oral performance, 53
— Oral prose narratives, 73
— Oral Tradition, 53, 55, 74
— proverbs, 59-63
— society, 60
— speech norms, 73
— Tales, 64-71
— schematic and thematic structure, 64
Experimental realism, 221

Fables, 114
Fall, Aminata Sow, 279, 286-287, 294
Family feuds, 8
Fantasy world of tales, 54
Female
— body, 288
— education, 277
— oppression, 289
— writers, 287, 295
Feminism
— in Franchophone African Literature, 275-296
Feminist ideology, 279
Festival of Arts and Culture, 1977, 265
Festival International des Franco phonies, 268
Fiction writing, 170
Fictional diaries, 159
Fictional reality, 216-217, 223
Folk
— music, 120
— songs, 119
— stories, 110
Folklore, 173
— Festival, 1967, 266

Index 301

Folktales, 7-8, 23, 107, 109-110, 112-113, 123-124, 134
Force-Bonte (First Franchophone African novel), 154
Foreign
— culture and ideology, 136
— linguistic medium, 138
Formulaic repetition, 74
— in song, incantation, etc, 74
Fox tales, 15
Franchophone
— Africa, 1-3, 17, 45, 80, 254-255, 257, 277
— African
— fiction, 221
— Literature, 34, 220-221
— novel, 153- 173, 179-192
— city novel, 185-187
— early novels, 183-185
— Epic novel, 188-191
— novelists, 237
— societies, 258
— women, 294
— writers, 157
— authors, 128
— black Africa, 102
— female writer, 281, 286
— fiction, 173, 222
— literary works, 3
— novel, 215-237
— oral culture, 47
— oral literature, 17
— Theatre, 270
— growth of, 265-267
— role of France and its Agencies, 267-271
— women's writings, 279-280, 295
— writer, 275
Freedom fighters, 166
French
— African territories, 257
— black Africa, 257
— colonial administration, 257
— colonial authority, 181
— colonialism, 1
— culture, 91
— education, 277
— educational system, 13
— ethnology, 158
— literary culture, 120
— literary tradition, 109, 121
— Literature, 109
— police, 241

— romantic literature, 219
— school system, 109
— society, 220
— speaking Africa, 256
— speaking communities, 1
— translations, 1, 18, 45, 80
— vocabulary, 15
— West Africa, 282

Gesticulations, 189
Gestures, 189
Government-controlled theatres, 265
Greek mythology, 31
Greeting formulae, 55-57
Griots, 9, 26-28, 31, 33, 36-40, 110, 113-114, 117, 122, 185

Hare tradition, 5, 17
Hispanophone Africa, 2
Historical threats, 11
History
— definition of, 1
Homo Africanus, 5
Hopi (American Indian tribe), 15-16
Human
— activities, 8
— tales, 7

Iconoclastic Realism, 235
Ideophones
— use of, 76-77
Illusion
— (varying degrees and types), 219-221
Illusion of Reality, 217-219, 233
Illusions
— reality of, 221
Incantations, 50, 57
Independence, 2
— and National Theatres, 257-262
Indigenous
— African theatres, 256
— culture, 136
— language, 14, 136, 143
— literature, 17
— machine, 184
— tongue, 265
— tradition, 46
Inter-African Theatre Competition, 268
Intercontinental miscegenation, 169
International community, 19
Internecine wars, 101, 184, 192
Intertexuality, 170
Introductory and Closing Formulae, 54-55

Islamic conquests, 114

Jeunesse du Rassemblement Democratique African, (JRDA), 260
Joachim, Paulin, 138

Keita, Aoua, 277, 280, 285
Kestleloot, Lilyan, 3
Koranic schools, 108, 116
Kossonho, Eugene, 88
Konte, Lansana, 262
Kourouma, Ahmadou, 121-122, 125, 127, 144-146, 148, 160
KWA languages, 7

Language, 6, 131-133
— as a political weapon, 150
— role of, 131
— use of, 72-73
Languages and Literature
— relationship between, 132-136
Language
— creations, 3
— habits, 15
— of African Literature
— attitudes to, 137-150
Lanson's Gustave, 3
Laye, Camara, 157, 183-184, 222, 240, 275
Legends, 7-8, 23, 27-28, 30, 114, 118-119, 134, 181
— and folktales
— differences between, 7
Les inconditionnels, 137-140
Les realistes, 137, 140-148
Lexical items, 143
Liberal feminist tradition, 285
Liberalism to militancy, 275-296
Liberation war in Angola, 166
Linguistic
— boundaries, 265
— competence, 136, 138, 141
— devices, 79
— medium, 133-135, 146
— realism, 143
Literary
— artefacts, 236
— artist, 138, 196, 201, 203, 206
— communication, 138
— creativity, 135-137, 139, 149
— criticism, 220, 278
— critics, 83-84, 88, 192
— culture, 121
— expression, 138

— forms, 134
— genres, 275, 279
— history, 154
— illusions, 217, 226
— image, 218, 230
— scene, 144, 278-279
— scholars, 180
— texts, 149
— themes, 197, 207, 212
— theoretician, 83
— works, 143-144, 147-148, 183, 243, 276
— writers, 275
Literature
— meaning of, 3-4
Local languages, 5, 264-265
Logocentric language, 291
Lusophone Africa, 2
Lusophone freedom-fighters, 166
Lusotropicalism, 166

Malinke language, 144
Marabouts, 28, 31, 38-39, 117-118, 184-185
Melisma or vowel extensions, 77
Memorisation, 50
Metaphor, 78
Migration, 8
Mimetic
— mode, 223
— Realism, 221-226
— repetition, 74
Mimics, 189
Misanthrope, 291
Misogynist, 291
Misovire, 291-292
Mixed tales, 7
Modern
— African Literature, 131-152, 215-237
— historical overview, 133-137
— literary critic, 83
Modes of vocalisation or voices, 49
Motifs, 25-27, 29-30
Monarchs, 31, 33, 36, 39
Monologue, 63
Moore, Gerald, 83
Mother country, 158, 165
Mother tongue 13, 15, 136, 138, 141-142
Music, 51
Myths, 7-8, 23, 27-28, 30, 114, 119, **134**

Narrative
— Devices, 53-63
— pattern, 67

— structure, 206-212
— Techniques, 39-42
National
— Festival of Arts and Culture, 1973, 260
— languages, 138, 150, 264
— Theatres in Franchophone Africa
— development of, 253-271
Native
— community, 123
— languages, 13
— and literature, 15
— population, 11
Negritude, 107, 109-110
— literature, 218, 220, 222
— movement, 231, 275
— philosophy, 83, 95
— poetry, 83-106, 218-219, 275
— poets, 84-86, 87, 90, 96, 98, 100, 104
— writers, 276
Negritudist assumptions, 220-221
Negro, 86
— art and exotism, 182
— philosophy, 220
— poetry, 182
Nkat minkana, 46-47, 53, 63-64, 77, 79
Nkobo or speech art, 79
Nkrumah, Kwame, 259
Non-formal education, 14
Norman invasion, 5
Nwapa, Flora, 276, 288

Objectivisation of time, 15
Oracles, 52, 191
Oral
— artists, 8-9, 49
— delivery devices, 63
— Delivery
— linguistic techniques, 71-77
— expression, 144, 147
— genres, 7, 10, 26, 58
— indigenous text, 128
— legacy, 47
— literary artefact, 9
— literary items, 58
— literary scholarship, 45
— Literature, 1-4, 13-14, 17, 46, 112, 120
— categorisation of, 2
— problems of, 2
— Literature
— Collections, 1
— gatherings, 8

— traditions, 5
— medium, 57, 172
— of expression, 147
— method, 63
— narration, 144
— narrative, 79
— Performance, 47-49, 71
scholarship, 47
— novels, 180
— performance, 48-49
— poetry, 119
— style, 63-64
— text, 45-46, 107, 112
— tradition, 7, 16, 23, 27, 43, 108, 145, 172
— trappings, 26
— version of poem, 126
Oraliture, 172-173
Ousmane, Sembene, 162-163, 168, 171, 182, 196, 199-201, 203, 205, 210-212, 231, 242-243, 245, 249-250, 275

Pageard, Robert, 3
Pedagogy, 59
Performance strategies, 53-63
Performing
— groups, 258
— theatres, 262
Personification, 79
Plagiarism (literary theft), 170, 278
Playwrights, 253, 258-259, 263-264, 268, 270
Ploche, 73
Poems, 10, 125-126, 190
Poetic language, 9
Poetry, 9-10, 126, 169
Political
— classes, 116, 286
— denunciation, 167
— independence, 163, 257
— play, 263
— theatre, 260
Post-negritude friction, 218
Praise
— chants, 50
— Epithets, 55-57
— names or eulogistic courtesies, 55
— singing mode, 50
Pre-colonial Africa, 3
Pre-Islamic ages, 119
Prose, 10, 26-27, 169
— fiction, 221
— literature, 218
— narratives

— subjectivity in, 64, 73
Protagonists, 30-31
Proverbs, 10-11, 50, 57-63, 119-120, 134, 188
— as expressive formulae, 57
— as figurative statements, 57
— in formulaic utterances, 57
Publishing industry, 269
Puppet Festival, 264

Racial
— and ethical incompatibility, 202
— discrimination, 185
— Realism, 221, 231-237
Radical realists, 237
Radio-France International (RFI), 268
Recitative mode, 49-51, 53, 55
Religions
— affiliations, 116
— differences, 186
Repetition, 74
Resilience
— definition of, 1-2
Revolt and Revolution (distinguished), 239
Revolution
— abortive type, 243-245
— threshold of, 239-242
Revolutionary
— Consciousness, 248-252
— Masterpiece, 245-246
— movement, 99, 294
— poets, 99
Riddles, 10-11, 134
Romantic modes, 280

Sahara desert, 4
Sankara, Thomas, 261
Sartre, Jean-Paul, 83-84, 86, 107, 110
Sassine, Williams, 171
Scenic parallelism, 75-76
Script writers, 258
Self-government, 2
Senghor, Leopold Sedar, 84, 94, 99-105, 107, 110-113,115, 117-118, 121-122, 126, 133, 138, 140, 142, 184, 262, 275
Senghorian Reconciliation Perspectives, 99-105
Slave trade, 1-2, 11-12, 14, 190
Social
— conflict, 156-157
— evils, 184
— group, 133, 135-136
— messages, 61

— problems, 285
— realist, 287
— responsibility, 196, 202
— structure, 95
Socialist realism, 249-250
Socio
— cultural group, 112, 116
— economic transformation, 206
— historical background, 24-26
— linguistis, 7
— political image of Africa, 236
Song mode, 49,51, 53
Songs, 125-126, 134, 169, 189-190
Speech
— act, 46
— behaviour, 46-82
— Devices, 77-79
— mode, 49-50
— performance, 72
— tools, 10
— tradition, 58
Spider tradition, 5, 17
Storytelling, 79
— sessions, 114
Structure of Tales, 69-71
— with human characters, 69-71
— with supernatural characters, 69-71
Superstition, 191
Supportive Proverbs, 57-63
Surrealism, 95

Tale
— embedding, 66-67
— merging, 66-67
— songs, 49, 51-53
Tales, 110-111, 114, 118-120, 123, 127-128
— as written literature in French, 121-127
— translation of, 121
Tales in Africa, 15
Tansi, Sony Labou, 144, 146-148, 167-168, 170, 268
Theatre, 169
— designer, 253
— during the colonial era, 254-257
— experts, 271
— groups, 260, 263, 267
— industries, 253, 265
— infrastructural inadequacies, 255
— of disillusionment, 255, 262-265
— of French Community, 257
— organisations, 267
— practice, 261, 267

— role of France, 255
— troupes, 264, 267, 270
Theatrical
— expression, 255
— tradition, 255
Thematic concerns of the Novels, 196-201
Theme of colonialism, 167
Tortoise tradition, 6
Toure, Ahmed Sekou, 259-260, 262, 265
Towa, Marcien, 99-100, 103
Trade unionsim, 200
Tradition
— translation and preservation of, 112-120
Traditional African
— beliefs, 222
— calendar and metric systems, 190
— culture, 218, 221, 226
— heritage, 173
— memory, 180
— oral technique, 190
— society, 226, 235
Traditional
— audience, 123
— community, 114, 154
— education, 109
— folklore, 45
— literary artist, 133
— patriarchal system, 289
— practices, 199
— religion, 202
— social structures, 13
— society, 133-134, 279
— techniques, 39
— verse, 10
Types of speech modes, 46
Unistructure and tale embedding, 66-67,
Use of Language, 72-73

Verbal
— artistry, 64
— arts, 80
— communication, 45, 77
— modes of, 49-53
— expression, 48
— Formulae
— use of, 53-63
— or stylistic repetition, 73-75
Voice parts, 53
Von Franz, Marie-Louis, 113

Wali, Obi, 148
War diary, 166
War songs, 190, 251
Western
— civilisation, 128, 134, 281
— colonialism, 11
— colonisation, 2
— culture
— influence of, 122
— education, 134, 240, 276-277, 284
— negative influence of, 286
— feminist, 292
— intervention, 134
— philosophy, 240
Westernised Independence Era, 1
White man, 2-5, 84, 86, 89, 92-94, 98, 101-105
William Pontry School, 254, 256
Women and mass movement, 246-248
World civilisation, 101
World literature, 275
Writer-reader relationship, 150

Yoruba folktales, 225

www.ingramcontent.com/pod-product-compliance
Lightning Source LLC
Chambersburg PA
CBHW070301010526
44108CB00039B/1436